John Forrest Dillon

The Laws and Jurisprudence of England and America

John Forrest Dillon

The Laws and Jurisprudence of England and America

ISBN/EAN: 9783337233426

Printed in Europe, USA, Canada, Australia, Japan

Cover: Foto ©Suzi / pixelio.de

More available books at **www.hansebooks.com**

THE

LAWS AND JURISPRUDENCE

OF

ENGLAND AND AMERICA:

BEING A SERIES OF LECTURES DELIVERED BEFORE
YALE UNIVERSITY

JOHN F. DILLON, LL.D.,

STORRS PROFESSOR, YALE UNIVERSITY, 1891-1892;

Author of Commentaries on the Law of Municipal Corporations; Member L'Institut de Droit International; late Professor of Real Estate and Equity Jurisprudence in Columbia College Law School; formerly Circuit Judge of the United States for the Eighth Judicial Circuit, and Chief-Justice of the Supreme Court of the State of Iowa.

Finis et scopus quem leges intueri, atque ad quem iussiones et sanctiones suas dirigere debent, non alius est quam ut cives feliciter degant. — BACON: *De Aug. lib. viii. aph.* 5.

There are two, and only two, foundations of law — equity and utility. — BURKE, *Tract on the Popery Laws.*

BOSTON:
LITTLE, BROWN, AND COMPANY.
1894.

Copyright, 1894,
BY JOHN F. DILLON.

UNIVERSITY PRESS:
JOHN WILSON AND SON, CAMBRIDGE, U.S.A.

A. P. D.

The years of professional studies, circuit journeyings, and judicial itinerancies, whereof this book is in some measure the outcome, as well as the time required for its preparation, have been taken from your society and companionship. The only reparation possible is to lay these imperfect fruits upon your lap. As to you, indeed, they justly belong, this formal DEDICATION serves alike to accredit your title and to manifest my grateful sense of obligation and affectionate regard.

PREFACE.

NOTHING can be less ambitious than this volume. The introduction to the first lecture shows the circumstances under which the lectures were given, and the scope and purpose of the course. I have, however, added some notes in the line of further development or illustration. It might have been more artistic to have recast the whole, working the notes into the text; but if this had been done, the loss would have exceeded the gain, since the lectures thus remodelled would not have been the lectures delivered, and they would moreover have contained details not adapted to oral discourses. Besides, it is a prized privilege of the teacher to make use of the first person, as this enables him to address his hearers more directly and more forcibly than in any other way. It is of set purpose, then, that I publish the lectures in their original form.

They are just what they are, and just what they purport to be, and nothing more, — namely, discourses to a class of law students, given largely to inspire a patriotic and just regard for the laws and institutions of our country, to incite enthusiasm in the study of the law rather than to impart technical instruction, to awaken inquiry rather than to satisfy it upon subjects of vital moment to the profession lying somewhat outside of the ordinary legal curriculum. It is due to me and to the reader that the book be judged from this point of view and no other. While it therefore disclaims any pretension to profound research or exhaustive treatment, as inconsistent with its main purpose, it deals, nevertheless, with the interesting subjects of legal education; trial by jury; the origin, development, and characteristics of the common law; written constitutions, legislation, case-law, the law reports, the doctrine of judicial precedent, codification, and law reform.

There is one purpose which runs through all the lectures, in virtue of which only can the book make any claim to unity of design: that purpose is to delineate the characteristics and to exhibit the excellences of our legal system as it now exists, with a view to show that for the people subject to its rule it is, with all its faults, better than the Roman or any other alien system. It is an argument intended to be so earnestly and strongly put as to amount to a protest against the *Continentalization* of our law. I have a profound conviction of the superiority of our system of law, at least for our people; but I know that this estimate is not so fully and firmly held by the body of lawyers and law teachers as I think it ought to be. I have therefore thought it a fitting, if not needful, aim to inspire on the part of the profession a more thorough appreciation of it. But while I confess to a desire to set forth its excellences, I am not conscious of any inclination to veil its imperfections.

An attempt, proper in oral discourse — at all events one which falls within the plan of these lectures — has been made at popular, or perhaps it were better to say non-technical, treatment of the subjects discussed, and to invest them with their appropriate literary and historical appanages; but always, it will be found, with a serious purpose in view. It may be that the continuous labors of forty years in the profession — twenty on the bench and twenty at the bar — have inclined me to approach and to consider legal questions too slightly on the theoretical and too much on the practical side. This is a general habit with lawyers under the common-law system; but it is a habit which has been characteristic of such lawyers from the beginning, and to which, more than to all other causes, that system owes its distinctive character, its merits as well as its defects.

As the result of studies, reflections, and experience, I have formed upon many of the topics discussed decided opinions, which I have freely expressed. They represent my matured views and convictions. The legal system of England and America is substantially developed, — as fully, I mean, as it is practicable to develop a system which must necessarily expand with the life and growth of the active communities which it governs and regulates. The pressing want of our substantive law is an authoritative, scientific, and comprehensive arrangement of its vast and scattered materials, — a work which is yet in its formative stages. What has thus far been projected has made but little real advance, and has not always proceeded on the right plan or principles. My judgment is that, for this purpose, our law must be treated as substantially unique and distinctive, and arranged according to its real character, — arranged, so to speak, from within and not from without.

Among many professed legal reformers and speculative writers it seems to be taken for granted that the Roman law will supply all or most of the needed aid and models. This is a radical mistake. Our laws and jurisprudence must be analyzed and resolved into their constituent principles, and these must be arranged according to their own nature and historical development. The resulting arrangement will necessarily be as unique and distinctive as the materials with which it deals, which cannot be recast except to a limited extent in moulds furnished by the Civil or Continental law. A Roman basilica cannot be transformed into a Gothic cathedral. We cannot sever ourselves from our past in respect of our law any more than in respect of our history. We can no more change the essential character of our legal system and legal institutions than we can change our language, or the traditions, habits, usages, sentiments, and genius of our people. Such a change would be impossible if attempted, and unwise if it were possible. The English and Roman systems are on many points so different in their conceptions, growth, essential character, and scope, as, in my judgment, to predestinate to certain and signal failure any attempt to remodel ours as a whole after the Roman system or any of its modern European adaptations.

The meagre results in this direction of the labors of Austin and his successors, though men of ability and learning, confirm me in this opinion. At all events, they have not produced any comprehensive and systematic analysis and re-arrangement of the corps or body of our laws in a shape ready or fitted for legislative action. They have supplied us with studies and sketches in abundance, but have only partially furnished working plans and detailed specifications. The necessary work has hardly been begun. I feel constrained to say this, although mindful of the influence and value of their labors in arousing the attention of the profession to the defects in our system of laws and jurisprudence and the necessity of amending and improving it. They have given us, indeed, skeleton forms, but these are practically useless unless clothed with flesh and blood, and made vital by legislative breath, — things seemingly yet far off. What worth there may be in the views on these subjects, and others scarcely less important, presented in this volume, must be left to the thoughtful consideration of the profession, and above all to time and experience to determine.

J. F. D.

NEW YORK, January, 1894.

CONTENTS.

LECTURE I.

Our Law in its Old Home. — Definition of Law and Jurisprudence. — Law more than a Body of Commands. — Ethical Nature and Foundation of Law. — Respective Fields of Law and Morality. — General Characteristics of the English System of Law. — Mainly the Work of the Lawyers and Judges of England 1–33

LECTURE II.

The Education and Discipline of the English Bar, and herein of the Inns of Court, their History, Character, and Purposes. — Origin, Antiquity, and Establishment of the Inns of Court (Note A). — Status of Serjeant-at-Law, Ceremonials on taking the Coif, the Difference between a Serjeant and a Queen's Counsel, etc., etc. (Note B) 34–74

LECTURE III.

The Education and Discipline of the English Bar, and herein of the Inns of Court, their History, Character, and Purposes (concluded). — The Literary Associations of the Inns of Court (Note A). — Studentship in the Inns of Court, and Mode of being called to the Bar (Note B) 75–107

LECTURE IV.

Westminster Hall: Its History and the Characteristics of the System of Law developed and perfected therein; and herein of Judicial Tenure and Compensation, Trial by Jury, and Judicial Precedent 108–142

LECTURE V.

Our Law in its New Home — America: Its Expansion, Development, and Characteristics in the Political and Judicial Systems of the United States . . . 143–168

LECTURE VI.

Our Law in its New Home — America: Its Expansion, Development, and Characteristics in the Political and Judicial Systems of the United States (continued) 169–195

LECTURE VII.

Our Law in its New Home — America: Its Expansion, Development, and Characteristics in the Political and Judicial Systems of the United States, and herein of our Written Constitutions, their Rationale, Limitations, and Guarantees (concluded) 196–215

LECTURE VIII.

Our Law: Its Excellences and Defects. — Doctrine of Judicial Precedent and its Consequences. — Case-law and its Uneven Development. — Unfortunate Separation of Legal and Equitable Rights and Remedies. — Unsatisfactory Condition of our Law of Real Property 216–241

LECTURE IX.

Our Law: Its Uncertainty and Enormous Bulk. — Suggestions as to the Scope and True Methods of Amending the Laws; and herein Codification considered. — The True Office and Use of Adjudged Cases (Note) . 242–263

LECTURE X.

Our Law. — The Vast Size and Rapid Accumulation of Case-law considered specially with Reference to the Practicability of Limiting its Growth by Legislative Action restricting the Publication of the Reports of Adjudged Cases. — Remedies Proposed by Lord Bacon and Lord Westbury for the Overgrown Bulk of our Statute and Case-law. — The Doctrine of Judicial Precedent and its Effects. — Judgment of the American Bar Association concerning the Publication of the Law Reports
264–292

LECTURE XI.

Our Law: Blackstone and Bentham as Types and Exponents of the Conservative and the Radical Forces, to whose Free Play it owes its Progress, as well as its Distinctive Form and Character. — The Literary, Institutional, and Historical Value of Blackstone's Commentaries. — Their Great Influence in moulding the Laws and Jurisprudence of America 293–315

LECTURE XII.

Our Law: Blackstone and Bentham as Types and Exponents of its Conservative and Radical Forces, to whose Free Play it owes its Progress, as well as its Distinctive Form and Character. — Bentham's Place in our Legal History. — Character and Influence of his Writings and Labors upon English Law and its Reformation (concluded) 316–347

LECTURE XIII.

PAGE

Our Law: A Century's Progress and Development. — Important Contributions to our Laws made by the United States. — Specific Changes in the Laws of both Countries upon Subjects of Great and Permanent Interest. — Present Condition of our Laws and a Forecast of their Evolution 348–389

TABLE OF CASES CITED 391, 392

AUTHORS CITED 393–398

INDEX 399–431

YALE LECTURES

ON

ENGLISH AND AMERICAN LAWS AND JURISPRUDENCE.

LECTURE I.

OUR LAW IN ITS OLD HOME. — DEFINITION OF LAW AND JURISPRUDENCE. — LAW MORE THAN A BODY OF COMMANDS. — ETHICAL NATURE AND FOUNDATION OF LAW. — RESPECTIVE FIELDS OF LAW AND MORALITY. — GENERAL CHARACTERISTICS OF THE ENGLISH SYSTEM OF LAW. — MAINLY THE WORK OF THE LAWYERS AND JUDGES OF ENGLAND.

A FEW months since, I received from the authorities of Yale University a letter stating that its Law School had a WILLIAM L. STORRS LECTURESHIP, which provided for the appointment each year of a different professor to give a course of about twelve lectures on legal topics, and asking me to occupy the place for the current college year, 1891–1892. My appreciation of this honor was such as to tempt me, in spite of my many engagements, to accept the appointment.

The subject matter of the lectures being left to my judgment, I have been not a little embarrassed

> **Lecture I.**

in determining the character and scope of this brief course. The object of lectures upon the law may be twofold: First, with the primary view to impart instruction; second, not primarily for the purpose of instruction, but rather to awaken and stimulate a real interest, — to set, if happily it may be, the hearer thinking, and to inspire enthusiasm in the study of the law, to the end that the hearer may be incited afterwards to pursue the subject on his own motion, and for the very love of it, by personal recourse to the appropriate and authentic sources of knowledge. Were I to select some single topic with a view to expository, technical treatment, I should run the risk of repeating more or less what has been already taught, and taught by lecturers who by constant use keep their equipment bright; whereas mine has so long hung idle upon the wall that it has become rusty, and its use unfamiliar. On the whole, I have determined, wisely or otherwise, to pursue the latter plan, thinking that in the long run some observations on subjects which lie beyond the marches of the ordinary legal curriculum, yet relating to matters of living and vital interest to the student of our laws, might be quite as fruitful in results as technical and didactic lectures.

The course proposed may be thus outlined: —

> **Course of lectures outlined.**

A consideration of Our Law in its Old Home, its definition, and distinctive character; the education and discipline of the English bar, and herein of the Inns of Court, their history, character, and purposes; of Westminster Hall and the characteristic qualities of the English system of law which is indissolubly associated with this illustrious building, and herein of judicial tenure, of the trial by jury, and the doctrine of judicial precedent. This will be followed by a consideration of Our Law in its New Home, its American expansion, development, and modifications, including written constitutional limitations; and this will lead to an examination of the English and American system of law and jurisprudence in its general features, wherein will appear its excellences and defects. This will be succeeded by a consideration of the conservative and radical forces in our law, of which Blackstone and Bentham are types and exponents, and of the true end, methods, and limitations of legal reform. And finally I shall attempt to trace the progress of law in this country during the first century of our national existence, with a view to exhibit its present condition, and then to mark out the probable, if not necessary, lines of its future growth and improvement.

Compendiously expressed, it may be said that these lectures, so far as unity of design can be predicated of them, relate to *Our Law in its Old and in its New Home,* — *England and America.*

What do I mean by the expression "our law"? Simple as it seems, this is a most important inquiry. It lies at the threshold, — nay, more, it lies at the very foundation of all legal studies scientifically conducted. What is meant will be made more clear by first stating, negatively, what is not meant. By the phrase "our law," I do not mean moral law; on the contrary, I mean to exclude it, — so far, at all

Lecture I.

Does not include ethics or morality.

events, as moral law stands distinguished from civil or municipal law.

As soon as the development of man's intellect enables him to distinguish right from wrong, he inevitably comes under the sway of what is termed moral law, and thenceforth it is impossible for him to do any act, however momentous or however minute, having a moral quality, of which that law does not take cognizance. Conscience having its imperial and divine seat in every breast, susceptible of having its vision made more comprehensive and more acute, its touch more delicate, and its decrees more perfect by enlightened education, yet, incapable of being torn from the breast of man, — conscience is a universal judge, holding its assize at every man's door, sitting in judgment upon every act and every omission partaking of a moral quality, to condemn or to approve.[1] It administers in its own way and by its own methods what may, indeed, be termed the moral code: and yet it is absolutely essential to a correct legal conception of law to define its province, and to separate it for purposes of definition, classification, study, and administration,

---

[1] By the metaphorical language of the text, in which conscience is personified, I do not imply that conscience is a separate, special, or exceptional moral faculty in our nature. On the contrary, I am inclined to agree with those who deny this, and maintain that conscience is the ethical manifestations or revelations of our whole moral nature, — which is indivisible, — and not those of a supposed single and distinct sense or faculty. Those who are curious on this subject will find it discussed at length by Professor Lorimer ("The Institutes of Law," Edinburgh and London, 2d ed., 1880, chap. vi., pp. 186-204). Unlike this distinguished writer, I am unable to see that the question whether conscience is a separate faculty or not has any special bearing on practical jurisprudence.

from the domain of ethics or morality, — that is to say, for all the purposes of the lawyer and the judge, or, more comprehensively, for all the purposes of jurisprudence, which concerns itself only with civil laws properly so called; namely, rules of conduct which are enforced or enforceable by the State.

Lecture I.

But this does not imply, as I shall show more fully after defining the term "law," that rules regulating civil conduct may not, so to speak, be *imported* by the tribunals, when necessary for the purposes of the actual decision of causes, from the field of morality. Such rules, however, become invested with the quality of law only when and to the extent that the judges authenticate or adopt, or set upon them the *imprimatur* of the State, — that is, recognize and enforce them by their judgments. This is not, as charged by the Benthamic school, a usurpation by the judges, but a legitimate and often necessary function of the judicial office. In the past, large additions to our legal rules, notably in equity and commercial law, have been made in this way, and further additions must, whenever the necessity arises, continue to be made, and in fact are daily made, from this unexhausted and perennial source. It is a mistake to suppose that this process has ceased. In consequence of modern inventions, aggregations of capital, and changed social conditions, I am inclined to think that at no previous period has this method of legal growth and change been in more constant and active operation than at the present time. Even the accepted general doctrines of courts of equity (and this is measurably true of courts of law) are not stereotyped, but

When ethical rules become legal rules.

Lecture I.	possess, within recognized limits, a progressive and flexible character.¹
Austin's "Province of Jurisprudence determined," a valuable contribution to the science of law.	Austin rendered, perhaps, no greater service to jurisprudence than in his elaborate chapters on the "Province of Jurisprudence Determined," wherein he defined the boundaries of jurisprudence, and separated it from the domain of ethics or morality.²

¹ *Re* Hallett's Estate, Law Reports, 13 Chancery Division, p. 710, *per* Sir George Jessel. This great equity judge there says: "The rules of courts of equity are not, like the rules of the common law, supposed to have been established from time immemorial. They have been established from time to time, — altered, improved, and refined from time to time. In many cases we know the names of the chancellors who invented them, — as, for example, the separate use of a married woman, the restraint on alienation, the modern rule against perpetuities, and the rules of equitable waste. We can name the chancellors who first invented them, and state the date. The older precedents in equity are of very little value; the doctrines are progressive, refined, and improved."

² Mr. Justice Markby, after expressing his approval of Austin's conception of law and of sovereignty, and his sense of our indebtedness to him for drawing so firmly the distinction between law and morals, thus proceeds: "Austin, by establishing the distinction between law and morals, not only laid the foundation for a science of law, but cleared the conception of law and of sovereignty of a number of pernicious consequences to which in the hands of his predecessors it had been supposed to lead. Laws, as Austin has shown (Lecture VI., p. 275), must be legally binding; and yet a law may be unjust. Resistance to authority cannot be a legal right, and yet it may be a virtue. But these are only examples. Into whatever discussion the words 'right' and 'justice' enter, we are on the brink of a confusion from which a careful observance of the distinction between law and morals can alone save us. Austin has shown not only what law is, but what it is not. He has determined accurately the boundaries of its province. The domain he assigns to it may be small, but it is indisputable. He has admitted that law itself may be immoral, in which case it is our moral duty to disobey it; but it is nevertheless law, and this disobedience, virtuous though it may be, is nothing less than rebellion " (Markby, " Elements of Law," 2d ed., London, 1889, § 12, p. 4). The justness of these observations may be admitted without admitting the correctness or sufficiency of Austin's definitions of law and sovereignty.

Continental, and particularly German, commentators upon the law have not always, if indeed they have ever, fully made this separation, — a separation so essential to the advancement of legal science. I quite agree with Professor Amos, who, referring to this subject, says: —

"It cannot be denied that the best and most
" philosophical thinkers of Germany, cognizant as
" they are of the true relations of law and morality,
" and of legal and moral terms, have to a certain
" extent contributed to popular confusion by their
" reluctance to abstract, even provisionally, law
" from its moral surroundings. This abstraction
" has nowhere been so completely achieved as by
" Englishmen. The result of this philosophic tend-
" ency in Germany has been to merge the scien-
" tific treatment of law in the larger region of
" general ethical inquiry; and consequently, instead
" of the science of law making an even and inde-
" pendent progress of its own, it has undulated with
" every wave of ethical speculation, and has conse-
" quently suffered the retardation incident to the
" growth of the most involved because the most
" composite branch of intellectual research."[1]

Lecture I.

Continental view of relations between law and morality.

---

[1] Amos, "The Science of Law," New York, 1876, chaps. i., ii., iii. A most striking illustration of the correctness of Professor Amos's observations may be found in the work of Professor Lorimer above cited. It is written in the spirit and pervaded by the doctrines of the German philosophic school. It has all the speculative interest and charm that a vigorous and captivating style can give it, but it is essentially an exotic. As a practical lawyer brought up in the English school, and for a lifetime accustomed to its views and methods, it may be that I underestimate the value of speculations of the German philosophers; but I am unable to see that their views and methods are capable of being transplanted with any considerable advantage

Lecture I.

Science of law to be distinguished from the science of politics.

Again, by the phrase "our law" I do not mean to include what may be called the science of politics or government, although this also stands closely related to law, and in many points in direct contact with it. Strictly speaking, the science of politics or of government falls within the domain of the statesman or legislator.[1]

Our law is synonymous with the lex terræ.

I mean by "our law" what Magna Charta calls the *lex terræ*, the law of the land, — the law of the

into our jurisprudence. Professor Lorimer treats of the principles of jurisprudence from the standpoint of nature, and his work is professedly intended to exhibit jurisprudence as a branch of what he calls the science of nature. Like the Continental jurists generally, he not only does not firmly discriminate law from morality, but insists that jurisprudence is only a compartment of the doctrines of natural law, — *Naturrecht*, — which is the ideal standard by which all enactments and legal principles are tested. Venturing no opinion concerning other and unfamiliar systems of law, it is my judgment that *our* law must be primarily — I do not say exclusively, but primarily — studied, not from the standpoint of nature, — *Naturrecht* or *Rechtsphilosophie*, — but from the lessons of recorded experience, especially as these are embodied in our statutes, law reports, commentaries, and history. Fruit grown on this native soil is indigenous, hardy, and suited to our wants. *Naturrecht* has been called "jurisprudence in the air," and Continental stock grown in England and in this country has so far borne no very promising fruit, but rather — if I may be pardoned a simile that has often occurred to me — orchids, having, indeed, a weird beauty, curious to look upon, but living on the air, and sending down no strong and stringy roots into the soil. I have often been led to doubt the permanent intrinsic value of Austin's labors; but conceding his definition of law to be inadequate even to the extent of being misleading, it must be admitted, I think, that we are largely indebted to him, among other things, for the clear and effectual partition of the fields of law and morality.

[1] The relation of law to politics, or the science of government, and the necessity for the purposes of the lawyer of marking and observing the distinction between them, are treated with his accustomed clearness and elegance by Sir Frederick Pollock in his "Introduction to the History of the Science of Politics," London, 1890, *passim*.

land as it actually exists in distinction from what in the view of the law reformer or of the legislator or of the jurist it is conceived or believed it ought to be. "Law" and "legislation" are by no means synonymous. The work of consciously changing the law from what it is to what it ought to be is the work of the legislator. This work may, and indeed usually does, fall largely into the hands of and is moulded by the lawyer in his capacity as a statesman or legislator, or the adviser of these; and thus legislation, especially in modern times, has become the usual and effective instrument for changing or amending the law, or making needful or special additions to it.

One might, à priori, think it were easy to define law. Grave mistake! Whoever has studied this subject feels an overpowering sense of its difficulties, — difficulties which seem to be beyond the reach of the most enlightened and trained intellects, and to overwhelm them with a consciousness of their own insufficiency. It requires a bolder man than I to propound a definition of the law of the land which shall be at once comprehensive and accurate. Volumes have been written upon this precise subject, with, to me at all events, no satisfying result.

Blackstone's definition, following Hobbes's,[1] is the

Lecture I.

Difficulty of defining the term "law."

---

[1] Hobbes's definition of law is thus: "Law in general is not counsel, but command; nor a command of any man to any man, but only of him whose command is addressed to one formerly [that is, already by having agreed to be his subject] obliged to obey. And as for civil law, it addeth only the name of the person commanding, which is *persona civitatis*, the person of the Commonwealth.

"Which considered, I define civil law in this manner. Civil law is to every subject those rules which the Commonwealth hath com-one best known to the profession, and is in these words: —

Blackstone's definition of law.

"Municipal law is a rule of civil conduct, pre-"scribed by the supreme power in a State, com-"manding what is right and prohibiting what is "wrong."[1]

I cannot, after much reflection, but regard this definition as both inadequate and incorrect. To make it cover the actual body of the whole civil law of a State, the word "prescribed" and the word "command" here used must be given an elasticity of meaning, or an artificial meaning, not consonant with the general or appropriate use of these words.

Austin's definition.

Austin's definition of law is similarly defective, and the same criticism applies. "Law," according to Austin, "is the aggregate of rules set by men as "politically superior or sovereign to men as politi-"cally subject."[2]

---

manded him by word, writing, or other sufficient sign of the will, to make use of for the distinction of right and wrong, — that is to say, of what is contrary and what is not contrary to the rule." Leviathan, chap. xxvi., "of Civil Laws," English ed., 1651, p. 137. Commenting on this Sir Frederick Pollock says: "Right and wrong in the legal sense are that which the State has allowed and forbidden, and nothing else. To understand this is one of the first conditions of clear, legal, and political thinking, and it is Hobbes's great merit to have made this clear beyond the possibility of misunderstanding. No one who has grasped Hobbes's definition can ever be misled by verbal conceits about laws of the State which are contrary to natural right, or the law of nature not being binding. All such language is mischievous, as confusing the moral and political grounds of positive law with its actual force." "History of the Science of Politics," pp. 60, 61.

[1] 1 Blacks. Com., 44. See Hammond's notes in his edition of Blackstone, vol. i., pp. 120-165, on the "Nature of Laws"

[2] Austin, "Jurisprudence," vol. i., lect. i., 5th ed. Campbell's, p. 86 et seq. Professor Clark, of the University of Cambridge, in his

The definitions of Blackstone and Austin are apt and accurate as applied to the great body of what we may call the *ordained* or *enacted* law of a State. But there is a large body of law to which the term "rules prescribed" or "commands" or "rules set" by a sovereign does not apply, except by subjecting these words to a strain which alters or greatly expands their proper meaning.

This subject has been carefully considered by Professor Holland in his "Elements of Jurisprudence," and I may adopt as sufficiently accurate for my present purpose (although with a conscious sense of its inadequacy) his conclusion that law may be defined as a general rule of civil conduct or of external human action, enforced, or at all events purporting to be enforced, by a sovereign political authority.[1] Consequently we can recognize as laws proper only such rules as are enforced or enforce-

Lecture I.

Holland's definition of law.

"Practical Jurisprudence: A Comment on Austin," 1883, devotes the sixteen chapters of Part I. to "The Definition and Origin of Law," and the sixteen chapters of Part II. to "The Form of Law," where the voluminous literature and learning concerning these subjects are well summarized and critically discussed.

[1] This is the result of Professor Holland's elaborate discussion of the subject in chaps. i.-viii., in his "Elements of Jurisprudence," 2d ed., London, 1882; more particularly pp. 18, 34, 35, 43, 62, 66, 69. His definition avoids the error of Blackstone's and Austin's limitation of law to something that is "commanded" or "prescribed" or "rules set by a sovereign." Pollock's review and comments thereon, see "Essays in Jurisprudence," London, 1882, pp. 1-18. Sir William Markby approves of Austin's definition of law, and sums up his own conception of the term "law" as follows: "That it is the general body of rules which are addressed by the rulers of a political community to the members of that society, and which are generally obeyed." Markby, "Elements of Law," chap. i., § 9, p. 3. "Rules addressed," etc., mean the same things as Blackstone's "rules prescribed" or Austin's "rules set," and are open to the same criticism.

Lecture I.

Result summed up.

able by a sovereign political authority, — that is, the State. As a result, law, as the lawyer has to deal with it, is concerned only with legal rights; and by legal rights are meant only such rights as are recognized and enforced by the power of the State. The thing to remember is that *coercion by the State* is the essential quality of law, distinguishing it from morality or ethics. Nothing is a legal right unless it implies a capacity residing in one person of controlling, with the assent and assistance of the State, the actions of others; and that which gives validity, or at least effect, if not existence, to a legal right, is in every case the force which is lent to it by the State. Duty is the correlative of right, and duty in a legal sense implies a sanction or amenability to sanction, which sanction it is the function of the judicial tribunals to apply and enforce. Whatever rights and duties they thus recognize and enforce are legal rights and duties, and for practical purposes none others fall within the domain of law so far as lawyers and courts are concerned. A moral right, if disregarded, will be viewed with public censure or disapprobation, but that is all; a legal right, however, if disregarded, will be enforced by the public will of the organized society which is called the State.[1]

While we must for all purposes of legal science and jurisprudence keep the boundaries of law and ethics distinct, it would be a most serious error for the lawyer to conceive or suppose that he has to do only with constitutions and statutes and decided

---

[1] Holland, *passim*, chaps. iii., iv., vii., viii.

cases, and that these constitute all there is of law. Law, even municipal or civil law, is vastly more than Blackstone's and Austin's stereotyped and imperfect definition makes it, — "a command of the sovereign," "a rule of civil conduct prescribed by the supreme power in a State," — if by this is meant something always originating with and created *de novo* by the legislature, — a mere product of sovereignty, of legislation, — and which, therefore, the legislator can determine, fix, and mould, as clay in the potter's hand, at his pleasure.

Lecture I.

What the sovereign authority in other countries (Parliament, for example, in Great Britain), or Congress or a State legislature in this country, acting within constitutional limits, commands, is indeed law; and nothing in a legal sense is law, in whatever shape existing, which the State will not enforce. And yet it is true that the body of such commands, even if the State may by artifice of speech be supposed to command whatever it permits to its judges, does not represent the totality of the civil or municipal law of any given State.[1] If you ask me to define

Origin, nature, and ethical foundations of law.

[1] In the scholarly and able address of Mr. James C. Carter before the American Bar Association (Reports of the Association for 1890, p. 217), this eminent lawyer condenses and states with clearness and force the argument against the Austinian conception and definition of law, and he shows that the law of a State is much more than the body of commands proceeding from the legislature or sovereign. Mr. Carter ascribes the unwritten law mainly to custom. I think it is derived, especially in modern times, still more largely from the general sense of justice and right as interpreted and ascertained by the judges than from "custom" in the usual sense of that word. Sir Henry Maine's last two Lectures (XII. and XIII.) in "Early History of Institutions" materially undermined, or at least limited, Austin's theory of command and sovereignty.

Lecture I.

Origin, nature, and ethical foundations of law (continued).

law, I can, speaking as a lawyer, do no better than to adopt Professor Holland's definition already given. If you ask me to enumerate all of the ultimate sources whence legal rights and duties originate, and how these are evolved, I hide my diminished head, and confess my inability satisfactorily to formulate an answer. Law is not ethics, it is true; but except so far as laws are abitrary or conventional regulations, or are mere usages and customs not having a moral quality, — if there be any such, — they have an ethical foundation. Laws are to be found in part expressed in written constitutions and statutes, and in part the evidences thereof will be found in judicial decisions, in the commentaries and works of learned men; and yet, with all their voluminousness, the law is not to be found in these alone. These constitutions, statutes, judicial decisions, and treatises are numbered by thousands. They are almost unknown to the mass of men; they are at best imperfectly known to lawyers; and yet so it is that any man who in good faith obeys the dictates of a pure and honest heart, whose civil conduct toward his fellow-men is guided by the sense of justice and right which is graven on his heart by the supreme Law-giver, — will find such a course of conduct, except in the rarest instances, to be in perfect conformity with the requirements of the laws of his country. This is to me conclusive proof of the essential ethical nature and foundation of our laws, and also conclusive proof that laws are something more than a body of *commands* in any real and proper sense of the word.

If you will critically examine the long catalogue of

legislative enactments found in the Revised Statutes of the United States, or in the statute books of any of the States or of Parliament, you will find that the most of them relate to positive regulations of expediency, and not to the great and permanent doctrines of general or universal justice or jurisprudence. Prolific as the various legislatures are in the exercise of the function of legislation, yet how infinitesimal compared with the vast aggregate of our laws and jurisprudence is the work of any given legislature, or even the combined work of all the legislatures, from the beginning down to this present. Thus much as to the differentiation in general of law and legislation, and as to the essential nature of law as the equivalent of the enlightened, ethical, permanent justice of the State.

These views are enforced by considerations of the necessity, purpose, and effect of our American written constitutions, since these are our supreme law; and in these the people have embodied not only their deliberate judgment as to the best form in which to mould the framework of their government, but they have also infused and incorporated therein their highest, their best, their loftiest conceptions of the fundamental rights and duties on which the organic, permanent justice of the State rests.

In considering, therefore, what law is, under the limitations of our written constitutions, Federal and State, it is first of all necessary to get rid of the idea that law is whatever the populace of the moment may determine to be their sense of expediency or right, even though enacted by a legislative majority. An adequate and just regard for

Lecture I.

Constitutional limitations as affecting law.

Lecture I.

law, and the obligation of all men, including those in authority, not only to recognize their subjection to law, but to cherish, preserve, and obey it, can, as I think, in no way be better inculcated, strengthened, and enforced, than by correcting the erroneous conception that law is in its essence the mere product of the popular will or of a legislative majority of the hour, and by contemplating the higher and purer sources of law, and thus to become saturate with the great truth that law and legislation are not, in this country at any rate, necessarily equivalents, but that law in its more engaging and nobler aspects, and in its essential nature, is "the beneficence of civil society acting by rule;" is "the absolute "justice of the State enlightened by the perfect rea- "son and morality of the State," as ordained, established, and declared in the constitutions.

Law in its nature is therefore opposed to all that is fitful, capricious, unjust, partial, or destructive; and happily legislative enactments of this character will in general be found to be in conflict with some one or more of the express provisions of the organic law, and therefore void.[1]

Retroaction of moral upon civil law.

Kant's philosophy is to me, I am sorry to confess (for it may be my fault), in general unprofitable enough in practical results; but there is one noble passage of his that made on me an impression that years have never effaced or dimmed: "There are "two things which, the more I contemplate them, "the more they fill my mind with admiration, — "the starry heavens above me, and the moral law "within me."

[1] See *post* Lecture VII.

Not less wondrous than the revelations of the starry heavens, and much more important, and to no class of men more so than to lawyers, is the "moral law" which Kant found within himself, and which is likewise found within and is consciously recognized by every man. This moral law holds its dominion by divine ordination over us all, from which escape or evasion is impossible. This moral law is the eternal and indestructible sense of justice and of right written by God on the living tablets of the human heart, and revealed in his Holy Word. It is considerations of justice and right that make up the web and woof and form the staple of a lawyer's life and vocation. The lawyer's work and business are, it is true, with human laws; but let me repeat, the lawyer makes a grievous mistake who supposes law to be the mere equivalent of written enactments or judicial decisions. Theoretically, and for many purposes practically, lawyers must discriminate law from morality, and define and keep separate and distinct their respective provinces. But these provinces always adjoin each other; and ethical considerations can no more be excluded from the administration of justice, which is the end and purpose of all civil laws, than one can exclude the vital air from his room and live. A thousand times have I realized the force of this truth. If unblamed I may advert to my own experience, I always felt in the exercise of the judicial office irresistibly drawn to the intrinsic justice of the case, with the inclination, and if possible the determination, to rest the judgment upon the very right of the matter. In the practice of the profession I always feel an abiding

Lecture I.

Retroaction of moral upon civil law (continued).

Lecture I.	confidence that if my case is morally right and just it will succeed, whatever technical difficulties may appear to stand in the way; and the result usually justifies the confidence.
Practical importance of correct theory as to nature of law.	The views which one holds as to the sources and nature of law are not of speculative interest merely, but have direct practical bearings of the most important character, — as, for example, on the true method of legal education, and on the true function and scope of legislation. If law were simply commands or rules prescribed or set by a sovereign, the natural way to learn it would be by a study of such commands or rules and their application; whereas the law can only be thoroughly and comprehensively learned by a consideration of the various relations of individuals to the State and to each other, out of which relations legal rights and corresponding duties arise, only part of which take the form of a legislative command.[1]
Concluding observations on the relations between law and morality.	It is obviously with such relations that the legislator has necessarily to deal whenever he enters upon the work of legislation; and we shall see in the course of these lectures how essential it is to understand both how law and legislation are differentiated from as well as related to each other.[2]

The subject of the relations of law and ethics is full of delicate and difficult considerations. It is

---

[1] This subject, namely, the theory of law in its relations to legal study, is presented in the two valuable reports of the Committee on Legal Education, 1891, 1892, to the American Bar Association. Report, 1891, pp. 336, 337; Report, 1892, pp. 355–359; reprinted by the United States Bureau of Education, see "Report on Legal Education," 1893, pp. 33–36.

[2] See *post* Lectures IV., VIII., IX., X.

more easy to be lured into than to avoid a field of unprofitable speculation where, like Milton's metaphysical angels, one "finds no end in wandering mazes lost." In what I have said I have resolutely resisted this temptation. Where the legislative will is silent, and there is no customary law or precedent, the judges frequently have no guide but what is well termed in our law "equity and good conscience."[1] In such cases I do not believe it is possible, or, if it were, that it is desirable, to separate dogmatically the domain of law from that of ethics. I therefore venture, in concluding this topic, upon the following observations. Legislation belongs to or is a branch of ethics; the legislator in the exercise of the function of legislation not only regards ethical considerations, but such considerations are generally the foundation or animating principle of his enactment. In modern times the judicial and legislative functions are not only discriminated, but separated. Yet the separation, while theoretically complete, is perhaps never actually so; and therefore judges, in and by the very exercise of their duty of adjudication, are, as I have said above, obliged in many cases, where the legislative will is silent and the case is novel, to legislate. Now, so far as the separation of the judicial and legislative functions is actually complete, it is easy to distinguish the provinces of law and morality. But in so far as

Lecture I.

Relations between law and morality.

---

[1] Chancery relieves "according to the principles of conscience, good faith, honesty, and equity." 1 Spence's Equity, Part II., Book I., chap. iii., pp. 335–330; *Ib.*, Book II., chap. i., p. 407, and illustrations.

Lecture I.

the judges are compelled, as they not infrequently are, to exercise what is really a creative power and to make a new rule, — in a word to exercise, albeit covertly or circuitously, the function of legislation, — it seems to me that they are rightfully, because necessarily, within the domain of ethics, and that in such cases the domains of ethics and law are not and cannot be delimited in advance, nor until the line is drawn by the judges in and by the opinion and judgment which are given in the particular case.

The term "jurisprudence" defined.

The process of marking out what is meant by the term "law" would be incomplete unless we also marked out what is meant by the word "jurisprudence," which is in such familiar use. Well, "jurisprudence" is almost as difficult to define as "law," because of the varied senses in which that word is used by our judges and commentators. Our older law writers do not use the word. For example, I do not recollect that it occurs in Lord Hale's "History of the Common Law." Professor Holland devotes the first chapter of his "Elements of Jurisprudence" to a consideration of the meaning of the term. He reaches the conclusion that it "ought to be used without any descriptive epithet" to denote the "formal science of actual, positive law;" and it is his opinion that "jurisprudence deals with the "various relations which are regulated by legal "rules, rather than with the rules which regulate "those relations." While he criticises as improper the current use of the word as the equivalent of "law," as in the phrases "English jurisprudence," "equity jurisprudence," and the like, he admits that it is unobjectionable to speak of "criminal" and "civil," and "public" and "private," jurisprudence. I do not doubt that Professor Holland's definition of the term marks out its meaning with scientific correctness for the purposes of his work, and as descriptive of jurisprudence in the abstract; but his definition is more limited than its ordinary use in our legal literature. Law, as I have shown, is the collective and appropriate name for the entire body or system of rules, regulations, principles, and enactments which are recognized and protected by the State, and which the State will compulsorily enforce when required. Accordingly, I use the word "jurisprudence" as synonymous broadly with the whole science of the law as law is thus defined, and as embracing not only legal relations but the entire body of legal doctrines, whencesoever derived, applicable to such relations. I therefore venture to state that it is a correct use of the term to refer to branches or heads of general jurisprudence by such qualifying words as "English" or "American jurisprudence," "equity jurisprudence," "criminal jurisprudence," and the like. Shortly stated, jurisprudence is concerned with the whole body of the law, and signifies the science of law, or the scientific knowledge of jural relations and the legal principles, doctrines, and rules which govern such relations.[1]

Lecture I.

The term "jurisprudence" defined (continued).

[1] Jurisprudence is defined, its methods and purposes set forth, its relations to law and ethics thoughtfully considered, and what is more important, wise and sound views are inculcated and enforced, by Sir Frederick Pollock in his "Oxford Lectures and other Discourses" (London, 1890, Papers I., II.), as well as in his previous book, "Essays in Jurisprudence and Ethics" (London, 1882, particularly Papers I.,

Lecture I.

Our law always has been and is a system distinct from the Civil or Roman law.

Again, by the phrase "our law" I mean the English and American system of law as distinguished from all other legal systems, and particularly from the Roman or Civil law. It is a most remarkable fact that if one casts his eye over the map of the enlightened world he will find, generically speaking, but two systems of law or jurisprudence, — the one of England, the other of Rome. The legal systems of the nations of the continent of Europe and of the South American States are based upon the Roman law; but the Roman law never obtained controlling authority in or among any people who speak the tongue of England. "None of the great nations," says Mr. Justice Markby, "founded on the continent of Western "Europe after the fall of the Roman Empire, has "constructed an independent legal system of its "own. France, Italy, Austria, Germany, Holland, "and Spain have every one of them adopted the "Roman law as their general or common law, and "have only departed from it so far as particular occa-"sions might require. Every gap not filled up by "special legislation, or specially recognized custom, "has been supplied from the Roman law, and even "modern codes to a very large extent only contain "the ideas of the Corpus Juris in a nineteenth-"century dress."[1]

II., XI.). "Amongst civilians the teaching of Jurisconsults by a system of treatises or commentaries is called Doctrine; the decision of the Courts is called Jurisprudence; the other source of law is Legislation. An accomplished civilian rarely confuses these terms." Mr. Justice Bradley, of the United States Supreme Court, manuscript letter to the author.

[1] Sir William Markby, "Elements of Law," 4th ed., London, 1889, § 85.

It was for some time the received notion that the Roman law ceased to exist in Europe until it was revived upon the discovery of the Corpus Juris at Amalfi when that city was taken by the Pisans in 1135. But Savigny and others have shown that this was altogether a mistake, and that the law of the Romans in general displaced the law of the conquerors, and was adopted as the law of the land. By one nation alone, in the territorially small kingdom of England, was the force of Roman law combated and resisted. English lawyers, English judges, and English parliaments, as often as it was attempted to introduce the Corpus Juris as an authority in England, stubbornly resisted it. Glanvill, Fleta, and Bracton were saturate with the Roman law, and incorporated principles of the Roman law in their works professing to treat of the laws of England. But it is interesting to note that in a case quoted by Fitzherbert in his Abridgment, decided in the 35th Henry VI., the court is represented as agreeing that "Bracton was never accepted as an authority in our law." Markby refers to this, and also to the case of Stowel against Lord Zouch,[1] wherein Saunders in argument is reported to have said: "And to this purpose he "cited Bracton, not as an author in the law, for he "said that Bracton and Glanvill were not authors in "our law; but he said he cited him as an ornament "to discourse where he agrees with the law."[2]

Lecture I.

The Common law a system distinct from the Roman law.

[1] Plowden's Reports, vol. i., p. 357.
[2] Elements of Law, § 89, p. 55, note. Markby adds: "As far as I am aware, neither Bracton, Fleta, nor Glanvill is ever quoted in the Year Books. . . . I am not aware upon what authority the state-

Lecture I.

Fortunate results of the successful exclusion of the Roman law as a system from England.

It would be a curious and not uninstructive speculation to consider what would have been the effect if the Roman law had acquired the same foothold and influence in England that it acquired on the continent of Europe. I cannot forbear quoting on this point — for I think they will interest you — a few striking sentences from Sir Frederick Pollock: —

"From the storm floods that made wreck of the "Roman Empire there emerged, defaced but not "broken, the solid fabric of Roman law. Not by "any command or ordinance of princes, but by the "inherent power of its name and traditions, Roman "law rose again to supremacy among the ruins of "Roman dominion, and seemed for a time supreme "in the civilized world. In only one corner of "Europe it finally failed of obedience. Rude and "obscure in its beginnings, unobserved or despised "by the doctors and glossators, there rose in this "island of England a home-grown stock of laws "and a home-grown type of legal institutions.[1] "They grew in rugged exclusiveness, disdaining "fellowship with the more polished learning of the

---

ment of Bracton's influence on English law rests." *Ib.*, § 89, note. "All the writers I have named (Bracton, Fleta, Glanvill) attempted to introduce the principles of the Roman law into English courts by incorporating them into works professing to treat of the laws and customs of England. But the attempt met with little success. It was perhaps due to this very admixture of Roman law that the authority of even so accomplished a writer as Bracton was repudiated so emphatically by the judges." *Ib.*, § 89, text. The subject of the connection of the civil and common law is learnedly discussed by Professor Hammond in the notes to his edition of Blackstone's Commentaries, vol. i., pp. 39–65.

[1] See *post* Lecture V.

"civilians, and it was well that they did so; for, had English law been in its infancy drawn, as at one time it seemed likely to be drawn, within the masterful attraction of Rome, the range of legal discussion and of the analysis of legal ideas would have been dangerously limited. Roman conceptions, Roman classification, the Roman understanding of legal reason and authority, would have dominated men's minds without a rival. It is hardly too much to say that the possibility of comparative jurisprudence would have been in extreme danger; for, broadly speaking, whatever is not of England in the forms of modern jurisprudence is of Rome or of Roman mould. In law, as in politics, the severance of Britain by a world's breadth from the world of Rome has fostered a new birth which mankind could ill have spared. And the growth of English politics is more closely connected with the independent growth and strength of English law than has been commonly perceived, or can be gathered from the common accounts of English history."[1]

Lecture I.

Effect of the exclusion of the Roman law.

---

[1] Oxford Lectures, London, 1890, Lecture II., pp. 46, 47, 48. It is an interesting fact that the work which most satisfactorily illustrates the important subject referred to in the last sentence in the text quoted from Sir Frederick Pollock was written in distant Australia by Chancellor Hearn of the University of Melbourne, — "The Government of England," 2d ed., London, 1887. Professor Dicey makes this acknowledgment: "Professor Hearn's 'Government of England' has taught me more than any other single work of the way in which the labors of lawyers established in early times the elementary principles which form the basis of the [English] constitution." Preface to "The Law of the Constitution," 2d ed., London, 1886. I can truly say that in my judgment Mr. Hearn's work merits the high estimation in which it is thus held.

26 LAWS AND JURISPRUDENCE.

<small>Lecture I.</small>

<small>Vast expansion and influence of the English law.</small>

When the lawyers, the judges, the nobility, and the commons of England so persistently and successfully resisted the innovation of the Roman law, they little foresaw, perhaps, the great and beneficent consequences in future times of their action; for such is the wide and vast expansion and influence of English laws that in our day they more than rival the law of the Roman Empire. You may recall Webster's famous description of England as "a power to which Rome in the height "of her glory is not to be compared;—a power "which has dotted over the surface of the whole "globe with her possessions and military posts, "whose morning drum-beat, following the sun and "keeping company with the hours, circles the earth "with one continuous and unbroken strain of the "martial airs of England."[1] In this magnificent passage the flag of England is made to symbolize the military power of England. But to the lawyer it also and equally symbolizes the reign of English law. Wherever, in either hemisphere, you find an English settlement, there also will be found the law of England. More powerful than armies, the English law holds under subjection in India over 240,000,000 of people.[2] It supplies the rule of action in all the British colonies and possessions. Our own country has become the theatre of the

---

[1] Webster's Works, vol. iv., p. 110, Little & Brown's ed., 1851.

[2] "In 1877 British India comprised 1,500,000 square miles, and contained about 240,000,000 of inhabitants." Kolb, "Condition of Nations," 1880, translated by Mrs. Brewer, p. 155. "Far more numerous than the Christians are the Mohammedans, and the Empress of India undoubtedly rules over many more followers of the Prophet than does the Turkish Sultan, nearly 41,000,000, in India." *Ib.*, p. 157.

most wonderful extension and development of English law, since that law constitutes, as I shall show in a subsequent lecture, the basis of the system of law in all, or in all but one or two of the States of the American Union; and even in these it has so modified or supplemented the Roman system as almost to dominate it.

Now the form of this law, or rather its want of form or of scientific or methodical arrangement, is as remarkable as its history. The main body of this unique system of laws, everything in fact that goes under the comprehensive description of the Common Law, is "unwritten," using this word in distinction to positive or statutory law. This so-called unwritten law constitutes the great bulk of the English and American system of law. Of this system the lawyers and the judges are the visible artificers. "The State has," as Professor Holland says, "in general, two, and only two, articulate " organs for law-making purposes, — the legislature " and the tribunals. The first organ makes new " law; the second attests and confirms old law, " though under cover of doing so it introduces " many new principles."[1]

The existing body of English case law has been mainly the work, the stupendous work, of judges and lawyers extending in almost unbroken reach through several hundred years. It has not been excogitated by any single brain; it is not the product of any determinate number of minds, but it has been the slow work of ages, constantly growing and ever changing. It is never stationary, and

Lecture I.

Lawyers and judges are the main artificers of the English law.

[1] Elements of Jurisprudence, chap. v.

28   *LAWS AND JURISPRUDENCE.*

Lecture I.

never can be. It can never reach a fixed and final form. English law in the shape in which we have it is thus essentially a growth, a historical development, — the work, I repeat, chiefly of the lawyers and judges of England through a succession of centuries.

As the lawyers and judges of England are the main builders of the English law (at least as respects its repositories and its external and authoritative form), it is at all events interesting — and in my judgment it is in no small degree necessary to a thorough conception of the manner in which they have wrought this great work, and of their fitness for it — to understand the methods of the legal education, training, and discipline of the bar, and the nature of the powers, functions, and duties of the judges. And here it is to be observed that the judges in England are not a distinct branch of the profession, but are merely eminent members of it, selected for judicial office by reason of qualifications and character.[1] So that, in fact, the fashioning of the laws of England is, in its last analysis, the work, not of lawyers and judges, but in a broad sense the work of the bar, of whom the judges are an integral, and in virtue of the functions and powers of the judicial office a most important, part.

Repositories of English law.

The extant English judicial records do not begin until 1194 (Mich. 6 Rich. I.). We have a series of

---

[1] "From an early time our judicial system has been independent of Continental culture, and singularly independent of the other departments of the government. The judges have not been a special branch of the profession, but selected, under an efficient criticism of skilled opinion, from the profession at large." Pollock, "Oxford Lectures," London, 1890, p. 25. See *post* Lecture II.

such records from 1384 (6 Rich. II.). The first law treatise by Glanvill was not written before 1187. The law reports begin in 1292.[1] The knowledge of the laws of England prior to the twelfth century is in many points obscure and uncertain. From that time, however, the growth and development of these laws can be traced in the parliamentary and official records, treatises, and law reports.

By the time of Edward I., if not before, we reach the important era when the judicial office is separated from the kingly office, and when justice is administered by the judges and in the judicial courts.[2] I have not time to unfold all that this simple statement implies, or to set forth its great, permanent, and beneficent consequences. To this fact may indeed be traced nearly all that in the course of these lectures I shall say concerning the merits and value of the laws of England and America as they now exist. I can only remark that administering justice by and through the judges and in the courts theoretically means, and for two hundred years has actually meant, that the judges are free from any

Lecture I.

Merits of our legal system due to the mode of its evolution in the judicial courts.

---

[1] Markby, "Elements of Law," § 90. 5 Harvard Law Review, 1892, p. 252, Professor Thayer's paper on "The Jury and its Development."

[2] "We may say," remarks Freeman, "that in the time of Edward I., A. D. 1272-1307, the English Constitution definitely put on the same essential form which it has kept ever since. . . . From that time English constitutional history is not merely an inquiry, however interesting and instructive, into something which has passed away. It is an inquiry into something that still lives; it is an inquiry into laws which, whenever they have not been formally repealed, are in full force at this day. Up to the reign of Edward I. English history is strictly the domain of antiquaries. From the reign of Edward I. it becomes the domain of lawyers." Freeman's "Growth of the English Constitution," chap. ii.

Lecture I.

Merits of our legal system due to its judicial evolution.

control or interference by the Crown or Parliament, and that the King, though in legal theory the fountain of justice, cannot pronounce any judgment, or in the slightest degree infringe or authorize an infringement upon the legal rights of the least of his subjects.[1] It means that the judges must be selected from the bar; and until very recently the common law judges had to be of the degree or estate of serjeant-at-law, long the highest, and never in point of learning an inferior, rank in the profession.[2] The judges act under the solemnity of an oath of office. They sit in public. They must hear arguments on both sides. They do not possess arbitrary power, but are bound by positive enactments and by the decisions of their predecessors. They must deliver judgments openly, and in important causes state the grounds and reasons therefor. They have the power to enforce their judgments and decrees. Publicity as a restraint upon judicial tyranny, oppression, and corruption, both in its grosser and subtler forms, is of the highest and most wholesome consequence. The discontinuance of the salutary practice of giving reasoned opinions is justly regarded as one of the worst innovations of servile judges of the Stuart period.[3]

[1] See *post* Lectures IV., VIII.
[2] See *post* Lecture II.
[3] Hearn, "Government of England," 2d ed., pp. 66, 71, 78, 558, 562, 563. Lord Bacon condenses the matter thus: "Let not the judgments of the courts be given in silence, but let the judges produce the reasons of their sentence openly and in full audience of the court, so that what is free in power may yet be limited by regard to fame and reputation." Bacon, "Advancement of Learning," Book VIII., chap. iii., Aphorism xxxviii., Devey's Translation, Bohn Libraries. The importance of judicial opinions, and of their publicity, is

The essential attributes of courts of justice, if I may attempt to define them, are that they shall be held by judges appointed or selected for that purpose; that cases and controversies therein shall be cast in some form of pleadings resulting in specific issues of law or fact, in which, on issues of fact, only competent evidence is admissible, and if not documentary, to be given under the sanction of an oath, with the right to cross-examine; that there shall be a public trial or hearing resulting in a judgment or

Lecture I.

Essential attributes of courts of justice.

enforced by Burke in his great and (considering that he had never been called to the bar) wonderful Report of April 30, 1794, from the committee appointed to inspect the Lords' Journal in relation to their proceeding upon the trial of Warren Hastings. "Works of Edmund Burke," vol. xi., 4th ed., Little, Brown, & Co., Boston, 1871, pp. 29–40, 153. It was in the course of this report that he made the following most weighty observations: "English jurisprudence has not any other sure foundation, nor, consequently, the lives and properties of the subject any sure hold, but in the maxims, rules, principles, and judicial traditionary line of decisions contained in the notes taken, and from time to time published (mostly under the sanction of the judges), called Reports." *Ib.*, p. 42. "To give judgment privately is to put an end to reports; and to put an end to reports is to put an end to the law of England. It was fortunate for the Constitution of this kingdom that in the judicial proceedings in the case of ship-money the judges did not then venture to depart from the ancient course. They gave and they argued their judgment in open court. Their reasons were publicly given, and the reasons assigned for their judgment took away all its authority. The great historian, Lord Clarendon, at that period a young lawyer, has told us that the judges gave as law from the bench what every man in the hall knew not to be law." *Ib.*, p. 44. "All courts," says Lord Brougham, "ought to sit and give their judgments in public, and the fullest liberty should be given to the publication through the press of all their proceedings." "The British Constitution," vol. ii., p. 322, Black's ed., Edinburgh, 1872. And elsewhere he observes that: "With an enlightened bar and an intelligent people, the mere authority of the bench will cease to have any weight at all, if it be unaccompanied with argument and explanation." Further as to Law Reports, see *post* Lectures VI., IX., X., and XIII.

<small>Lecture I.</small> decree, which the court has the inherent power, by its own officers, process and machinery, to enforce. Such a court is the tribunal to which Mr. Justice Blatchford, speaking for the Supreme Court of the United States, refers in the great Minnesota case, wherein he affirms the right of a party to "a judi- "cial investigation by due process of law under the "forms and with the machinery provided by the "wisdom of successive ages for the investigation "judicially of the truth of a matter in contro- "versy."[1] The difference between judicial courts constituted of judges, and any form of legislative tribunal not constituted of judges but of commissioners or other officials by whatsoever name they may be called, is of vital moment to the rights and liberties of the citizen.

<small>Judicial judgments as the source and evidence of individual rights.</small> I shall hereafter take especial occasion further to show that the rules of English law are all-embracing in their protective energy, and that they have, in the main, been the work of the courts which have defined, established, and enforced them. They have their source or authoritative evidence in the adjudged rights of individuals. These rights, secured by the decisions of the courts, make the Constitution of England; they are not created by and are not the product of the Constitution.[2] These glorious characteristics, these fundamental principles, these crowning excellences of the English law, have been inherited or adopted in all their amplitude in this country. Not only so, but

---

[1] Chicago, etc., Railway Company v. Minnesota (extent of legislative power to fix railway rates), 134 U. S. Rep. 418, 457, 1889.

[2] See on this subject *post* Lecture VII.

we have in our constitutions, Federal and State, placed them beyond the range of legislative power, — beyond the courts, beyond Congress, beyond the States, — thus giving them a scope, a legal security and solidity, theoretically, at least, greater than they have in the old country.

Lecture I.

We have thus not only all the necessary safeguards of the essential rights and liberties of the subject or citizen, but in the official records of the realm, in the records of the courts and in the reports of their judgments and opinions, we have data that enable us to trace the history and evolution of our law for the last six hundred years with all needed fulness and precision.

English lawyers and judges being thus the chief artificers of English law, I shall in the next two lectures show you where and how, since the period when they became so influential, they have been educated, trained, and prepared for their office and work.

LECTURE II.

The Education and Discipline of the English Bar, and herein of the Inns of Court, their History, Character and Purposes. Origin, Antiquity, and Establishment of the Inns of Court (Note A). Status of Serjeant-at-law, Ceremonials on taking the Coif, the Difference between a Serjeant and a Queen's Counsel, etc., etc. (Note B).

Lecture II.

Unique character of the Inns of Court.

I POINTED out in my last lecture how largely the laws and legal institutions of England had been moulded and fashioned by the lawyers of England. I am now to consider where and how they have been educated and trained in the learning and duties of their profession, and this will lead me to present in outline one of the most ancient and to me one of the most interesting objects of curious and instructive study, — The Inns of Court, their history, character, faculties, and purposes.

These institutions, so intimately associated with English law and lawyers, like so much else connected with the law of England, are absolutely unique. We have in this country nothing which in the least degree resembles them. The subject abounds with materials from which to draw a picture rich in historic interest and replete with professional instruction. But alas for my unpractised pencil! I must rely upon your taste, knowledge, and reading, to fill in the sketch, which I can only "crayon out" (to use Burke's phrase), and to supply the necessary shades and coloring.

The Inns of Court, and Westminster Hall where the great courts were held for so many centuries until their removal in 1882 into the new Royal Courts of Justice building, are the visible wellsprings and fountains of English, and derivatively of American, law. Neither the history of the English nation nor the special history of the English law can ever fail to be of surpassing interest to the statesmen, the legislators, the judges, the lawyers, the students of law, and even the people, of this country. In a general view the history of England "during the last six centuries is the history of the progress of a great people toward liberty;"[1] and Magna Charta and the Petition of Rights and Bill of Rights are the basis of American, as well as of English liberty.

There are now, and for centuries have been, four great coequal societies or Inns of Court: Lincoln's Inn, Gray's Inn, the Inner Temple, and the Middle Temple. With these there have been connected until very recently about ten smaller Inns known as Inns of Chancery, most of which were subordinate to one or another of the Inns of Court. But these Inns of Chancery have ceased to exist.[2]

Lecture II.

The four great Inns

[1] Mackintosh, "History of England."
[2] In a late publication, "The Inns of Court and Chancery," by Mr. W. J. Loftie (Macmillan & Co., 1893), it is said (p. 74) : "There are, as a fact, no Inns of Chancery. The Inns of Court, whose offspring they were held to be, have cut them adrift;" and they have nearly all, he adds, sold their property.

Lecture II.

What are the Inns of Court? They are thus defined: "*Inns of Court*, colleges or corporate "societies in London, to which all barristers and "serjeants-at-law and all aspirants to these dignities "must belong; also the buildings belonging to these "societies in which the members of the Inns dine "together, and barristers have their chambers. *Inns* "*of Chancery*, colleges in which young students "formerly began their law studies. They are now "occupied chiefly by attorneys, solicitors, etc."[1] This gives, as we shall see, a very general and incomplete idea of the singular and composite character of the Inns, and is, moreover, inaccurate in ascribing to them in a legal sense a corporate character. We must make a closer study.

The name "Inns of Court," whence derived.

Even the name of these societies and of their places of residence or habitation — Inns of Court — does not to a modern ear, at least in this country, accurately denote their character; it tends rather to mis-describe them. Modern usage associates the Saxon word "inne," as well as the French word "hôtel," wholly with houses of public entertainment. But at the time when the Inns of Court and of Chancery were established, the Norman French was much in use, and in that language they were called "hostels," — a word signifying, as thus used, not a public place of entertainment, but the private city or town mansion of a person of rank or wealth, — as, for example, the hostel of the Earl of Lincoln. The word "inn" is the equivalent of the word "hostel;" and when the hostel of the Earl of Lincoln was let to the lawyers and students of law, it naturally

---

[1] Imperial Dictionary, 1883, "Inns of Court."

acquired the name of Lincoln's Inn. The name of Gray's Inn and of most of the Inns of Chancery had a like origin; and the houses, as well as societies collectively, came to be called the Inns of Court and the Inns of Chancery.

The phrase "Inns of Court," therefore, signifies, primarily, the four great and Honorable Societies of Lincoln's Inn, Gray's Inn, The Inner Temple, and The Middle Temple; and, secondarily, the houses which these societies occupy and own.[1]

Lecture II.

What the phrase "Inns of Court" signifies.

---

[1] The houses of the Inns of Court were anciently described by the old French word "hostel," meaning not a public place, such as is denoted in our language by the modern word "hotel," but the city mansion or place of residence of a person of rank or wealth. The word continues to have this meaning in French usage. In the Latin law records the Inns were called *hospitia;* while the name of *diversoria* was given to public houses of entertainment or public inns. Pearce, "Inns of Court," chap. iii.; Herbert, "Antiquities of the Inns of Court and Chancery," 168. The Earl of Lincoln built his "hostel" in or about the time of Edward II., and Gray's Inn, Clifford's Inn, and Furnival's Inn were anciently the hostels or inns of noble families. Thavie's Inn was called after John Thavie, or Tavie, of London, whose will was proved in 1350, is extant among the records of Guildhall, and is referred to by Coke in the Preface to the 10th volume of his Reports (p. xxii). We are told that Coke regarded Thavie's will with so much interest that he procured a transcript of it, which he was in the habit of showing to his learned friends. In Thavie's will the testator directed that "all of that *hostel* (hospicium) in which the apprentices of the law were wont to dwell should be sold, and out of the produce a proper chaplain found to pray for the souls of himself and his wife." "John Thavie's old hostel is thus shown," says Serjeant Pulling, in his "Order of the Coif" (pp. 132-136), "to have been used by the apprentices of the law as an Inn of Court more than five hundred years ago. The possession of the smaller hostels or inns seems originally to have been acquired by the apprentices of the law in somewhat the same way as Thavie's Inn, — viz., by hiring from the actual owners, — this temporary possession being in after times made permanent by lease or purchase. . . . The story of the greater Inns — the Inns of Court as they came in time to be exclusively called — does not essentially differ from that of the lesser Inns. The societies

Lecture II.

The Inns of Court (including under this general name the late Inns of Chancery) are among the

of the Inns of Court, like those of the lesser Inns, came into possession as tenants or lodgers, and at last they became sole proprietors." The history of the acquisition by the societies of the Inns of the freehold or reversion of their valuable properties is given by Dugdale, Foss, Pearce, Pulling, and others. Places of public entertainment were, at least as early as the fifteenth century, called common or public hostels; the keepers of which in London in 1473 obtained an order to change their name from "hostelers" to "innkeepers." The word "inn" — Saxon "inne" — means a dwelling or abiding-place, and came in popular use to mean "a large lodging-house, hotel, house of entertainment" (Skeats' Dictionary); "a house of entertainment for travellers" (Johnson's Dictionary). The English word "inn" was used as the equivalent of the hostels or houses where the lawyers and students dwelt or abode, and hence Johnson gives as a secondary definition of the word "inn": "A house where students were boarded and taught; whence we still call the colleges of common law *Inns* of Court." What we call the Tabard Inn, of Southwark, — which, though destroyed in the great fire of 1676, lives in the immortal pages of Chaucer's "Canterbury Tales" (written not many years prior to A. D. 1400), as the place from which the pilgrims started for the shrine of the holy blissful martyr Thomas à Becket, — was described not by the word "inn," but by the word "hostelry": —

> "Befel that, in that season on a day,
> In Southwark at the Tabard as I lay
> Ready to wenden on my pilgrimage
> To Canterbury with devout coráge,
> At night was come into that hostelry
> Well nine and twenty in a company
> Of sundry folk."

"Dr. Johnson," says Rendle, "has a choice little selection of quotations from great writers on the subject of inns; the two sadder ones touch me most: from Spenser, where the word is perhaps used in its more extended sense: —

> ' "Palmer," quoth he, "death is an equal doom
> To good and bad, the common inn of rest;"'

from Dryden, who seems to paraphrase Spenser: —

> ' Like pilgrims to the appointed place we tend;
> The world's an inn, and death the journey's end.'"

"The Inns of Old Southwark," by William Rendle, London, 1888, chap. i., pp. 7, 8.

most remarkable antiquities of London. The mists of a remote period hang densely about their foundation. The legal antiquary cannot fix upon the exact time of the origin of these Inns, but it can be nearly approximated.[1] They carry the mind back to the depths of the Middle Ages. They antedate the discovery and settlement of America. They existed long before Columbus lifted the veil from the New World. They touch upon the borders of Magna Charta and the Crusades. King John lodged at the new Temple previously to signing Magna Charta, and pending the negotiations with his barons, which, in 1215, had their glorious issue at Runnymede. A distinguished American lawyer and judge, — the Hon. Jeremiah Black, — who visited Europe for the first time in 1880, declared that he did so to see two things, — the Inns of Court, and Running-Mede. The Temple society of lawyers afterward inherited the name, and what was more important to it succeeded to the property, of the Knights Templars, which the society still owns.

In the quaint and curious edifices known as the Inns of Court, the lawyers and judges of England, the artificers and builders of English law, have been trained and educated for centuries. Changes,

Lecture II.

Origin and antiquity of the Inns.

---

[1] "It is natural that the mist which veils any system built up in remote periods should hang most densely about its foundations; and an attempt to ascertain exactly the time from which each of the Inns of Court has been established as a seat of legal education has little prospect of success." — Smith, "History of Education for the English Bar," p. 2.

"*The original institution* of the Inns of Court nowhere precisely appears.... They are voluntary societies which have for ages submitted to government analogous to that of the seminaries of learning." — Lord Mansfield in Rex v. Gray's Inn, 1 Douglas, 353.

replacements, and additions have from time to time been made in the buildings; and the present structures, as a whole, excepting of course the Temple Church, and the old halls, notwithstanding the admiration with which they are regarded by their members, offer externally to the eye no imposing presence, and no striking architectural beauty; quite the reverse. The interest is historical and intellectual. The chambers are in sober fact mostly dismal and dingy; but they are associated with the lives and names of the great sages in the law who have conferred glory and renown upon the legal profession and advanced English law to its present height and proportions.[1]

---

[1] In "Pendennis," chapter xxix., — "The Knights of the Temple," — Thackeray gives a graphic account of some of the features of the social life at the Inns, and takes off, in his quiet way, the pride with which they are regarded by the members. The following extracts may interest the reader: "A well-ordained workhouse or prison is much better provided with the appliances of health, comfort, and cleanliness, than a Foundation School, a venerable College, or a learned Inn. In the latter place of residence men are contented to sleep in dingy closets, and to pay for the sitting-room and the cupboard, which is their dormitory, the price of a good villa and garden in the suburbs, or of a roomy house in the neglected squares of the town. . . . Nevertheless, those venerable Inns, which have the Lamb and Flag and the Winged Horse for their ensigns, have attractions for persons who inhabit them, and a share of rough comforts and freedom, which men always remember with pleasure. I don't know whether the student of law permits himself the refreshment of enthusiasm, or indulges in poetical reminiscences as he passes by historical chambers, and says, 'Yonder Eldon lived — upon this site Coke mused upon Lyttleton — here Chitty toiled — here Barnwell and Alderson joined in their famous labors — here Byles composed his great work upon Bills, and Smith compiled his immortal "Leading Cases" — here Gustavus still toils, with Solomon to aid him:' but the man of letters can't but love the place which has been inhabited by so many of his brethren, or peopled by their creations as real to us at this day as the authors

More than six centuries have elapsed since the Inns of Court were founded, and the original Westminster Hall was at that time more than a century old. What thoughtful lawyer or law student can survey them with indifference? Dr. Johnson, in a familiar and noted passage respecting famous places, declares "that to abstract the mind from all "local emotion would be impossible, if it were en- "deavored, and would be foolish, if it were possible. "Whatever withdraws us from the power of our "senses, — whatever makes the past, the distant, or "the future, predominate over the present, advances "us in the dignity of thinking beings. Far from "me, and from my friends, be such frigid philoso- "phy as may conduct us, unmoved, over any ground "which has been dignified by wisdom, bravery, or "virtue. That man is little to be envied whose "patriotism would not gain force upon the plain of "Marathon, or whose piety would not grow warmer "among the ruins of Iona."[1] As little to be envied

Lecture II.

Dr. Johnson's passage concerning famous places.

whose children they were; and Sir Roger de Coverley walking in the Temple Garden, and discoursing with Mr. Spectator about the beauties in hoops and patches who are sauntering over the grass, is just as lively a figure to me as old Samuel Johnson rolling through the fog with the Scotch gentleman at his heels, on their way to Dr. Goldsmith's chambers in Brick Court, — or Harry Fielding, with inked ruffles, and a wet towel round his head, dashing off articles at midnight for the 'Covent Garden Journal,' while the printer's boy is asleep in the passage."

[1] "Journey to the Western Isles: Inch Kenneth." Speaking of this extract, Boswell (Life of Dr. Johnson) says: "Had our tour (to the Hebrides) produced nothing but this sublime passage, the world must have acknowledged that it was not made in vain. Sir Joseph Banks told me he was so much struck on reading it, that he clasped his hands together and remained for some time in an attitude of silent admiration."

is the lawyer who can contemplate without emotion these venerable Inns and this illustrious Hall.

The Inns of Court were originally provided for the use of lawyers and students of law, and they have maintained that character to the present time. By a clause in Magna Charta, June 15, A. D. 1215, it was, to redress the grievance of compelling suitors to attend the sovereign wherever he might chance to be, ordained that the Court of "Common Pleas " should not thenceforth follow the Court [the " King], but be held in some certain place." This certain place was established in Westminster Hall, which distinctively became, and has remained until recently, the principal seat of the great judicial courts.[1] The fixed location of this court, called by

---

[1] The authorities clearly establish that the Court of Common Pleas existed from time immemorial, and was not created by the clause in Magna Charta which required this court to be held in some certain place. Serjeant Pulling in his "Order of the Coif," after referring to the authorities (chap. iii., p. 89 *et seq.*), says that they "quite refute the idea of those who speak of the Court of Common Pleas as *created in the time of Edward I.*, or originating in the clause of Magna Charta, which provided for its sittings being in *aliquo certo loco*. The words of this clause in Magna Charta have evidently led to a variety of mistakes with reference to the Common Pleas. The evil which was designed to be dealt with by the clause in question was the continual change in the place of sitting of the courts. Incidentally no doubt it had the effect in time of bringing about the establishment at Westminster Hall of not only the Court of Common Pleas, but the other courts which grew out of the old *Aula Regia*; but it is free from dispute that for ages after Magna Charta, as well the Common Pleas, as the King's Bench and Exchequer, were held in a variety of places and were certainly not *de facto aut nomine* what in modern times they became, 'His Majesty's Courts at Westminster.' They were each of them in their turn held at Winchester, Gloucester, Windsor, Lincoln, or York, as much as at Westminster, and neither of the places named could therefore exclusively be called the *certus locus* in which the courts were obliged to be held."

Sir Edward Coke "the lock and key of the common law," had another important consequence. It drew as with a magnet the lawyers together from all parts of the kingdom, and formed them into one body, — who to the great advantage of the law henceforth gave themselves wholly to its study and practice.[1] There is, however, another interesting consideration which I must not omit to mention. According to the weighty opinion of Sir William Blackstone,[2] this clause in Magna Charta concerning the Common Pleas had a most influential, if not decisive, effect at a critical time on the fortunes of the common law in its struggle to prevent the intrusion of the civil law into England. This clause localized the great courts, and such localization concentrated the common lawyers who were dispersed throughout the kingdom, and formed them into an organized body for the study of the "law of the land" as distinguished from the civil law, which alone was taught at Oxford and Cambridge; and for the accommodation of "the professors of the municipal law," as the lawyers were called, they acquired the properties which afterwards received the name of "the Inns of Court and of Chancery." These became collegiate houses or seminaries where the common law was taught and degrees therein conferred, as I shall hereafter describe. And thus the Inns of Court, their history, powers, purposes, and associations, have a profound interest to all who like myself rejoice that the common law as a compet-

Lecture II.

Localization of the courts and concentration of the lawyers.

---

[1] 1 Blacks. Com., 23. Pulling, "The Order of the Coif," London, 1884, chap. iii., p. 89 *et seq.*
[2] 1 Blacks. Com., 23-25.

44 LAWS AND JURISPRUDENCE.

Lecture II.

When the societies assumed their modern form and mode of government.

ing system with the civil law retained its mastery in England.

I have said above that the exact date of the origin of the several Inns of Court cannot be determined. It seems to me probable from the researches which have been made that houses for the reception of students of the law were established soon after Magna Charta. The attendance gradually increased, and by the time of Edward III., 1327, the original of what we now know as the Inns of Court existed, although we are not advised as to their constitution, mode of government, or the nature of the distinction, if it then existed, between the Inns of Court and the Inns of Chancery. The records of Lincoln's Inn go back only to 1423, those of the Temple and of Gray's Inn not quite so far. Foss's opinion is that the Inns did not assume their modern form of societies " bound by established rules, gov-" erned by a controlling body, and empowered to " confer legal degrees," until about the beginning of the sixteenth century; and that in the reign of Henry VIII. they were fully established upon the system which in form and substance prevails at the present time.[1]

The sites of the Inns.

The Inns, with their adjacent gardens, are in our day in the very heart of London. All is quiet

[1] The curious student or inquirer will find in Note A, at the end of this lecture, some of the results of the researches of learned antiquaries and writers on the subject of the origin, antiquity, and establishment of the Inns briefly summarized, and the sources of more detailed information pointed out. As to the origin (which is somewhat obscure) of the faculty of the Inns to confer the rank of barrister-at-law, see Goldsmith's " English Bar; Or Guide to the Inns of Court " (London, 1843), p. 84, wherein is given the substance of the Sixth Report of the Common Law Commissioners concerning it.

within the Close, but the swelling tide of life and business flows tumultuously along the adjacent Strand and on the bordering Thames. But when the sites of the Inns were chosen they were in the suburbs, between the place where the King's Courts were held at Westminster and the city of London, thus enabling the members conveniently to attend the one and draw their supplies of provisions from the other.[1]

Lecture II.

Why chosen.

The Inner and Middle Temple were located on the Thames, and near three hundred years ago were alluded to by Spenser in the "Prothalamion," published in 1596, as

———— "Those bricky towers
The which on Themmes brode aged back doe ride,
Where now the studious lawyers have their bowers;
There whilom wont the Templar Knights to bide,
Till they decayed through pride."

Lincoln's Inn in the same neighborhood is also finely situated, and the gardens of the Temple and

[1] 1 Blacks. Com., 23. Sir John Fortescue ("De Laudibus Legum Angliæ"), more than four hundred years ago, thus sets forth the reasons for the location of the Inns. The sites of the Inns were chosen not "within the city, where the confluence of people might disturb the quietness of the students, but somewhat several in the suburbs of the same city, and nigher to the King's Courts, that the students may dayly at their pleasure have access and recourse thereto without weariness." "For this place of study is situate nie to the King's Court, where the same laws are pleaded and argued, and judgments on the same given by judges, men of gravity, ancient in years, perfect and graduate in the same laws: wherefore every day in court the students in those laws resort by great numbers into those Courts, wherein the same laws are read and taught as it were in common schools." (Chap. xlviii.) See note A at the end of the present lecture. The river Fleet, — whence the name of the celebrated street and prison, — flowing past the foot of Holborn Hill, separated the Inns of Court from the city.

of Gray's and Lincoln's Inn, and the ground known as Lincoln's Inn Fields, are among the most attractive portions of the great metropolis. Lord Bacon belonged to Gray's Inn. In it he had his home for many years. He is its chiefest glory. His many faults and weaknesses have not obscured his original brightness. Shakespeare, Bacon, Milton, Burke, — in this order Choate ranked the four greatest Englishmen.[1] If regarding Bacon in the aspect of his varied and wonderful powers and achievements in science, philosophy, literature, and law, in each of which he was pre-eminent, we assign to him the intellectual primacy, it would be easier to deny his title than to disprove it. May we not fitly pause for a moment and contemplate this extraordinary man in connection with the Inn he loved so well? Here he lived in his unworthy struggle for power, and here he retreated when he had been precipitated from it. His Essays, the most delightful and best known of all his writings, are dated from his "Chamber in Graie's Inn."[2] From his lodgings in this Inn, attended by the officers of the Chan-

---

[1] Rufus Choate's letter to Charles Sumner. Brown's "Life of Choate" (Little, Brown, & Co.), p. 112.

[2] It is generally thought that the gardens of Gray's Inn were laid out in or about 1597 by Lord Bacon, who was at that time the treasurer of the Inn. Lamb (Essay "On Some of the Old Actors") in his description of the gardens of Gray's Inn, after entering his protest against the marring of their beauty by the ugly, "accursed Verulam buildings," thus gives his judgment upon them, and recalls Bacon's relation to them: "They are still," he says, "the best gardens of any of the Inns of Court, — my beloved Temple not forgotten, — have the gravest character; their aspect being altogether reverend and law-breathing. Bacon has left the impress of his foot upon their gravel walks." What Lamb thought of the Temple gardens he tells us in the Essay on the "Old Benchers": "Indeed, it is the most

cery, the students of law, the judges and the nobility of England, he rode in state, clothed in purple satin, on May the 7th, 1617, to be installed in Westminster Hall as Lord Keeper of the Great Seal. He had at length attained the summit of human greatness; but his fall came speedily and justly.

As the price of regaining, after his disgrace, the coveted liberty to live in London, Bacon had been compelled by Buckingham to part with York House, in which he was born, and in which he wished to die. "Solitary and comfortless," without children or the companionship of wife, he again sought, with the weight of years and cares and the greater weight of debts and public disgrace pressing upon him, a home in his old Inn. Here he imagined his strength to revive, and here he gave himself with undistracted devotion to the "studies, arts, and sciences to which," as he truly declared at his installation as Lord Keeper, "in my own nature I am most induced." Like so many others, when they have realized the vanity of worldly fame, or felt the ingratitude or injustice or even the deserved displeas-

Lecture II.

Bacon's disgrace.

elegant spot in the metropolis." Pepys has these two characteristic touches in his diary:—

"4th May, 1662. When church was done my wife and I walked to Gray's Inn to observe the fashions of the ladies, because of my wife's making some clothes."

"17th August, 1662. I was very well pleased with the sight of a fine lady that I have often seen in Gray's Inn Gardens."

The earlier extract shows that woman's love of the becoming and beautiful in dress, and the later that man's admiration of loveliness in woman, have undergone no change in the two and more centuries which have since gone by, nor are they likely to undergo any in the future, whatever may be the changed civil, legal, and political rights of women.

ure of their fellow-men, he found solace in books and studious contemplation and intellectual employment. His death was pathetic. He was destined to become a martyr to his love of science. In experimenting upon the effect of cold in arresting putrefaction he caught a fatal illness, but he demonstrated the possibility of the great industry of our day of preserving meats in ice, and their transportation across continents and oceans in refrigerator cars and ships. His accidental illness thus contracted was so severe as to prevent his reaching his beloved Inn, and dying within its walls.

In his earlier life he so enjoyed the quiet of the gardens of the Inn and the prospect it afforded that he built therein a summer house for study and reflection. The records of the Society show that the sum of £7 15s. 4d. at one time and £60 6s. 8d. at another, laid out for planting elm-trees in these gardens, were allowed to Mr. Bacon. A catalpa-tree which Bacon planted in the gardens of the Inn he loved so well grew with his rise and lofty advancement, survived his inglorious fall, and while, it is said, it lives to interest the beholder,[1] yet such is the indestructible nature of the works of genius that his

---

[1] Bacon "is said to have designed the gardens of Gray's Inn, and to have planted the old catalpa tree still standing there in 1885." Hutton's "Literary Landmarks of London," article "Bacon." Tradition says that a catalpa-tree was planted by Bacon, and Douthwaite adds: "It is one of the oldest in England, and may well have been brought from its native land by Raleigh." Douthwaite, "Gray's Inn: Its History and Associations," p. 185. It was pointed out to me in 1889. As to the relations of Bacon and Gray's Inn, Douthwaite, *ubi supra*, p. 207. "Bacon's chambers in Gray's Inn were in the building now known as No. 1 Gray's Inn Square." *Ib.*, p. 209. *Post* Lecture III., Note A.

fame, which he confidently committed to an indulgent posterity, will for ages outlive the trees he planted and watered and enjoyed.¹ The works of our hands are perishable; only the creations of the intellect have the heritage of immortality.² Bacon died leaving an assured though tarnished fame; but Lord William Russell, who was beheaded on Lincoln's Inn Fields, a martyr to the eternal cause of human liberty, left to the world for all coming time the legacy of a spotless life, and the unfading record of a high and heroic example.³

Lecture II.

Bacon's tarnished but enduring fame.

We possess on many points but little satisfactory and definite information of the Inns of Court and Chancery until the time of Henry VI. (A. D. 1422–1461). Sir John Fortescue was his nominal Chancellor, and in his "Panegyric on the Laws of England" we have a sketch of the Inns as they

Fortescue's sketch of the Inns of Court.

---

¹ The solemn and touching words of Lord Bacon's will, in which he expresses his reliance upon the justice of future times, are: "For my name and memory I leave it to men's charitable speeches, to foreign nations, and the next ages."

² "The beings of the mind are not of clay;
Essentially immortal, they create
And multiply in us a brighter ray
And more beloved existence. . . .
  Shylock and the Moor,
And Pierre, cannot be swept or worn away —
The keystones of the arch! though all were o'er,
For us repeopled were the solitary shore."
  Byron, "Childe Harold," canto iv. verse iv.

³ "The scaffold was erected in Lincoln Inn Fields, a place distant from the Tower; and it was probably intended by conducting Russell through so many streets to show the mutinous city their beloved leader, once the object of all their confidence, now exposed to the utmost rigors of the law."— Hume, "History of England," chap. lxix.

Lecture II.

then existed.[1] This was over four hundred years ago. He describes them as composed of four large Inns having about two hundred students each, and ten lesser Inns called Inns of Chancery, having about one hundred students each, about eighteen hundred in all, and situate in the suburbs of the city. The students were chiefly young men of birth, many of them being attended with servants; and although he mentions that it was costly to live at the Inns, he does not give the order or course of instruction or study.[2] More than a century later, in the reign of Queen Elizabeth (A. D. 1558-1603), Lord Coke[3] gives a full account of the Inns of Court at that time, — their names, constitution, readings, moots, etc., — and he describes the Inner Temple, Gray's Inn, Lincoln's Inn, and the Middle Temple, as the "foure famous and renowned Colleges or houses of Court." "All these," with the Serjeants' Inn and the Inns of Chancery, are, he adds, "not

They constitute a legal university.

"farre distant one from another, and altogether doe "make the most famous Universitie for profession of "law onely, or of any one humane science, that is in "the world, and advanceth itself above all others. "In which houses of Court and Chancery the read-"ings and other exercises of the lawes therein con-

---

[1] "De Laudibus Legum Angliæ," written between 1461 and 1470. Sir Walter Raleigh calls Fortescue that Notable Bulwark of our Laws, — "History of the World," Part I., Book II., chap. iv., § 16.

[2] In 1470 the "Paston Letters" (vol. i., p. 41) speak of "your college the Inner Temple," and also subsequently of the Middle Temple. Margaret Paston sent her husband in term time supplies of provisions from the country, as, for example, "xjxx rabets by the berer hereof." "Paston Letters," vol. ii., p. 21.

[3] Preface to the third part of the Reports.

"tinually used are most excellent, and behooveful for "attaining to the knowledge of these lawes."[1]

Lecture II.

[1] In 1586 in the various Inns of Court and Chancery the number of students in term was 1,703, and out of term was 642, as appears from a MS. in Lord Burghley's collection. Pearce, "Inns of Court," p. 79.

Stow in his "Survey of London" (1598) enumerates as then existing the several societies, fourteen in number, corresponding nearly with those recognized at the present day, of which four are the Inns of Court, properly so called, — Encyclopædia Britannica, 9th ed., "Inns of Court."

In the grant of James I. to "the Inner and Middle Temple" these are described as "being two of those four colleges the most famous of all Europe" for the study of the law.

Edward Wynne, the author of "Eunomus," which originally appeared in 1767, gives (Dialogue II.) an interesting account of the Inns of Court in his time. Space does not permit it to be here set out at length. I can only subjoin an epitome of it with a few extracts. He points out that the common or municipal law was not taught in the two great Universities, but was taught in London by learned men of the law who set up schools for that purpose : —

"It seems to me not improbable that the abolition of the Law Schools by the prohibition that issued 19 Henry III. might in part give occasion to a more regular course of instruction, and fix the places of residence that we enjoy at this very day." See Note A at the end of this lecture.

"'Those writers who have called the Inns of Court and of Chancery by the name of an University do by no means degrade the term in its more genuine and strict acceptation." He runs a parallel between them and the Universities, and points out that the number of the Inns is not much less than the number of the colleges. In each instruction is given and degrees are taken. The internal government of the Inns in its nature and institution is, he maintains, as perfect as in colleges. But there is no instance, at least in print, until 1762, " of a voluntary concurrence of all of the Inns of Court to establish one common set of regulations [in respect of legal education], which regulations, well considered, reflect great honor on the present establishment," — "Eunomus," vol. ii., Dialogue II. (2d ed., 1774), pp. 232–255.

"Lord Coke," he says, "in his preface to the third Report, reckons fourteen Inns of Court and Chancery, comprehending the two houses of Serjeants' Inn, *all of which*, except Serjeants' Inn on Fleet Street, *are more or less dedicated to the law at this day*" (1774), — "Eunomus," 2d ed., vol. iv., notes, p. 95.

Lecture II.

I cannot in this sketch enter minutely upon the details of the student's life. He had his chambers or residence in the Inn. The mode of instruction was principally readings and mootings. Minute regulations as to dress and discipline were ordained, and attendance on religious services was made compulsory.

Branches of the legal profession in England.

And here I may observe that the legal profession in England has for centuries been divided into two distinct branches: (1) Barristers or counsel who constitute the higher or upper class of lawyers, and who alone have the right to appear in the Superior Courts, and who become such by being "called" by one of the four Inns of Court; (2) Attorneys (officers of the common law courts) and solicitors (officers of the courts of chancery). None of this lower branch has any right to practise in the courts, but they instruct the barrister or counsel in respect of matters in litigation therein. In 1845 and 1875 was chartered "The Incorporated Law Society," composed of attorneys, solicitors, proctors, and others, *not being barristers* practising in the courts of law and equity in the United Kingdom. This great, and, we may truly call it, Honorable Society has succeeded in securing legislation (6 & 7 Vict. c. 73, 23 & 24 Vict. c. 127) under which preliminary, intermediate, and final compulsory examinations are required on the part of all persons seeking to become attorneys or solicitors. Without further observations touching the division of the profession in England, I now resume my sketch of the Inns of Court.

There are three ranks or degrees among the members of the Inns of Court: (1) Benchers, or the governing body;[1] (2) barristers, that is, persons actually called to the bar; (3) students, that is, members keeping their terms at the Inns with a view to being called to the bar.

The degrees of legal precedence among the members of the bar are these: (1) The highest in rank are the Queen's counsel, the words of appointment in the patent being "one of our council learned in the law." These cannot be retained or employed in causes in which the Crown is concerned unless specially permitted. They "lead" in cases, and receive double the fees of an ordinary barrister. They give opinions on cases or questions submitted to them. They do not accept conveyancing or pleading, or admit pupils to their chambers. Seniority determines precedence. They cannot maintain an action for fees, or act in a case except through an attorney. They rank serjeants, unless the serjeant has a patent of precedence. (2) The degree of serjeant-at-law, the most ancient and formerly the highest rank at the bar. He is required by the King's writ to take the office, the admission to which was formerly attended with expensive ceremonies, of which only one remains, — that of presenting gold rings with mottoes to the

---

[1] "They are self-elected. They vary in number from twenty in Gray's Inn to seventy and upwards in Lincoln's Inn and the Inner Temple. The meetings of the benchers are variously denominated a 'parliament' in the Inner and Middle Temple, a 'pension' in Gray's Inn, and a 'council' in Lincoln's Inn." — Encyclopædia Britannica, 9th ed., "Inns of Court."

Lecture II. Sovereign, the Lord Chancellor, the judges, and others.[1]

[1] In Modern Rep., 9, the following curious circumstance relating to the *rings* given by serjeants on their call is recorded: " Seventeen serjeants being made, November 4th (21 Car. II.), Serjeant Powis, one of the new-made serjeants, coming a day or two after to the King's Bench bar, Chief-Justice Keeling told him he had something to say to him, viz.: that the rings which he and the rest of his brethren had given weighed but 18*s.* apiece; whereas Fortescue says (" De Laudibus ") that the rings given to the Chief-Justices and Chief Baron ought to weigh 20*s.* apiece, and that he spoke not this expecting a recompense, but that it might not be drawn into a precedent, and that the young gentlemen there might take notice of it."

Fortescue (" De Laudibus," chap. l.) says, " every serjeant shall make presents of gold rings to the value in the whole of £40 (at least) English money. I well remember when I took upon me the state and degree of a serjeant-at-law that my bill for gold rings came to £50." Mr. Waterhouse in his edition of " De Laudibus " (London, A. D. 1663), commenting on the above, says the rings were " old-fashioned gold rings with inscriptions. Forty pounds sterling is near as much as two hundred pounds now." The cost of the rings was but a small portion of the expense, and hence, anciently, only those were created serjeants " who have sufficient learning in the laws and an estate to support the dignity and equipage of it." Mr. Serjeant Robinson's account of the rings bestowed by him on his creation as a serjeant is given in Note B at the end of this lecture. Mr. Serjeant Sleigh, of whom I have elsewhere made mention, related to me, when he was on a visit to the United States, the following incident. Mr. Sleigh, in 1868, being in the goldsmith's shop in London to order rings on his own call to the order of the coif, a lady alighted from her carriage, came in, and wished to see the proprietor. Mr. Sleigh politely stepped aside, and thereupon the lady threw down a box containing many rings, offering them for sale, saying: " We have no use for them, you know; they were given to my dear papa when he was Lord Chancellor." In the biography of her dear papa I find the following entry in his diary at the time he was created Chief-Justice of the Queen's Bench. " October 15 [1849]. Have been trying to find a motto for my rings when I am called serjeant. Nothing better turns up than '*Justitiæ tenax*' (Juv. Sat., viii. 25). I shall be the first peer ever made a serjeant, as hitherto all peers who have worn the coif had put it on before they were ennobled; but I suppose there is no objection to the order being reversed " (" Life of John, Lord Campbell," by his daughter, the Hon. Mrs. Hardcastle (Am. Ed.), vol. ii., chap. **xxix.**,

The order of the serjeants-at-law can be traced historically for eight hundred years. It is intimately associated for this long period with the growth of the English law. It is older than the oldest peerage. It is older than the earliest Westminster Hall, — the one built by William Rufus. Chaucer describes the "wary and wise serjeant of the law that had often been seen at the Parvis of old St. Paul's," and the order was then very ancient.[1] The serjeants for ages constituted the entire profession. Selden shows that for seven hundred years the coif has been their distinctive mark. For more than six hundred years, and until the Judicature Acts of 1875, the judges had always been serjeants-at-law, — no small security for fit appointments.[2] But by several acts of

Lecture II.

Antiquity and decay of the order.

p. 331). What became of the rings presented by her dear papa, — who knows? Her dear papa relates that "Erskine's full-bottom wig was purchased and exported to the coast of Guinea, when he ceased to be Lord Chancellor, for the purpose of making an African warrior look more formidable to his enemies in the field of battle," and he wished, or affected to wish, that his own uncomfortable wig had been exclusively reserved for the like use. *Ib.* p. 346.

[1] "A serjeant of the law, ware and wise,
That often hadde ben at the parvis,
Ther was also, full rich of excellence.
Discreet he was and of great reverence,
He semed swiche; his words were so wise,
Justice he was ful often in assise,
By patent, and by pleine commissiun,
For his science, and for his high renoun,
Of fees and robes had he many on."

Chaucer, "Canterbury Tales." See Pulling, "The Order of the Coif," p. 3.

[2] Pulling, "The Order of the Coif," 3, 5, 23, 38, 274. Serjeant Robinson's "Bench and Bar," chaps. xxii., xxiii. His account of the ceremonials on taking the coif, of the status of the serjeant-at-law, and of the difference between a serjeant and a Queen's counsel, as well as other points of interest, is given in Note B at the end of this lecture.

Lecture II. Parliament in recent times the ancient rights and exclusive privileges of the order have been much impaired, and by the prolific creations of Queen's counsel the value of the degree or estate of the serjeant much diminished; and finally by the Judicature Acts (36 & 37 Vict. c. 66, § 88) it was enacted that "No person appointed a judge of either of the "said courts shall henceforth be required to take "or to have taken the degree of serjeant-at-law." This does not, it will be observed, abolish the order. The Crown may still create new serjeants; but this enactment, in connection with the previous unfriendly legislation, the large number of Queen's counsel, and the spirit of the age which is against exclusiveness of privileges, has practically doomed the order to destruction.

Its approaching extinction. I had the pleasure of a personal acquaintance with Mr. Serjeant Sleigh, the one who had then the most recently taken the coif, and who, alluding to the approaching end of the order, pleasantly said to me on one occasion: "Behold the last serjeant! or, as you would say, 'I am the last of the Mohicans.'"[1] It is now understood that no new serjeants will be called; and with the death of the last of the present survivors — now very few in number — this ancient and venerable order will cease to exist. Although I cannot but think the order, if its distinctive privileges were to be maintained, has outlived its usefulness, and although as an American lawyer my interest in it may be said to

---

[1] Mr. Serjeant Sleigh assumed the coif in 1868. There were, however, several expectant judges created serjeants after Mr. Serjeant Sleigh's creation. Robinson, p. 299.

be wholly one of sentiment, I cannot refrain from saying that I witness its certain doom with the same feeling of sadness and regret which Wordsworth so tenderly expressed concerning the decay and final extinction of the Venetian republic after her glorious history of a thousand years: —

Lecture II.

"Men are we, and must grieve when even the Shade
Of that which once was great has passed away."

I conclude this brief reference to this venerable order by remarking that serjeants-at-law are not wholly unknown in the history of the profession in this country. In the Province of New Jersey, at the May term, 1755, the Supreme Court appointed serjeants. In 1763 it was ordered "that no person "for the future shall practice as a serjeant in this "court but those that are recommended by the judges "to the Governor for the time being, and duly called "up by writ, and sworn agreeably to the practice in "England." At the May term, 1764, this order was vacated, and the former practice for "the court only "to nominate and appoint such persons as the court "thought fit and proper for that service by rule of "court without writ" was restored. The number of serjeants was subsequently fixed at twelve. Serjeants were necessary to pass a common recovery. They alone conducted examinations for admission to the bar. Only as late as 1839 was the degree of serjeant-at-law formally abolished in New Jersey.[1]

Serjeants-at-law in this country.

[1] The above is taken from the "History of the Supreme Court of New Jersey," by Mr. Francis Bazley Lee, in vol. i., series ii., of "The Supreme Courts of the States and Provinces," 1892, p. 66. Such facts as the above are interesting, moreover, as showing how closely our laws and practice were modelled after the English original. Indeed,

Lecture II.

The ordinary barrister-at-law.

(3) The lowest degree in the ranks of barristers is the ordinary barrister-at-law or counsellor.[1]

The subject will be resumed in the next lecture.

Mr. Lee's article shows his statement to be correct that "the Supreme Court of New Jersey remains to-day in organization much as it was nearly two centuries ago." *Ib.*, p. 58.

[1] Sometimes called "utter barristers." "There is also the practitioner 'below the bar,' the lowest in the ranks of the forensic hierarchy, who limits his practice to those special branches of the law designated pleading and conveyancing, and is precluded by the fact of his not having been 'called' from appearing in court,"— Encyclopædia Britannica (9th ed.), "Inns of Court."

NOTE A.

ORIGIN, ANTIQUITY, AND ESTABLISHMENT OF THE INNS OF COURT.

Much has been written concerning the origin, antiquity, and establishment of the Inns of Court and the several Inns of Chancery. Foss in his elaborate work, "Judges of England," has examined the subject with laborious care and seeming impartiality. His conclusions seem, in general, to be well warranted by the researches he has made and the facts and records to which he refers. It is the purpose of this note merely to state concisely, by way of supplement to the text, the general results reached by him and the other writers to whom reference is made.

Note A.

Henry III. prohibited the continuance of schools of law *within* the city of London in 1235. This mandate did not include the establishments outside of the city, and of course did not apply to those establishments probably then existing in the suburbs *outside* of the walls of the city for the reception of students of law, and which afterwards developed into and became the Inns of Court as we now know them. The purpose of this prohibitory order of Henry III. has been much disputed. By some it is supposed that the schools of law were suppressed within the city to encourage the establishments in the suburbs of the city for teaching the common law. Such is Blackstone's opinion (1 Com. Introd. 24). Foss is of a contrary opinion (vol. ii., p. 201), and so also is Lord Coke (2 Inst. proem). Mr. Philip Anstie Smith in his "History of Education for the English Bar" (London, 1860) discusses the subject, and doubts whether at this time "any legal university existed" (p. 4). Pearce, "Inns of Court," chap. i., p. 18 ("Early Schools of Law"), gives the Latin text of the prohibition, and the opinions of Coke, Selden, and Blackstone as to its purpose.

Henry the Third's prohibition of law schools.

60   LAWS AND JURISPRUDENCE.

Lecture II.
Origin of the Inns of Court.

From the time of the order of suppression in 1235 "there is," says Foss, "a total silence among historians, till the present reign (Edward III., 1327–1377), as to the places where and the manner in which the study was pursued." Foss, vol. iii., p. 375. That learned author regards it as beyond dispute "that during the hundred years before the accession of Edward III. (1327) there were some establishments for the reception of law students." In a case in the Year Book in 29 Edward III., the judges refer to a certain exception taken "amongst the apprentices in hostels;" which implies "a place and means of learning and a degree recognized in the courts." *Ib.*, 377. "Although it is the fashion," he says, "to attribute to the reign of Edward III. the institution of the several Inns of Court, it is to be lamented that legal antiquaries have given us nothing but tradition as the groundwork of that hypothesis, and have left us ignorant, not only of their original constitution, but of the precise distinction between them and the now called Inns of Chancery." *Ib.*, 375. Foss does not mean to deny that the establishments which gradually grew into what were or became known as the Inns of Court and of Chancery existed in the time of Edward III., for this fact seems to be beyond controversy. To give only one proof: There is the record of a lease in 18 Edw. III. (1344), of Clifford's Inn to the apprentices of the bench, "apprenticiis de banco," at an annual rent of ten pounds. *Ib.*, 383.

Lincoln's Inn.

"Lincoln's Inn is considered the most ancient of our legal seminaries, and is supposed to have been so occupied," says Foss, "previous to this reign" (Edward III.). *Ib.*, 380. Spilsbury says, without doubt or qualification, that "Lincoln's Inn is the most ancient of the Inns of Court." "Lincoln's Inn," by William Holden Spilsbury, London, 1873, chap i. But he admits that the precise date of foundation is not known. *Ib.*, p. 16.

Gray's Inn.

Referring to Gray's Inn, Pearce ("Inns of Court," p. 315) says: "Our legal antiquaries agree in the opinion that in the reign of Edward III. this [Gray's] Inn was the residence of a society of students of the law, whose successors have remained, first as tenants, and subsequently as proprietors there, from that time to the present day." Foss, summarizing the evidence, traditionary and documentary, on this point, considers it insufficient to prove that Gray's Inn was established in the reign of Edward III., though he does not deny the strong probability that such was the fact. Referring to Fortescue's account, given below, written between 1461 and 1470, in the time of Henry VI., Foss thus states his own guarded conclusion: "The evidence of Fortescue, — although he does not name the four Inns of Court, — and of some further facts which we shall advance in their proper place, may be taken as demonstrative of Gray's Inn having been occupied by students of the law, certainly as early as the reign of Henry VI. (1422-1461), and probably before." Foss, vol. iii., p. 382. Mr. W. R. Douthwaite, the historian of the Gray's Inn, claims an origin for it as far back as A. D. 1300. He says: "The exact date of its foundation as an Inn of Court is not known. But we can at once step back to 1311, at which time the Inn can boast of a bencher, — one Ralphe Andrewe, — whose pedigree is preserved in the Harleian Manuscript. This brings the foundation back at most to 1300, for even in those days it took time to make a bencher. The same doubt hangs over the date of foundation of all four Inns of Court. Now and again some writer whose zeal on behalf of his Inn outran his love of strict accuracy has proved to his own satisfaction the priority of one or the other of them; but the jealous eye of a sister has always found a flaw in the pedigree, and the Inns are to-day, as they were in the time of Elizabeth, 'the four equal and Honorable Societies of the Inns of Court.'" Mr. Douthwaite, article "Gray's Inn," Green Bag Magazine (Boston), vol. v., p. 65; "Gray's Inn: Its History and Associations," by W. R. Douthwaite, London, Reeves and Turner, 1886, chap. iii.

Mr. Loftie reviews the evidence *pro* and *con* and says: "The evidence of the existence of the society [Gray's Inn] before the time of Henry VIII. is, however, extremely weak." "Inns of Court and Chancery," 1893, chap. x., p. 67. The author means probably the society organized on its existing plan. "In the fine old Hall of Gray's Inn as it now exists Queen Elizabeth witnessed masques. It is one of the two buildings now remaining in which the plays of Shakespeare were performed in his lifetime, — the other being the Middle Temple Hall." Douthwaite, *ubi supra*.

As to the Temple, Dugdale, who wrote two hundred years after

Note A.

Gray's Inn (continued).

Lecture II.

The Temple.

Fortescue, refers to the tradition that it was "demised to divers professors of the common law" in the reign of Edward III. Dugdale admits that this rests upon tradition; but he adds, "That they were seated here in King Edward the Third's time is out of all doubt." Record evidence tending to establish this fact is, however, not wholly wanting. We have above referred to the lease of Clifford's Inn in the 18th of Edward III., 1344, to the apprentices of the bench. If Clifford's Inn was at this time a dependency of the Inner Temple, the inference that the common lawyers were then settled in the Temple would be very strong; and it is one which accords with known contemporary facts. Foss, vol. iv., p. 26; but see *Ib.*, pp. 141, 279, as to connection between Clifford's Inn and the Temple. "It is beyond dispute that the Temple was inhabited by a law society in the reign of Edward III." Reeves, "History of the English Law," Finlason's Ed., Reeves & Turner, 1869, vol. ii., p. 439.

The reign of Richard II. (1377-1399), is contemporary with Chaucer, and Foss concedes that the evidence is sufficient "to establish the fact that the Temple was then occupied in some manner by students of the law; and Chaucer's description of the Manciple, generally understood to have been written about 13 Richard II. (1389), may be adduced as further testimony in its support, if the first line is to be taken as referring to this house: —

'A gentil Manciple was ther of a temple
Of which achat ours mighten take ensample,'" etc.

But "in the reign of Richard II. scarcely anything is to be found illustrative or explanatory of the distinction between the Inns of Court and the Inns of Chancery." Foss, vol. iv., pp. 26, 27.

Inns as legal seminaries.

"There is no direct evidence of the existence during this reign [Henry IV., 1399-1413] of any of the four modern Inns of Court as legal seminaries." Foss, vol. iv., p. 141. But there is such evidence at this period of the existence of two of the modern Inns of Chancery, — Clifford's Inn and Furnival's Inn. *Ibid.* There is also such evidence in the reign of Henry V., (1413-1422), of Gray's Inn, and of the following Inns of Chancery, viz.: Lyon's Inn, Staple Inn, and Chester Inn, sometimes called Strand Inn. *Ib.*, pp. 199, 200.

In the reign of Henry VI. (1422-1461), flourished Sir John Fortescue. He was a member of Lincoln's Inn and a bencher. He was chief-justice of the King's Bench, and nominal if not actual Lord Chancellor in the reign of Henry VI. His is deservedly one of the great names in our law. His work "De Laudibus Legum Angliæ" was written at Berry in France when in exile between the years 1461 and 1470. In chapter 49 he gives an account of the Inns of Court, of which he says "there are four in number," and of the "ten lesser Inns, sometimes more, which are called Inns of Chancery." He does not give the names of any of either class of Inns. "Every word of his account of those places of legal study," says Foss (vol. iv., p. 249), "becomes most interesting, as the first authentic proof of their existence in that character [as legal seminaries], and the earliest description of their object and exercises."

Note A.

Fortescue's account.

Extract from Chapter Forty-Eight of Fortescue's "De Laudibus," concerning the Situation of the Inns of Court and of Chancery, and the Mode of Study therein, — Amos's Edition, 1825.

"Wherefore the Laws of England being learned and practised in those three several languages [English, French, and Latin], they cannot be so well studied in our Universities, where the Latin is mostly in use;[1] but they are studied in a publick manner and place much more commodious and proper for the purpose than in any University. It is situated near the King's Palace at Westminster, where the Courts of Law are held, and in which the Law-Proceedings are pleaded and argued, and the resolutions of the Court upon cases which arise are given by the Judges, men of gravity and years, well read and practised in the laws, and honoured with a degree peculiar to them. Here in Term-time the students of the law attend in great numbers, as it were to public schools, and are there instructed in all sorts of Law-Learning, and in the practice of the Courts; the situation of the place where they reside and study is between Westminster and the City of London.

Chapter 48 of Fortescue.

Site of the Inns.

---

[1] "Which reason, however, can hardly be deemed a satisfactory one." Foss, vol. iv., p. 249. See more fully, 1 Blacks. Com., 20–25, and Professor Hammond's notes to his edition of Blackstone.

64   LAWS AND JURISPRUDENCE.

Lecture II.

which as to all necessaries and conveniences of life is the best supplied of any City or town in the Kingdom: the place of study is not in the heart of the City itself, where the great confluence and multitude of the inhabitants might disturb them in their studies, but in a private place, separate and distinct by itself in the suburbs, near to the Courts of Justice aforesaid, that the students at their leisure may daily and duly attend with the greatest ease and convenience."

Extract from the celebrated Forty-Ninth Chapter of Fortescue's "De Laudibus," relating to the Inns of Court and the Inns of Chancery, — Amos's Edition, 1825.

Chapter 49 of Fortescue.

"But, my Prince, that the method and form of the study of the law may the better appear, I will proceed and describe it to you in the best manner I can. There belong to it ten lesser Inns, and sometimes more, which are called the Inns of Chancery, in each of which there are an hundred students at the least, and in some of them a far greater number, though not constantly residing. The students are, for the most part, young men; here they study the nature of Original and Judicial Writs, which are the very first principles of the law. After they have made some progress here, and are more advanced in years, they are admitted into the Inns of Court, properly so called: of these there are four in number. In that which is the least frequented there are about two hundred students. In these greater Inns a student cannot well be maintained under eight and twenty pounds a year; and if he have a servant to wait on him (as for the most part they have), the expense is proportionably more. For this reason the students are sons to persons of quality, — those of an inferior rank not being able to bear the expenses of maintaining and educating their children in this way. As to the merchants, they seldom care to lessen their stock in trade by being at such large yearly expenses. So that there is scarce to be found throughout the Kingdom an eminent lawyer who is not a gentleman by birth and fortune; consequently they have a greater regard for their character and honour than those who are bred in another way. There is, both in the Inns of Court and the Inns of Chancery, a sort of an Academy or Gymnasium, fit for persons of their station, where

Number of Inns and of students, etc.

Mode of life and study.

they learn singing and all kinds of music, dancing, and such other accomplishments and diversions (which are called Revels) as are suitable to their quality, and such as are usually practised at Court. At other times, out of term, the greater part apply themselves to the study of the law. Upon festival days, and after the offices of the church are over, they employ themselves in the study of sacred and profane history: here everything which is good and virtuous is to be learned; all vice is discouraged and banished; so that knights, barons, and the greatest nobility of the Kingdom often place their children in those Inns of Court, not so much to make the laws their study, much less to live by the profession (having large patrimonies of their own), but to form their manners, and to preserve them from the contagion of vice. The discipline is so excellent that there is scarce ever known to be any piques or differences, any bickerings or disturbances amongst them. The only way they have of punishing delinquents is by expelling them the society, — which punishment they dread more than criminals do imprisonment and irons; for he who is expelled out of one society is never taken in by any of the other. Whence it happens that there is a constant harmony amongst them, the greatest friendship, and a general freedom of conversation. I need not be particular in describing the manner and method how the laws are studied in those places, since your Highness is never like to be a student there; but I may say in the general that it is pleasant, excellently well adapted for proficiency, and every way worthy of your esteem and encouragement. One thing more I will beg leave to observe, viz. : that neither at Orleans,— where both the Canon and Civil Laws are professed and studied, and whither students resort from all parts, — neither at Angiers, Caen, nor any other University in France (Paris excepted), are there so many students who have passed their minority as in our Inns of Court, where the natives only are admitted."

Note A.

Chapter 49 of Fortescue (continued).

A recent writer questions not only the correctness but the authenticity of "most of the observations in the chapters (48, 49) on the Inns of Chancery and the Inns of Court as spurious additions made more than a century after Fortescue's death." He insists that "the account thus given of the Inns of Court

Comments on Fortescue's relation.

Lecture II.

Comments on Fortescue's relation (continued).

bears on the face of it evidence of being composed just before the date of publication [the first edition appeared early in the reign of Henry VIII., 1537], and many ages after the death of Fortescue, containing statements that Fortescue could not have made, — for example, as to the number of the Inns, and their use as places of abode, of study, and of diversion; but the accounts quite accord with the days of Elizabeth and Chancellor Hatton." Serjeant Pulling's "The Order of the Coif," London, 1884, pp. 153, 158. The learned author does not claim that the entire chapters (xlviii. and xlix.) are fabrications, or undertake to point out more minutely what is spurious. I have of course no means of ascertaining by independent research how far his sceptical observations are warranted. But if they be so, it is certainly most remarkable that Dugdale, Coke, Blackstone, Reeves, Crabb, Selden, Foss, and other learned writers and legal antiquaries have accepted without question the account in the published editions of Fortescue's work as genuine. If genuine, as would seem likely, there can exist no doubt of its substantial correctness. Apparently the statements of Mr. Serjeant Pulling are not well considered. It is not correct to say that Fortescue's work was not published until many ages after his death. The first publication of "De Laudibus" was in 1537, and more than a dozen editions have since appeared. The exact date of Fortescue's birth, while not certain, is very near the year 1400. Record evidence exists that in 1476 he was in the discharge of his official duties. Tradition has it that he died when ninety years of age. See "Governance of England," by Sir John Fortescue, edited by Charles Plummer, Oxford, 1885, pp. 72, 85. Foss says that "De Laudibus" was written between 1461 and 1470; but Plummer fixes the period of its composition more closely at 1468–1470. The first publication was therefore within seventy years after it was written, and probably within fifty years of Fortescue's death. It would appear, on the whole, that no good grounds exist to impeach the accuracy or authenticity of the 48th and 49th chapters of "De Laudibus."

The following are Foss's conclusions as to the time when the societies of the four Inns respectively assumed their more modern constitution or order of government: —

"Although Fortescue does not name the four Inns of Court,

we have," says Foss (vol. iv., p. 254), "sufficient evidence to show that they were the same [in the time of Henry VI., 1422-1461] as those now in existence.[1] We shall therefore proceed to give an account of them separately," commencing with Lincoln's Inn, "as its records afford the earliest proofs of its antiquity." "From the reign of Edward III. till that of Henry VI. we find no mention whatever of Lincoln's Inn. In the latter, however, we have its Black Book, which is the earliest existing record of the proceedings of that or of any other Inn of Court. It commences in 1423. In it are contained the orders of the society, and the admittances into it from that date. . . . All these facts and dates seem to establish one of two things: either that the society received its first formation at this period, or that if it previously existed, as no doubt it did, a new system of government was now introduced into it. (Vol. iv., pp. 255, 258, 259.)

Note A.

Foss's conclusions as to time when the Inns assumed their modern constitution, etc.

"We are quite in the dark as to the precise time when the lawyers were first established in the Temple; and equally so as to the period when the division into the two houses called the Inner Temple and the Middle Temple took place; . . . but that it took place before the reign of Henry VI. may be presumed from Fortescue describing four Inns of Court, which could not be reckoned without them. (Vol. iv., pp. 267, 270.)

"Although no reasonable doubt, therefore, can be entertained of the existence of Gray's Inn as a house of reception for students previous to the composition of Fortescue's work, it may very fairly be questioned whether they held it till about 1506 in the form in which we afterwards find it, — of a society bound by established rules, governed by a controlling body, and empowered to confer legal degrees. The evidence afforded by the books of the society all tends strongly to confirm the idea that about the latter date an entirely new system was established, or at least that its constitution was subjected to a 'radical reform.' (Vol. iv., pp. 275, 276.)

"The reign of Henry VIII. may be regarded as the period when, beyond doubt, all the four Inns of Court were estab-

[1] Sir William Dugdale ("Origines Juridiciales," 3d ed., A. D. 1680) says. "The four Inns of Court mentioned by Fortescue are extant, and eight Inns of Chancery, of which only two are the same as in Fortescue's time, namely, Clifford's Inn and Thavie's Inn." p. 142.

lished upon the system which, making allowance for subsequent changes in the manners and habits of men, prevails at the present day." — (Vol. v., p. 110.)[1]

NOTE B.

CEREMONIALS ON TAKING THE COIF, THE STATUS OF A SERJEANT-AT-LAW, THE DIFFERENCE BETWEEN A SERJEANT AND A QUEEN'S COUNSEL, AND OTHER POINTS CONCERNING THE TWO GRADES IN THE PROFESSION, ETC., ETC.

Mr. B. Coulson Robinson, who became a serjeant in 1865, published in 1889 a book entitled "Bench and Bar: Reminiscences of One of the Last of an Ancient Race." This was written, it will be observed, after the Statute of 1875 made it no longer necessary that a common-law judge should be a serjeant at the time of his appointment, when it was understood that no more new serjeants would be created, after the sale of Serjeants' Inn, and when there were "only eleven serjeants either on the bench or retired from it, and six who are still [1889] supposed to be practising serjeants, although most of them have ceased to follow up the profession" (p. 298); and hence his reference to himself as "One of the last of an Ancient Race." The following concise relation concerning the present and former status of a serjeant-at-law, the difference between a serjeant and a Queen's counsel, the ceremonial of taking the coif, the final sale of the Serjeants' Inn, and the practical extinction of the Order of the Coif, is extracted from it (chaps. xxii., xxiii.) : —

"It may not be out of place to describe the process of a barrister's conversion into a serjeant-at-law, and the status he thus occupies in the profession. It will not be long before there will exist no living representative of the race."

---

[1] "The sixteenth century was the real period when the Inns of Court were first regularly constituted, there being no books or records or reliable chronicles showing that there were before that period, even in the greater Inns. either governors, treasurers, or readers, — or indeed any regular order of government." — Pulling, "Order of the Coif," 1884, p. 155.

OUR LAW IN ITS OLD HOME. 69

"The position of serjeant-at-law is undoubtedly the oldest, and was, until comparatively recent times, the very highest dignity a barrister could achieve below that of a judge. It dates from about the middle of the thirteenth century. Until the year 1875, the judges were invariably selected from that rank; and so strictly was the rule adhered to that even a Queen's counsel, who had spent half his life under that title, was obliged, on his appointment as judge, to become a serjeant perhaps the day before he was sworn in as a member of the bench.

"The little round black patch on the top of the wig distinguishes a serjeant from the other members of the bar." (pp. 290, 291.)

"The position of Queen's counsel is of comparatively modern date. The first was Lord Bacon, — who is always so called, although he never bore that title, — but his position had nothing to do with the rank as it at present exists. He acted merely as the Queen's private adviser, while the Attorney and Solicitor General were the advisers of the Government. No other appointment of Queen's or King's counsel was made for many years, until Sir Francis North (afterwards Lord Guildford) was so created in the reign of Charles II.; and from that period the title seems to have grown, and to have gradually assumed its present significance. The Queen's counsel will soon have it all their own way, for it is now resolved that no fresh serjeants are to be appointed, although the existing ones maintain the same rank and privileges they have always enjoyed.

"The cause of their decline from their high estate originated in the throwing open the Court of Common Pleas to the whole bar indiscriminately. Until the year 1846, — with a small interval from 1834 to 1839, — that court was entirely monopolized by the serjeants. No other member of the bar could be heard within its precincts, although the serjeants were allowed to practise in them all. But the Common Pleas was considered to be their peculiar region, and when they [the serjeants] went into the Queen's Bench or the Exchequer they had to sit in the back rows, unless indeed they had a patent of precedence. By an order made, however, by Chief-Justice Cockburn, some time before I became a serjeant [1865], they obtained the privilege of sitting in the front one, in all the courts.

"I am often asked what is the difference between a Queen's

Note B.

Of Queen's counsel.

Decline of order of serjeants.

Lecture II.

Difference between a Queen's counsel and a serjeant.

counsel and a serjeant. In the first place, I may state that the former is created by patent and the latter by writ under the Great Seal. As to rank, there is no difference whatever between a serjeant who has obtained a patent of precedence and a Queen's counsel; but with regard to serjeants who have no patent it is otherwise. Theirs is an intermediate grade between Her Majesty's counsel and the rest of the bar; so that every newly created Queen's counsel takes precedence of an unpatented serjeant, however long he may have worn the coif. The Queen's counsel always appear in black silk gowns, in and out of term. The serjeant has several additional robes: black cloth in term time, except on saints' days when purple cloth is worn, while black silk was the robe out of term at *nisi prius*, — which means trial before a jury. A scarlet gown is only worn by them at the churching of the judges at St. Paul's in Trinity term and at the Guildhall banquet, — at the latter of which occasions some of them had always the privilege of attending with the judges. When I became a serjeant [1865], it was *de rigueur* that these habiliments should be worn at the prescribed times; but shortly afterwards the rule was gradually disregarded, and latterly black silk has been our only wear in court.

"Another distinction is, that the serjeant holds a rank quite independent of the profession, while a Queen's counsel has no recognized position out of it, so that, while in general society a serjeant would rank above a Queen's counsel, in matters relating to the profession he would rank below him, — unless he had a patent of precedence; then their relative positions would depend on the date of their respective appointments. And, again, the serjeants are also quite independent of the sovereign, while, as I have said before, the Queen's counsel are always assumed to be in the service of Her Majesty, as her private advisers, though I need hardly say they are very seldom honored with her confidence.[1] When I was called to the bar there were sixty-

---

[1] "The serjeant differs in many important respects from the King's counsel. He has to take a very remarkable and ample oath, by which he binds himself to plead for all, however humble their condition." Woolrych, "Lives of Eminent Serjeants-at-Law," vol. i., Introduction, p. 27, where the form of the oath is given. See also form of oath: Foss, vol. i., p. 24 ; Preface to 10 Coke Reports, p. xxii. Form of writ: Foss, vol. i., p 24; *Ib*, vol. iv., p. 21 ; Manning, "Serviens ad Legem," p. 33. Coif and dress: Foss, vol. i , p. 25 ; *Ib.*, vol. iv., p. 243 ; Pulling, *passim* and illustrations. Rings : Foss, vol. iv., p. 242; *ante*, pp. 53, 54, and note.

three Queen's counsel; there are now about three hundred." (pp. 293-296.)

Note B.

"The power of conferring the coif rested — in fact, still exists — with the Lord Chancellor, but he never exercises it except at the recommendation of the chief-justice of the Common Pleas." (p. 300.)

"On the creation of a serjeant, a number of gold rings (about twenty-eight) had to be bestowed by him on several persons of different grades, — the Queen, the Chancellor, the judges, and I think the masters of the Common Pleas. Even the chief usher of that court received one, but it dwindled down to a hoop of not much greater breadth than a curtain ring and about one tenth of its thickness. Her Majesty's ring was a very massive affair, — nearly an inch long, — with enamel in the middle and massive gold ends; on the former was engraved, — as indeed was the case with all of them, — a motto specially chosen for the occasion. The Chancellor's and the judge's rings were about one third of an inch in breadth, but luckily for me not very thick, — as I had to pay for them. The greater number I never saw, for the goldsmith always undertook to distribute the gifts to those who by immemorial custom had a claim to them. It was only the Queen's, the Lord Chancellor's and the colt's of which we had personal inspection. I may state that the 'colt' is generally a young professional friend, who attends the new serjeant on his being sworn in before the Lord Chancellor, and who is an ancient and necessary appendage to the ceremony. He walks in (pone) behind his principal, and it is said that the term 'colt' is merely a parody on that Latin word.

Ceremonials on creation of a serjeant-at-law.

"The ceremonial itself is very simple. You go in full official dress with your colt before the Chancellor in his private room, where the Queen's writ conferring the rank upon you is read. The oath of allegiance is then administered by the Chancellor; after which you kneel down before him, and he pins the coif (consisting of a patch of black silk with a white crimped border) on the top of your wig, and you become a serjeant-at-law. You are henceforth addressed by the judges who are serjeants as 'brother,' but the relationship ends there; we never take the same liberty. In court we address them as 'my lord,' and in private as 'judge.'

"On rising from your knees and receiving the congratula-

Lecture II.

tions of the Lord Chancellor, the colt advances and presents the Queen's ring to the Chancellor, requesting him to beg Her Majesty's acceptance of it in the name of his principal; another is presented to the Chancellor, and a third is kept by the colt as his own perquisite.

Serjeants' Inn.

"The next thing to be done was to get yourself proposed as a member of the mess at Serjeants' Inn, — that is, if you wished it, which, of course, every newly-made serjeant did. But it was not compulsory. There were formerly three different clubs or societies of serjeants, each called Serjeants' Inn. One in Holborn, near Hatton Garden, which has, I believe, for centuries ceased to exist; another in Fleet Street, which, although bearing the name, has for many years had no connection with the serjeants in fact. The only recognized Inn of late years was that in Chancery Lane, the whole of which was sold a few years ago, and the proceeds divided amongst the serjeants. Of this sale I shall have a few words to say presently. The property consisted of a long range of buildings in Chancery Lane, let out in offices, an ancient and not very picturesque hall, a remarkably handsome dining-room, a reading-room, spacious kitchens and cellars, and other conveniences adapted to an ordinary club-house.

"On being elected to the mess a practising serjeant had to pay an entrance fee of three hundred and fifty pounds; a judicial one — that is, any one so created as a preparative to a judgeship — paid five hundred pounds; and, for some time after my joining, every member paid fifteen pounds a year as commons, but this sum at last dwindled down to zero, and we paid nothing for our board or for the other conveniences the Inn afforded us." (pp. 301-304.) [1]

---

[1] "Previous to the actual call or creation of serjeants," says Pulling, "there were in former times stately ceremonies of the Inns of Court; the newly elected serjeants assembling each in the hall of the Inn, when learned addresses were delivered, and a purse of gold *de regardo* or by way of retaining fee given to each of the new serjeants, who were then *rung out* of the society by the chapel bell, — a usage kept up, at all events at Lincoln's Inn, to a very recent time." "The Order of the Coif," p. 229.

Lord Campbell being appointed chief-justice of the Queen's Bench, writes, March 5, 1850: "This morning began with 'ringing me out' of Lincoln's Inn. The prospect of the ceremony made me rather uncomfortable from the time I knew Brougham was to preside in it. . . . Brougham tried to play me

In answer to the adverse criticism which was made on the action of the serjeants in selling their Inn and dividing the proceeds amongst themselves, the insinuation being that it was public property, Mr. Serjeant Robinson says: "That Serjeants' Inn was a private club, and that our funds were derived from private sources, may surely be sufficiently established from this, that the fifteen judges would never have acted as they did if there had been a scintilla of proof or even of suspicion to the contrary. There was not one of the serjeants who did not deeply regret the necessity of parting with our venerable hall and its appendages, but not a voice was raised against our right to proceed to a partition. With the certainty that no more serjeants would be created, judicial or otherwise, and that our income of £1,500 or £2,000 a year would thus be cut off from us, it was impossible that the establishment could be maintained on the same liberal scale as of yore; we should be gradually dying off, like the members of a tontine, until the property ultimately vested in the survivor to do as he please with, for there was no one else who could have the slightest claim to it. The Inn was accordingly sold, and the proceeds divided amongst the members." (Chap. xxiii., p. 313.)

Note B.

Sale of Serjeants' Inn.

Pulling on this subject says: "Under the private Act in 1834 the society [of Serjeants' Inn] was constituted a corporation, and this incorporated society still continues, though without worldly property, for its accounts have all been wound up. Its only remaining possessions [1884], the interesting old pictures, have been presented to the National Portrait Gallery, and now form part of that collection." "The Order of the Coif," chap. v., p. 127, note.

Mr. Serjeant Ballantine records ("Experiences," chap. xvii.) that in 1872 he was elected treasurer of Serjeants' Inn, and

a dog's trick by running off with my fee of ten guineas as a retainer to plead, when become a serjeant, for the society of Lincoln's Inn. I made him disgorge the money at the House of Lords by threatening to sentence him to the gallows as a thief, and by commencing my judicial career with a notorious culprit I was sworn in before the Chancellor at four o'clock. . . . First I was made a serjeant and then my patent writ as chief-justice was handed to me. . . . I dined twice at the Serjeants' Inn, my admission to which cost me near seven hundred pounds." "Life of John, Lord Campbell," chapters xxix., xxx., by his daughter, Mrs. Hardcastle.

Lecture II.

annually re-elected until 1875, when he accepted a retainer to go to India; and that on his return, "being reinstated, I remained treasurer until the abolition of the Inn; and if I have no other word inscribed on the roll of fame, I shall be recorded as the last treasurer of one of the most ancient, and at one time the most honored, of the institutions of Great Britain. . . . The order to sell the property was made at the last meeting, held on April 27, 1877."

Bibliography.

Mr. Herbert has an interesting account of the Antiquity and Dignity of Serjeant-at-law,— "Antiquity of the Inns of Court," chap. x., p. 358, London, 1804. Mr. Serjeant Woolrych has two excellent volumes entitled "Lives of Eminent Serjeants-at-Law," London, 1869. Mr. Serjeant Pulling has written a history of the order, under the title, "The Order of the Coif," London, 1884, with illustrations; it is a work of careful research and of exceeding interest. Serjeant Wynne published a tract in 1765, entitled "Observations touching the Antiquity and Dignity of the Degree of Serjeant-at-Law, with Reasons against laying open the Common Pleas" ['to all barristers to practice in that Court as serjeants do now']. See also first Report of the Common-Law Commissioners on the subject of "Serjeants' Inn and the Inns of Court," and Serjeant Manning's Report of the "Serjeants' Case," Longmans & Co., 1840; Crabb's "History of English Law," London, 1829, pp. 182, 416; Wynne's "Eunomus," Dialogue II., § 53; Pearce, "Inns of Court," pp. 428–440; Fortescue, "De Laudibus," chap. l., "Of the State, Degree, and Creation of a Serjeant-at-Law;" "The Tenth Part of the Reports of Sir Edward Coke," Introduction, p. xx.

LECTURE III.

THE EDUCATION AND DISCIPLINE OF THE ENGLISH BAR, AND HEREIN OF THE INNS OF COURT, THEIR HISTORY, CHARACTER AND PURPOSES (CONCLUDED). THE LITERARY ASSOCIATIONS OF THE INNS OF COURT (NOTE A). STUDENTSHIP IN THE INNS OF COURT, AND MODE OF BEING CALLED TO THE BAR (NOTE B).

I RESUME the subject of the last lecture. Each of the Inns of Court has numerous buildings of its own, consisting of chambers or rooms let for hire, mainly to the barristers and students;[1] and belonging to each Inn is a large library hall, a spacious kitchen, and also a commodious and beautiful hall used for readings, dining, etc., and a chapel for religious service. The Inner Temple owns and in common with the Middle Temple uses for the latter purpose the exquisite Temple Church built by the Knights Templars (in imitation of a temple near the Holy Sepulchre), and which was dedicated in A. D. 1185, over seven hundred years ago. In the

Lecture III.

Buildings and halls.

Temple Church.

---

[1] "The whole number of inhabited houses in the Inner Temple is said to be forty-two, which seems large in comparison with the twenty-three of Lincoln's Inn, but is exceeded considerably by the fifty-six at Gray's Inn." Loftie, "Inns of Court and Chancery" (Macmillan), 1893, p. 32. According to the census of the city in 1891 there were nine hundred and eighty-two employers in the Inner Temple, and eight hundred and fifty-seven in the Middle Temple. Loftie, p. 24.

Lecture III.

chapels and the Temple Church some of the most eloquent and pious of the English divines have exercised their sacred office, among whom may be mentioned as familiar to us the names of Hooker, Donne, Hurd, Tillotson, Heber, and Warburton.

Literary associations.

Chambers or apartments in the Inns are let to others as well as to members of the profession. These have been thus occupied by some of the most famous of the poets and writers of England, and this gives to the Inns an added interest. How close and intimate are the ties between the people of our race in this new country and their ancestors in the old appears not only in our laws and institutions but in our whole history. It was reserved, so far as I know, for an American, Mr. Hutton, to make the first compendious survey of what I may call literary London, and to display its landmarks and the footprints of its great poets, writers, and authors. I quite agree with his observation that "London has no associations so inter-"esting as those connected with its literary men, "and that to the cultivated reader the Temple owes "its greatest charm to the fact that it was the birth-"place of Lamb, the home of Fielding, and that it "contains Goldsmith's grave."[1] These names are here put by way of example only, — of eminent example, if you please, — but there are other names equally illustrious to which Mr. Hutton refers in the body of his book, and there are also some others which he has omitted to notice.

After a day of labor in the contentious arena of the court room, where my life has been so largely

[1] Hutton, Introduction to "Literary Landmarks of London."

spent, I have filled up the tranquil leisure of an evening, or the other precarious leisure that comes to the active lawyer or the judge, by literary recreations, and in course of these have made notes of the distinguished men of letters who have had chambers or lodgings within the Inns. Time allows me only to cast a hasty glance over these notes, and merely to pronounce the names of Chaucer, Beaumont, Sidney, Chapman, Bacon (who equally belongs to philosophy, law, and literature), Fielding, Cowper, Johnson, Boswell, Goldsmith, Horne Tooke, Sheridan, Hallam, Lamb, Macaulay, Thackeray.[1] Destined as you are for a profession which yet happily retains its claim to be regarded not only as a learned but liberal calling, I trust you will not tax against me the few moments of your time which this reference to the literary celebrities of the Inns has taken, and without which even this outline sketch — for it is nothing more — would be manifestly deficient. So long as the world shall recall the unselfishness of Sidney; so long as it shall remember "The Canterbury Tales," shall admire the sturdy morality of Johnson and read the history of "Rasselas, Prince of Abyssinia;" so long as it shall delight in "The Vicar of Wakefield," "The Traveller," and "The Deserted Village," — so long will these works and their authors remain associated in men's memories with the Inns wherein they lived and studied, rejoiced and suffered, toiled and

Lecture III.

Eminent men of letters who have resided within the Inns.

---

[1] I have made some extracts from these notes, which, in the hope that they may be regarded with sufficient interest to be worth the small space they occupy, I have reproduced in a note (A) at the end of this lecture.

Lecture III.

wrought, while they became immortal. This is not a digression, but belongs to my subject; though if it be considered a digression, I pray you to pardon it to the love of literature. It would lead me too far afield to mention with proper comment the great names in the law who constitute the pride and glory of the respective Inns; and I therefore resume my main purpose, namely, a consideration of the Inns in connection with legal education, and their exclusive faculty of calling persons to the bar.

Ancient legal education in the Inns.

From the institution of the Inns down to about the period of the civil disturbances of 1640, the exercise of readings was the principal mode of legal instruction therein. The Inns were established for this purpose among others, but provision was made only for instruction in the common law.[1]

Readings and mootings.

The instruction so far as given in the Inns was mainly by readings and mootings. The ancient readings continued only about "three weeks in every Lent and every August of each year," until they fell off in consequence of the excessive and sumptuous practices which will be referred to pres-

---

[1] In Mr. Smith's paper on "Ancient Legal Education in the Inns of Court," 1856, vol. i., Juridical Society Papers, 385, it is said: "On the whole, the system of education anciently in use at the Inns is entitled to more respect than it often receives, although the slight esteem of it is not surprising. . . . At all events, the system in these legal colleges was obviously suited to their special objects, — the cultivation of a learned acquaintance with the laws, and readiness and skill in applying them. There is something pleasing in the co-operation of the different grades of the societies in their common occupation. Benchers and readers, utter and inner barristers, and students appear to have been combined in the pursuit of legal knowledge." See also Smith, "History of Education of the English Bar," London, 1860, chaps. ii., v., vi.; Douthwaite, "Gray's Inn: History and Associations," chap. iv.; Pearce, "Inns of Court," chap. iv.

ently. Mootings were arguments of put cases or doubtful questions in the law, between benchers and barristers, in the hall of the Inn, in the presence of the students.

The reader was annually elected by the benchers from the most eminent or learned of the barristers, and the office was considered one of great distinction. The readings consisted of an analysis and exposition of some leading statute, or important section of a statute, in the light of the common law and the adjudged cases. Many of these readings, relating "to the grounds and originals of the law" extending back to the time of Edward VI., are still extant, and the more important of them have been published.[1]

The original object of the readings and the kindred exercises of mootings was instruction, but in the course of time the readings were attended with expensive entertainments given to the nobility, judges, and gentry of the kingdom; the expenses

Lecture III.

What the readings consisted of.

---

[1] "The readings were, from the very foundation of these seminaries, looked upon as a vital part of their constitution." Pearce, "Inns of Court," chap. iv., p. 65. Lord Coke (1 Inst., Preface) enumerates, after his laborious and learned manner, five excellent characteristics of the ancient readings. We owe to this exercise twenty-three readings on "Fines" (27 Edw. 1., chap. i.), by Sir Edward Coke, reader of the Inner Temple (*temp.* Elizabeth) ; a reading on "Sewers" (23 Henry VIII., chap. v.), by Robert Callis, reader of Gray's Inn, A. D. 1622, republished as late as 1824, and known as "Callis on Sewers;" on the "Statute of Uses" (27 Henry VIII., chap. iii.), by Sir Francis Bacon, also reader at Gray's Inn (*temp.* Elizabeth) ; and many other readings by such lawyers as Littleton, Dyer, Plowden, Fitzherbert, and Finch. Many of these readings are still regarded with great, and often with authoritative, respect in the courts of Westminster Hall. An alphabetical list of principal Readings on Statutes is given in Clarke's Bibliotheca Legum (2d ed.), p. 402.

fell upon the reader, and often amounted to £1,000 in the course of two or three weeks, — a sum equal in value to more than three times that amount in our day. This expensive honor finally caused the disuse of readings. During the period when these sumptuous entertainments were given by the readers, the Inns of Court were at certain seasons the scene of fantastic plays and masques, and riotous revels, which were likewise conducted on an extravagant scale, and were scarcely consistent with the purpose of the Inns as seminaries of legal learning. These were often attended by the Sovereign, the court, and the nobility, and reached their height in the reign of Elizabeth. They continued until the rebellion of 1640; but when the spirit of the Puritan obtained ascendency, entertainments of this character were denounced by an act of Parliament as "the very pompes of the Divell."[1]

As legal colleges or universities the Inns of

---

[1] Pearce, "Inns of Court," p. 113. See Gardiner's "History of England," vol. vii., chap. lxxiii., as to Inns of Court masque of 1633, the prevailing immorality of the stage, the prosecution and cruel punishment of Prynne, — who was sentenced by the Star Chamber to be imprisoned for life; to a fine of £5,000; to be expelled from Lincoln's Inn; to be incapable of practising his profession, degraded from his degree in the university, set in the pillory, where both his ears were to be cut off. In reading the history of that era, even as drawn by the calm and temperate Gardiner, we feel our blood grow warm, and conclude that Cromwell was necessary and that he came none too soon. Milton's "Comus" prefigured and heralded the coming elevation of the literature of the drama, though destined to be delayed beyond the Restoration.

"The Czar of Muscovy, Peter the Great, was present at the Christmas revels in the Temple, 1697-8. The last of the revels in the Inns of Court took place in the Inner Temple Hall, on the elevation of Mr. Talbot to the woolsack in 1733." Pearce, "Inns of Court," p. 128.

Court were chiefly deficient in the want of a general, comprehensive, and systematic course of instruction. The course was essentially practical, — exclusively and distinctively English. The main purpose was instruction in the common law and its statutable modifications and additions. It must have been contemplated that much the greater part of a legal education should be acquired in other modes than from the brief readings and occasional mootings. Accordingly the custom of reading in attorneys' offices, or with a barrister or private tutor, has long prevailed in England.[1] It is called by Lord Campbell "the pupilizing system," which is much the same as reading in lawyers' offices in this country, although the pupil is in chambers at one of the Inns of Court.

Lecture III.

Defective system of legal education in the Inns.

The Inns of Court maintained their primary and leading character as largely intended for legal instruction until the fifteenth century, when they became, as I have said, places of gayety and revelry. Their efficiency as seminaries of instruction declined, and from the middle of the seventeenth century the instruction in them was nominal, the real instruction being chiefly conducted in private offices. It is only in our own time that the function of the Inns as places of legal instruction has been restored. In 1852 the four Inns, acting in concert, jointly, established a uniform system for the legal education of the students, and to that end created five

Modern legal education in the Inns.

---

[1] Smith, "Legal Education," p. 157. For an excellent sketch of the instruction given at that time in the Inns of Court, see Chancellor Hammond's article in Steiger's "Cyclopedia of Education," p. 515, title "Law Schools."

professorships; and students were required, as a condition of eligibility to be called to the bar, to attend for one year the lectures of two of the readers, or if this were not done to pass a satisfactory public examination. The readerships were filled by eminent jurists, and the prescribed course of instruction was minute and quite comprehensive. In 1872 an enlarged and amended scheme of legal education was promulgated by the four Inns.

At the present time (1892) the Council of Legal Education of the Inns of Court has the superintendence of all matters relating to the education and examination of students for the purpose of being called to the bar, or of practising under the bar. This council consists of twenty benchers, five of whom are nominated by each of the four Inns. Before a person can be admitted into either of the Inns as a student he must satisfactorily pass an examination in the English and Latin languages and in English history. A public examination is also required and must be satisfactorily passed as a condition of being called to the bar. The scheme of instruction has been much enlarged, and it embraces an examination in the Roman as well as in the English law. The details concerning the legal education now required of both branches of the profession are set forth in the Report on Legal Education, prepared by a most competent and learned committee of the American Bar Association, with the active assistance of the United States Bureau of Education, and submitted to the Association at its meeting in 1892. That report is the most complete view of the subject that has ever been presented. An attentive perusal of it will, I think, fully support the observation I made on the floor when the subject was under discussion, to the effect that if the Association had never done anything else to justify its existence, that report alone would constitute such justification.[1] Since the making of that report we are informed that a new scheme of lectures has been determined upon by the Council of Legal Education, which would seem to indicate that the subject in England is not yet upon a perfectly satisfactory basis.[2]

Lecture III.

Report of American Bar Association the subject.

[1] On the subject of legal education and admissions to the bar three valuable reports have been made to the American Bar Association. The first was submitted in 1879 by a committee consisting of Mr. Carleton Hunt, Mr. Henry Stockbridge, and Mr. Edmund H. Bennett, and is printed in the Report of the American Bar Association for 1879, p. 208. No definite result was reached, and the subject was revived in 1890, and a report made which will be found in the Report of the Association for 1891, p. 301. The report was re-committed, and a final report made which appears in the Report of the Association for 1892, p. 317. The committee were effectively aided by the United States Bureau of Education, which has published as an official document the committee's report of 1892, with tables and data "showing what is taught, and what methods of instruction are pursued in the leading law schools of the various countries, and giving the latest statistics available." The membership of this committee during the three years of its existence has been as follows: In 1890 William G. Hammond, George M. Sharp, and Henry Wade Rogers; in 1891 the same gentlemen, with the addition of J. Hubley Ashton; in 1892 the gentlemen last named, with the addition of Samuel Williston. The report as published by the Bureau of Education, 1893, contains much matter not found in the report as printed in the proceedings of the American Bar Association.

[2] "A new scheme of lectures is about to be started by the Council of Legal Education. Everything will depend on the working of it. On paper it is certainly better than the old one; and if it be worked with zeal and intelligence the Inns of Court may possibly within a few years be not much inferior as a centre of legal instruction to an average second-rate American law school." Sir Frederick Pollock in Law Quar. Rev., vol. viii., 19 (1892).

Lecture III.
Criticism on English course of legal education.

Foreign jurists and teachers have always marked and condemned as inadequate the limited scope of legal instruction in England. Thus MM. Durand and Terrel in substance observe as follows:—
"What distinguishes the English course of legal "education is its practical character. We may "justly praise the organization of the English "bar, but cannot condemn too strongly its want "of theoretical studies. This education makes good "lawyers and even good judges, but cannot create "accomplished jurists who are able to advance "the science of jurisprudence."[1]

I must admit the general truth of the criticism, but must also insist that a system of education which makes good lawyers and good judges cannot be regarded as a failure, although defective in a more general and scientific view. Doubtless it is a system capable of improvement, and one that ought to be improved. However it may be in England, it is certainly true in this country that the subject of legal education, both as respects the scope and methods of instruction, is in an unsettled and unsatisfactory state. Wherefore I hope you will indulge me in some observations thereon, although my brief experience of three years as a law teacher in Columbia College does not enable me to speak with any considerable weight of

[1] MM. Durand and Terrel, Preface to Professor Lioy's "Philosophie du Droit." They say: "Ce qui caractérise l'enseignement anglais, c'est donc son caractère pratique. Si l'on peut louer justement l'organisation du barreau anglais, on ne saurait condamner trop énergiquement ce défaut d'études théoriques. Cette éducation peut faire de bons avocats et même de bons magistrats, mais elle ne saurait créer de veritables savants qui fassent avancer la science du droit." Preface, cxxvii.

authority. All will agree, I think, that there are few questions which more intimately concern the well-being, not only of the profession but of the people, and especially a free people.

The following are in my judgment the more material considerations belonging to the subject under the general conditions which surround it in this country. These conditions are in some respects peculiar, and particularly those that *practically* limit the course of instruction to two or three years.

1. We must take things as they are, and shape our course accordingly. Practically, the law schools in this country are limited, or rather they are forced to limit themselves, to a two or at most a three years' course.[1] Excuse the homely phrase, but we must "cut the garment according to the cloth." Keeping this in mind, the primary object aimed at is to teach the great principles of law and jurisprudence; but these are to be taught with special and direct reference to our system of law, and not some other. Nearly every law student contemplates admission to the bar and the practice of the law as a profession. This in connection with the short course compels the teaching to assume almost exclusively a practical character, and to be directed (if it will not mislead to say so) toward making the student a lawyer rather than a jurist. I would that every student might receive what I may call a juristic training; but this is not, as things now stand, practicable to the full extent that is desir-

Lecture III.

Scope and methods of legal education in this country.

Limited terms of study.

---

[1] Report of Committee of the American Bar Association, 1892, above mentioned, printed by the United States Bureau of Education: "Report on Legal Education" (1893), pp. 13, 15.

Lecture III.

Teaching of the law too practical and technical.

able. In saying this I must also take leave to say that I decidedly think the actual course of instruction in our law schools is too intensely practical and technical; that law if not taught too much as an art is taught too little as a science; and that the course of instruction can have and should have a broader scope than it has when the student is confined to the usual text-books written for practising lawyers, and the designated illustrative cases, since the oral instruction rarely goes beyond this range. To supply this want, the Civil Law, for purposes of comparative jurisprudence, and because of its more orderly and scientific arrangement, should, in its great outlines and essential character, be made an element of instruction to a greater extent than it is in our American law schools. Except in this view and in this incidental or subordinate way, I doubt its utility in the short course of legal study to which our law colleges are confined. I have long been of opinion that less than a three years' course of study ought not to be adopted.

"Case system" and "text-book system" of instruction.

2. The law must be learned from text-books, adjudged cases, and oral instruction, including therein lectures and class exercises. There is a great deal of current discussion as to the relative merits of what is termed the " case system " and the " text-book system." My experience does not enable me to pronounce any judgment concerning the merits of this controversy. I am not even sure that I exactly understand the question in dispute.

The difficulties in the way of teaching our law are many and great. Our law consists of, or is to be found in, constitutions and statutes, and what is called case-law or judiciary law. In our legal system the only authoritative sources, or, more accurately, the authoritative evidences of the latter and of the true meaning of the former, are to be found in the reported judgments of the courts. Now, fortunately for our jurisprudence, but unfortunately both for the teacher and the student, our case-law is embodied in many thousands of volumes of reports; and of these reports any system of instruction with which I am acquainted necessarily makes use. Our elementary treatises, numbering many hundreds of volumes, are written not for the purpose of the teacher, or primarily for the purpose of the instruction of students, but for the use of the practising lawyer. They are, therefore, not specially adapted to the use of the student or the teacher of law. It is a work which belongs to the future, but it is a work which I think must sooner or later be done, — to cast our law into a more orderly, methodical, and scientific form; and when this shall be accomplished the work of the teacher and the student will be made much easier and more satisfactory than it now is. The great drawback to-day, alike of the teacher and the student, is the non-existence of elementary works written by lawyers of competent learning and experience, designed for the specific purpose of enabling the teacher to teach and the student to learn the elements, the great primordial and essential principles of our jurisprudence. And by reason of the inorganic shape, if I may so express it, in which our law is found, comes the urgent need of oral instruction and exposition; for, after all, private law in its essence consists largely in certain great principles of justice and right, to acquire knowledge of which is the primary object of legal education.

The importance and value of the reports as authoritative examples, expositions, and applications of these principles, cannot be overrated; but it is easy to underrate the necessity and importance of elementary treatises. In the voluminous and unmethodized state of our law they are indispensable. It is not too much to say that under existing conditions they are absolutely necessary to the student, to the lawyer, and to the judge.

My conclusion is that in any well-considered system of legal education, oral instruction (including therein lectures, recitations, colloquies, moot-courts, etc.), text-books, and cases must go together. If I were to assign a relative value to the three, I would say the first in importance is the oral work of the teacher, and that he must use both the text-books and selected cases, not according to any rigid or prescribed system, but in such way that, according to his skilled judgment, the principles of law — the end to be sought — can be the most easily and thoroughly mastered.

I believe, as an indifferent observer (although I attach little weight to my own judgment), that the discussion concerning the competing systems of "instruction by case-law" and "instruction by text-books" has already had one beneficial result, and that result is to show that neither of these methods should be the exclusive method; that possibly (though I do not state this upon personal knowledge of the matter) somewhat more of oral exposition and elementary instruction could be profitably carried into the case system, and somewhat more of the case system into what is known as the text-book system.

Lecture III.

If I could realize my notion, under existing conditions, of the expedient mode of legal instruction, I would assume that the students' minds were wholly uninformed. I would call the class into the lecture-room, and selecting a subject, would orally outline or chalk out in the most elementary way its place in and its relations to the legal system, and the great principles that underlie it. Then, if the particular subject were well treated in some text-book, I would require that to be studied, and also to be studied some of the leading cases upon it. Whether on any given subject the case-system or some other system should predominate would depend, of course, on circumstances. The student should then be required to recite both upon the text-book and upon the selected cases, and to state, analyze, and discuss the latter, — the professor's function being to see that the principles were mastered, and the mode in which they were applied in the selected cases fully understood.

Advisable mode of instruction suggested.

The great test of the teacher is: Does he inspire enthusiasm in the student? Does he set him thinking? Does he make him work? If so, the particular mode in which he accomplishes this is comparatively unimportant.

I close with a brief reference to the legal character and faculties of the Inns. Their legal character has been clearly ascertained by numerous

Lecture III.
Legal character of the Inns of Court.

decisions.[1] The adjudged cases establish the following points: The Inns are voluntary societies, and not corporations; they have no charters, either from the Crown or Parliament. They are self-governed. The courts cannot interfere with the internal management of their affairs. In respect of their acts or orders affecting members, they are not subject to the jurisdiction of the Courts of Westminster Hall proceeding according to the common law. They cannot be compelled by *mandamus* or otherwise to admit persons to become students or members of the society with the view of being called to the bar. This rests alone with the society. When admitted as members, the visitatorial power of the judges attaches, and the action of the society in refusing to call a member to the bar, or in expelling him from the society, or in depriving him of his gown, — that is, disbarring him, — may be reviewed by the judges on an appeal (but in no other mode), against the orders complained of. The power to call members to the bar seems not to be oppressively or illiberally exercised, since it appears that during a period of twenty years only three students had been refused admission to the bar by the four Inns of Court.

[1] The principal cases concerning the legal constitution and powers of the Inns of Court, and the extent of judicial control over them, are Booreman's case, March Rep. 177; Townshend's case, cited 2 T. Raymond, 1028; Rakestraw v. Brewer, Abridg. Cases in Equity, 102; Hart's case (Rex v. Gray's Inn), 1 Douglas, 354; Lord Rosslyn v. Jodrell, 4 Campbell, 303; 1 Starkie Rep. 148; Wooler's case, 4 Barn. & Cress. 855; May v. Harvey, 13 East, 197. In Hart's case, *supra*, the judges sustained the benchers of Gray's Inn in refusing to call Mr. Hart to the bar, for the reason, among others, that he had knowingly become security for money borrowed of others to a much greater amount than he was able to answer.

The most important faculty which the Inns exercise is the *exclusive power*, as legal colleges,[1] *to confer the degree of barrister-at-law or counsellor*, which is an indispensable qualification to practise in the courts of common law. A barrister can be created in no other way than by a call by one of the four Inns of Court. He cannot be created by letters patent, or be admitted as with us, by the authority of the court. The Inns of Court being independent of royal or executive power, no person called to the bar is indebted for the station to any authority except the governing body of the Inn of Court to which he belongs. To this cause has been attributed, in part, the spirit of independence, which, in the history of constitutional liberty, has been so often displayed by the Inns of Court, and which has at all times characterized the members of the bar in asserting legal rights committed to their advocacy or defence.[2] "Rare Ben Jonson," who, it is said, assisted his stepfather, a brick-layer, in erecting, in the reign of Elizabeth, a wall for Lincoln's Inn, dedicated a

Lecture III.

Exclusive power to call to the bar.

[1] Blackstone styles the Inns of Court "our Juridical University" (1 Com. 25); and Lord Coke, in a passage before quoted, styles them the "foure famous and renowned colleges or houses of Court," which "altogether doe make the most famous Universitie for the profession of law, onely, that is in the world, and advanceth itself above all others." *Ante* Lecture II.

[2] "Intrepidity in the discharge of professional duty is so common a quality at the English bar that it has, thank God, long ceased to be a matter of boast or praise. If it had been otherwise, gentlemen, — if the bar could have been silenced or overawed by power, — I may presume to say that an English jury would not this day have been met to administer justice. Perhaps I need scarce say that my defence shall be fearless, in a place where fear never entered any heart but that of a criminal." Sir James Mackintosh's Speech in Defence of Jean Peltier, for a libel on the First Consul of France, delivered in the King's Bench, Feb. 21, 1803.

play¹ "to the noblest nurseries of humanity and liberty, the Inns of Court."

A person who contemplates a call to the bar is required to be admitted as a student, — that is, to become a member of one of the four Inns, which any person of respectable character and educational attainments has no difficulty in doing; to dine in the common hall of the Inn a few days in the course of every term, that he may be seen and known, and if unfit, the more readily detected before his final application to be called to the bar; to keep in this manner, ordinarily twelve terms, and in addition, under more recent regulations before mentioned, to attend the lectures of the readers or professors in the Inn; and satisfactorily to pass a public examination for the purpose of ascertaining his fitness to be called to the bar. Having complied with these conditions, the student or member is eligible to be called, and, unless some good reason appears, is called to the bar.²

From this brief sketch it will be perceived that the Inns of Court are *sui generis* in their character.

---

[1] Every Man out of his Humour.

[2] The hospitality of the Inns in the matter of calls to the bar is shown in the case of Mr. Benjamin. "On January 13, 1866, Benjamin (Judah P.) was admitted a student of Lincoln's Inn, and in Trinity Term of the same year, after six months' probation, was, by special grace, called to the bar. He was made a Queen's counsel of the County Palatine of Lancaster, with a patent of precedence dating from July 29, 1872, and afterwards full Queen's counsel. In April, 1875, he was made a bencher of Lincoln's Inn." "A Generation of Judges," London, 1888, article "Benjamin."

That the reader may understand the preparation required and the mode of being "called" to the bar in the Inns, I reprint as a note (B) at the end of this lecture extracts from Mr. Serjeant Robinson's recent account thereof.

As to jurisdiction, powers, privileges, and rank, all the four Inns stand on a footing of perfect equality. Within them are collected the great body of the profession of the law in England. The membership of the four Inns in 1873 was about eight thousand, of whom six thousand were barristers and the rest students.[1] This legal community in all its professional relations is governed by its own officers, laws, and usages. The chambers are let to students and barristers. The latter have their offices in them. Unmarried members attended by servants frequently live within them, and at their option take their meals in the dining-hall of the Inn. Each Inn, as I have said, has not only its chapel, but its kitchen;[2] not

Lecture III.

Governed by their own officers, laws, and usages.

---

[1] Spilsbury, "History Lincoln's Inn," ed. 1873, p. 18.

[2] "In all the Inns of Court and Chancery the important concern of eating and drinking seems to have occupied the most attention; instruction, such as it was (consisting of public readings or lectures, and the mootings, or arguing of cases), was a secondary object." Herbert, "Inns of Court," p. 223.

"Another apartment [of Lincoln's Inn] forming an essential appendage to all collegiate establishments, and without which even the splendid Hall would be only suited for the imaginary feast of the Barmecide, is the kitchen, — forty-five feet square and twenty feet high; and connected with the kitchen are cellars capable of holding upwards of one hundred pipes of wine, and above these, butlers' pantries," etc. Spilsbury, "Lincoln's Inn," p. 120.

"In term-time Mr. Pen showed a most praiseworthy regularity in performing one part of the law student's course of duty, and eating his dinners in the Hall. Indeed, that Hall of the Upper Temple is a sight not uninteresting, and with the exception of some trifling improvements and anachronisms which have been introduced into the practice there, a man may sit down and fancy that he joins in a meal of the seventeenth century. The bar have their messes, the students their tables apart; the benchers sat on a high table on the raised platform, surrounded by pictures of judges of the law and portraits of royal personages who have honored its festivities with their presence and patronage." Thackeray, "Pendennis," chap. xxix.

only a large library,[1] but an ample dining-hall and drawing-room adorned with the busts and portraits of its eminent members. Each member is thus within the eye and in a degree under the fraternal guardianship of all the others; and heretofore, however it may be under recent regulations, benchers, barristers, and students have participated in the educational as well as the social life of the Inn.[2]

Thus much for the Inns of Court which are so intimately and immemorially associated with the social life, education, discipline, character, and achievements of the English bar. It is indeed a quaint and curious picture; and if it is not also a picture replete with interest and instruction, the fault is surely mine. The English bar have made, or at all events have determined, the character and form of the English law. The English lawyer is distinctively a specialist. From the earliest period of the Inns his life and training tended to make him such. Where and how he wrought, and what is the character of the product of his professional studies and labors, — this is the subject which I shall attempt to portray when we meet again.

---

[1] The number of volumes in 1881 in the library of the Inner Temple was thirty thousand; of the Middle Temple twenty-eight thousand; of Lincoln's Inn forty-three thousand; and of Gray's Inn thirteen thousand. Encyclopædia Britannica, 9th ed., art. "Inns of Court;" Loftie, "Inns of Court and Chancery" (Macmillan), 1893; Douthwaite, "Gray's Inn, History and Associations," London, 1886.

[2] Works mainly consulted in the foregoing sketch of the Inns of Court: Blackstone Com., Introductory Lecture; Smith's "History of Education for the English Bar;" Pearce, "Guide to Inns of Court," London, 1855; Spilsbury, "Lincoln's Inn and Library," 2d ed., London, 1873; Herbert, "Antiquities of Inns of Court," London, 1804; Encyclopædia Britannica, 9th ed., art. "Inns of Court," by Mr. J. Claude Webster, Barrister; Foss, "Judges of England;" Pulling, "The Order of the Coif," London, 1884. See *ante* Lecture II., Note B, at end.

NOTE A.

THE LITERARY ASSOCIATIONS OF THE INNS OF COURT
REFERRED TO IN THE PRECEDING LECTURE.

GOWER is said to have been a member of the Middle Temple. "PHILIP SIDNEY was a member of Gray's Inn." Hutton, "Literary Landmarks of London," article *Sidney*.

"BEAUMONT was entered a member of the Inner Temple, Nov. 3, 1600." *Ib.*, v. *Francis Beaumont*. "Beaumont and Fletcher wrote a masque entitled 'The Masque of the Inner Temple and Gray's Inn,' which seems to have been performed alternately by the two societies, the title being varied accordingly. In 1612 it was played at Whitehall before the court. 'The Masque of Flowers,' a seventeenth century pageant, was performed in 1613 at Gray's Inn, and repeated in 1887 on the occasion of the Queen's Jubilee;" and it was also repeated in the hall of the Inner Temple. Loftie, "Inns of Court and Chancery" (Macmillan, 1893), pp. 48, 70.

"LORD BACON, as a member of Gray's Inn, lived at No. 1 Coney Court, which was unfortunately burned down in 1678. The site is occupied by the present [1868] row of buildings at the west end of Gray's Inn Square, adjoining the gardens in which the great philosopher took such delight." Jesse's "London," vol. iii., "Gray's Inn." "He [Bacon] is said to have designed these gardens, and to have planted the old catalpa tree still standing there in 1885." Hutton, "Literary Landmarks of London," v. *Francis Bacon*. See *ante* Lecture II.

SELDEN (John), the learned legal antiquary and writer, had lodgings in the Inner Temple, died in 1654, and was buried in the Temple Church.

"FIELDING became a student of the Middle Temple in 1737, and was called to the bar three years later, when 'chambers were assigned to him in Pump Court.'" Hutton, "Literary Landmarks of London," v. *Fielding*. I do not know a more charming autobiography than Gibbon's. It is a striking proof

Note A.

Literary associations of the Inns of Court.

Lecture III.

Literary associations of the Inns of Court.

of his genius that he could make so interesting the narrative of a life so externally uneventful. His vanity and self-satisfaction with his labors, so freely displayed, are fairly justified by his success, and they give a real human interest in the story of his life, which is interspersed with reflections and episodes most felicitously expressed. Take, for example, his reference to "our immortal Fielding, who was," he says, "of the younger branch of the Earls of Denbigh, who drew their origin from the counts of Habsburg. Far different have been the fortunes of the English and German divisions of the house of Habsburg: the former have slowly risen to the dignity of a peerage; the latter, the Emperors of Germany and Kings of Spain, have threatened the liberty of the Old and invaded the treasures of the New World. The successors of Charles the Fifth may disdain their brethren of England; but the romance of Tom Jones, that exquisite picture of human manners, will outlive the palace of the Escurial and the imperial eagle of the house of Austria." Thackeray, in the "English Humourists," quoting the above passage, adds: "There can be no gainsaying the sentence of this great judge. To have your name mentioned by Gibbon is like having it written on the dome of St. Peter's. Pilgrims from all the world admire and behold it." Quotation from "Pendennis," referring to Fielding, *ante* Lecture II., p. 40, note.

COWPER " had been entered at the Middle Temple (April 29, 1748) before he left school, and he took chambers there in 1752. . . . On the 14th of June, 1754, Cowper was called to the bar. . . . In 1756 he lost his father. . . . Three years after his father's death he removed from the Middle to the Inner Temple, and purchased chambers there (they cost him £250), in an airy situation." Southey, "Works of Cowper," London, 1835, vol. i. chap. ii.

Cowper, "after leaving Westminster School, went into solitary lodgings in the Middle Temple; but in 1754 or 1755 [Southey fixed a later date, 1759] he took chambers in the Inner Temple, where for a number of years he devoted much of his time to composition, and not a little of it to thoughts of love, — for it was here that he met the first great sorrow of his life, in the refusal of his family to permit his marriage with his cousin, — and it was here that his mental derangement led to his attempt at suicide." Hutton, "Literary Landmarks of

London," *v. William Cowper.* It was in 1763 that he attempted suicide by hanging himself in his chambers in the Temple. Cowper's narrative thereof is given at large in Southey's "Cowper," *ubi supra,* chap. v. "Eventually he was removed to an asylum at St. Albans, and recovered the use of his faculties; but he never returned to live in London, and even the place of his residence in the Temple is unknown." Loftie, "Inns of Court and Chancery," 1893, p. 29. In a poem written years after the melancholy termination of his residence in the Temple, he touchingly refers to that sad event, and to the tenderness with which the Saviour's compassion and love had healed his wounds: —

Note A.

Literary associations of the Inns of Court.

> "I was a stricken deer that left the herd
> Long since; with many an arrow deep infixt
> My panting side was charged, when I withdrew
> To seek a tranquil death in distant shades.
> There was I found by One who had himself
> Been hurt by the archers. In his side he bore,
> And in his hands and feet, the cruel scars.
> With gentle force soliciting the darts
> He drew them forth, and heal'd, and bade me live."

DR. JOHNSON. "I have this day moved my things, and you are now to direct to me at Staple Inn [Holborn], London. I am going to publish a little story-book ['Rasselas'], which I will send you when it is out." Letter of Johnson to Miss Porter, March 23, 1759, in Boswell's "Johnson," Birkbeck Hill's Ed., vol. i., pp. 340, 516, art. 50. "He retired to Gray's Inn, and soon removed to chambers on the Inner Temple Lane [No. 1], where he lived in poverty, total idleness, and the pride of literature." Murphy, "Essay on Johnson." He remained at No. 1 for about five years from 1760. "Johnson's house in Inner Temple Lane has since been removed, giving place to the more imposing, but less interesting, Johnson Buildings, which stand upon its site." Hutton, "Literary Landmarks," etc., *v. Samuel Johnson.*

BOSWELL. "In July, 1763, Boswell removed to 'the bottom of Inner Temple Lane, where Johnson was living, in order to be nearer to the object of his devotion.'" Hutton, "Literary Landmarks of London," *v. James Boswell.* May 24, 1763, Boswell gives a characteristic account of his first visit to

Lecture III.

Literary associations of the Inns of Court.

Johnson's Chambers at No. 1 Inner Temple. Boswell entered his name at the Inner Temple with a view to be called to the bar. He did not carry out this purpose then, but in 1775 he again entered his name, and eleven years later was duly called. Loftie, *ubi supra*, p. 30.

GOLDSMITH. "In 1764 Johnson found Goldsmith in a humble set of chambers at No. 2 Garden Court, Middle Temple, near the New Library and behind Fountain Court. He then went to Gray's Inn. The proceeds received for 'The Good-Natured Man' gave Goldsmith a feeling of unlimited wealth; and he took chambers, consisting of three rooms, on the second floor of No. 2 Brick Court, Middle Temple." Hutton, "Literary Landmarks," etc., *v. Goldsmith*. The "Vicar" was written in 2 Garden Court in 1764. "The Good-Natured Man" brought him £500; whereupon he bought the chambers, No. 2 Brick Court, Middle Temple, for £400, where he remained until his death, in 1774, about nine years. "The Deserted Village" and "The Traveller" were written in 2 Brick Court. Thackeray in his "English Humourists" refers to his own residence in that house in 1855. Loftie, "Inns of Court and Chancery," 1893, pp. 42, 43.

Irving ("Life of Goldsmith," chap. xxiii.) relates Goldsmith's extravagance in fitting up these chambers, and adds: "He gave dinners to Johnson, Percy, Reynolds, Bickerstaff, and other friends, and supper parties to young folks of both sexes. . . . Blackstone, whose chambers were immediately below, and who was studiously occupied on his 'Commentaries,' used to complain of the racket made by 'his revelling neighbor.'" Hutton, who quotes the above, adds: "In 1885 No. 2 Brick Court was precisely as Goldsmith left it when carried to his grave. The house, erected in 1704, and the little court are the house and court he knew so well." Hutton, "Literary Landmarks," etc., *v. Goldsmith*. "Goldsmith died, and was buried, where the happiest and most peaceful years of his life had been spent, in the Temple. His funeral took place at five in the afternoon of the 9th of July, 1774, when his staircase on Brick Court was crowded with mourners of all ranks and conditions in life, conspicuous among them being the outcasts of both sexes, who loved and wept for him because of the goodness he had done. The exact position of Goldsmith's grave is not known. The plain monument with the simple inscription, 'Here Lies Oliver Goldsmith,' was placed, in 1860, on the north side of the Temple Church, as near as possible to the spot where his remains are supposed to lie." *Ib.*

Note A.

Literary associations of the Inns of Court.

Speaking of Goldsmith's life in No. 2 Brick Court, Middle Temple, 1767, when Goldsmith was thirty-nine years of age, Forster says: "Among his happiest hours were those passed at his window, looking over into the Temple gardens. Steam and smoke were not yet so all-prevailing but that, right opposite where he looked, the stately stream which washes the garden foot might be seen, as though freshly 'weaned from her Twickenham Naiads,' flowing gently past. Nor had the benchers thinned the trees in those days; for they were a race of benchers loved of Charles Lamb, who refused to pass their treasurer's account 'twenty shillings to the gardener for stuff to poison the sparrows.' So there Goldsmith sat, with the noisy life of Fleet Street shut out, and made music for himself out of the noise of the old Temple rookery. . . . Let us leave him to this happiness for a time, before we pass to the few short years of labor, enjoyment, and sorrow in which his mortal existence closed." Forster's "Goldsmith," vol. ii., book iii., chap. xix.

"It was," says Mr. Martin, "but a biscuit toss from Crown Office Row [where Charles Lamb was born] to No. 2 Brick Court, Middle Temple, where Goldsmith died only ten months before the birth of Lamb; and was buried somewhere in the buryingground of the Temple Church. Within it the benchers put up a tablet to his memory. The inscription on that tablet may have first been spelled out by Mary to her small and eager brother. Doubtless the two children knew the exact spot of his grave, — known exactly to none of us to-day, — as they knew every corner and cranny of the Temple grounds and buildings." Martin, "Footprints of Charles Lamb," 1890, pp. 13, 14. "No memorial indicates the grave to the pilgrim or the stranger, nor is it possible any longer to identify the spot in the burial-ground of the Temple Church which received all that was mortal of this delightful writer." Forster, "Life of Goldsmith," vol. ii., book iv., chap. xxi. Forster, himself a member of the Inner Temple, in 1852, accompanied by Sir Frederick Pollock, at that time treasurer of the Temple, visited "the burial-ground of the Temple in the hope of identifying the grave, but did not succeed in

Lecture III.

Literary associations of the Inns of Court.

the object of our search. We examined unavailingly every spot beneath which interment had taken place, and every stone and sculpture on the ground." *Ib.*

This record is to me inexpressibly sad. Early in life Goldsmith had written "whatever vicissitudes we experience in life, however we toil, or wheresoever we wander, our fatigued wishes still recur to home for tranquillity; we long to die in the spot which gave us birth." "Citizen of the World," letter ciii. Alas! he had no home in the true sense of the word, and yet we cannot doubt that the well-known lines closing with the pathetic image of the hunted hare expressed his heart's sincerest desire:—

> "In all my wand'rings round this world of care,
> In all my griefs,— and God has given my share,—
> I still had hopes, my latest hours to crown,
> Amid these humble bowers to lay me down;
> . . . .
> And, as a hare, whom hounds and horns pursue,
> Pants to the place from whence at first she flew,
> I still had hopes, my long vexations past,
> Here to return,— and die at home at last."

TOOKE (John Horne) in 1756 was entered at the Middle Temple.

"SHERIDAN was entered a student at Middle Temple in 1772." Hutton, "Literary Landmarks," etc.

SOUTHEY entered Gray's Inn in 1797. Hutton, "Literary Landmarks."

MOORE (Thomas) entered his name as a student in the Middle Temple in 1799, but did not live within it. Ford, the dramatist, Wycherley, Shadwell, and Congreve had chambers in the same Temple. Loftie, p. 49.

LAMB. Lamb commences his "Old Benchers of the Inner Temple," to a lawyer the most delightful of all his essays, thus: "I was born, and passed the first seven years of my life, in the [Inner] Temple." He was educated at Christ's Hospital, as everybody knows who has read his two essays on that famous school. From his birth, in 1775, till 1795, Lamb lived in Crown Office Row, Temple; then after residing elsewhere till 1801, he again removed to the Temple. "And so," says Mr. Benjamin Ellis Martin in his late interesting volume

("The Footprints of Charles Lamb," 1890, p. 55), "on Lady Day, March 25, 1801, he and Mary moved into the Temple, there to begin, near their childhood home, that life of 'dual loneliness,' never again broken in upon, — consoled by their mutual affection, cheered by their common tastes, brightened by the companionship of congenial beings. In the Temple they remained for seventeen years, living in two sets of chambers during that period," — eight years at No. 16 Mitre Court Buildings, and then on the third and fourth floors of No. 4 Inner Temple Lane, looking back into Hare Court, with its pump and trees, which trees came into the window. "Do you know it?" wrote Lamb to Manning. "I was born near it, and used to drink at that pump when I was a Rechabite of six years old. Here I hope to set up my rest, and not quit till Mr. Powell, the undertaker, gives me notice that I may have possession of my last lodging." The hope thus expressed was not realized. At the end of the seventeen years he finally left the beloved Temple grounds, living chiefly at Enfield and Edmonton, and dying in his home at the latter place in 1834, in his sixtieth year. Thus, for more than half his life, his home was within the Temple Close. His Essay on the "Old Benchers" appeared in 1821, after he had ceased to live in the Temple, and when he looked back with fond recollections upon the scenes of his earlier life.

Note A.
Literary associations of the Inns of Court.

I cannot refrain from confessing to a kindly regard for the memory of Samuel Salt, Esquire, barrister of the Inner Temple and one of its benchers; and this springs not from anything that he did in or for his profession, nor indeed from anything that Lamb says concerning him in the "Old Benchers," but solely from the fact that he was the lifelong friend of Lamb's parents, and as long as he lived of Charles Lamb and his unfortunate sister.

I extract the following concerning Lamb's life in the Temple and concerning his benefactor from Mr. Martin's "The Footprints of Charles Lamb," 1890: "'Cheerful Crown Office Row (place of my kindly engendure)'" — to use Lamb's own words — "has been only partly rebuilt; and that end of the block wherein lived his parents stands (A. D. 1890) almost in the same state as when it was erected in 1737. . . . Under the 'Chamber Book of the Inner Temple' I have hunted up its numer-

Lecture III.

Literary associations of the Inns of Court.

ous occupants. By this archive and by the books of accounts I have been enabled to trace Samuel Salt from his first residence within the Temple, in 1746, until he settled down in his last chambers, wherein he died in February, 1793. The record reads: a 'parliament,' — meaning one of the fixed meetings of the benchers of the Inner Temple, — '13th May, 1768. At this parliament: It is ordered that Samuel Salt, Esquire, a barrister of this society, aged about fifty, be and is hereby admitted for his own life to the benefit of an assignment of Ground Chamber No. 2, Crown Office Row, he having paid for the purchase thereof into the treasury of this society the sum of £150.'"
"So that it was in No. 2, — the numbers having remained unchanged, — of Crown Office Row, in one of the rear rooms of the ground-floor, which then looked out on the Inner Temple Lane, some of which rooms have been swept away since, and others have been slightly altered, that Charles Lamb was born, on the 10th February, 1775. For Samuel Salt, Esquire — one of 'The Old Benchers of the Inner Temple,' whose pensive gentility is portrayed in Elia's Essay of that title — had in his employ as 'his clerk, his good servant, his dresser, his friend, his "flapper," his guide, stop-watch, auditor, treasurer,' one John Lamb [father of Charles], who formed, with his wife and children, the greater part of the household 'of Samuel Salt, Esquire.' . . . To John Lamb and to his children Salt was a lifelong benefactor, and never until death had made an end to the good man's good deeds did there fall on the family any shadow of change or penury."

"HALLAM was a bencher of the Middle Temple." Hutton, *v. Hallam.*

"MACAULAY, between 1829 and 1834, occupied chambers at No. 8 South Square, Gray's Inn, in a building that has since been torn down to make way for the extension of the library." Hutton, *v. Macaulay.*

THACKERAY "loved the Temple and lived for some time, or, to speak more strictly, 'occupied' chambers which have now disappeared, at 10 Crown Office Row. He had been called to the bar in 1834, and he shared his apartments with Tom Taylor. He often speaks of the Temple, in which the scene of so much of 'Pendennis' is to be found." Loftie, p. 27.

DICKENS was not of the Inns, but some of the most delightful

scenes in "Martin Chuzzlewit" are laid in Fountain Court, Middle Temple; and who does not recall Serjeant Buzfuz? _{Note A.}
With the reflections so well expressed by Mr. Loftie in concluding his account of the "Inns of Court and Chancery," I may fitly conclude these scattered notes concerning their literary associations. "The proud Templars actually did march through the courts still called after them, and were actually buried in the church. Here, too, we think of Johnson and Goldsmith, of Cowper and Lamb, of Thackeray and Dickens, as well as of the eminent lawyers who were nourished in these old walls. The Middle Temple contains in its hall almost the only tangible relic of Shakespeare that exists in London. Some see a similar association in the hall of Gray's Inn, but there Bacon is the most commanding figure. I never pass Lincoln's Inn gate tower without remembering that it was new when Sir Thomas More walked through it as chancellor. Memories of this kind crowd on us among the Inns of Court and Chancery."

NOTE B.

STUDENTSHIP IN THE INNS OF COURT, AND MODE OF BEING CALLED TO THE BAR, REFERRED TO IN THE PRECEDING LECTURE.   Note B.

Mr. Serjeant Robinson, in his book, "Bench and Bar," before mentioned (*ante* Lecture II., Note B), describes in a clear and interesting manner the preparation for and the mode of being called to the bar sixty years ago, and adds that "the mode of proceeding is much the same now (1889) as it was formerly."   Mode of call to the bar.

"It may not be uninteresting to the general reader to gain an insight into the process by which certain of the liege subjects of Her Majesty acquire the right to disguise themselves in the costume of the wig and gown. I entered as a student at the Middle Temple in April, 1833, A. D. There are four distinct establishments that have the exclusive privilege of granting the degree. A candidate must attach himself to one of them,

104   LAWS AND JURISPRUDENCE.

Lecture III. although it is quite immaterial by which of the four portals he seeks to enter the profession. These Inns of Court, as they are called, are Lincoln's Inn, the Inner Temple, the Middle Temple, and Gray's Inn. There are several other establishments called Inns, such as Clement's Inn, Staple Inn, Clifford's Inn, New Inn, Barnard's Inn, etc.; but they are not Inns of Court, and have nothing to do with the bar, except that some of them are dependencies of the four superior ones, whilst others, originally in the same predicament, have now a totally separate existence. [But see *ante* Lecture II.]

"They form for the most part communities of attorneys, and have accumulated considerable wealth. In these confiscatory times, some of them have thought it expedient to subject themselves to deliberate suicide, lest a worst fate might befall them. Like the French Huguenots of old, they have thought it better to break up their ancient houses and homes, and disperse, each with his share of what was for centuries recognized as a joint title and assured possession, rather than live in constant fear of an arbitrary statute that might doom them to forfeiture and annihilation. [See *ante* Lecture II. as to the sale of Serjeants' Inn.]

Studentship in the Inns of Court. "Any one wishing to become a student at an Inn of Court had to furnish himself with a certificate of respectability signed by two barristers, who vouched for his eligibility in that respect. He had then to go through the formality of what was technically called an examination, the crucial part of which occupied about a minute and a half. One or two questions in Latin or in general literature were put to him, in the perfunctory style in which one asks a passing acquaintance after his health, being quite indifferent as to what answer he might give. The pursuit of knowledge by the examiner as to a youth's proficiency was not very ardent in those days, and the most superficial candidate for the honors of admission might have come off with great credit to himself. I believe the examination now is just a trifle nearer the real thing, but I never yet heard of any man being plucked in this preliminary 'little go.' If I had, I should expect the next intelligence I got of him would date from an idiot asylum. [But see *ante*, pp. 82, 83, as to present educational requirements of persons applying for admission to the Inns as students.]

"The next important step was the payment of one hundred

pounds into the treasury of your selected Inn, while you entered into a stringent bond with two sureties that you would obey the rules and regulations of the establishment, attend church (in my case the Temple) every Sunday with strict regularity, and pay up your commons and other dues whenever they were demanded. As to the third of these stipulations, the sureties were mere substitutions, — if you did not pay your debts they would pay for you; but it was never understood that they could observe the rules of the Inn for you, or even that they could go to church for you when you were profligate enough to stay away.

"These preliminaries satisfactorily got through, no future penance was required to qualify you for a call to the bar except a certain display of assiduity in eating and drinking, and it was prescribed in this wise: It was necessary that you should keep twelve terms; and as there were four terms in the year, this stage lasted three years. A term was of three or four weeks' duration, and in the middle of each there was what was called a grand week, and the remainder was divided into periods called half-weeks. Now, keeping a term meant that you had dined in the hall at least once in grand week, and also once in each of two half-weeks. To partake of three dinners was *de rigueur*, but they need not be in consecutive terms. You might take your time about them, spread them over ten years if you liked; but to render yourself eligible for a call you must have completed your tally of twelve. Keeping a term then was not so harrowing a curriculum as many are found to be in these educational times.

"The dinners took place every day in term time, Sundays included. Each day at five o'clock the benchers in their gowns walked in procession up the hall and took their seats on the dais, where their dinners were served. One long row of tables, each accommodating twelve persons, ran down the sides of the hall. The bar was seated at the upper end according to seniority, and below them sat the students. I may mention here that by an old custom, still kept up at the Middle Temple, a porter goes round the different courts and avenues, half an hour before dinner, blowing a bullock's horn to remind all whom it may concern that dinner-time is at hand.

"The bar and the students were parcelled off into messes of four men each, every one being treated to the same bill of fare.

Note B.

Keeping terms.

Lecture III.	Menus were, therefore, quite unnecessary, even had they been in ordinary use. We had a bottle of wine (invariably port) to each mess, soup, a sirloin of beef, a fruit tart, cheese and bread, with an unlimited supply of small beer, — certainly the best of the three classes of that beverage, which are described as strong table, weak table, and *lamen*-table. After dinner, which lasted about an hour, the benchers marched out as they had marched in, and retired to what was called the parliament chamber, to finish their repast with wine and dessert, whilst we were left to our own devices. (Chap. ii.)
Tuition.	"Having achieved a right to studentship, the next thing to do was to look out for a pedagogue, under whose tuition I might become initiated into the science and subtle mysteries of the law, of which I was then as profoundly ignorant as an Ojibewa Indian. This was usually accomplished by paying one hundred guineas a year, for as many years as were considered expedient or convenient, to a barrister or special pleader, for the privilege of what was called having the run of his chambers. (Chap. iii., p. 24.)
Ceremony of being called to the bar.	"In Easter Term, 1840, I was called to the bar. As a preparative for investiture, the aspirant, who has sufficiently dined, must get himself proposed by one bencher and seconded by another in the parliament chamber, where the official business of the Inn is conducted; and if his character is unimpeached, the fiat for his call goes forth. But no one could claim to be called as a matter of right. The benchers might reject the candidate's application, if they pleased, but always subject to an appeal to the body of judges as visitors of the Inn; and their decision was final. (Chap. iv., p. 30.)

"The actual ceremony of being called was very short and simple. On the appointed day, while the benchers and bar were in the hall prepared to sit down to dinner, I, happening to be the senior of nineteen infatuated beings, habited for the first time in the full panoply of gown, wig, and bands, and each brimful of hope and speedy distinction, walked up the hall and stood in a row before our venerable superiors. We then took a short oath that we would do our duty to the Inn, to the public, and to our clients, — should we ever have any, — and the formal business was at an end. We sat down to our repast as usual, and, as soon as the benchers had returned from the bench table, private friends were allowed to flock in and partake of wine and dessert at the table assigned their particular host; and the revels were generally kept up to a late hour. Next day, with light hearts, but many of us with aching heads, after the severe trials of the night before, we had to take divers oaths before a judge in the Bail Court, containing allusions not very complimentary to the Pope, or the Pretender, whoever that might be." (Chap. iv., p. 32.)

Note B.

LECTURE IV.

WESTMINSTER HALL: ITS HISTORY AND THE CHARACTERIS-
TICS OF THE SYSTEM OF LAW DEVELOPED AND PERFECTED
THEREIN; AND HEREIN OF JUDICIAL TENURE AND COM-
PENSATION, TRIAL BY JURY, AND JUDICIAL PRECEDENT.

Lecture IV.

Westminster Hall: its history and associations.

WESTMINSTER HALL (that is, the original building) had been built by William Rufus (A. D. 1087–1100) more than a century before the clause in Magna Charta, heretofore considered, required the Court of Common Pleas to be held "in some certain place."[1] It was originally built as an annex to the King's palace of Westminster, and its earlier uses, as I shall presently show, were for royal ceremonies and festivities. After Magna Charta (and probably in consequence of it) it is certain that Westminster Hall became the seat of the great judicial courts, including, for a long period and until our own day, the Court of Chancery, after its establishment as a distinct jurisdiction. It has never ceased to be used as the place where the ceremonials of the coronation of the English monarchs are solemnized with the accustomed splendor, and as the place for the trial of peers and of official personages charged with great crimes and misdemeanors. But

[1] See *ante* Lecture II.

its most distinctive character has been acquired by reason of its having been for centuries the seat of the great courts of justice of the realm. Hawthorne, visiting England in 1855, thus records in his "English Note-Books" his impressions of it. "We entered "Westminster Hall. . . . After the elaborate ornament of the rooms we had just been viewing, this "venerable hall looks extremely simple and bare. ". . . But it is a noble space, and all without the "support of a single pillar. . . . I love it for its "simplicity and antique nakedness, and deem it "worthy to have been the haunt and home of "History through the six centuries since it was "built. . . . The whole world cannot show another "hall such as this, so tapestried with recollections "of whatever is most striking in human annals."

Lecture IV.

Hawthorne's impressions.

Among the most finished pieces of word-painting in the language is Macaulay's well-known reference to the main hall as the place for the trial of the impeachment of Warren Hastings. You recall his words: "The place," he says, "was worthy of such a "trial. It was the great hall of William Rufus; the "hall which had resounded with acclamations at the "inauguration of thirty kings; the hall which had "witnessed the just sentence of Bacon and the just "absolution of Somers; the hall where the eloquence "of Strafford had for a moment awed and melted a "victorious party inflamed with just resentment; the "hall where Charles had confronted the high court "of justice with the placid courage which has half "redeemed his fame." The great essayist by his love for dramatic effect and by his immediate subject, — which was the trial of the extraordinary man

Macaulay's description.

Lecture IV.

The chief glory of the place.

to whose valor and genius Britain's monarch owes to-day her title of "Empress of India" and her rule over the 240,000,000 of her Indian subjects,[1] — overlooked the less striking but after all the chief glory of the place as the external or visible source whence English justice for more than six centuries has gone forth in its silent but exhaustless flow to the "business and bosoms" of men throughout the entire realm, and whose principles are the rich inheritance of all English-speaking people in every part of the globe. When Westminster Hall is mentioned, the world thinks of it, and above all the lawyer thinks of it, as the seat of the judicial courts and the fountainhead of English justice. Its permanent glory is derived, not from coronation ceremonies or the imposing spectacle of an occasional state trial, but from its being immemorially associated with the history and development of the English law, with the renown of great judges, with the fame of learned lawyers and eloquent advocates. The history and associations of a building so illustrious, one which has given its name to the distinctive system of law which for ages has been administered in it, may fitly occupy a few moments of the time of those who are engaged in studying that system, since this will serve as an introduction to a view of the nature and characteristics of the system itself.

The Hall of William Rufus.

Macaulay's statement that Westminster Hall, where Hastings was tried, "was the great hall of William Rufus," if taken literally, is incorrect. Lord Campbell fell into the same mistake when he said that "William Rufus built the magnificent

[1] *Ante* Lecture I., p. 26.

"hall which is looked upon with such veneration by "English lawyers, and which is the scene of so many "venerable events in English history. This being "completed at Whitsuntide, 1099, the Chief-Justiciar, "Flambard, sat here in the following Trinity Term; "and the Superior Courts of Justice have been held "in it for seven hundred and fifty years."[1] The precise facts are these: The first great hall was indeed built by William Rufus, and was completed in 1099, when that monarch held therein his court — probably the Curia Regis — for the first time; so that it is now nearly eight centuries since "that sacred "spot [not the existing building] was first applied "to legal uses."[2]

Lecture IV.

The original hall of William Rufus had to be renovated, if not rebuilt, within a hundred years. As a result of floods, fire, and time, it was necessary again to renovate or rebuild the hall in the time of Edward III.; another fire intervened in 1386 in the time of Richard II.; and in the work of restoration the edifice was altered, enlarged, strengthened, and beautified. In this re-edification and improvement it is considered not improbable that there was brought into requisition the taste if not the active superintendence of William of Wykeham,[3] — of William of Wykeham, the Magnificent; for such may justly be called the accomplished minister and Chancellor of Edward III. and Richard II. The hall *as it now exists*, "in its "perpendicular Gothic style, its stately roofs, its

Rebuilding.

The existing hall and its uses.

---

[1] Campbell, "Lives of the Chief-Justices," vol. i., chap. i.
[2] Foss, "Judges of England," vol. i., *William Rufus.*
[3] Foss, iv., p. 20.

Lecture IV.

Devoted mainly to legal uses since 1399.

"hammer-headed beams and angels' heads," was finished under Richard II. in 1399:[1] From that date it was devoted mainly to legal uses. It is reasonably clear that it has been thus used from the time of Henry III., when the Curia Regis, more than six hundred years ago, came to an end, and its powers were distributed into the several benches of Westminster Hall. And it is probable that it was thus used from a period soon after Magna Charta. The spot, therefore, has been consecrated to judicial uses for nearly eight centuries, and the present building was continuously the seat of the great courts of justice for nearly five hundred years, until their recent removal to the new Law Courts Building, known as the Royal Courts of Justice.[2]

[1] "To the ill-fated Richard II.," says Jesse (reprinted in "Memories of Westminster Hall," vol. i., chap. ii.), "we are indebted for the magnificent old hall as it now stands. Under his auspices, it was greatly strengthened and beautified, the present matchless roof having been added, and the exterior coated with thick walls of stone. At its completion, in 1398 [1399], it must have presented nearly the same appearance which it wears at the present day. As an apartment, it is said to be the largest in Europe, and its massive timber roof is perhaps the finest specimen of similar scientific construction in the world." "The actual history of Westminster Hall," says Serjeant Pulling, who has made a careful study of it, "shows it to have been originally designed not for a hall of justice, but for a banqueting hall; that it was so used for ages after it was first erected in the time of William Rufus; that Rufus's building was destroyed and an entirely new hall built before the Courts of Law were fixed there, and that the existing Westminster Hall dates back, not to the days of William Rufus, but to Richard II." Pulling, "The Order of the Coif," London, 1884, p. 70.

[2] The erection of the new building and the removal thither of the great courts of the kingdom is so notable an event in the judicial history of England that I have subjoined an account of the erection and character of the building, and of the ceremonies attending its inauguration, in a note (A) at the end of this lecture.

But all things change, even in England. In the course of time the location of the courts in Westminster Hall, while the Chancery Courts were held near the Inns of Court, became inconvenient, and the rooms in which all of these courts were held insufficient in size and uncomfortable. This occasioned a movement, sanctioned by Parliament in 1865, to concentrate all of the courts and to provide a new building for their accommodation, resulting in the completion in 1882 of the Royal Courts of Justice Building in the vicinity of the Inns of Court. This vast and imposing pile was inaugurated by the Queen with impressive ceremonies, December 4, 1882; the Common Law Courts were thereupon removed from Westminster Hall, and the Chancery Courts from Chancery Lane, and courts were on January 11, 1883, regularly opened in their new home. But Westminster Hall, notwithstanding such removal, will remain in the lawyer's memory as the Mecca of English law and justice. Its antiquity, the great events of which it has been the theatre, above all the objects to which for so many ages it has been devoted, and the splendid and enduring results which have been attained in the establishment and development of the system of English law and English legal institutions, combine to make it to all men one of the most interesting of monuments, and to the lawyer a monument absolutely unique, which he may be pardoned for regarding with affectionate veneration.

Lecture IV.

The new Law Courts Building.

The Lord Chief-Justice, on taking his seat for the first time in the new building, in a short address to the bar and the public most appropriately remarked "that though they had left Westminster Hall, he

Removal thither of the great judicial courts.

"trusted they had not left behind them the tradi-
"tions of that great and illustrious building, and that
"they would follow them in this their new habitation;
"and especially he hoped that the unbroken tradition
"— unbroken since he had known it — of mutual
"dependence and harmony between bench and bar
"would continue unbroken, — relations without
"which the bar might probably, and the bench cer-
"tainly would, find it impossible to discharge their
"most important functions." And thus the new Law
Courts Building, as the successor for judicial purposes of Westminster Hall, began its history. If,
like Westminster Hall, it shall stand for centuries
as the seat of English justice, it will surely witness
great events, and important, though I hardly think
structural or revolutionary, changes in the system of
English law. It will in its turn become illustrious
with a history of its own; but the old name of Westminster Hall, more enduring than the hall itself, will
still be associated in the professional mind with that
distinctive system of law and jurisprudence which
furnishes the rule of conduct to the many millions
of people on both hemispheres who have adopted
the institutions of England, and "who speak the
"tongue that Shakespeare spake; the faith and
"morals hold which Milton held."[1]

To me, and I think to lawyers generally, the real, the deepest interest in Westminster Hall, rich as it is in historic associations, is not so much in the building itself as it is in the system of law which, during so many centuries, has been therein fashioned and gradually advanced

[1] Wordsworth, Sonnet, "English Freedom."

toward its present perfection by the combined learning, experience, and labors of so many generations of the lawyers and judges of England. I do not hesitate to say that the system of law taught in the Inns of Court, and which has been developed, applied, and enforced in Westminster Hall and the Courts of Chancery, comprehensively known as the system of English jurisprudence, while having, it must be confessed, some grave defects, is upon the whole, as exemplified in the judicial history of England since 1688, and of its colonies and of the United States, the best system of practical justice, adapted to the needs of the peoples whose conduct it regulates, which the world has ever seen,—the Civil or Roman law not excepted. Except the peculiar American doctrine of written constitutional limitations on legislative power, our system of laws is, in its seminal principles, in its main features and substance, but a prolongation of the English system, modified to suit our changed conditions.

Lecture IV.

Speaking generally, the chief excellences of the English system are that the rule of law, the rule of equal law, the same rule applicable to all alike, pervades and permeates every part of English institutions and polity, and that such rule is applied in the great courts of law by judges having an independent and stable tenure of office; and next to this, the two most striking characteristics of the system are the trial by jury, and the doctrine of the authority of adjudged cases as precedents. Upon each of these subjects I venture to submit some observations for your thoughtful consideration now and hereafter.

The chief excellences of English law.

Lecture IV.

Its rule of legal equality.

The distinguishing feature of English law — that which makes it unique, which constitutes its crowning glory, which raises it high up over every other existing or competing system — is that, under English institutions and polity, law, the rule and reign of law, of equal law, is everywhere predominant and supreme. In a subsequent lecture I shall recur to this point, and endeavor to bring out in sharp relief, with the requisite details and illustrations, this noblest characteristic of English law.[1] It must suffice at this time to say that under that law arbitrary power is unknown; that all men under its sway are governed by and are responsible to the law, and to the law alone; that no man is punishable or can be punished except for a violation of law, — a violation established by public proofs in open court; that the irresponsible power which is recognized by the Continental systems and enforced in administrative or other special tribunals has no existence in the English law, where but one rule — one equal rule — applies everywhere and always to all persons alike, official and non-official; and what is fully as important is that this rule of equality before the law is administered and enforced in and by and through the great law courts, and not, as on the Continent, by any mere administrative or exceptional tribunals.[2]

[1] *Post* Lecture VIII.

[2] English liberty, as it is described in the text, has constitutionally existed since Magna Charta; but it has not been at all times actually and securely enjoyed by the subject in its full measure except since the Revolution of 1688. Fortescue, who wrote A. D. 1461–1470 (see *ante* Lecture II.), compares the legal rights of Englishmen in his day with those of the people of France, and the outlines of the picture, as

It is well known that in England by virtue of various acts of Parliament, and in this country by legislative enactment, a great variety of petty offences, mostly of a police character, may be prose-

Lecture IV.

he drew it more than four hundred years ago, still remain true, with this difference that what was then theory is now fact as well. " Englishmen," he says, "are not sued at law, but before the ordinary judge, where they are treated with mercy and justice, according to the laws of the land; neither are they impleaded in point of property, or arraigned for any capital crime, how heinous soever, but before the King's judges, and according to the laws of the land." " De Laudibus," Amos's Ed., chap. xxxvi., p. 137; and see Mr. Amos's excellent and learned notes; also his Note B to chap. viii. Since Magna Charta, these have been among the fundamental rights of Englishmen. Prior to 1688, however, these rights were sometimes flagrantly denied or violated; but they were never permanently overthrown or destroyed. In times of high prerogative, these rights were often nipped at the top, but they died not at the roots. Bacon praised the Star Chamber Court as "one of the sagest and noblest institutions in this kingdom." And among its merits he declares, borrowing his language from the Civil law, that this court "discerneth principally of four kinds of causes, forces, frauds, crimes various of stellionate, and the inchoations or middle acts towards crimes capital or heinous, not actually committed or perpetrated." Bacon, " History of King Henry VII.," Am. Edition of Montagu's Works of Bacon, vol. i., p. 333. In summing up his view of the reign of Henry VII., Bacon (*Ib.*, pp. 381, 382) says: "He did much to maintain and countenance the laws, which nevertheless was no impediment to him to work his will; for it was so handled that neither prerogative nor profit went to diminution. . . . Justice was well administered in his time, save when the King was a party; save also that the Council-table intermeddled too much with ' meum' and ' tuum.'" Very large and important exceptions, it must be admitted. Entertaining such notions as Bacon did concerning the Star Chamber and the prerogative, we need not be surprised at his attempt by means of the old writ, *De non procedendo Rege inconsulto*, to prevent the courts or judges from adjudging causes in which the interests of the Crown were concerned. Had Bacon succeeded, administrative law in the Continental sense would, as Professor Dicey well observes, have been established in England. Dicey, " Law of the Constitution," 2d ed., London, 1886, lectures v., iv.; see *post* Lecture VIII. That the full and secure enjoyment of the constitutional guarantees of English liberty belong, however, to the later periods of

cuted by summary proceedings before justices of the peace and inferior municipal officers, without the intervention of a grand or petit jury. M. Boutmy has sharply criticised the extent of the powers of the local magistracy in England in this respect, and the manner in which their powers are exercised. He admits that, " with regard to such civil and criminal " proceedings as come before the Superior Courts, " England has been for a long period in advance of " all other European nations ; " but he contends that, " with regard to administrative matters and " minor offences, a single phrase describes accurately " the powers of the county magistracy, — ' absolut-" ism shielded by impunity.' "[1] There may be some ground for the criticism in England; but even there his picture is perhaps overcolored, since the powers of the magistrates are conferred, limited, and regulated by acts of Parliament.[2] I am familiar with

English history, is nowhere more strikingly shown than by referring to the solemn representations and request of the judges of both benches and of the Exchequer, in June, 1591, addressed to Lord Chancellor Hatton and Lord Treasurer Burghley, that measures be taken to the end that Her Majesty's subjects " maie not be committed or deteyned in Preson by commaundemente of any noble man or Counsellor against the lawes of the Realme." Sir Henry Ellis reprints " this very curious and honest document levelled at some arbitrary proceedings of the Privy Council." Ellis, " Original Letters Illustrative of English History, 3d Series," Letter 433, p. 87. I should insert it here if space there were. Such specific and realistic examples show, as it seems to me, more forcibly than any general statement can do, the immense progress which has since been made in the security and enjoyment of individual liberty and rights.

[1] Émile Boutmy, " The English Constitution," Eaden's translation, London, 1891, p. 167.

[2] Stephen, " History of the Criminal Law of England," London, 1883, vol. i., chap. iv., pp. 122–126, under the head of " Courts of a Summary Jurisdiction."

the matter in this country, and I have considered it fully elsewhere.[1] I content myself with saying in this place that the power of summary procedure within the limits to which it is confined by our constitutions and the decisions of the courts is not, as I think, incompatible with the essential rights and liberties of the citizen, and does not detract from the praise — for its freedom from arbitrary power — to which I have said the system of English law is justly entitled.

Lecture IV.

The deserved confidence which the whole world feels in the justice which is distributed by the English courts is almost wholly due to the character of the English judges. They are selected from the most eminent of the profession. They hold their office during good behavior. Ample salaries enable them to give without distraction or anxiety their time and energies to the duties of their high place. A stable and permanent tenure secures that independence, both of popular and royal power, which is essential to a good judicial system and to the fearless administration of justice.[2]

Character of English judges; tenure and compensation.

Let me here, as I pass along, inculcate and enforce a great lesson. It is not too much to say that a stable and independent judiciary is the strongest hope of our own country.[3] That was the system our fathers gave us, and it is the one that still obtains in the selection of Federal judges, and

---

[1] Dillon, "Commentaries on the Law of Municipal Corporations," 4th ed., vol. i., §§ 432–439, and the cases cited.
[2] See *ante* Lecture I.
[3] See *post* Lecture VII.

Lecture IV.

of State judges in seven or eight of the States. But forgetting the nature of judicial power, we have unfortunately discarded this vital principle in the other States of the Union. The best interests of the country are concerned in retrieving this mistake. The mode of selection is not so important perhaps as the tenure and compensation; the one should be during good behavior, and the other adequate and beyond legislative diminution. It is with pleasure that I see in the comparatively recent action of several of the States the first steps of a return, in the lengthened term and more ample salaries, to the principles which the founders of our government borrowed from England and embodied in the Federal and early State constitutions. I shall only add that whenever we depart from these sound notions, whenever we weaken the independence or degrade the dignity of the judicial office, either by the mode of selection, or by a restricted tenure, or by the inadequate compensation of the judges, or in any other way, we make a most serious mistake.[1]

American departure.

Trial by jury.

I am not able to state how the trial by jury is regarded in its practical workings at the present

---

[1] "Everything which compromises or lessens the independence of the judicial power compromises the good administration of justice. The judiciary should be the organ of the law, and not an instrument of government [or party]; *it renders judgments not services.*" M. Glasson, "Elements du Droit Français," p. 212; 11 Am. Law Rev., 677. Mr. Merrill (11 Am. Law Rev., 677) says, "It is difficult to know whether, in popular estimation, the judges are always, in point of fact, entirely independent of the executive." M. Glasson pays a high compliment to the "traditional integrity, great enlightenment, and the gravity of morals" of the French judges.

time by the lawyers, the judges, and the public, in England, or whether it there maintains its ancient popularity. Probably it does; for there judges of ability and experience preside in the courts and have not been shorn of their power so to control the course of trials as to prevent unjust verdicts or the miscarriage of justice.¹ But in this country, I think it is not too much to say that its favor in civil causes has much declined. Many of our best lawyers, of the largest experience, in their lighter moods openly ridicule it, and in their more serious moods openly denounce it. This state of opinion is deeply to be regretted; for no institution can long survive its usefulness, or flourish, when it ceases to cling about the popular heart and to draw life from the popular favor.² I have given some thought and reflection to this subject, but have only time, on the present occasion, to state shortly the conclusions reached: —

Lecture IV.

I. I consider the trial by jury an essential part of our judicial system. It is a cherished tradition. It is more. Its roots strike down deep into the experience, the life, and the nature of the people who have developed and perfected it.³ It gives an individuality to our legal system. It is a vital part

An essential part of our judicial system.

¹ A vigorous defence of the trial by jury in England is made by Mr. Best, 1859, published in vol. ii., "Juridical Society Papers," p. 183.

² "No political institution can endure which does not rivet itself to the hearts of men by ancient prejudice or acknowledged interest." Hallam, "Middle Ages," vol. i., chap. ii., part ii.

³ The historical development of the jury, from its germ in certain practices in public administration adopted by the Normans from the Frankish law, and by the Normans carried into England at the Conquest, through its various enlargements, changes, and transmutations, until it finally shaped itself into the institution of the jury as it now

Lecture IV.

of it. Its shortcomings are not inherent. If judges will do their full duty, jurors will do theirs. I have tried literally thousands of cases with juries, and the instances are few where I had reason to be dissatisfied with their verdicts.

Mr. Justice Miller's views of the jury system.

I recall with interest the views of the late Mr. Justice Miller and the change of opinion on his part on the subject of trial by jury. His opinions are of value, for by general consent he ranks among the ablest judges who have ever held a seat on the bench in this or in any country. He said to me at one time that his notion of an ideal trial court was a court composed of three judges to try all civil issues of law or fact. Some years afterwards, as the result of more observation and experience, he told me he had changed his views, and that he thought juries better judges of fact than

exists, I have seen nowhere presented in such succinct, compact, and satisfactory a manner as in the articles of Professor Thayer, of Cambridge, the "Jury and its Development," published in the Harvard Law Review, 1892, vol. v., pp. 249, 295, 357. Many points in this interesting history, formerly obscure, have been illuminated and made clear by the recent researches of careful students and inquirers in Europe and Great Britain; and the results of the old knowledge and the new are embodied with learning and diligent care in these articles. Nor is this subject of antiquarian interest only. Many questions arise in connection with the functions of the jury, and the relation of the court to the jury and its powers over them, in which a judge is likely to slip if he is not familiar with the story of the origin and evolution of the jury itself. Besides, it is obviously true, as Professor Thayer points out, that the unique English Law of Evidence is "the child of the jury;" is, indeed, its "greatest and most characteristic offshoot," without which it would never have grown up, and without which it cannot be understood. Control over Juries by the Courts, *Ib.*, 312, and by New Trials, *Ib.*, 384. As to Trial by Jury in England, 2 Juridical Society Papers, 183 (Best), *Ib.*, 236 (Sir Fitz James Stephen); Unanimity of Jury, *Ib.*, 7; Report of American Bar Association, 1891, pp. 32, 281.

judges. We have to lament the recent death of this great magistrate; but not long before that event he wrote a paper on "The System of Trial by Jury," in which he expressed his deliberate and final appreciation of the worth and value of trial by jury.[1] It is a cherished right. It is protected from legislative overthrow by the National and by all of our State constitutions. It is a historical and essential part of the free institutions of England. It equally belongs to our own free institutions. It springs out of them, and tends to support and perpetuate them.

Lecture IV.

The jury is part of our free institutions.

[1] "I must confess," says Mr. Justice Miller, "that my practice in the courts, before I came to the bench, had left upon my mind the impression that as regards contests in the courts in civil suits, the jury system was one of doubtful utility; and if I had then been called upon, as a legislator, to provide for a system of trial in that class of actions, I should have preferred a court constituted of three or more judges, so selected from different parts of the district or circuit in which they presided as to prevent, so far as possible, any preconcerted action or agreement of interest or opinion, to decide all the questions of law and fact in the case, rather than the present jury system. . . . An experience of twenty-five years on the bench, and an observation during that time of cases which come from all the courts of the United States to the Supreme Court for review, as well as of cases tried before me at *nisi prius*, have satisfied me that when the principles above stated are faithfully applied by the court in a jury trial, and the jury is a fair one, as a method of ascertaining the truth in regard to disputed questions of fact, a jury is in the main as valuable as an equal number of judges would be, or any less number. And I must say that in my experience in the conference room of the Supreme Court of the United States, which consists of nine judges, I have been surprised to find how readily those judges come to an agreement upon questions of law, and how often they disagree in regard to questions of fact, which apparently are as clear as the law. I have noticed this so often and so much, that I am willing to give the benefit of my observation on this subject to the public, that judges are not pre-eminently fitted over other men of good judgment in business affairs to decide upon mere questions of disputed fact." Mr. Justice Miller in an article on "The System of Trial by Jury," Am. Law Review, vol. xxi., pp. 861, 863.

Lecture IV.

It is my firm conviction that the love of liberty, — of liberty regulated by law, — and a general and habitual reverence for and obedience to the Constitution and the laws, are the only ties which can surely hold together our vast republic. These are the sources of our greatness and the foundation of our hopes. Let us never forget the truth so nobly expressed by Burke: "Justice is itself the great "standing policy of civil society; and any eminent "departure from it, under any circumstances, lies "under the suspicion of being no policy at all."

No acceptable substitute for jury in criminal cases.

In criminal cases there is no substitute for the jury that would be acceptable to the profession or endured by the people. In the solemn act of passing upon the guilt of those charged with offences against the public, the jury represent the majesty of the people as a whole;[1] and when acting under the guidance of a capable judge, their verdicts are almost always right. In the occasional cases where the offender has been almost more sinned against than sinning, but which cannot be anticipated or excepted from the criminal code, and where the offender is consequently technically guilty and a judge would feel bound so to decide, the jury administer an irregular equity, not capable of being defined and formulated, nor of a nature to be expressly sanctioned by the lawgiver, but which satisfies the judgment and conscience of the community without overturning the criminal statute, which still stands intact.

II. But civil controversies, especially in modern times, are much more complicated than criminal

---

[1] Professor Amos, "Science of Law," chap. x., Am. Ed., p. 267.

trials, and the verdicts of juries are much less satisfactory. This is largely owing to obvious causes:

1. Juries ought always to be, but too frequently are not, composed of the better class of citizens in respect of intelligence, moral character, and business experience.[1]

2. Judges have been deprived in many of the States of some of the powers necessary to secure a true verdict, and they fail to exercise there and elsewhere the power to correct the mistakes of juries by an adequate exercise of the right to grant new trials. In some of the States, moreover, statutes have been passed which degrade

Lecture IV.

Causes of dissatisfaction with jury trials.

Curtailment of the powers of the judges.

---

[1] In "De Laudibus" (chap. xxix.), Fortescue discusses the question "why there is not a jury of twelve men in other countries." After adverting to the fact that jurors were required to be "good and lawful men of the neighborhood to the vill where the fact was done . . . who have lands and revenues to the value of 100 shillings," says that "England is so thick-spread and filled with rich and landed men" that it is everywhere practicable to obtain "a substantial jury within the description before observed." "Other countries, my Prince, are not in such a happy situation, — are not so well stored with inhabitants. . . . Wherefore, in those countries they must make up a jury . . . of people of inferior rank, who have no proper notion of shame or infamy, who have no estates or characters to lose; so prejudiced and incapable in point of education as not to be able clearly to discern on which side the truth lies . . . ; other parts of the world cannot furnish juries of so great sufficiency or equally qualified." This was written four centuries ago. The whole chapter goes to show that character and intelligence in jurymen were from the first considered indispensable. In this country we have rejected rank and property qualification as conditions of eligibility, — necessarily and rightly so under the fundamental principles of our political institutions. But there never was a time and never a country where it was so important, as now and here, to require juries to be composed of substantial citizens, men of intelligence, moral character, and varied experience in the affairs of life. If the trial by jury is to regain its former popularity the reform must begin here; and to secure it, the legislatures and the courts must work hand in hand.

the judge as the presiding and guiding intelligence at the trial, into an officer whose functions rather resemble those of a mere moderator. He is forbidden to charge upon the facts, forbidden to sum up the case upon the evidence, forbidden to express any opinion upon the value of the testimony, and is expressly required to confine his charge or instructions to a barren, and to the jury often unintelligible, statement of the law of the case; and is sometimes required to give or refuse instructions in the precise form in which they are adroitly framed by counsel.[1]

[1] *Missouri.* — When the evidence is concluded, and before the case is argued or submitted to the jury, "either party may move the court to give instructions on any point of law arising in the cause, which shall be in writing, and shall be given or refused; the court may, of its own motion, give like instructions." 2 Wagner, Mo. Sts., p. 1046, § 47; 1 Rev. Sts., Mo., 1889, p. 566, § 2188. The construction of the statute, or at all events the settled practice in Missouri, is, that if there is *any* testimony, however slight, relative to the issue, such evidence must be submitted to the jury. Hays v. Bell, 16 Mo., 496. Houghlating v. Ball, 19 Mo., 84; McKoun v. Craig, 39 Mo., 156.

Wisconsin. — The statute of Wisconsin, after requiring that the charge shall, in all cases, unless waived by counsel, be in writing, and providing that if any judge shall "make any comments upon the law or facts to the jury on the trial of any cause, without the same being reduced to writing before it is given, any judgment which shall be rendered upon the verdict shall be reversed," adds, "Each instruction asked by counsel to be given the jury shall be given *without change or modification*, the same as asked, or refused in full." 2 Rev. Sts. Wis. — Taylor's — p. 1496, § 15; Sanborn & Berryman, Anno. Sts. Wis., § 2853 (1889).

Illinois. — "Section 52. Hereafter no judge shall instruct the petit jury in any case, civil or criminal, unless such instructions are reduced to writing." Rev. Sts. Ill., Hurd, 1801, p. 1049; Starr & Curtis, Anno. Sts., p. 1814. "Instructions asked, and not given, must be marked 'refused,' those allowed must be marked 'given,' and there shall be no modification, or qualification, or explanation thereof, except in writing." Rev. Sts. Ill., Hurd's Ed., 1877, p. 740, §§ 52, 53,

I repeat that if the judges will do their full duty, the jurors will do theirs. If we are to expect satisfactory verdicts, the presiding judge must in his charge make the way of the jury plain and clear, and he must have the legal power, as well as the ability, to do this. To do this well is one of the

<small>Lecture IV.</small>

<small>Province and duty of the judge.</small>

54. And "juries in all criminal cases shall be the judges of the law and the fact." *Ib.*, p. 405, § 431; Rev. Sts., Hurd, 1891, p. 1049; Starr & Curtis, Anno. Sts., p. 1814.

Mississippi. — All instructions must be in writing, and no judge in any case, civil or criminal, shall sum up or comment on the testimony; but it shall be lawful for the judge to charge the jury upon the principles of law applicable to the case, at the request of either party. Rev. Code, 1871, § 643; Anno. Code, 1892, § 732.

Arkansas. — "The reading of law books to the jury *shall be allowed* in all cases, and after the argument or submission of a cause to the jury, the court shall then charge and expound the law to the jury." Act of Jan. 19, 1861, Laws of Arkansas, 1861, p. 325. Since repealed. The present practice is as follows: "Section 5131. *Fifth,* When the evidence is concluded, either party may request instructions to the jury on points of law, which shall be given or refused by the court; which instructions shall be reduced to writing if either party require it." Digest of the Statutes of Arkansas, 1884, p. 997.

Iowa. — Either party may request instructions to the jury on points of law, which shall be given or refused, or given as modified by the court in writing. The court may also, of its own motion, charge the jury in writing, and no oral explanation thereof shall be allowed. Code of Iowa, 1873, §§ 2784, 2788; Rev. Code, 1888, p. 958. And so in criminal cases. Code, 1873, §§ 4440, 4441; Rev. Code, 1888, p. 1392.

North Carolina. — "No judge, in giving a charge, shall give an opinion whether a fact is fully or sufficiently proven, such matter being the true office and province of a jury; but he shall state, in a plain and direct manner, the evidence in the case, and declare and explain the law arising thereon." Battle's Revisal of 1873, p. 197, § 237. This law has been replaced by the following: "Section 414 (1885, c. 137). Every judge at the request of any party to an action on trial, made at or before the close of the evidence, before instructing the jury on the law, shall put his instructions in writing, and read them to the jury; he shall then sign and file them with the clerk as a part of the record of the action." Anno. Code, Civ. Pro., Clark, 1892, p. 396. Similar statutes exist in some of the other States.

supreme tests of judicial capacity. But it is possible for the judge to show the jury their duty plainly, and yet not infringe upon their domain. Lord Chief-Justice Cockburn's charge in the Tichborne case, though admitted to be one of the most remarkable intellectual performances from the bench ever witnessed, is thought by some who have examined it to have trespassed upon the legitimate province of the jury. Mr. Justice Stephen's charge in the Maybrick case, which I read carefully at the time, is justly open, as it seems to me, to this criticism, — at least as we in this country view the respective functions of the judge and jury.[1]

[1] Referring to Lord Chief-Justice Cockburn and his mode of charging a jury, the author of a late volume, "A Generation of Judges, by their Reporter," London, 1888, says: "His summing up [in the Tichborne case], which all agree to be a marvel of lucidity, has been criticised, especially across the Atlantic, —whence our cousins canvass legal proceedings in England with keen interest and intelligence, — as too unfavorable to the defendant." The writer adds these sagacious and just general observations in respect of the judge's functions and duties in jury trials: "There are, in fact, two distinct courses for a judge to take in summing up to a jury. He may either recapitulate the facts and leave all the responsibility to them; or, having formed an opinion on the various issues in the case, he may point out to the jury the considerations tending to that conclusion, giving them, at the same time, all the considerations which have an opposite tendency. The first plan is that of a weak judge, and the other is the one adopted by Cockburn. By the first view of the judge's duty, juries are deprived of the best part of the experience, training, and intellectual superiority of the judge; while, in the plan adopted by Cockburn, they have the full benefit of the judge's assistance. There can be no question of the superior advantages of Cockburn's system in the hands of a man like him; the only danger is that it may be adopted by weaker judges who cannot do justice to the facts in all their bearings."

I had the pleasure in 1875 to hear Lord Chief-Justice Cockburn charge a jury at the Queen's Bench in London, and I must say I never heard anything more admirable. It was the work of a master.

The implications from such legislation as I have referred to above, although not pleasant to contemplate, may be useful to weigh and consider. Such legislation implies the existence of a judicial system that works in an imperfect and unsatisfactory manner. Soften or disguise the fact as best one may, such legislation implies a distrust either of the capacity or of the integrity of the judges. Doubtless it is the former; for integrity in the benches of our courts is a common and almost universal possession. Such legislation, therefore, implies a distrust of the capacity of the judge to deal with the evidence in summing up so as not to be likely to do more harm than good, and it overlooks the need on the part of the jury for intelligent judicial instruction and guidance.

Lecture IV.

The remedy is not in the line of these statutes which are based upon the assumed continued existence of the cause of such statutes, but the true remedy is to remove the cause by securing judges who are competent to the full discharge of the high and delicate duties of the judicial office. Taking the judges as they run, I very much doubt whether such legislation has the approval of the body of the bar of the States which have adopted it. It has, doubtless, often originated, not in a public demand, or in any demand on the part of the bar at large, but with some lawyer in the legislature who likes to control juries by declamatory rhetoric, and who has been disappointed by the conscientious discharge on the part of some independent judge of his whole duty. Under the practice required by these statutes, mistaken verdicts are greatly multi-

Remedies suggested.

Lecture IV.

Granting new trials.

plied. At the same time, as an indirect although unintended consequence of other legislation, judges have been led to pay too much respect to erroneous and eccentric verdicts. I have known judges who boasted that they had never exercised their power to set aside verdicts. This is a useful power in the court, and one which it is sometimes necessary to use to prevent a miscarriage of justice, and when thus necessary should be unhesitatingly exercised.

The scintilla doctrine.

The evil is increased by the prevalence in some of the States of the false principle known as the *scintilla* doctrine, — namely, if there is a *scintilla* of evidence the case must go to the jury; whereas the true doctrine is that approved by the Supreme Court of the United States, — namely, that no case ought to be submitted to a jury where the evidence in favor of the party who asks the submission is so weak that a verdict in his favor ought to be set aside by the court.[1] The injustice often produced by the *scintilla* doctrine and by the

---

[1] The Supreme Court of the United States, after some apparent fluctuation of opinion, has rejected the *scintilla* doctrine, and adopted for the Federal courts the English rule on the subject, namely, — "that in every case, before the evidence is left to the jury, there is a preliminary question for the judge, not whether there is literally no evidence, but whether there is any (including all the inferences which the jury can justifiably draw therefrom) upon which the jury can *properly* find a verdict for the party producing it." *Per* Mr. Justice Miller in Pleasant *v.* Fant, 22 Wallace, 116. The same principle has been often reaffirmed. The following are some of the later cases: Bowditch *v.* Boston, 101 U. S., 16; Schofield *v.* Chicago, etc., R. R. Co., 114 *Ib.*, 615; Marshall *v.* Hubbard, 117 *Ib.*, 415; Louisville & N. R. R. Co. *v.* Woodson, 134 *Ib.*, 614.

Judges and Juries. — Some years ago in a public address before one of the State Bar Associations I gave expression to views similar to those expressed in the text. The numerous letters I received con-

refusal of the trial-court to interfere with unsound verdicts, is made final by the refusal of the appellate court, except in cases of the most flagrant wrong, to interfere with the discretion of the trial-court refusing a new trial. If the courts will clearly instruct juries, and will exercise when they ought to do so the power to set aside verdicts and grant new trials, there will be less complaints about trial by jury, and

Lecture IV.

Defects in the jury system remediable.

cerning them showed the deep interest of the profession in the subject. The general tenor of the views expressed are indicated in the extracts below given.

A judge of the Supreme Court of Missouri, who had been eminent for more than a quarter of a century, wrote : " I agree with you so heartily in your suggestions about judges and juries that I cannot refrain from so saying. I have, as you know, no personal interest in the tenure of the judges; but the changes made every few years, from political considerations alone, tend to destroy the boasted independence of the judiciary, and to make the courts the organs of popular opinion. The abandonment of the good behavior tenure is a mistake; the limit of our recent constitution to a small salary is a greater one."

A very able judge, of large experience on the bench of the Supreme Court of another State, wrote: " I fully approve of your remarks upon jury trials and the *scintilla* doctrine. It seems to me that one great difficulty juries have to contend with is the mass of instructions given in particular cases. They not unfrequently are lost in a maze of instructions. Brief, pointed instructions, calling attention to the points at issue, will generally, so far as I have observed, be followed by satisfactory verdicts."

A distinguished lawyer in Illinois, speaking of the trial by jury, said: " After much experience, reading, and cautious consideration, I have come to the conclusion that the jury is a costly, cumbrous, and uncertain tribunal for the trial of civil cases, and dangerous where the judges dare not, or cannot, or will not restrain them. It cannot last. In civil cases jury trial in England nominally exists; but it is *practically* abolished by the judges in many cases, as every advocate knows and feels. In a large portion of the cases, the presiding judge on the circuit intimates to the barrister that *he* does not need a jury, and the barrister knows that it is damaging to his cause if after that he insists on a jury."

132 · LAWS AND JURISPRUDENCE.

<small>Lecture IV.</small> less agitation for a change in the law whereby verdicts may be rendered by a less number than the whole of the jury, — a change which I believe to be based upon no necessity and in the highest degree unwise.

It is mainly to the causes above mentioned, some of which are produced by unwise legislation, but all of which, happily, are remediable, that the trial by jury has declined to such an extent that it has come in many cases to be an avowed maxim of professional action, — a good case is for the court; a bad or doubtful case is for the jury.

<small>Doctrine of judicial precedent.</small> Another distinctive feature of the system of law which we have derived from England and the Courts of Westminster Hall is the doctrine of judicial precedent. In the Continental systems of jurisprudence the decision of a cause is of no authoritative force, in the sense in which we use the word "authoritative," in any other court, or even in the same court; hence reports of decisions have comparatively little practical effect, and are relatively few. But not so in England and in this country, and the result is that the doctrine of judicial precedent has already produced a mountainous mass of law reports, and the number, notwithstanding all efforts to check production, is increasing with undiminished rapidity. The reports are extant in a regular series from the reign of Edward II.[1] They embody the wisdom of the bar and the bench for many generations. They contain the record of the development of the common and the equity law of the realm. "English

---
[1] See *ante* Lecture I., p. 29.

jurisprudence," says Burke in a passage before quoted, "has not any other sure foundation, nor, "consequently, the lives and property of the sub- "ject any sure hold, but in the maxims, rules, "principles, and juridical traditionary line of deci- "sions contained in notes taken from time to time, "and published mostly under the sanction of the "judges, called Reports."[1]

Lecture IV

The growth of legal literature and the multiplication of the reports are marvellous, and perhaps it is not too much to add, alarming. Lord Coke, after enumerating the legal treatises of his time, says: "Thus have you *fifteen* books or treatises, and as "many volumes of reports, besides the abridge- "ments of the common law and divers great volumes "of the statutes and acts of Parliament."[2] Since that time, however, these fifteen treatises have multiplied into as many hundreds; and of English, Colonial, and American reports we have an unnumbered multitude. In twenty-seven years, since 1865, the council of law reporting in England have issued a large number of volumes, and I estimate that more than sixty volumes of reports are annually published in this country. We stand appalled at this amazing and continuing growth. The lawyer finds the reports to be indispensable. The lawyer who reads and uses them is more than a match for the lawyer who does not. We complain of the number of reports and of the conflicting judgments to be found in them, but this is only one side of the account; on the other side, no lawyer

The enormous mass of our legal literature.

[1] *Ante* Lecture I., p. 31, note.
[2] Preface to the third part of his Reports.

Lecture IV. or judge can estimate how much he is indebted to them, and how much he is dependent on them, until he reflects how much legal doctrine has been settled, and how utterly lost he would feel if by some great calamity all the law treatises and reports were suddenly destroyed. Where this multiplication of law reports is to end, what is to be its final issue, what the form and shape which our law will in the future assume, no one is wise enough to foresee. Some affirm that this is either no evil, or a necessary evil. Others assert that it is not only an evil, but one which is even now almost insupportable; that it is bound to break down under its own weight; and that we must in this respect assimilate our jurisprudence to the civil law or the Continental models. Others propound what goes under the vague name of codification as the only panacea. Certain it is that we have here presented one of the gravest problems connected with our law. I only advert to it at this time in passing, but I shall hereafter offer thereon some more extended observations.

The growth and excellence of our legal system. I have now finished all that the limits of this course allow me to say concerning the development, general nature, and essential characteristics of the system of English law. The basis of our American law is the system thus outlined, and with which the Inns of Court and Westminster Hall are indissolubly associated. It is not a perfect system. The common law was, indeed, crude; and its imperfections have not been wholly remvoed and its deficiencies supplied by legislation, by the courts of law, and by the splendid system of equity jurisprudence with which the common law has been supplemented. Our legal system still exhibits but too many touches and traces of its origin; it is doubtless capable of amendment in many respects; but point me, who can, to any system worthier of higher admiration for its substantive principles, or which has accomplished better results, or which day by day distributes better justice to those subject to its sway. To the building up of this system many generations of judges and lawyers have brought their wisdom, learning, and experience. The workmen have died, but the work, like the building of the cathedral of Milan or of Cologne, has gone steadily on. Those glorious edifices are, we are told, at length finished, and already begin to show decay; but the law, being a living growth whose roots are in the life of the people, ever advances toward an unattainable completion. The majestic intellectual structure of our jurisprudence, massive, grand, and venerable, standing unmoved in the tide of history, has witnessed the rise and fall of dynasties; but amidst all these changes its peaceful workmen, "carrying a trowel to build but no torch to burn," have kept on with their labors, now strengthening its foundations, now removing some unsightly angle, anon lighting up or clearing out some dark passage, now adding to its size and improving its symmetry and usefulness, and at all times carrying its walls still higher toward the skies; thus preserving and adapting it, albeit at times tardily, to the ever-changing and multiplying wants of society.

Lecture IV.

The law a living growth.

136   *LAWS AND JURISPRUDENCE.*

Lecture IV.

Justly entitled to our admiration and praise.

For this system with its popular institutions, the grand and petit jury; for its regard for individual rights which raises it above and distinguishes it from every other; for Magna Charta; for the writ of Habeas Corpus; for the Petition of Rights and Bill of Rights; for its grand historic associations; for Hampden and ship money; for Burke's lofty accusation of Hastings; for the verdict of the honest and independent jury which acquitted the seven bishops; for the illustrious names which have adorned it, — Hale, Holt, Somers, Hardwicke, Mansfield, Kent, Story, Marshall; for the social order it has given and the liberty it has propagated and secured; for the even-handed and enlightened justice it has dispensed; for the light which for many years it supplied to my dim vision as a judge, — I must be pardoned if I feel something of the admiration of an enthusiast, the veneration of a worshipper, the homage of a disciple, and the gratitude of a cit-

The great expansion of our law.

izen. I would inspire you with the same love! It is worthy of it. What a marvellous growth it has had! It has followed the flag of England wherever it has been planted throughout the globe. If a member of one of the Inns of Court or a lawyer from Westminster Hall or the new English Law Courts buildings shall visit to-day the august judicial tribunal of the nation which sits at Washington, or any court on the Atlantic sea-board, or on the Lakes, or on the Mississippi, or at the base of the Rocky Mountains (where Pike's Peak stands in stately grandeur like a monarch of the Middle Ages, with his lesser barons grouped around him), or on the shores of the Pacific Ocean, or beneath Indian skies, or

"By the long wash of Australasian Seas
Far off,"

or in our schools of law, he will find lawyers and teachers quoting from, and judges guided by, the decisions of Westminster Hall. Such and so vast is the intellectual empire of our law! Such and so glorious are its peaceful and beneficent conquests! Our lines have fallen upon a wonderful period in the history of the world and of civilization. Not only all the past but all contemporary experience is at our service, and it is literally true that we " stand " at the confluence of the greatest number of streams " of knowledge flowing from the most distant sources " that ever met at one point."[1] The law, " like all " human systems, will ever advance nearer to per- " fection, and ever fall short of it."[2]

Your special duty in your day and generation

Lecture IV.

Its vast empire and beneficial conquests.

---

[1] Mackintosh's "Lectures on the Law of Nature and of Nations," given in the Inns of Court, June, 1799. These lectures filled the hall of Lincoln's Inn "with an auditory such as never before was seen on a similar occasion." "All classes were there represented; lawyers, members of Parliament, men of letters, and country gentlemen crowded to hear him." "Life of Sir James Mackintosh," by his son (Boston: Little, Brown & Co., 1853), vol. i., p. 107.

[2] Sir William Jones's Preface to the Speeches of Isæus. The law, " like all human systems, will ever advance nearer to perfection, and ever fall short of it. In the course of his inquiries he [the student of the law] will constantly observe a striking uniformity among all nations, whatever seas or mountains may separate them, or how many ages soever may have elapsed between the periods of their existence, in those great and fundamental principles, which, being clearly deduced from natural reason, are equally diffused over all mankind, and are not subject to alteration by any change of place or time; nor will he fail to mark as striking a diversity in those laws, which, proceeding merely from positive institution, are, consequently, as various as the wills and fancies of those who enact them."

Lecture IV.

The duty of amending and improving our law.

will be to carry forward the work of improving the law, so that you may leave it in a better condition than you found it. This can only be done by an adequate conception of the sources, the nature, and the end of law. Our law is a complex system of conventional and positive rules, and of fundamental principles of natural justice based upon the reason, the experience, and the conscience of mankind. The cultivated lawyer does not undervalue positive regulations, or forms, or precedents, but his vision is not bounded by them, and he delights to ascend to higher altitudes, which offer to him a broader horizon and a more glorious prospect. He is thus enabled to perceive that the law in its great living and essential principles may be and often is something more than the "command" of the sovereign or of a legislative body, — is something deeper than these; that it has innermost and invisible springs in the realms of an elevated morality, hard by the throne of God;[1] and that its waters, — which are meant, like the leaves of the tree of life, for the healing of the nations, — although they may be colored or tinctured by "the soils through which they run,"[2] never lose the sweetness and purity derived from their original source, however far they may flow, or to whatever uses they may be applied.

[1] *Ante* Lecture I.; *post* Lecture VII.

[2] The fine sentence of Lord Bacon from which the quotation is made is in these words: "For there are in nature certain fountains of justice whence all civil laws are derived, but as streams; and like as waters do take tinctures and tastes from the soils through which they run, so do civil laws vary according to the regions and governments where they are planted, though they proceed from the same fountains." Bacon, "Advancement of Learning," Book II.

NOTE A.

THE NEW ROYAL COURTS OF JUSTICE.

The removal in 1882-1883 of the Common Law courts from Westminster Hall and of the Chancery courts from various buildings in Chancery Lane and rooms in Lincoln's Inn, in which they had long been held, to the new building known as the Royal Courts of Justice, marks so important an event in the history of the English courts of justice that it seems fitting to make a more detailed reference to it. The following account is abridged from a contemporary publication relating thereto. The inadequacy and inconvenience of the court rooms adjoining Westminster Hall having long been felt, the Incorporated Law Society set on foot a movement to secure a new site and new building in the vicinity of the Inns of Court. Steps had been previously taken by the officials of the Chancery Division for better courts and offices than the inconvenient, ancient, and dingy rooms situate in various parts of Chancery Lane and Lincoln's Inn. After much discussion, the scheme ripened in successive acts: "The Courts of Justice Building Act, 1865" (28 Vic., chap. 48); "The Courts of Justice Concentration (Site) Act, 1865" (28 Vic., chap. 49); and "The Courts of Justice Act, 1868" (28 & 29 Vic., chap. 63). The competition between the site on the Thames Embankment and on the Strand and Carey Street, in the vicinity of the Inns of Court, was settled in favor of the latter location. This involved the acquisition of between seven and eight acres of land and the demolition of about four hundred and fifty old buildings and rookeries. The designs of Mr. Street for the new building were accepted, and in 1874 the work of construction was commenced. The building occupies an area of four hundred and seventy by four hundred and sixty feet, the central hall being two hundred and thirty feet long, forty-eight feet wide, and eighty-two feet high. There are over seven hundred rooms and offices in addition to the nine-

Note A.
History of the new courts building.

teen courts. The work of construction occupied about eight years. The last case tried in the old courts at Westminster was the celebrated case of Belt v. Lawes, in which judgment was given December 28, 1882. The new building was inaugurated by the Queen with imposing ceremonies, December 4, 1882. The Lord Mayor and Aldermen of London, the Lord Chancellor, the Lord Chief-Justice, and the entire body of the judges from Westminster Hall received the Queen on her arrival at the grand entrance, and the First Commissioner of Works, on her Majesty's taking her position on the dais, presented a silver key to the Queen, saying: "May it please your Majesty, — Your Commissioners of Works and Public Buildings have been charged with the erection of this building during the last eight years. It is now complete. It has fallen upon me to announce to your Majesty that it is ready to be constituted by your royal command as the central place in which, in accordance with the ancient laws of your kingdom, justice shall be administered in the future by your Majesty's courts."

Her Majesty, handing the key to the Lord Chancellor, said: "My Lord Chancellor, — I deliver into your charge with this key the care of these courts of law. I trust that the uniting together in one place of the various branches of judicature in this my Supreme Court will conduce to the more efficient and speedy administration of justice to my subjects; and I have all confidence that the independence and learning of the judges, supported by the integrity and ability of the other members of the profession of the law, will prove in the future, as they have in times past, a chief security for the rights of my crown and the liberties of my subjects."

The Lord Chancellor replied with the following eloquent speech, which was received with deep attention, and made a profound impression, particularly the reference to the architect [Mr. Street], who had untimely passed away, and the glories of her Majesty's happy reign: "May it please your Majesty, — In the name and on behalf of the assembled judges of your Majesty's Supreme Court of Judicature, I accept the charge which your Majesty has been pleased to lay upon me ; and I ask permission to offer to your Majesty the humble expression of our loyal devotion to your Majesty's person and throne, and of our gratitude for the part which your Majesty has been graciously pleased to take in the solemnity of this day. This building, now complete, was authorized by your Majesty, with the concurrence of Parliament, in the year 1865, and it has been in progress for more than eight years under the hands of a great architect, to whom it has not been permitted to see this day. Your Majesty, whose strength of sympathy is so well known to us all, will, I am sure, share the feelings of your subjects when they think of those who are no longer with us, — of the architect whom we have lost, and of that great prelate, venerable as much for his wisdom and virtue as for his great office, from whose lips we might have hoped, not many months since, to hear the Divine blessing invoked upon us to-day. Man passes away, but his works remain. This building will remain, as we trust, to a remote posterity, one of the most magnificent public works of the time in which we live. These Royal Courts of Justice, stately enough to satisfy even those who are most accustomed to Westminster Hall, will not, like Westminster Hall, recall the memories of Norman or Plantagenet, of Tudor or Stuart kings; but they will be forever associated with the name of your Majesty, and with the glories of a reign happy beyond all which have preceded it in those qualities of the sovereign which have caused your Majesty to be so universally beloved and revered, in the advancement of all the arts of civilization, and in the general peace and prosperity of the British people. Among the legislative improvements which have distinguished your Majesty's reign, not the least has been the consolidation and union of the several branches of the Supreme Judicature, which formerly exercised divided jurisdiction. To give full effect to that great change it was necessary that the different courts and offices should be brought together in one edifice fit for the duties which they have to perform. This has at last been done; and your Majesty, by your gracious presence here to-day, has given a signal proof of your care for that justice which will here be administered in your name. It was, indeed, fitting and worthy of your Majesty that these Royal Courts should be dedicated to their future use by the Sovereign of these realms, whose noblest prerogatives are justice and mercy, and from whom all jurisdiction within the British dominions is derived."

Note A.

The Lord Chancellor's speech (continued).

Lecture IV.

The new Courts of Justice, though inaugurated on December 4, 1882, were not actually opened for business until January 11, 1883; and the case of Belt v. Lawes served to connect the old and new courts, since it was the last case adjudged in the old, and an application for a rule for a new trial therein was the first business transacted in the new building.

The Lord Chief-Justice's speech.

The Lord Chief-Justice, when taking his seat with Baron Pollock and Mr. Justice Manisty in the Lord Chief-Justice of England's Court, addressing an audience (composed of a large number of members of the bar and professional gentlemen, as well as many ladies) which crowded every part of the court, said: "In taking their seats for the first time he did not propose to make any general observations; all such observations had been made, in a manner which it would be vain for him to attempt to imitate, by his noble friend, the Lord Chancellor, upon the occasion when her Majesty was graciously pleased to declare these courts open. He wished to say only two things before beginning the business of the day. First of all, he would say that, though they had left Westminster Hall, he trusted they had not left behind them the traditions of that great and illustrious building, and that they would follow them in this their new habitation; and especially he hoped that the unbroken tradition — unbroken since he had known it — of mutual dependence and harmony between the bench and the bar would continue unbroken, — relations without which the bar might probably, and the bench certainly would, find it impossible to discharge their most important functions."

LECTURE V.

OUR LAW IN ITS NEW HOME — AMERICA : ITS EXPANSION,
DEVELOPMENT, AND CHARACTERISTICS IN THE POLITICAL
AND JUDICIAL SYSTEMS OF THE UNITED STATES.

IN the preceding lectures I discussed the subject of Our Law in its Old Home, — England, — and some of its essential and distinguishing features. In the present lecture and the next I shall consider Our Law in its New Home, — America, — and its expansion and development in the institutions of the United States. In this I have a distinct purpose. I am concerned that you, as persons destined to the profession of the law, shall have an adequate and just appreciation of the real character of our laws, of their excellences and their defects. It is my deliberate opinion that our laws as they exist are deserving of high regard and admiration. It is, in my judgment, a great error to assign (as I fear some are inclined to do) to our laws a place inferior to the Roman law, or its Continental adaptations.

Professor Pollock, in his excellent lectures, lately published (1890),[1] speaking of the United States, says:

"We find a marked tendency in American authors "to take a Continental rather than an English view

[1] Oxford Studies, lecture i.

"of the general theory of jurisprudence. Not only
"our positive and analytical method finds little favor
"with them, and their theoretical work is mostly
"akin to that of the German philosophical and his-
"torical schools, but they treat the common law
"itself as an ideal system to be worked out with
"great freedom of speculation and comparatively
"little regard to positive authority. Decided cases
"are treated by them not as settling questions, but
"as offering new problems for criticism. There
"are even one or two American writers of great
"ability, for whom, as for the German expounders
"of *Naturrecht*, legal science appears to consist in a
"perpetual flux of speculative ideas." [1]

I confess that I do not know to whom the learned professor in the last sentence refers; and I think he is mistaken in the general statement that American authors display a tendency to take a Continental rather than an English view of our jurisprudence, and to adopt German and Continental rather than English methods in the study and prosecution of legal science or the decision of legal problems. But if Professor Pollock is not mistaken, then the observations in this lecture and the next are all the more timely.

Our government, state and national, embodies and rests upon the fundamental principle of the absolute and essential civil and political equality of all its citizens, whose collective will, expressed by majorities, is the rightful and only source of all political power. By this principle we must stand or fall. In adopting it, we reversed the

[1] See *ante* Lecture I., p. 7, and note.

doctrines of the governments of continental Europe, which doctrines were "that all popular and consti-"tutional rights, all useful and necessary changes in "legislation and administration, can only emanate "from the free will and concession of the monarch "or instituted government." You may recall the discussion of this subject by Mr. Webster in the celebrated *Hülsemann* correspondence.[1] The political doctrine he asserted, so familiar to us, and the elevated style and sustained dignity, force, and logic of this remarkable state paper, combined to fix upon it the attention of the contemporary world. Is this fundamental principle sound? As applied to our government, it has now stood the test of more than a century, overcoming our fears, strengthening and establishing our faith. I do not purpose to discuss its soundness; the stage of discussion ended more than a century ago. We then adopted it; we staked everything upon it. Our institutions to-day have no other foundation; and with it "we must sink or swim, live or die, survive or perish."

Lecture V.

President Lincoln's celebrated phrase in his Gettysburg oration, wherein he described ours as the "government of the people, by the people, for the people," is not a mere flourish of rhetoric, but a definition historically and legally exact. It is a government *of* the people, because it was ordained by their sovereignty; *by* the people, because it is carried on by their representatives and servants;

Lincoln's famous description legally exact.

[1] Letter of Daniel Webster as Secretary of State to Chevalier J. G. Hülsemann, Sept. 30, 1850. Webster's Works (Little & Brown, Boston, 1851), vol. vi., p. 488.

for the people, because it is maintained and conducted solely for their benefit and behoof. Well might the martyr President utter the fervent and effectual prayer that it might not "perish from the earth." We believe and maintain, indeed, that our government rests upon the broadest, deepest, and most secure of all possible foundations, since it rests upon the consent and interest of *all;* in a word, upon the sovereignty of society at large, which possesses all the powers necessary to preserve and secure the general welfare and safety, — "powers which," even Blackstone admits, "no climate, no "time, no constitution, no contract, can ever destroy "or diminish." It would seem to result that our self-governed nation is fitted to live, that it ought to live, and that it will live so long as it promotes the interest of the people, protects their rights and liberties, and safeguards the common weal.

Professor Émile Boutmy, member of the Institute of France, has recently written a work, entitled "Studies in Constitutional Law — France — England — United States." I have found it an interesting and suggestive book. He treats of the differences, not only in the structure and form, but also in the genius, of the constitutions of England and the United States on the one hand, and of France on the other. In the preface to the second edition he states that though tempted to do so, he has refrained from entering upon certain extra-constitutional questions in the United States which he says have lately arisen and will certainly be some of the problems of the future. These he thus enumerates:

"The rapidity with which the growth of landed "estates has begun and progresses; the immense "extent of the *latifundia*; the approaching exhaus- "tion of the available soil, — that seemingly inex- "haustible treasure; the increase of tenant farmers "(a class hitherto almost unknown, and now by "degrees replacing the yeomen who work their "own estates); the appearance of the agrarian "question; the radical and socialistic character of "the remedies proposed, — these things all show an "alteration of the ancient basis on which the polit- "ical fabric was erected. But if it is certain "that the United States will tend to enlarge and "strengthen the action of the central government "in proportion to their advance in population and "material civilization, one cannot say as yet whether "this centralization will be for the benefit of a sin- "gle federation or of several. The question of "secession is not yet closed. Will the government "of Washington alone profit by the powers taken "from the thirty-eight States, or will these powers "be divided among three or four governments at "the head of federations fixed by natural geo- "graphical divisions ? These are serious questions, "which I could not have entered upon without giv- "ing more space to speculative conjectures than was "compatible with my original plan." [1]

Lecture V.

Boutmy's speculations and fears.

Professor Boutmy is not only an intelligent but a candid observer and careful student of our history; nevertheless, I must say that I certainly

Not justified by existing conditions.

---

[1] "Studies in Constitutional Law — France — England — United States." By Émile Boutmy. Dicey's translation (Macmillan), London, 1891.

fail to see anything in existing conditions that justifies his fears. I do not observe any alarming growth of landed estates threatening a monopoly of this source of wealth. The vast increase of personal property effectually renders anything like a monopoly of wealth in this country impossible. Happily every industrious man may readily accumulate money and property; and so far as we can foresee, that will be the condition for many generations to come. There may remain some existing tendency as the result of the Civil War, or from other causes, to enlarge and strengthen the central government; but if so, it is comparatively slight, and not in any degree alarming. In my judgment there is no such tendency whatever at this time. Professor Boutmy asserts that the question of secession is not yet closed, and expresses a fear that such centralized power may finally inure to, and be divided among, three or four federal governments fixed by natural geographical divisions. He is mistaken. If anything in our history can be said to be settled, it is the question of secession. Other questions may be open; but that question is closed, and is so regarded universally, South as well as North. And I shall point out presently that the natural geographical situation under existing conditions is that of one entire nation extending, as now, from the Atlantic to the Pacific, and from Canada to Mexico.

Let us rise, if we may, to adequate conceptions. We have already a population of 65,000,000, — a number greater than all the other peoples who speak the English language, — inhabiting forty-four States and four Territories, reaching in unbroken continuity from ocean to ocean, and from the Lakes to the Gulf of Mexico. Behold the map of our country! How fortunate that the great mountain-ranges and the intervening rivers run from north to south, — nature's eternal ligaments. If the Rocky Mountains or the Mississippi River had been co-incident with what was erewhile known as Mason and Dixon's Line, the nation might not have come out of the Civil War undivided. Since then we have spanned these mountain-ranges not only with telegraph lines but with five transcontinental railways, whereby our Atlantic and Pacific possessions are brought within a week of each other, and the mountains themselves have ceased to be physical barriers or lines of territorial division. Consider not only our territorial extent, but the variety of climate, soil, productions, and resources, — territory suited to the most varied agriculture; vast plains adapted to grazing; coal and iron lying side by side; long stretches of mountain-ranges rich with deposits of the precious metals. If we apply to the future the law of our past growth (and why may we not?), there are those present who will live to see our country with a population of 100,000,000 of people.

Shall we, the lawyers and law students of America, be insensible to the responsibilities growing out of our twofold relations and duties, — duties as citizens toward our country, and duties as lawyers toward its laws and jurisprudence? I offer no apology for this line of remark, since it is impossible properly to estimate the merits and value of any system of laws, dissociated from the political

Lecture V.

Duties and responsibilities of the legal profession in the United States.

institutions out of which those laws spring or to which they relate, and since also it ought never to be forgotten that our primary and fundamental relation is that of citizens. It is not uncommon to hear it said that although our government has not as yet gone to pieces, it is liable to do so; at any rate, that the practical workings of our institutions are unsatisfactory, and have failed of real success. As more than any other class the lawyers of a century ago shaped and moulded our institutions,[1] so it is especially the duty of the legal profession of to-day to show, in their lives and conversation, that they appreciate at their undiminished value the free and popular institutions of their country.

Success of American popular institutions. Our institutions failed of success! I deny it; a thousand times I deny it! In the name of every man who, like myself, has come through the terrible ordeal of poverty and knows what it is, — in the name of the unnumbered thousands of generous youth who must yet walk barefoot upon the heated ploughshares of this ordeal, I deny it; for the genius of our institutions will attend them, unseen, throughout the fiery trial, and give them a safe deliverance. What, let me ask, is the cause of our unexampled growth, our matchless prosperity? Not alone, or

---

[1] In one of the greatest of all his speeches, "For Conciliation with America," March 22, 1775, Burke observes concerning the American Colonies: "*In no country, perhaps, in the world, is the law so general a study.* The profession itself is numerous and powerful, and in most provinces it takes the lead. The greater number of the deputies sent to Congress were lawyers. I hear that they have sold nearly as many of Blackstone's 'Commentaries' [then recently published] in America as in England." "The Works of Edmund Burke," 4th American Ed., Little, Brown, & Co., Boston, 1871, vol. ii., pp. 124, 125; see *post* Lectures XI., XIII.

chiefly, a favored climate and a fertile soil, but the magnetic force and marvellous power of our free institutions, whose chief glory is that all men are equal before the law, whose priceless benefaction is that all men have equal opportunities.[1] A teacher of law who fails to inculcate a rational but hearty and sincere love of country fails in the discharge of a high and peremptory duty.

<small>Lecture V.</small>

It is with the laws and the legal institutions of such a nation, — founded upon the sovereignty of the public will; with the cherished traditions and rich heritage of its past history and achievements; with its present greatness and grandeur; with the bright visions of the future which it opens to our view, and which, expanding illimitably as we gaze, swell our hopes and exalt our pride; a homogeneous people, widely distributed over a territory of more than imperial extent, with a common language, with common interests, with common aspirations and hopes, — it is with the laws and legal institutions of such a country that we have to do, and which are placed under the special guardianship of the bar of America.

<small>The laws and legal institutions of a great nation.</small>

The lawyers and students of law of America ought especially to remember that the strength of the nation largely depends upon its laws, and the manner in which they are administered. Are the laws just, and are they justly administered? The inquiry must be answered by the divine test: "By their "fruits ye shall know them. Do men gather grapes "of thorns, or figs of thistles?" Justice is the fruit

<small>The nation's strength largely depends upon the just administration of its laws.</small>

[1] *Ante* Lecture IV.; *post* Lecture VII.

of good laws well executed; and "justice," says Sir James Mackintosh, in one of his famous lectures delivered in Lincoln's Inn Hall, "is the permanent interest of all men and of all commonwealths."[1] Conscious of its general truth, we give a ready assent to this sentiment, without pausing to inquire why it is that justice is of such supreme importance to the nation as well as to the individual. It is the justice of good laws well enforced that restrains and punishes the criminal; that erects the only effectual barrier against the uncurbed and multitudinous passions of men as they come surging on with the power of the ocean, and proclaims, " Thus far and no farther;" that protects with absolute impartiality every right recognized by the law, whether of natural persons or corporate, of the weak or the strong, against any who menaces or invades it; that stands as the impersonation of the highest attribute of God, not passively with her scales in equipoise, but with flaming sword, to guard the injured and the innocent, and to strike down the high-handed or the fraudulent wrongdoer. The most satisfactory ideal I have ever been able to form of justice is embodied in the picture of a judge courageous enough "to give the devil his due," whether he be in the right or in the wrong.

It is to protect and enforce public and private rights that courts, with their judges and officers, their jurisdiction and machinery, are established and maintained. Their usual function, their most obvious use, is to decide civil and criminal causes.

[1] *Ante* Lecture IV.

But this is far from the measure of their usefulness. We readily see how important the administration of justice is to the individual; but why is it of importance to the nation? What, let it be asked, is the nation but the aggregate of individual citizens? In our time, certainly in our country, no government is secure that does not rest upon the interest and affection of the governed. Ordinarily, when things are moving on in the even, accustomed tenor of their way, we lose sight of the vital dependence of national life upon national justice. But let the safety of the nation be threatened from within or without, in the pressure and stress of such an exigency, which comes sooner or later to all nations, then is instantly perceived and felt the vital relation between the national justice and the national existence. If all *interests* in the State, those of labor and those of capital, which are always closely allied and rarely antagonistic except as the result of laws which operate unjustly upon the one or the other; if all *persons* within the State, regardless of birth, race, religion, or condition, feel that the State is the highest embodiment of practical beneficence, and surely to be relied on to do equal justice to all men and all interests, — then in the moment of public peril all persons rise and rally, dilated and transfigured by a sublime and irresistible patriotism, bringing as freewill offerings their treasure and their lives to defend and preserve the laws and institutions which they have found to be so dear Then especially it is that the strength of popular institutions such as ours is revealed and demonstrated.

Lecture V.

Dependence of national life upon national justice.

If these observations be well founded, can the

lawyer, the statesman, or the citizen conceive any inquiry more important than one involving an examination into the character and condition of the laws and jurisprudence of his country? I therefore purpose to attempt in this and the two following lectures a survey, necessarily brief, of the general nature of our system of laws and its practical workings, with a view to see how far it is consonant with our political institutions and adapted to the temper and wants of our people, and with the further view to see how far it deserves, on the one hand, the eulogies so often pronounced upon it, or on the other, the complaints so frequently made against it. Such a survey will, moreover, tend to define the extent to which the "choice and tender business" (as Sir Matthew Hale expresses it) of introducing changes therein seems to be practicable and expedient.

It is observed in respect of the constitution of the human mind that it "continually oscillates between an inclination to complain without sufficient cause, and to be too easily satisfied."[1] Either extreme is injurious. If we erroneously conceive an institution or system to be perfect, it induces self-satisfaction and inactivity. If we magnify its defects, it may discourage the needful attempt to remedy them. Let us come, then, to this inquiry, not as partisans, nor with the zeal and bias of the advocate, but with the "cold neutrality of impartial judges." "Paint me as I am" was the command of Oliver Cromwell to Lely. "If you leave out the wart, the scars, or the wrinkles, I will not pay you a shilling."

[1] Guizot, "History of Civilization in Europe," lecture i.

Now the great fact, which, as we approach this subject, meets our view, is that the common law (including in the phrase "common law," as here used, the supplemental equity system of the Court of Chancery which grew out of the common law and constitutes a part of it) underlies the whole system of American law and jurisprudence. The expression, "the common law," is used in various senses: (*a*) sometimes in distinction from statute law; (*b*) sometimes in distinction from equity law; and (*c*) sometimes in distinction from the Roman or civil law. I use it in this lecture in the latter sense. I do not stop to inquire how the common law came to be introduced here and adopted by us. I deal with the fact as it exists, which is that the common law is the basis of the laws of every State and Territory of the Union, with comparatively unimportant and gradually waning exceptions. And a most fortunate circumstance it is, that, divided as our territory is into so many States, each supreme within the limits of its power, a common and uniform general system of jurisprudence underlies and pervades them all; and this quite aside from the excellences of that system, concerning which I shall presently speak. My present point is this: That the mere fact that one and the same system of jurisprudence exists in all of the States, is of itself of vast importance, since it is a most powerful agency in promoting commercial, social, and intellectual intercourse, and in cementing the national unity. This view is so important that I must take leave to dwell upon it for a moment.

Lecture V.

The common law underlies the whole system of American laws and jurisprudence.

Vast importance of this fact pointed out.

Lecture V.

Jurisprudence, as I have heretofore pointed out,[1] is not something in the air — something lifted up above and abstracted from the life of men — but an eminently practical science, which has to do directly with the conduct and relations of men, and with their conduct and relations as members of a particular State. It therefore necessarily partakes of a national character, — as, for example, Roman jurisprudence, German jurisprudence, English jurisprudence, etc., referring thereby to the principles and character of the distinctive legal systems of these several peoples. The Roman law affiliates the legal systems of continental Europe and gives them a common, an organic character. So the common law affiliates the legal systems of England and the United States, and also the legal system of each of the American States with the legal system of all of the other States of the Union. It makes them all akin. It gives them an organic character. It is a living bond of union, since it is the cause and medium of a constant and active intercommunication and intercourse, making the people of the whole country neighbors. The legal systems of our forty-four States have not only the same general character, but they are substantially uniform and identical. So completely is this the case that I speak from my observation and experience when I state that a thoroughly educated and trained lawyer of any one State, having access

The common law gives to the legal systems of the States a homogeneous character.

[1] See *ante* Lecture I., pp. 21, 22. Accordingly, Burke says: "The science of jurisprudence is the pride of the human intellect. A science which, with all its defects, redundancies, and errors, is the collected reason of ages, combining the principles of eternal justice with the infinite variety of human concerns."

to the statutes and reports, is competent to deal with, and in fact our lawyers daily do deal with, questions and cases arising in and governed by the laws of any of the other States. Undoubtedly there are frequent inconveniences, and occasional mischiefs, growing out of diversities in local legislation, and undoubtedly these could be materially reduced, and ought to be; but after much experience and reflection I am of opinion that these inconveniences and mischiefs are somewhat exaggerated, for, after all, the common law gives to our legal system in all of the States not only a distinctive but essentially a homogeneous character.

Lecture V.

And now the inquiry presents itself: What is the general character of the common law? what its adaptation to our people and our situation? what its merits? what its defects?

General character of the common law.

The first observation I would make is that the common law, as well as the institutions which it developed or in the midst of which it grew up, is *pervaded by a spirit of freedom, which distinguishes it from all other systems, and peculiarly adapts it to the institutions of a self-governed people.*[1] It is clearly established by the learned researches which have been more recently made that the elements of this law and of English polity are of Germanic origin.[2] The Saxon conquerors of Great Britain were not mere bodies of armed invaders. They went to England, during two or more centuries, in families

[1] See *ante* Lecture IV.
[2] Stubbs's "Constitutional History," chap. i. *et seq.*; Freeman, "Growth of the English Constitution," *passim.*

and communities. What manner of men were they? Guizot, certainly no partial witness, dwells upon the fact that the distinguishing character of the Germans was "their powerful sentiment of personal liberty, personal independence, and individuality." He affirms and repeatedly reiterates that they it was who "introduced this sentiment of personal inde-"pendence, this love of individual liberty, into "European civilization; that this was unknown "among the Romans, unknown in the Christian "Church, and unknown in nearly all the civili-"zations of antiquity. The liberty which we "meet with in ancient civilizations is political "liberty,—the liberty of the citizen, not the per-"sonal liberty of the man himself."[1]

Conquering and colonizing England in this manner, our Saxon ancestors carried with them "from "lands where the Roman eagle had never been "seen, or seen only during the momentary incur-"sions of Drusus and Germanicus,"[2] their language, their religion, their customs, their laws, and their organizations. These were indigenous — homebred, without trace or tincture of the Roman law and institutions.[3] They borrowed nothing from antiquity or from surrounding peoples. They founded, and in the course of centuries their successors and descendants — the people of England — built up, their institutions on their own model. Macaulay speaks of this with his accustomed vividness: "The foun-"dations of our Constitution," he says, "were laid

---

[1] History of Civilization in Europe, lecture ii.
[2] Freeman, "Norman Conquest," chap. i.
[3] Digby, "History of Real Property," 11, 12.

"by men who knew nothing of the Greeks but "that they had denied the orthodox procession and "cheated the Crusaders, and nothing of Rome but "that the Pope lived there. Those who followed "contented themselves with improving on the origi-"nal plan. They found models at home, and there-"fore they did not look for them abroad."[1] In words well known the author of the "Spirit of the Laws," referring to the English Constitution, says, "This beautiful system has been found in the forests of Germany" (*Ce beau système a eté trouvé dans les bois*).[2]

This love of personal freedom and independence was impressed upon the institutions they founded, or adopted or modified. Learned investigators differ concerning the extent to which Roman law existed and prevailed in England at the time of the Saxon conquest, and the extent to which its principles have been incorporated into English laws, usages, and institutions. As a system, it was, as I have already pointed out, early and sturdily rejected.[3] But there is a universal assent to these propositions, namely, that the Saxon spirit of freedom was embodied in the various local courts; that it was in these popular tribunals that the principles of law and local government were cultivated and disseminated; that the Saxons breathed into the English government and institutions "a spirit of "equity and freedom which has never entirely de-"parted from them,"[4] and that in the course of time

[1] Essay on History. [2] Montesquieu, book xi., chap. vi.
[3] See *ante* Lecture I., pp. 22–26.
[4] Mackintosh, "History of England," vol. v., chap. i.; Reeves, "History of the Common Law," Introduction by Finlason.

the common law intertwined its roots inseparably into the constitution, polity, local and municipal institutions, the civil and criminal jurisprudence, the family relation, and the rights of person and of property. So from an immemorial or early period the local territorial subdivisions of England, such as towns and parishes, enjoyed a considerable degree of freedom, and were permitted to assess upon themselves their local taxes and to manage their local affairs. The rate-payers were thus dignified by being an integral part of the communal life; the foundations of municipal liberty were laid; political power was decentralized; knowledge of the laws and reverence for and obedience to them were constantly taught by a participation in their administration and enforcement. This is exactly the opposite of the systems prevailing on the Continent, where the central power absorbs, governs, and regulates everything, thereby destroying municipal freedom and the capacity to enjoy and exercise it, as well as the power to defend and preserve it.[1]

In this country the system of decentralizing political power, and of intrusting the direction of local affairs to the local constituencies, has from the earliest colonial periods been carried to a much greater extent than in England. As you pass from one end of this country to the other, alike in the older regions and in the newest organized settlements, you will see the affairs of each road-district, school-district, township, county, village, and city locally self-managed, including the administration of local justice. Every township in the United States has

[1] Hearn, "Government of England," chap. i., § 8.

OUR LAW IN ITS NEW HOME. 161

a local court, with power to summon a jury of the vicinage, thereby bringing justice home to the business and bosoms of the people, and making it their own affair. We are somewhat apt to look with disdain upon the courts held by justices of the peace; but in reality we have few more useful institutions. The eyes of the ordinary justice have not, indeed, been couched to the "gladsome light of jurisprudence." He may be prone to make technical mistakes; but in general he manages, by himself or the jury, to work out substantial justice in the decision of the disputes arising out of the every-day affairs of the people. It is in no slight degree instructive to trace the institutions of this new country back to the germs of the Saxon or Anglo-Saxon polity; for when we touch to-day, not only in the towns of New England but even in our frontier settlements, the electric chain wherewith Providence hath bound the ages and the generations of men together, we discover that we are in historic communion with rude and remote ancestors, although separated from us by seas, mountains, and centuries.

Whoever among you may have read the graphic picture which Freeman in the opening of his work on the "Growth of the English Constitution" draws of democratic institutions in the Swiss Cantons of Uri and Appenzell, will never forget it. These, he says, have existed from the earliest times They are, he insists, a continued survival of the earliest notions and usages of old, Teutonic freedom,— "an "immemorial freedom, a freedom only less eternal "than the rocks that guard it, that puts to shame "the antiquity of kingly dynasties, which, by its

Lecture V.

Freeman's description of Swiss freedom in Uri and Appenzell.

11

<small>Lecture V.</small>

"side, seem but as innovations of yesterday. There
"year by year, on some bright morning of the
"spring-tide, the sovereign people, not intrusting
"its rights to a few of its own number, but dis-
"charging them itself in the majesty of its cor-
"porate person, meets in the open market-place or
"in the green meadow at the mountain's foot, to
"frame the laws to which it yields obedience as
"its own work, to choose the rulers whom it can
"afford to greet with reverence as drawing their
"commission from itself. Such a sight there are
"but few Englishmen who have seen; to be among
"those few I reckon among the highest privileges
"of my life. This is a sight such as no other cor-
"ner of the earth can set before the traveller. . . .
"The men of Appenzell have kept one ancient
"rite, which surpasses all that I have ever seen or
"heard of in its heart-stirring solemnity. When
"the newly-chosen landammann enters on his
"office, his first duty is to bind himself by an oath
"to obey the laws of the Commonwealth over
"which he is called to rule. His second duty is
"to administer to the multitude before him the
"same oath by which he has just bound himself.
"To hear the voice of thousands of freemen pledg-
"ing themselves to obey the laws they themselves
"have made is a moment in one's life which can
"never be forgotten, — a moment for whose sake
"it would be worth while to take a far longer and
"harder journey than that which leads us to Uri or
"Appenzell."

<small>New England town-meetings.</small>
The assembly of citizens here described are mere local assemblies, not assemblies of a nation, but of a

district; and it seems not a little remarkable that this learned writer should have said that such meetings of the whole body of citizens in their primary capacity as men could be seen in no other part of the world. For more than two hundred years before that passage was written, New England town-meetings had been continuously held, where every citizen was entitled to meet and vote, — to determine and settle their local affairs, and to elect the public officers by which those affairs were to be administered for the coming year. And in essence the same powers are now exercised by the whole body of the citizens of the thousands of municipal and public corporations in the American States.[1]

The States of this country bind together the congeries of local institutions, which they create, or recognize and regulate, independent of Federal control, thus happily preventing a concentration at the national centre of the governmental power and duty of legislating for and regulating the affairs of local communities throughout the country, — a country of such extent that it would be impossible for Congress to become accurately acquainted with their exact situation, wants, and interests.

So, in the ascending scale, the Federal Constitution constitutes the States and the people of all the States into a national government. It defines the relations of the States to each other and to the general government, and limits, as amended, the

American municipal freedom.

The States of the Union.

---

[1] As to local self-government in England, see Dillon, "Municipal Corporations," 4th ed., Little, Brown, & Co., 1890, vol. i., § 8 et seq.; in the United States, §§ 8 a, et seq., 19 b, et seq.; as to the legal character of the New England town, Ib., § 28.

Lecture V.

Magna Charta made part of our fundamental law.

power of the States under any pretext to deprive any citizen, however humble, of the great primordial rights of freedom and equality before the law.[1] Magna Charta remains to-day one of the main foundations of English liberty.[2] Its chief glory is the provision " that no freeman shall be imprisoned " or disseized of his freehold but by the lawful judg-"ment of his peers or the law of the land." This memorable provision, long ago embodied in the State constitutions, has been carried into the Fourteenth Amendment of the Federal Constitution, thereby placing the rights of life, liberty, and property, as against invasion by the States, under the protection of the national authority. The ancient lawgivers, to induce the highest possible veneration and esteem for the laws, taught that they came from heaven and were sacred. If any human work ought to be regarded with sanctity by us, it is the Constitution of the United States. Unmatched and matchless instrument; bulwark and guaranty of national life, of general prosperity, and of countless bless-

---

[1] *Post* Lecture VII.

[2] "The whole of the constitutional history of England is little more than a commentary on Magna Charta." Stubbs's "Constitutional History," vol. i., chap. xii. Magna Charta "is the keystone of English liberty." Hallam, "Middle Ages," vol. ii., chap. viii. M. Boutmy gives an interesting account of the causes which led to Magna Charta and the nature of that great document. I can only give a few sentences. "The resistance [to the King] had to be political if the victory when gained was not to prove barren; it had to be, of necessity, general, national, — nay, even democratic, — if the victory was to be gained at all. . . . This is what imparts grandeur and originality to the mighty drama, of which the first act ended with the great charter, and which reached its climax with the constitution of Parliament about 1340." Boutmy, "English Constitution," Eaden's translation, 1891, chap. i., pp. 28, 29. See *post* Lecture VII.

ings, — making the States and the people thereof one great, free, happy, united nation!

If the Supreme Court during the period of active national development covered by the long official career of Chief-Justice Marshall had put a narrow and inelastic construction upon the Federal Constitution, so that it could not have expanded with the growth and answered the necessities of a great people, it would have been calamitous to an extent no words can portray, and no imagination conceive. His views left it possible for the national growth to take place in accordance with the natural process of evolution. Marshall's judgments upon the national Constitution are among the most original and massive works of the human reason. They are almost as important as the texts of the Constitution which they expound. Some of them were, indeed, criticised at the time; but they have immovably established themselves as right in the general judgment of lawyers, public men, and the people. Although changes in political parties have been reflected in the *personnel* of the bench; although unforeseen crises in the national life have been reached and passed, it is remarkable that on not one of his many judgments has been written the word "over-ruled," and equally remarkable that no political party proclaims or holds tenets or doctrines inconsistent with the principles on which those judgments rest. They have become primal lights, shining with the steadfast fidelity of the North Star or the Southern Cross, for the guidance of the inquirer after American con-

166   *LAWS AND JURISPRUDENCE.*

Lecture V.

stitutional law. For nearly fifty years after his death the nation failed to show in any overt manner an adequate appreciation of the simplicity, worth, and dignity of his character, and of his unequalled judicial fitness and qualities; at all events, it failed to display any public memorial of gratitude for those labors which not only so greatly contributed to make the Supreme Bench illustrious, but which enabled the country to attain unto its present stature without any strain upon the Constitution.

Statue to the memory of the Great Chief-Justice.

The bar and the nation have, though tardily, shown themselves worthy of the inheritance of such a name and of such labors, by erecting a statue to his memory, executed by the gifted son of his loved and eminent associate, to the end that the chief executive, the legislator, the suitor, the lawyer, the judge, and the citizen, may in all coming time, as they go to or return from the Capitol, be reminded of the thoughtful though severely plain features, the calm majesty, the placid courage, the lofty character, the inestimable public services of him whose uncontested and unenvied title is that of the Great Chief-Justice. The most satisfactory estimate of Marshall and of his labors which exists will be found in the address of your distinguished Kent professor, delivered in 1879, before the American Bar Association.[1]

The grand and petit jury.

Consonant with the popular character of our institutions are the grand and petit jury. They are

[1] Annual address of Edward J. Phelps before the American Bar Association, at Saratoga Springs, N. Y., 1879, reported in the transactions of the Association for that year at pp. 173-192.

expressions of the free and practical spirit of the common law. They have a value, a deep value, too often overlooked, beyond the specific functions they exercise. The jurors acquire and disseminate a knowledge of the laws among the local communities from which they come, and to which they return. We ought, doubtless, to reform the abuses of administration in the jury system; but the complaints against the system, so far as well grounded, arise largely from inexperienced or incapable judges, or from unwise statutes curtailing the powers of the judge in jury trials to those of a mere moderator. I have made the jury the subject of much observation and reflection, some of the results whereof I expressed in my last lecture. I will not here repeat them, further than to reaffirm that in my judgment the jury is both a valuable and an essential part of our judicial and political system. It is not simply to be venerated as a reminiscence, but to be prized for its usefulness. Its roots strike deep into the soil, and cling to the very foundation stones of our jurisprudence. The system belongs to free institutions, and tends to fortify and perpetuate them. I quite agree with Chief-Justice Taney, than whom few judges have had wider experience, and none, perhaps, more capable of forming a sound and unimpassioned judgment. He has left on record his deliberate opinion that our liberties are closely bound up with the preservation "in full vigor and "usefulness of the great principles of the common "law and trial by jury."[1] I protest against the

Lecture V.

Chief-Justice Taney's opinion of the trial by jury.

---

[1] Tyler, "Memoir of Roger Brooke Taney, LL.D., Chief-Justice of the Supreme Court of the United States," Baltimore, 1872, p. 328.

Lecture V.

continentalization of our law. I invoke the conservative judgment of the profession against the iconoclast who in the name of reform comes to destroy the jury; against the rash surgery which holds not a cautery to cure, but a knife to amputate. Twelve good and lawful men are better judges of disputed facts than twelve learned judges.[1]

[1] See *ante* Lecture IV

LECTURE VI.

OUR LAW IN ITS NEW HOME — AMERICA : ITS EXPANSION, DEVELOPMENT, AND CHARACTERISTICS IN THE POLITICAL AND JUDICIAL SYSTEMS OF THE UNITED STATES (CONTINUED).

RESUMING the subject of the last lecture, I commence by saying that it is no part of my purpose to institute a comparison between the civil and the common law, the one or the other of which constitutes the foundation of the jurisprudence of every civilized Christian state.[1] It is true that, abstractly considered in its entirety as a system of jurisprudence, the civil law, elaborated during many centuries and matured by Rome in the height of her civilization, was at one time superior to the common law, whose foundations were laid in the twilight of the nation, and which had not in many points kept pace with the progress of the English people. The feudal system in its day made serfs of masses of men. It was a system in its nature at war with commerce. It was inimical to peaceful pursuits. Out of its logic sprang the most baleful doctrine that has blighted the English law, — *the*

Lecture VI.

The civil and common law.

General effects of feudalism.

[1] See *ante* Lectures I., V.; *post* Lecture VIII.

170   *LAWS AND JURISPRUDENCE.*

<small>Lecture VI.</small>

doctrine of tenure.[1] To gratify ancestral pride and maintain family splendor, the feudal aristocracy tied up landed property in the iron fetters of tenure; and although it constituted the chief wealth of the nation, it was withdrawn from commerce and could not serve as a basis of credit. The feudal system is the principal source of the land-laws of Great Britain, which still press with such weight upon the agricultural and industrial classes. What singular phenomena we frequently witness as the results of opposing forces. For example, feudalism as a military system was by its very nature compelled to ignore the rights of woman. She could not render military service. Upon marriage her legal identity was lost, — merged in that of her husband; and the old common law pressed this fiction inexorably to all its logical consequences, — consequences which often so shocked the moral sense as to lead the Court of Chancery timidly to take the wife partially under its benign protection. At the same time it is curious to observe that it was

<small>Effect on domestic life and manners.</small>

feudalism, in its effects upon the domestic life and manners in the castle, that gave to woman, to the wife and mother, an importance they never before had, and have never since lost. Having done its work, feudalism is happily gone; but its choicest flower — the elevation, companionship, and recognized dignity of woman — still lives, and its fragrance fills the air. Nevertheless, her legal rehabiliment — perhaps it were better to say her new birth — is the work of our own times.[2]

---

[1] See *post* Lecture VIII.   [2] More at large, *post* Lecture XIII.

But with the growth of commerce, the world's great civilizer; with the advancement and elevation of the people and their constant progress toward liberty; with the establishment and growth of the principles of equity under the great Hardwicke and a long succession of illustrious equity judges; with the disappearance from the law courts of the refinements, subtilities, and artificial logic of the schoolmen, which so long poisoned the common law, — and taking law and equity as together constituting one connected system of laws and jurisprudence, as that system exists at this time in Great Britain and in America, it is, I think, with all of its defects, the best system of enlightened and practical justice that the world has ever witnessed.

Lecture VI. The unequalled excellence of the existing legal systems of England and America.

The Roman law conquered the nations of continental Europe; but the English people, as I have already pointed out, resisted it, and as a system it obtained no foothold on English soil.[1] Many of its principles have been introduced one by one into, and have thereby enriched, the English law, notably commercial and equity law; but the common law has always maintained itself intact as a competing, distinctive system. It must be confessed that it lacks the artistic symmetry of its great rival; but it was better adapted than the civil law to the institutions and character of the English people, *and is for them at least, as it is for us, the better system.*[2]

---

[1] See *ante* Lecture I.
[2] Wherefore Sir Matthew Hale well says : " Of its common municipal law this great kingdom has been always tender, and there is great reason for it. For it is not only a very just and excellent law

Lecture VI.

The sources of this excellence.

It is not a speculative system. It has not been wrought out by *doctrinaires* and built up from without as a work of conscious art. Its merit is that it is based upon the experience of mankind; has grown out of real transactions, actually litigated and recorded. The foundation, or at least the distinguishing feature, of our legal system is the conviction that the only knowledge which can be relied on in framing statutes or rules of conduct must come from experience and not speculation. The principles of a judicial judgment, settled and announced after the argument of counsel, limited to the precise state of facts which the particular case presented, added that much, but only that much, to the existing mass of legal doctrine. The chief value of our system of law as we now have it is that it embodies the lessons of time and long experience. "Everybody is wiser than anybody," said Talleyrand, and truly; and it is this general, accumulated wisdom that has been carried into our law. Lord Hale in his short tract on the "Amendment and Alteration of Laws," every word of which is golden, three times declares that "time is the wisest thing under heaven," and that "time and long experience is " much more ingenious, subtile, and judicious, than

in itself, but it is singularly accommodated to the frame of the English government and to the disposition of the English nation; and such as by a long experience and use is, as it were, incorporated into their very temperament, and in a manner become the complexion and constitution of the English Commonwealth." Sir Matthew Hale, "The History of the Common Law" (4th ed., Runnington, 1779), chap. iii., p. 51. And much more to the same effect will be found in Fortescue's "De Laudibus," written two centuries before. See particularly chaps. xxviii., xxx., xxxiii., xlv., xlvii., liv.

"all the wisest and acutest wits, coexisting in the world, can be."[1]

<small>Lecture VI.</small>

The most distinctive feature of the common law of England and America is the rule of judicial precedent, or the authoritative force of adjudged cases as rules of decision for like causes subsequently arising. In no other system of jurisprudence is such force given to judicial judgments.[2] The result is that elsewhere than in Great Britain and America the judicial reports are comparatively few, since judicial judgments have no authority, and no higher rank, theoretically at least, than the expositions or commentaries of private writers. The correspond-

<small>Doctrine of judicial precedent and its effects.</small>

---

[1] "It is most certain," says Lord Chief-Justice Hale, "that time and long experience is much more ingenious, subtile, and judicious, than all the wisest and acutest wits, coexisting in the world, can be. It discovers such varieties of emergencies and cases, and such inconvenience in things, that no man would otherwise have imagined. And on the other side, in everything that is new, at least in most things, especially relating to laws, there are thousands of new occurrences and entanglements, and coincidences, and complications, that would not possibly be at first foreseen. And the reason is apparent; because laws concern such multitudes, and those of various dispositions, passions, wits, interests, concerns, that it is not possible for any human foresight to discover at once, or to provide expedients against, in the first constitution of a law, . . . so that in truth ancient laws, especially that have a common concern, are not the issues of the prudence of this or that council or senate, but they are the productions of the various experiences of the wisest thing in the inferior world, — to wit, time, which as it discovers day after day new inconveniences, so it doth successively apply new remedies; and, indeed, is a kind of aggregation of the discoveries, results, and applications of ages and events; so that it is a great adventure to go about to alter it, without very great necessity, and under the greatest demonstration of safety and convenience imaginable." Hargrave's Law Tracts, "Amendment and Alterations of Laws."

[2] See more fully, *post* Lectures VIII., IX., X., XIII.

ing result is that the judicial reports in England now number more than three thousand volumes, and in this country not less than the same number, and they are increasing in both countries at the rate of over one hundred and fifty volumes a year.[1]

Where is this multiplication of reports to end? Is it to go on unchecked, indefinitely? Is it desirable or practicable to check it? How far is it an evil, and what is the remedy? These are inquiries of such serious moment that they may well engage our attention.

Bentham's admission as to the value of the law reports.

I suppose it to be undisputed up to this time that the law reports cannot be regarded otherwise than as an inestimable possession. At all events, it is not disputable. Even Bentham, the bitter opponent of what he derisively styled "judge-made law," and advocate of that to which he gave the name of "codification," declared of the "report books" (which in "Benthamese" stands for law reports) that the "greatest quantity of wealth possessed in "this shape by any other nation is penury in com-"parison of that which has been furnished by the "English common law. In this point of view (as a "rich storehouse of materials for legislation; such a "storehouse, that without it no tolerably adequate "system of laws could be made) *it is a blessing even* "*now.* As a light to the legislator, to assist him in "making real law (that is statute law), it is a match-"less blessing; but this sham law (that is, judge-"made law) as a substitute to real law, is a curse. "Time was when for want of recorded experience,

---

[1] See *ante* Lectures III., IV.; *post* Lecture X.

"the pen of the legislator could find no tolerably "adequate indications for guidance. Time was — "but that time is now, at least, at an end." [1]

Lecture VI.

To the subject of codification I shall presently make a brief reference; but since it is clear that down to the present time the law reports are such invaluable repositories of legal principles, the inquiry I wish now to make is *whether the publication of law reports has lived out the period of its usefulness;* that is, whether their continued publication is a benefit or an evil. Undoubtedly it were better that many of the volumes of reports of inferior or overworked courts had never appeared. Undoubtedly the weighty advice of old Bulstrode, so quaintly expressed in the dedication of his second volume, in the time of the Commonwealth, over two hundred years ago, has been too often disregarded: "That "as the laws are the anchor of the Republic, so the "Judicial Reports are as anchors of the laws, and "therefore *ought to be well weighed before put out.*" Undoubtedly, it is to be regretted, that so many cases have been, and that so many cases continue to be, reported containing nothing new or valuable.

The publication of law reports a continuing necessity.

But the inquiry is, Have we reached a stage in the history and development of our law when it is desirable that the doctrine of judicial precedent, as above defined, shall cease; that no more law reports shall be put out, and that the reports be superseded

---

[1] Letter IV. of "Jeremy Bentham, an Englishman, to the Citizens of the several American United States," on the Codification of the law, 1817; Bentham's Works, vol. iv., p. 460; *post* Lectures VIII., IX., X., XI., XII., XIII.

<small>Lecture VI.</small>

by extracting from them all that is valuable and transmuting it into statutable form? It does not appear to me that the general answer to these inquiries is difficult. The law as a result of the ever occurring changes in the condition of society and in legislation is constantly changing. How are these changes authoritatively to be authenticated? The old is to a great extent so well settled and known as to have become elementary and indisputable. It is the new that is unknown, and needs interpretation and definition. And as between the old reports and the new, the experience of every lawyer and judge is, I think, to the effect that the new are the most useful because the most needed; and while this is felt to be so, the publication of Reports of Adjudged Cases will of course continue.[1]

<small>The issue of the existing situation, — what?</small>

The inquiry, however, recurs, Is this to go on forever? If not, when and how is it to end? Will it break down under its own ever-increasing and insupportable weight, and end in eliminating the doctrine of judicial precedent from our law, and substituting the Continental system; or will it have its end in superseding the law reports by codification; or will it have some other issue?

I shall refer to certain features of this great subject in this lecture, reserving other aspects of it for future consideration. The matter is too vast and complicated to admit of short and summary disposition.

<small>Defects in our law which call for remedy.</small>

We have two great divisions of law, — statute-law and case-law. The statutes are frequently fragmentary, — in Bacon's phrase, " cross and intricate,"

---

[1] See *post* Lecture X.

superimposed one upon another. Case-law has to be sought in almost numberless reports and often among conflicting decisions. Our law is thus fairly open to the threefold objection of want of certainty, want of publicity, and want of convenience.[1] Its existing condition urgently calls for some remedy, if any practicable and expedient remedy can be found. The lawyer in an important case does not feel that he has discharged his full duty if he has not made a thorough examination of the multitudinous decisions and put the result upon his brief. The community,

Lecture VI.

Bulk and uncertainty of our laws.

[1] Amos ("Science of Law," chap. xiii.), classifies "the exact evils" to be provided against under four headings: —
 1. Actual uncertainty, owing to the multiplicity and conflict of decisions.
 2. Waste of labor in the process of ascertaining the state of the law.
 3. Want of publicity, preventing knowledge of the law by the community or laity.
 4. Want of knowledge, or the difficulty of acquiring such knowledge, on the part of the legislator, thus hampering him in his efforts to amend it.
 It seems to me that the mischiefs which call for remedy are the three I have mentioned in the text, namely: —
 1. *Want of certainty*, — that is, the existence of unnecessary uncertainty, arising mainly out of the partial and irregular development of case-law and conflicting decisions and piecemeal and desultory legislation. See *post* Lectures VIII., IX., X.
 2. *Want of publicity*, arising out of having to acquire a knowledge of the law by a resort to so many volumes of reports, thus necessarily confining a knowledge of even its leading principles to the profession of the law. See *post* Lectures IX., X.
 3. *Want of convenience (or voluminousness)*, caused by the vast number and multiplication of reports and statutes. See *post* Lectures IX., X., XIII.
 Of these, the first and third are the more serious; but the second is by no means unimportant, especially in a nation where suffrage is universal. I have known more than one instance of the results of the toil of years being swept away because men in business did not know the elementary principles of the law of negotiable paper.

178   *LAWS AND JURISPRUDENCE.*

Lecture VI.

which is conclusively supposed to know the law and required to obey it, does not attempt to acquire or affect to possess such knowledge.[1] Our condition is worse than the condition in England, since we have forty-four State courts of last resort, and no superior tribunal to harmonize conflicting decisions, except in the comparatively small number of cases involving Federal law. Still the inquiry comes back, What is the remedy? "Is there no balm in Gilead? Is there no physician there?" Still the question presses, Where or in what is all this to end?

Probable remedies suggested; expanded legislative action.

When we consider how purblind are the wisest and most sagacious in dealing with the future, I venture a forecast, and the reasons therefor, with unaffected distrust.

1. Our laws will, I believe, even if codification be not adopted, become relatively more and more embodied in legislative form. The greater certainty and convenience of a carefully considered enactment which covers the entire subject with which it deals, over the chaotic and unmethodized condition of the law when it has to be sought through volumes of reports and a variety of detached statutes, will constantly operate with no inconsiderable force in expanding the scope of legislative action; and this although codification, in the sense often or usually

---

[1] Tennyson's well-known picture borrows nothing from poetic coloring, but is severely drawn with the sober pencil of a judge.

"The lawless science of our law,
The codeless myriad of precedent,
That wilderness of single instances,
Through which a few, by wit or fortune led,
May beat a pathway out to wealth and fame."

attached to the term, be not undertaken. This tendency is specially observable in recent English legislation, and one cannot fail to perceive in the later English reports how much greater than formerly is the proportion of causes that turn upon statutory enactments. Every statute carefully thought out and fully covering an important subject (as, for example, the English act codifying the law of bills of exchange) is, in one sense, codification, — codification *pro tanto* ; at all events, it is *pro tanto* a remedy for the unsatisfactory condition of the law on that subject existing when the statute was enacted. In this silent, unperceived way, the English bar and people are being educated up to and gradually prepared for codification in some practicable, expedient form.

But ought the legislative action to be so expanded as to embrace codification within its remedial endeavors? Well, what is codification? The term is used in such a variety of senses that it must be defined before the question, *whether codification is an expedient remedy?* can be answered.

By one class of code advocates it is insisted that the essential idea of a code is a complete statement of the whole law of the land including both statute-law and case-law. In their view, the principles of true codification must assume that the law in its leading departments has practically attained its growth; that its fundamental principles are settled; that these can be and ought to be expressed in precise and logical form, without any necessary reference to old language, conceptions, or titles; that it is feasible to do this so as to cover the whole field of general law, and then to classify and arrange the result scientifically to the end of superseding the prior statutes and the law reports; and that any lesser attempt argues an inadequate appreciation of the mischief and of the needful remedy. To me, it has always seemed inexpedient, even if it were possible (which it is not), to attempt a scheme so ambitious as the embodying into a code or statutory form rules applicable to all the complicated transactions of modern business and society, with a view to supersede the reports.

Bentham as a law reformer, and his idea of a code.

The comprehensive scheme above outlined was Bentham's idea of a code. What is more visionary than the legal millennium he pictured to his fancy? " Every man his own lawyer! Behold in this," he exclaimed, " the point to aim at." Bentham never argued or tried a cause. His independent and vigorous intellect lacked the true legal wisdom that can only come from living contact with the law at the bar or on the bench. He had all the traits of a reformer, — enthusiastic, fierce, destructive. He is an unique, statuesque, eccentric figure in the English law. His sensitive nature personally unfitted him for the practice of his profession. But as we read his bitter, bold, sweeping denunciations of the evils in government and the law as he saw them, we fancy that we behold in him an ancient prophet with flowing robe and beard, coming with a new message to an unheeding world. His assaults were not wholly without effect, and they brought about at length some useful emendations in the law. They did much more. They set the lawyers thinking; they initiated the notion of legal reform. They originated and communicated an impulse in our law which is still felt and which has produced lasting consequences. The world is yet troubled over his ideas as to the rationale and true purpose of codification; and it is not impossible that a future age may accept as sound some of the ideas and notions, which we still regard as extravagant or chimerical.[1]

Lecture VI.

Bentham and law reform.

He believed it was possible to extract from the reports all that was valuable in them — nay, that this ought to be done, and done speedily — and to embody it in a code; whereupon he would have been willing, I fancy, to have burned the law reports, and himself to have applied the torch. Unfortunately there is no alchemy by which the value of the law reports can *all* be extracted and transmuted into statutory coin.

There are, I think, few advocates of codification who share in Bentham's extreme views; but there are many who believe, myself among them, that a far less radical scheme — one more suited " to human nature's daily food" — is not only feasible but desirable; namely, a thorough revision and systematic statement by experienced and master hands not of the whole law, but as far as it can be expediently done, of the law on the great subjects which relate to the ordinary business and life of the people; deducing and stating what is clear; removing what is archaic and obsolete; settling what is doubtful or obscure; never losing sight of the old landmarks; sailing ever close to the shore; using whenever they will best answer the purpose, old conceptions, language, and methods of classification, and making no

Within what limits codification is practicable and expedient.

[1] See *post* Lectures IX., XI., XIII.

changes except where it is demonstrably clear that change is improvement. Codification (if this is codification), within these conservative limits, has many advocates in England and in this country among lawyers and judges of ability and wide experience.

Of the opponents of codification of case-law in any form, some deny its practicability and some its expediency. Its practicability proceeds, in part, upon the truth so clearly expressed by Lord Mansfield, that "the law does not consist of particular "cases, but of general principles, which are illus-"trated and explained by these cases."[1]

The number of the cases is legion; but the principles they establish are comparatively few, capable, of course, of being thoroughly mastered, and capable also of direct and intelligible statement. The objection to the expediency of such a performance, assuming the work to be thoroughly done by the fittest men in the profession, is that the freedom of growth of case-law will thereby be arrested, and the inelasticity and imperativeness of the codified rule will work injustice, since the courts will be required to apply it in cases in which the facts and circumstances would take it out of the rule if the rule had not been cast in an inflexible statutory mould.

There is some plausibility, but on the assumption that the work of codification is kept within the limits and performed in the spirit and manner I have indicated, there is little real force in the objection. In my view, the codifier ought not to generalize any principle so that it could fairly apply to any other than the class of cases specially defined, and for which it

[1] Rex v. Bembridge, 3 Doug., 332, 1783.

was intended, to the end that the codified rule shall, unless purposely changed, be simply co-extensive with the uncodified rule, which the courts have no more power to change or to refuse to apply in the uncodified, than in the codified, state. If cases shall arise not within the rule, and not expressly provided for, they will be determined in the same manner as if no code existed. If mistakes be made, they can be speedily remedied by the legislature, which meets annually or biennially in all the States; and by a standing provision for periodical legislative revision. A rule could also be enacted that the code should be construed as a code of the common law of the State, and not strictly, like statutes in derogation of the common law.

In the law of procedure, America has heretofore led the way, under an able and eminent lawyer (Mr. David Dudley Field), in a reform which has spread not only over our own land, but has crossed the two oceans, and lies at the basis of the existing Judicature Acts of Great Britain. Fortunate man! to have had his life graciously prolonged so much beyond the common span, that he might witness the almost ecumenical triumph of the ideas of his earlier, but not more enthusiastic, days.[1]

Lecture VI.

Codification of the law of procedure; David Dudley Field's labors.

[1] Lord Chancellor Cairns, perhaps the ablest English judge of this generation, in a speech in the House of Lords in 1876, said: "The great change effected by the Judicature Acts came into operation on the first of November last, and I am bound to say that every day which has passed has satisfied me of the wisdom of Parliament in introducing that great scheme. So far as I can observe the working of the Judicature Acts, they have been in the highest degree satisfactory. There has been found in their working a degree of flexibility, of simplicity, of uniformity, and of economy of judicial time, which has secured the best results." Other eminent men hold like views:

Lecture VI.

It ought to gratify a laudable national and professional pride if we could, in like manner, lead the

Thus, the late Right Hon. Sir Alexander James Edmund Cockburn, Lord Chief-Justice of England, speaking of the Judicature Acts on the occasion of being presented with the freedom of the city of London, said: "I am happy to have this opportunity of saying it thus publicly, as the result of my own experience during the past few months, that this legislation has effected very great and salutary improvements in the condition of English law. It has in many respects brought the old maxims of the common law into harmony with the larger and more liberal principles of equity. It has improved our procedure, — simplified and improved it."

Referring to the general condition of the English law, he added: "There are still imperfections, numerous indeed, and serious too, which have to be removed, and the greatest work of all has yet to be accomplished. Your law is scattered over an area which makes it difficult to find what you want at the moment you want it. A Roman legislator complained 'that the works on Roman law had become the load of many camels.' How truly may that be said of the law of this land, with this exception, that for camels I could, if you would allow me, substitute cartloads. [He might have said carloads.] The truth is, that the unwritten law, in the reports and decided cases, and in the innumerable treatises which spring up like grass under our feet, has become at last a chaotic mass, a labyrinth in which no man can find his way, unless he has got a lawyer to go along with him and support him. Now, that is a state of things which I think is not creditable to us as a great nation. You have brought justice to every man's door; you must bring a knowledge of the law, at all events of its elementary principles, and, as far as you can, a knowledge of its principles to every man. Our law is to be found in thousands of volumes and in acts of Parliament without end, in acts of Parliament more or less unintelligible by reason of the uncouth, barbarous phraseology in which they are framed. . . . It is time that all that was removed. It is time that your laws should be reduced into intelligent phraseology; it is time that your laws should be digested. . . . No one but a lawyer knows what is law except as to the most elementary principles. This is not a state of things creditable to this country; and as a great politician once said, 'Register, register, register,' my advice, and I am very glad to have the opportunity to express it publicly here, to the legislator, lawyer, and the layman, is, 'Digest, digest, digest; codify, codify, codify.' I will not listen to the man who tells me that the thing is not capable of being done. Other nations have done it. . . .

way to a reform equally needed, and within the limits I have above indicated, equally practicable,

Lecture VI.

It is not only France that has done this, for other Continental nations have done the same; Prussia, Austria, and Italy have all admirable codes. . . . There are some people who run away with the strange notion that the law is made only for lawyers and judges to interpret. They do not seem to see the fact that the law is made for the community, and not merely for the body of lawyers. . . . Depend upon it, the time will come when the pressure of public opinion on this subject will not allow our law to remain in the state of chaotic uncertainty in which to a certain extent it is."

The present Chief-Justice of England, Lord Coleridge, at the public reception tendered to him by the Bar Association of New York City in 1883, in reply to the address of welcome, took occasion to say : —

" You are probably aware that we in England have been engaged for the last ten years, beginning in 1873, when as attorney-general I was responsible for passing the Judicature Act through the House of Commons, in endeavoring to cheapen and simplify and expedite our procedure upon the lines of those salutary statutes which the wisdom of Parliament enacted about thirty years ago (in 1852 to 1854). It was high time that something was done to expedite and amend and simplify the common law. It had become associated in the minds of many men with narrow technicality and substantial injustice. That was not the fault of the common law, but it was the fault, if fault it were, of the system of pleading, which looked at practically was a small part of the common law, but very powerful men had contrived to make it appear that it was almost the whole of it, — that the science of statement was far more important than the substance of the right, and that rights of litigants themselves were comparatively unimportant unless they illustrated some obscure, interesting, and subtle point of the science of stating those rights. It is a comfort to think that those subtleties, if there was any merit in them, have not entirely been banished from the earth, and I am told that there is a State in this progressive Union in which they are, at this moment, as alive as ever; and I venture upon this subject to make you a practical suggestion. You have lately procured, — may I say most wisely ? — a great National Park, in which the beauties and glories of Nature and the strange and eccentric forms which natural objects sometimes assume, may be preserved forever for the instruction and delight of the citizens of this great republic. Could it not be arranged, that with the sanction of the State, some corner in that one State should be preserved, as a kind of pleading park, in which the glories of the *negative preg-*

Lecture VI.

Progress of American jurisprudence; extract from Webster's eulogy on Justice Story.

in the substantive law common to both nations. I recall here Webster's remarks in his finished eulogy on Mr. Justice Story: "There is no purer "pride of country than that in which we may in-"dulge when we see America paying back the "great debt of civilization, learning, and science "to Europe; and in the august reckoning and "accounting between nations, returning light for "light, and mind for mind. Acknowledging, as "we all acknowledge, our obligations to the orig-"inal sources of English law, as well as of civil "liberty, we have seen in our generation copious "and salutary streams turning and running back-"ward, replenishing their original fountains, and "giving a fresher and brighter green to the fields "of English jurisprudence."[1]

To show that the bar and judges of England cordially acknowledge that the debt which we owe is being paid, may I be pardoned for giving an extract

nant, absque hoc, replication de injuria, rebutter and sur-rebutter, and all the other weird and fanciful creations of the pleader's brain, might be preserved for future ages to gratify the respectful curiosity of your descendants, and that our good old English judges, if ever they re-visit the glimpses of the moon, might have some place where their weary souls might still find the form preferred to the substance, the statement to the thing stated. I cannot help thinking that that would be a matter worthy of the liberality, of the genius and conservative instincts of the great American public. But it is really, to speak seriously, a great pleasure for me to find that slowly, and if I may say so, with wise hesitancy, you are gradually admitting into your system those changes which we have lately made, as and when they satisfy the needs, the temper, and the genius of your people."

The learned chief-justice seemed for the moment to forget that America had led the way in this reform.

[1] Webster's Works (Little & Brown), vol. ii., p. 297, 1845; *post* Lecture XIII.

from an autograph letter now before me, dated December 30, 1876, which I had the honor to receive from the late Lord Chief-Justice Cockburn. He says: "I pray you to believe that the respect "paid by the jurists of the United States to the "authorities of the Old Country, in regard to the "law which both nations have derived from a com-"mon source, is most cordially reciprocated. There "is scarcely a discussion of any importance in "which American decisions and American authors "are not cited, and the judgments and *dicta* of a "Marshall or a Story are as familiar to us as those "of a Mansfield or an Ellenborough. May this "ever be so! While as an Englishman I desire "that a community of origin and a community of "interests (when the latter are properly understood) "should draw the two nations closer, as a lawyer I "could wish that a common jurisprudence should "assist to cement the bonds of international "amity."[1]

Lecture VI.

Lord Chief-Justice Cockburn's acknowledgment.

2. In course of time, each State will have, as the result of permanent statutes and the lengthened line of its own judicial decisions, a jurisprudence of its own so ample that the necessity for going beyond

Future condition of the law in the several States of the Union.

[1] Lord Selborne, under date of October 26, 1892, writing to me in a similar strain of generous candor, in acknowledgment of the receipt of the medal awarded to him by the American Bar Association "for meritorious and distinguished services in advancing the science of jurisprudence and the administration of justice," says . "Whatever I may have been able to do, or endeavored to do, to advance the science, in the common pursuit of which your association and the bar of England are engaged (and I certainly cannot myself estimate it as worthy of so high an honor), it is to be attributed entirely to those masters of the principles of law, at whose feet I have been a learner; among whom not the least are the great American jurists."

188   LAWS AND JURISPRUDENCE.

<small>Lecture VI.</small> it will arise only in novel and exceptional cases, which will justify and reward the labor.

<small>Importance of the study of principles increasingly recognized.</small> 3. As the common law, happily, underlies substantially our whole jurisprudence, thereby giving it a general uniformity of character; as the labor of examining the multitude of reports becomes more and more onerous to the busy practitioner or the equally busy judge; and as the character for learning and ability of many of the benches of shifting judges is not such as to invest their judgments and decisions with special value, the combined result will be a tendency more and more to diminish the importance of the "case lawyer" and to make felt the importance of a knowledge of the great, living, fundamental principles of our law and equity systems, and to argue and decide causes with greater reliance upon these principles. We have happily at length reached, in law as in literature, the salutary stage, when, in the language of Dr. Johnson, "no <small>Ideal of a modern judge.</small> precedents can justify absurdity."[1] When recently crossing the bay of New York, the Statue of Liberty with its uplifted torch enlightening the world suggested to me that the true ideal of a modern judge was no longer a figure with bandaged eyes, but rather the figure of one who carries in his upraised hand the torch of truth lighted from on high, and who throughout the arguments of counsel and in the maze and labyrinth of adjudged cases walks ever with firm step in the illumination of its constant and steady flame.

[1] Life of Milton.

As, therefore, we must expect that adjudged cases will continue to be reported, and continue as heretofore to be used as authority and to serve as sources or evidence of legal principles, we are deeply concerned in whatever favorably or injuriously affects the value of the reports.[1]

<small>Lecture VI.</small>

The character of many recent American reports has deteriorated from several causes. To two of these I shall now allude because they arise from mistaken views and practices of the judges themselves, and are, therefore, readily remediable. Most of our appellate courts are crowded with causes, and the effect upon the judges is that they too often feel it to be an ever-pressing, paramount, all-absorbing duty to clear the docket. This mistakenly becomes the chief object to be attained, — the primary, instead of a quite subordinate, consideration. In the accomplishment of this end, the judges are as impatient of delay as was the wedding-guest in the Rime of the Ancient Mariner. Added to this, a majority of the appellate judges generally reside elsewhere than at the capital or place where the courts are held, and the desire is constantly felt to bring a laborious session to an end as speedily as possible, in order that they may rejoin their families and do their work in the fatigue-dress of their libraries, rather than under the necessary restraints of the term. They begrudge the time necessary for full argument at the bar. They dislike to hear counsel at length. They prefer to receive briefs. As a result, two practices have grown up too gen-

<small>Deterioration of modern law reports and the causes thereof.</small>

[1] See *post* Lecture X.

erally throughout the country, which have, as I think, done more to impair the value of judicial judgments and opinions than perhaps all other causes combined.

Lecture VI.

Superior value of oral over printed arguments.

The first is *that the submission of causes upon printed briefs is favored, and oral arguments at the bar are discouraged, and the time allowed therefor is usually inadequate.*

On this subject, I hold very strong opinions; but also hold that no opinion can be too strong. As a means of enabling the court to understand the exact case brought thither for its judgment; as a means of eliciting the very truth of the matter both of law and fact, there is no substitute for oral argument. None! I distrust the soundness of the decision of any court, of any novel or complex case, which has been submitted wholly upon briefs. Speaking, if I may be allowed, from my own experience, I always felt a reasonable assurance in my own judgment when I had patiently heard all that opposing counsel could say to aid me; and a very diminished faith in any judgment given in a difficult cause not orally argued. Mistakes, errors, fallacies, and flaws elude us, in spite of ourselves, unless the case is pounded and hammered at the bar. This mischievous substitute of printer's ink for face-to-face argument impoverishes our case-law at its very source, since it tends to prevent the growth of able lawyers, who are developed only in the conflicts of the bar, and of great judges, who can become great only by the aid of the bar that surrounds them. What lawyer will prepare for a thorough argument at the bar when he knows that he will not have the time to present it? It was not thus until a recent period. Nor are these views at all novel. Lord Coke refers to the benefits of oral arguments in language the most solemn and impressive. In cases of difficulty, he says: "No man alone with all his uttermost labors, "nor all the actors in them, themselves by them- "selves out of a court of justice, can attain unto a "right decision; *nor in court without solemn argument* "*where I am persuaded Almighty God openeth and en-* "*largeth the understanding of those desirous of justice* "*and right.*" This, I declare unto you, I do verily believe.

Lecture VI.

Lord Coke's opinion.

Formerly, whenever a new or difficult question arose, the judges of England invited argument and reargument, *always in open court;* and in the earlier days of the law, the matter was not only debated at the bar by the counsel for the parties, but was afterwards discussed by the judges openly at a time prefixed in the presence of the barristers and apprentices: "a reverend and honorable proceeding "in law, a grateful satisfaction to the parties, and a "great instruction to the studious hearers."[1] Truth

Former English practice.

---

[1] "Whereunto (in those cases that be *tortuosi* and of great difficulty, adjudged upon demurrer or resolved in open court), no one man alone with all his true and uttermost labors, nor all the actors in them, themselves by themselves out of a court of justice, nor in court without solemn argument, where (I am persuaded, Almighty God openeth and enlargeth the understanding of those desirous of justice and right) could ever have attained unto. For it is one, amongst others, of the great honors of the common laws, that cases of great difficulty are never adjudged or resolved *in tenebris* or *sub silentio supressis rationibus*, but in open court, and there upon solemn and elaborate arguments,— first at the bar by the counsel learned of either party [a] (and if the case depend in the Court of Common Pleas, then by serjeants-at-law only [b]); and after by the bench by the judges, where they argue (the

[a] See *ante* Lecture I. [b] See *ante* Lecture III.

Lecture VI.

is not apt to enter where she is not received with welcome and hospitality.

If our case-law is not to go on deteriorating, we must revive the former appreciation of the value of oral arguments. It is these that must be favored, and it is the submission wholly on briefs that ought to be discouraged.

Full consultation by the judges should always precede the writing of the opinion of the court.

The other practice among some, I fear many, of our appellate courts which injuriously affects our case-law *is the practice of assigning the record of causes submitted on printed arguments to one of the judges to look into and write an opinion, without a previous examination of the record and arguments by the judges in consultation.*

This course ought to be forbidden, peremptorily forbidden, by statute. What is the most difficult function of an appellate court? It is, as I think, after the record is fully opened and the argument understood, to determine precisely upon what point or points the judgment of the case ought to rest. This most delicate and important of all judicial duties ought always to be performed by the judges in full conference *before* the record is delivered to one of their number to write the opinion of the court; which, when written, should be confined to the precise grounds thus predetermined. In respect to oral arguments, the time allowed therefor, the will-

puisne judge beginning and so ascending) *seriatim* upon certain days openly and purposely prefixed, declaring at large the authorities, reasons, and causes of their judgments and resolutions, in every particular case (*habet enim nescio quid energiæ viva vox*) a reverend and honorable proceeding in law, a grateful satisfaction to the parties, and a great instruction and direction to the attentive and studious hearers." Sir Edward Coke's Preface to 9th Coke's Reports, p. xiv.

ingness to hear counsel and full conferences among the judges in the presence of each other prior to decision or assigning the record to a judge to write the opinion, the Supreme Court of the United States is a model for every appellate tribunal in the country.

Lecture VI.

The Supreme Court of the United States a model of excellence.

When the ideal of legal education shall be the mastery of principles, so that the first impulse of the lawyer in cases not depending upon local legislation will be to find the "principle" and not the "case" that governs the matter in hand; when arguments at the bar shall be mainly directed, first to an ascertainment of the peculiar and controlling facts of the case under consideration, and then to pointing out the principles of law which apply to this precise state of facts, each of which operations requires the disciplined exercise of intellectual qualities of a high order; when the bench shall be constituted of the flower of the bar, and appellate judgments shall not be given without a previous conference of the judges at which the grounds of the judgment shall be agreed upon before the record is allotted for the opinion to be written; when opinions shall be rigidly restricted, without unnecessary disquisition and essay-writing, to the precise points needful to the decision, we shall have an abler bar, better judgments, and an improved jurisprudence, in which erroneous and conflicting decisions will be few, and reduced to the minimum.

How our jurisprudence may be improved.

And here I must close. My purpose in this and the preceding lecture has been to show that our system of laws and jurisprudence is consonant with the

Lecture VI.

Advantages springing from the substantial identity of the English and American systems of law.

genius of our people and with our civil and political institutions; that it is an outgrowth of them, and powerfully supports and sustains them. It is, in its ground-work, the system that prevails wherever, on either continent, our language is spoken. In our law libraries we find the learning and labors of judges administering this system in law reports from India, South Africa, Australia, New Zealand, the Dominion of Canada, the Sandwich Islands, and the West Indies. All this is the heritage, by what I may call a species of tenancy in common, of the English and American lawyer, who wherever, within this wide horizon, he finds his language spoken, finds also individual and civil liberty, popular institutions, the grand and petit jury, legislative assemblies, Magna Charta, Habeas Corpus, equality before the law, the same sacred regard for individual rights, the same reverential affection for, and instinctive obedience to law. What incalculable advantages! We have the same legal literature. We have the same legal firmament, in which we behold Hale and Marshall, Hardwicke and Story, Blackstone and Kent, Erskine and Webster. We partake freely of the benefits of the labors of each other. Whoever achieves anything for the advancement or improvement of the law, achieves it not for his own country alone, but for all English-speaking and English-governed peoples. My further purpose has been to show that although this system is not without serious defects, mostly, however, of form rather than of substance, the remedy is not to substitute an alien system, but to engraft the needed amendments and changes on our own hardy, native stock.

OUR LAW IN ITS NEW HOME.

The special duty of the American lawyer is, of course, to improve and promote the laws and jurisprudence of his own country. What great and complex problems confront the American lawyer, growing out of our vast territorial extent and our distinct Federal and State systems of government and jurisprudence; out of the changes wrought by iron, steam, and electricity in business and all the modes of communication and transportation; out of the combinations of capital almost without limit in corporate form, affecting interests vital to individuals and to society. The law has to be adapted to these new situations and circumstances. What a weighty work! Truly it demands the most attentive study, the most penetrating observation, the most sedate consideration, the ripest judgment. Here will be found work for all. We have laid, as I have attempted to show, the foundations of a noble jurisprudence, and during the two centuries of our colonial and national life, the structure has been carried along so as to meet contemporary wants and needs. The work must, however, go forward with the progress of the States and the nation. What more generous ambition can inspire, what higher duty can engage, the American lawyer than to assist, in his day, in advancing this structure, and adapting it, by alteration and enlargement, to the changed and changing conditions of society; a work which must ever go on, yet never be completed.

Lecture VI.

Duty of the American bar to improve our laws: its scope and difficulty.

"Some unfinished window
In Aladdin's tower
Unfinished must remain."

LECTURE VII.

OUR LAW IN ITS NEW HOME, — AMERICA; ITS EXPANSION, DEVELOPMENT, AND CHARACTERISTICS IN THE POLITICAL AND JUDICIAL SYSTEMS OF THE UNITED STATES, AND HEREIN OF OUR WRITTEN CONSTITUTIONS, THEIR RATIONALE, LIMITATIONS, AND GUARANTEES (CONCLUDED).

Lecture VII.
Written constitutions the unique feature of American legal institutions.

THE absolutely unique feature of the political and legal institutions of the American republic is its written constitutions, which are organic limitations whereby the people by an act of unprecedented wisdom have, "in order to establish justice, to promote the general welfare and secure the blessings of liberty to themselves and their posterity," *protected themselves against themselves.* What renders this the more extraordinary is that these constitutions are self-imposed restraints. The spectacle is that of the acknowledged possessors of all political power voluntarily circumscribing and limiting the plenary and unrestrained use of it. History affords many examples where the holders of political power have been forced to surrender or to curtail it for the general good; but the example of the people constituting the American political communities in limiting, by their own free will, the exercise of their own power, stood alone when this sublime sacrifice was made, and it has not been followed in any country in Europe, nor successfully put in operation elsewhere than in the United States.[1] I said that in this way the people had protected themselves against themselves; and this they have done by making the Constitution in reality what, in its sixth article, it expressly declares itself to be, namely, "the supreme *law* of the land, binding the judges in every State, anything in the constitution or laws of any State to the contrary notwithstanding." This latter purpose they accomplished by providing that the Constitution should be interpreted and enforced by the judiciary as one of the departments of the government established by the Constitution, and that the judgment of the courts thereon should be, if necessary, carried into execu-

Lecture VII.

The supreme law of the land.

---

[1] Political and speculative writers there are in Europe who still maintain that it is idle, unwise, or at any rate self-contradictory, for the sovereign or supreme power in a State to put limits upon itself; but more than a century ago the people of this country did restrain the exercise of their own power by organic limitations upon all of the organs of the State. The wisdom and general efficiency of this political invention, for such it was, have been vindicated and established by our long experience. The device — the idea — the political conception, if I may so term it — of written constitutions, belongs to the statesmen who founded our political institutions. It is true, as the late Professor Dwight has pointed out ("Political Science Quarterly," vol. ii., no. 1, March, 1887), that in Harrington's "Oceana" appears "the first sketch in English political science of a *written constitution* limiting sovereign power;" that he declared that government should be an "empire of laws and not of men;" "that the exercise of all *just* authority over a free people ought (under God) to arise from their own consent," which is Jefferson's exact phrase in the Declaration of Independence; and doubtless true, also, it is, that Harrington's writings were familiar to our statesmen a hundred years after Harrington's death. At the very utmost, his speculations are but adumbrations of the work which was conceived, put into form, and made an actual, living, working reality by the great men who established the political and legal institutions of the United States.

Lecture VII.

Rationale and purposes of written constitutions.

tion by the executive by the whole power of the State.[1]

The devices which our constitutions provide to prevent precipitate action of the popular will are single and simple in principle, but elaborate, though not complex, in arrangement. They may thus be grouped and shortly stated: (*a*) Three co-ordinate departments, and the separation and distribution of all of the powers of the government into these departments, — each checking the other; (*b*) A system of representation with a double chamber, — each a check on the other; (*c*) The insertion of guarantees of primordial and fundamental rights, — Magna Charta enlarged and perfected, — into the Constitution; (*d*) Distribution of powers between the States and the Federal Union; and (*e*) An independent judiciary, made the guardian of the Constitution, with the crowning power and duty to declare unconstitutional statutes to be void, — all to the end that there may be secured "a government of laws and not of men."[2]

[1] United States *v.* Lee, 106 U. S. Rep., 196, 220, 1882.

[2] In the address of Rufus Choate, referred to below, the scheme of our written constitutions, and the manner in which they protect and secure all persons and all interests against the haste and passions of the hour, are presented with surpassing force and eloquence. "Addresses and Orations of Rufus Choate" (5th ed., Little, Brown, & Co., 1877), p. 133. I refer to this subject more fully throughout this lecture. I only add here that this system of checks and balances which the framers of our government contrived, and which in its totality constitutes our constitutions, has but the single ultimate purpose of curbing the unfettered exercise of the popular will, and it demonstrates how thoroughly they realized the dangerous and destructive force of that will if it were not put under effective restraints. Unrestrained, it would be (to borrow an illustration from Schiller) like the path of the lightning or of the cannon ball: —

Whatever rights and duties are enforced by the State in its judicial tribunals are legal rights and duties in the full sense of the term; these are truly law.[1] To have constructed our constitutions so as to provide *legal* sanctions for their provisions was the great, illustrious, beneficent, immortal, work of the statesmen and lawyers who were their authors. "I do not know," said Rufus Choate, "that I can "point to one achievement in American statesman- "ship which can take rank for its consequences of "good above that single decision of the Supreme "Court, which adjudged that an act of the legisla- "ture contrary to the Constitution is void, and that "the judicial department is clothed with the power" — and he might have added, charged with the duty — "to ascertain the repugnancy, and pronounce "the legal conclusion. That the framers of the "Constitution intended this to be so is certain; "but to have asserted it against Congress and the "executive, to have vindicated it by that easy "yet adamantine demonstration than which the "reasonings of mathematics show nothing surer, "to have inscribed this vast truth of conservatism

Lecture VII.

The legal sanctions of our constitutions.

"Direct it flies and rapid;
Shattering that it *may* reach, and shattering what it reaches."

If restrained, however, blessings attend its course, and it answers the description that follows: —

"But, my son, the road human beings travel,
That, on which BLESSING comes and goes, doth follow
The river's course, the valley's playful windings;
Curves round the corn-field and the hill of vines,
Honoring the holy bounds of property!
And thus secure, though late, leads to its end."

"The Piccolomini," Coleridge's translation, act i., scene iv.

[1] See *ante* Lecture I.

Lecture VII.

Choate's eulogium thereon.

"upon the public mind, so that no demagogue, not
"in the last stage of intoxication, denies it, — this
"is an achievement of statesmanship [of the judi-
"ciary] of which a thousand years may not exhaust
"or reveal all the good."[1]

[1] Address, July 3, 1845, before the Harvard Law School in Cambridge, Mass., on "The Position and Functions of the American Bar, as an Element of Conservatism in the State." "Addresses and Orations of Rufus Choate" (5th ed., Little, Brown, & Co., 1887), p. 133. This is a notable production, not only for its literary excellence, but as embodying the matured views of one of the most eminent lawyers who have adorned the profession in this country.

The distinctive character as well as the importance of the doctrine that the courts not only have the power but that it is their duty to declare statutes in plain conflict with the Constitution to be void, — a doctrine no longer questioned, daily acted on, and now laid up among the fundamentals of American jurisprudence, — justifies a historical reference to the origin and development of this great principle. The earliest case is Holmes *v.* Walton, referred to in State *v.* Parkhurst, 4 Halstead (N. J.), 444, decided by the Supreme Court of New Jersey in 1780. Virginia decided the same way in 1782 and 1788, — Commonwealth *v.* Caton, 4 Call (Va.), 5, 1782 ; " Case of the Judges," *Ib.*, 135, 1788, — and again in 1793 in Kamper *v.* Hawkins, 1 Va. Cas. 20. So in principle in South Carolina in 1792, in Bowman *v.* Middleton, 1 Bay (S. C.), 252. So in Rhode Island in 1786, in Trevett *v.* Weeden, often though erroneously referred to as the earliest case. See Cooley, "Constitutional Limitations" (4th ed.), 196 ; Bryce, "American Commonwealth," vol. i., 532 ; Arnold, "History of Rhode Island," vol. ii., c. 24. So in North Carolina in 1787, Bayard *v.* Singleton, 1 Martin, 48 ; see Ogden *v.* Witherspoon, 2 Haywood, 227, 1802. So in Massachusetts in 1788, Bancroft, "History of the Constitution," vol. ii., 473.

The views of contemporary statesmen and the early decisions, State and Federal, are fully given by Judge Elliott in his valuable article on " The Legislatures and the Courts : The Power to Declare Statutes Unconstitutional," " Political Science Quarterly," vol. v., 232–246. The question was put to rest in the Federal courts and in effect in the State courts by the decision of the Supreme Court of the United States in Marbury *v.* Madison, 1 Cranch, 137, 1803, in which the opinion was given by Chief-Justice Marshall. This is the "adamantine demonstration" referred to by Mr. Choate in the text. Of Marbury *v.* Madison, Chancellor Kent had previously

Other nations have what they call constitutions or fundamental laws; England, for example. But no provision is beyond the transcendent and omnipotent power of Parliament. And therefore De Tocqueville denied that England had in reality a constitution. His striking passage on this subject is: "The Parliament has an acknowledged right to "modify the Constitution; as, therefore, the Con- "stitution may undergo perpetual changes, *it does* "*not in reality exist;* the Parliament is at once a "legislative and a constituent assembly." In the American conception of the office and effect of a constitution, De Tocqueville's criticism is formally just. Belgium and France have written constitutions, but since they practically have no legal sanction, they are mere glittering declarations of abstract principles of political morality or action,

Lecture VII.

American constitutions discriminated from European.

said that it "approaches to the precision and certainty of a mathematical demonstration." 1 Com., 453. It deserves the high praise, for this doctrine established in Marshall's language, that ours was "a government of laws and not of men." "It lies," as Mr. Hitchcock well says, "at the very root of our system of government." "Constitutional History of the United States" (Putnam, 1890), p. 77. The following is Mr. Justice Miller's weighty comment thereon: "The immense importance of this decision [Marbury v. Madison], though in some respects *obiter*, since the court declared in the end that it had no jurisdiction of the case, may be appreciated when it is understood that the principles declared, which have never since been controverted, subjected the ministerial and executive officers of the government, all over the country, to the control of the courts, in regard to the execution of a large part of their duties. Its application to the very highest officers of the government, except perhaps the President himself, has been illustrated in numerous cases in the courts of the United States, and in the reports of the Supreme Court. Perhaps one of the latest and most instructive of these is the case of United States *v.* Schurz, 102 U. S. Rep., 378." Ann Arbor Address, 1887; Miller on the Constitution, p. 386. Carson, "Hist. Sup. Court U. S.," chap. xiii.

Lecture VII.

having no force except such as public opinion may give them. They are not laws, since their restrictions and directions will not be enforced by the courts.[1] We are told on good authority [2] that "during a period of more than fifty years no Belgian judge ever pronounced a parliamentary enactment unconstitutional," and that "no French tribunal would hold itself at liberty to disregard an enactment, however unconstitutional, passed by the National Assembly, inserted in the 'Bulletin des Lois' and supported by the force of the government."

American constitutions praised by foreign critics.

Foreign statesmen and lawyers, after observing the workings of our constitutions in this regard for more than a century, at length join in praising the wisdom of the American device. Thus, Professor Dicey in his Oxford Lectures [3] on the "Law of the Constitution," says: —

"This system [the American system], which makes the judges the guardians of the Constitution, provides the only adequate safeguard which has hitherto been invented against unconstitutional legislation"[4] "The glory of the founders of the United States is to have devised or adopted arrangements under which the Constitution became in reality as well as in name the supreme law of the land."[5]

---

[1] See *ante* Lecture I.
[2] Dicey, "The Law of the Constitution," 2d ed. London, 1886, lecture iv., p. 144.
[3] 1886.
[4] Lecture iii., p. 125.
[5] Lecture iv., p. 145. "The distinguishing feature of our institutions," says Judge Sharswood, "is what we term Constitutional Law.

The great fundamental rights guaranteed by the constitutions are life, liberty, contracts, and property. The two former are everywhere respected and protected by the legislatures and the courts. I recall only one notable exception to this statement, and that is found in the decision of the Supreme Court of Pennsylvania, affirmed by the Supreme Court of the United States, that the legislature could constitutionally prevent a man from pursuing what was, in fact, a lawful business, namely, the manufacture and sale of oleomargarine. I have commented on this elsewhere.[1] But we cannot close

Lecture VII.

Fundamental guarantees.

There are and have been constitutions, written and unwritten, organic or fundamental laws. But in all of them, so far as I know, the fundamental laws thus established have no sanction beyond the oath of those intrusted with the administration of them, the force of public opinion, and the responsibility of the representative to his constituent. With us the fundamental laws are, in the strictest sense of the words, *leges legum*. The vital principle of our system is that the act of the legislative body, contrary to the power confided to it by the constitution, is a nullity and absolutely void. The courts must so pronounce, and the executive must enforce their judgments with the whole force of the State. The judiciary is thus necessarily an important branch of the government. Our Bills of Rights are, therefore, not mere enunciations of abstract principles, but solemn enactments by the people themselves, guarded by a sufficient sanction." Sharswood, " Law Lectures," lecture i., p. 23.

[1] Dillon, "Municipal Corporations," 4th ed., vol. i., p. 211, note. I there said: " We cannot but express our regret that the constitution of any of the States, or that of the United States, admits of a construction that it is competent for a State legislature to suppress (instead of regulating) under fine and imprisonment the business of manufacturing and selling a harmless, and even wholesome, article, if the legislature chooses to affirm, contrary to the fact, that the public health or public policy requires such suppression. The record of the conviction of Powell for selling without any deception a healthful and nutritious article of food makes one's blood tingle." I appreciate, of course, the difficulties in the way of the courts when asked to disregard the false recital in the legislative act, and I recognize the further fact

Lecture VII.

Attacks on private property.

our eyes to the fact that to some extent the inviolability of contracts, and especially of private property, is menaced both by open and covert attacks. Property is attacked openly by the advocates of the various heresies that go under the general name of socialism or communism, who seek to array the body of the community against individual right to exclusive property, and in favor of the right of the community in some form to deprive the owner of it or of its full and equal possession and enjoyment.

Property, or the full measure of its rightful enjoyment, is also covertly invaded, not by the socialist, but at the instance of a supposed popular demand; in which case the attack is directed against particular owners or particular forms of ownership, and generally takes the insidious, more specious, and dangerous shape of an attempt to deprive the owners — usually corporate owners — of their property by unjust or discriminating legislation in the exercise of the power of taxation, or of eminent domain, or of that elastic power known as the police power, — such legislation resulting, and intended to result, in "clipping" the property, or "regulating" the owner out of its full and equal enjoyment and use. Among the people of our race the era of the despotism of the monarch or of an oligarchy has passed away. If we are not struck with judicial blindness we cannot fail to see that what is now to be feared and

---

that the courts cannot supply a panacea for legislative misdoings; but still I think that invasions of fundamental rights, such as the right to pursue what is *in fact* a lawful business, ought not to be dependent upon the epithets with which a legislative majority may see fit to characterize it.

guarded against is the despotism of the many, — of the majority. Speaking of Great Britain, Sir Frederick Pollock recently said that "at no time "has it been fitter for us to be put in mind *that the* "*effective power of law is not only the work but the test* "*of a civilized commonwealth,* and that law, as a great "English writer has said, is in its nature contrary "to such forces and operations as are 'violent and "casual.'"[1]

The statesmen who founded and shaped our democratic, or more accurately speaking republican, institutions, were fully alive to these great truths. They were neither visionaries nor socialists.[2] It is among the eternal lessons of history,

Lecture VII.

The wisdom of the founders of our institutions.

---

[1] Oxford Lectures and Other Discourses, London, 1890, lecture iv., p. 100. So, before the kingly office was separated from the judicial office, David prayed : " Give the King thy judgments, O God, that they may come down like rain into a fleece of wool, even as the drops that water the earth ; " that is to say, gently like the fertilizing rain, and not violently like the destructive deluge. Psalm lxxii., version of the English Prayer-Book.

[2] They were really English Whigs of the Chatham and Burke school. The contest with England did not originate in any sentimental or speculative notions of the rights of man, or in any hostility to monarchy or the form of the English government. The Colonies made but a single issue, — namely, that they ought not to be taxed by a Parliament in which they were not represented. This contest began and was settled years before the French Revolution, and had nothing in common with it. The colonists claimed nothing but English liberties, and wanted nothing beyond Magna Charta. It was a contest for English liberties. So they regarded it, and so it was regarded by their friends and supporters in England. Thus, in Burke's address to the King occurs the passage on the subject, which Lord Grenville said "was the finest that Burke ever wrote, — perhaps the finest in the English language, — beginning, 'What, Gracious Sovereign, is the empire of America to us, or the empire of the world, if we lose our own liberties?'" "Life of Sir James Mackintosh" (American Ed., Little, Brown, & Co., 1853, vol. ii.,

Lecture VII.

Restraints on popular power necessary.

which they well knew, that the mass of the people were subject to the influence of supposed temporary interests and of "violent and casual forces" which might be in conflict with their own vital and permanent well-being.

Burke, perhaps the deepest and wisest political thinker of any age, speaking on this subject, says:

"Society requires not only that the passions of "individuals should be subjected, but that even in "the mass and body, as well as in the individuals, "the inclinations of men should be thwarted, their "will controlled, and their passions brought into "subjection. This can only be done by a *power* "*out of themselves*, and not in the exercise of its "function subject to that will and to those passions

p. 475). The colonists had the English love of precedents, and rebelled according to English forms. As in the English Revolution James II. was declared to have "abdicated," so curiously enough in the indictment of George III., which the Declaration of Independence really is, they asserted that he "has abdicated his government here by declaring us out of his protection and waging war against us." Singular abdication that of a king who was at the time fighting his accusers with his combined armies and navies! There was, indeed, no choice, but there was no general inclination to found the new governments upon any other basis than the sovereignty of the people. The perils as well as the advantages of this form of government, unless the direct exercise of popular power should be restrained, were anxiously felt. This was the great problem to be solved. And in this consists the whole rationale of written constitutions and of the checks and limitations of which the constitutions essentially consist. They did not believe men to be angels, but very human. Accordingly the constitutions which they builded are, as Professor Bryce forcibly puts it, "the work of men who believed in original sin, and were resolved to leave open to transgressors no door which they could possibly shut," with the result that the constitutions they established, "if regarded simply in their legal provisions, were the least democratic of democracies." Bryce, "The American Commonwealth," vol. i., pp. 299, 300.

"*which it is its office to bridle and subdue. In this* *sense the restraints on men, as well as their liberties,* *are to be reckoned among their rights.*"[1] Realizing these truths and the necessity of safeguarding these vital and permanent interests, the founders of our political and legal institutions originated — and the device is, as I have said, the crowning proof of their wisdom — the American polity of constitutional restraints upon all of the departments of the governments which the people established.

Lecture VII.

All of the original States in their first constitutions and charters provided for the security of private property, as well as of life and liberty. This they did either by adopting, in terms, the famous thirty-ninth article of Magna Charta which secures the people from arbitrary imprisonment and arbitrary spoliation, or by claiming for themselves, compendiously, all of the liberties and rights set forth in the Great Charter.[2] I make this statement as to the action of the original States after a careful examination of their charters and constitutions. On the admission into the Union of subsequent States, the constitution of each contained similar provisions.

Provisions of the early constitutions securing life, liberty, and property.

When the Federal Constitution was formed there was inserted in it the provision, also original and

Of the Federal constitution.

---

[1] Burke's Works, American Ed. (Little, Brown, & Co.), "Reflections on the Revolution in France," vol. iii., p. 310.

[2] All of the constitutions of the forty-four States contain like provisions. Mr. Bryce, in his chapter on the "Development of State Constitutions" ("American Commonwealth," vol. i., chap. xxxviii.), did not fail to perceive that "they show a wholesome anxiety to protect and safeguard private property in every way. . . . The only exceptions to this rule are to be found in the case of anything approaching a monopoly, and in the case of wealthy corporations."

unique, "*that no State shall pass any law impairing the obligation of contracts.*"¹

The Fifth Amendment, inter alia, ordained that, — "*No person shall be deprived of life, liberty, or property, without due process of law; nor shall private property be taken for public use without just compensation.*"

This was not new language, or language of uncertain meaning. It was taken purposely from Magna Charta. It was language not only memorable in its origin, but it had stood for more than five centuries as the classic expression and as the recognized bulwark of "the ancient and inherited rights of Englishmen" to be secure in their personal liberty and in their possessions.² It was, moreover, language which shone resplendent with the light of universal justice; and for these reasons it was selected to be put into the Fifth Amendment of the Federal Constitution, as it had already been put into the charters and constitutions of the several States. Thus we see a general, fixed, and settled purpose in both the State and Federal constitutions to protect and secure personal liberty, contracts, and private property.

---

¹ Art. I., § 10. Encroachments from the general government were feared, and this fear led to the speedy adoption of the first amendments to the Constitution. Justice Miller, in the Slaughter-House Cases, says: "The adoption of the first eleven amendments to the Constitution, so soon after the original instrument was accepted, shows a prevailing sense of danger at that time from the Federal power." These amendments were promised and insisted upon. "I hope," said Jefferson, "that a Declaration of Rights will be drawn up to protect the people against the Federal government, as they are *already protected in most cases against the State* government."

² Burke, vol. iii., "Reflections on the Revolution in France," pp. 272, 273, American Ed. (Little, Brown, & Co.).

With these guarantees, — life, liberty, the inviolability of contracts and the sacredness of private property, — the republic set out on its untried course. One hundred years and more have vindicated the necessity and demonstrated the wisdom of these organic limitations. Their value is no longer a matter of speculation or conjecture, but of history.

<small>Lecture VII.

Efficiency of constitutional limitations in protecting contracts and property.</small>

The result of the provision ordaining contracts to be inviolable has been, says Mr. Justice Miller,[1] "to " make void innumerable acts of State legislatures, " intended in times of disastrous financial depression " and suffering to protect the people from the hard- "ships of a rigid and prompt enforcement of the " law in regard to their contracts, and to prevent the " States from repealing, abrogating, or avoiding by " legislation contracts entered into with other par- " ties." Hundreds of acts of State legislation have been declared void under this clause by the Supreme Court, and repudiation, whether intended or unintentional, with its consequent dishonor, has been prevented. Who is not glad that the States, or the people of the States, have not had the power to destroy or impair contracts?

So, likewise, the provisions in the State and National Constitutions protecting private property have up to this time been effective. If disregarded by the legislature, they have been enforced by the courts, — the Constitution being the *supreme* law. These have been, indeed, the great triumphs of our popular system of government, for these were sup-

[1] Michigan, Ann Arbor, Address, 1887; Miller on the Constitution of the United States, p. 393.

Lecture VII.

Successful workings of our constitutions.

posed to be its vulnerable spots. Disbelievers in republican institutions had predicted early shipwreck on these rocks, and when it came not, they simply postponed the period of fulfilment.[1]

[1] Thus Alison, in his famous chapter xc. of "History of Europe," published in 1839-1842, after referring to the universal and equal suffrage which prevails in the United States, says: " As a natural consequence of this state of things, there is, in opposition to the will or passions of the majority, no lasting security either for life or property in America, in cases where the public mind is vehemently excited. Hitherto, indeed, no direct attack on property has been made, — at least where it is vested in land, — for this simple reason, that the majority are themselves landowners, and therefore any such system would be an attack upon their own interests. But the system of spoliating that species of property in which the majority do not participate, and for which they feel no sympathy, has already been carried to a most frightful extent. . . . The determination now openly acted on in many of the States, particularly Arkansas, Illinois, and the democratic communities in the valley of the Mississippi, and even in the great and opulent commercial State of Pennsylvania, to repudiate their State debt and shake off the burden of their public creditors, after they have experienced the full benefit of their capital by expending it on railroads, canals, and other public improvements, is another example of the incipient spoliation of the fund-holders. Their property of all kinds has undergone the most violent attacks in America, except that in land, which, from its diffusion, was protected by the interests of the majority. But the period of danger to them is postponed only, not averted. The period when the attack on landed property, if the present system of government continues, will commence, may be predicted with certainty. It will be as soon as the majority of electors, in any of the States, have come, from the natural growth of other trades, to be persons without any interest in the soil, and when the back settlements have become so distant by the advance of civilization that it is less trouble to take their neighbors' fields than to go to the far West and seek possessions of their own. This is nothing peculiar to America; in every country in the world the majority, under similar circumstances and similar political institutions, would do the same." (Chap. xc., paragraph 64.)

" The rapidity with which the growth of landed estates has begun and progresses ; the immense extent of the *latifundia* ; the approaching exhaustion of available soil, — that seemingly inexhaustible treasure ; the increase of tenant farmers ; the appearance of the agrarian

These prophecies have happily hitherto proved false, — so historically and signally false that as strong an unbeliever in popular government as Sir Henry Maine, speaking of the American Union and its unexampled career, was constrained, in 1885, to confess and declare that, —

Lecture VII.

Sir Henry Maine's opinion as to the basis of American prosperity.

"*All this beneficent prosperity reposes on the sacred-*
"*ness of contract and the stability of private property ;*
"*the first the implement, and the last the reward, of*
"*success in the universal competition.*" [1]

For this frank and candid utterance of a truth which forced itself upon his convictions, I forgive all his doubts as to the success of popular government, and cancel the remembrance of his dismal forebodings.

Then came, as a result of the Civil War of 1861–1865, the Fourteenth Amendment of the Federal Constitution, adopted in 1868, which, among other things, ordained, —

SECTION 1. "*Nor shall any State deprive any*
"*person of life, liberty, or property, without due pro-*
"*cess of law; nor deny to any person within its*
"*jurisdiction the equal protection of the laws.*"

The Fourteenth Amendment to the Federal Constitution.

It was of set purpose that its prohibitions were directed to any and every form and mode of State action — whether in the shape of constitutions, statutes, or judicial judgments — that deprived any person, white or black, natural or corporate, of life, liberty, or property, or of the equal protection of the

question; the radical and socialistic character of the remedies proposed, — these things all show an alteration of the ancient basis on which the political fabric [of the United States] was erected." M. Boutmy, "Studies in Constitutional Law," 1888. See *ante* Lecture I.

[1] Essay on Popular Government, p. 51 (American Ed.).

Lecture VII.

The value of the Fourteenth Amendment.

laws. Its value consists in the great fundamental principles of right and justice which it embodies and makes part of the organic law of the nation. No person is wise enough to foresee the beneficence of the future operation of these principles if the courts are true and firm in maintaining this amendment in its full scope and purpose. I believe it will hereafter, more fully than at present, be regarded as the American complement of the Great Charter, and be to us — as the Great Charter was and is to England — the source of perennial blessings.[1]

The Fourteenth Amendment, while it does not deprive the States of their autonomy or of their power, subject to the Federal Constitution, to regulate their domestic concerns, does nevertheless in the vital matters specified in that amendment operate as an

[1] Speaking of Magna Charta, Sir James Mackintosh has an eloquent passage, which I quote: "It was," he says, "a peculiar advantage that the consequences of its principles were, if we may so speak, only discovered gradually and slowly. It gave out on each occasion only so much of the spirit of liberty and reformation as the circumstances of succeeding generations required, and as their character would safely bear. For almost five centuries it was appealed to as the decisive authority on behalf of the people, though commonly so far only as the necessities of each case demanded. Its effect in these contests was not altogether unlike the grand process by which nature employs snows and frosts to cover her delicate germs and to hinder them from rising above the earth till the atmosphere has acquired the mild and equal temperature which insures them against blights. . . . Her Bacons and Shakespeares, her Miltons and Newtons, with all the truth which they have revealed, and all the generous virtue which they have inspired, *are of inferior value when compared with the subjection of men and their rulers to the principles of justice."*

By the Great Charter, says Stubbs, "the barons maintained and secured the right of the whole people *as against themselves* as well as against their master. . . . The whole constitutional history of England is little more than a commentary on Magna Charta. "Constitutional History of England," vol. i., chap. xii., pp. 596, 597.

express limitation upon the powers of the States. It puts life, liberty, and property, upon precisely the same footing of security. It binds them each and all indissolubly together. It places each and all of these primordial rights under the ægis and protection of the national government. By this provision they are each and all adopted as national rights. Under the Fifth Amendment they are each protected from invasion by Congress or the Federal government. By the Fourteenth Amendment they are each protected from invasion by State legislatures, or by the people of the States in any form in which they may attempt to exercise political power. If these rights are not safe and secure, it is because, and only because, of the essential infirmity of constitutional limitations of the most peremptory character. This we cannot admit. The Fourteenth Amendment in the most impressive and solemn form places life, liberty, contracts, and property, and also equality before the law, among the fundamental and indestructible rights of all the people of the United States.

Lecture VII.

The scope and purposes of the Fourteenth Amendment.

It sets the seal of national condemnation upon Proudhon's famous maxim that "property is theft" (*La propriété c'est le vol*): "Property-holders are thieves." This pernicious doctrine has hitherto found no general acceptance among our people or their legislators; and under the Constitution as it now stands this doctrine can obtain no foothold as to any species of property, — if the courts are faithful to their high trust as the guardians and defenders of the Constitution. Bear in mind ever that this, like all other provisions of the Constitution, was put into the Constitution "to be enforced by the judiciary as

Its protection to property.

one of the departments of the government established by the Constitution."[1] The value, however, of these constitutional guarantees wholly depends upon whether they are fairly interpreted, and justly and with even hand fully and fearlessly enforced by the courts.

In view of these considerations, you must permit me to say that in my judgment the great, paramount, overshadowing duty of the legal profession in this country is to defend, protect, and preserve our legal institutions unimpaired and in their full efficiency. If there is any problem which can be said to be yet unsettled, it is whether the bench of this country, State and Federal, is able to bear the great burden of supporting under all circumstances the fundamental law against popular, or supposed popular, demands for enactments in conflict with it.[2] It is the loftiest function and the most sacred duty of the judiciary, — unique in the history of the world, — to support, maintain, and give full effect to the Constitution against every act of the legislature or the executive in violation of it. This is the great jewel of our liberties. We must not, "like the base Judean, throw a pearl away richer than all his tribe." This is the final breakwater against the

---

[1] United States v. Lee, 106 U. S. Rep., 196, 220, 1882.

[2] See comments of Professor Dicey on Munn v. Illinois and the Legal Tender Cases. "In no country has greater skill been expended in constituting an august and impressive national tribunal than in the United States. Moreover, the guardianship of the Constitution is confided not only to the Supreme Court, but to every judge throughout the land. Still it is manifest that even the Supreme Court can hardly support the duties imposed upon it." "Lectures on the Law of the Constitution," lecture iv., p. 163.

haste and the passions of the people, — against the tumultuous ocean of democracy. It must at all costs be maintained. This done, and all is safe; this omitted, and all is put in peril and may be lost.[1]

Lecture VII.

If these observations are at all timely, if they have aught of value, and especially if they shall excite further thoughts upon the important subjects which I have touched in such an imperfect way, I shall have accomplished all that I sought, and more than I timidly dare to hope. "I shall then," — I use in closing, slightly changed, the quaint and curious reflections of an old writer on the laws of England, — "I shall then, with the vanity of an author, com-"pare myself to one who in his travels over a bleak "and dreary country has picked up some plants, "which he afterwards transfers to some delightful "spot, in a milder climate, where they may attract "notice, even among more agreeable productions, by "those who would never have visited them on their "native soil. And if after all they should have any "medicinal virtues useful in life, they will be wel-"come, wherever they may be made to grow."[2]

Concluding observations.

[1] Judge Cooley, the eminent author of "Constitutional Limitations," in an address to the bar of South Carolina in 1886, uttered these wise and weighty words: "The habit of mind which consents to the doing of constitutional wrong, when it is supposed some temporary good may be accomplished, should be recognized as a foe to constitutional limitations and securities, and which therefore, at any cost, must be corrected."

[2] "Eunomus, or Dialogues concerning the Law and Constitution of England," vol. i., — Essay on Dialogue, p. xc., dated 1767, written by Edward Wynne, Barrister-at-Law.

LECTURE VIII.

Our Law, — its Excellences and Defects. — Doctrine of Judicial Precedent and its Consequences. — Case-law and its Uneven Development. Unfortunate Separation of Legal and Equitable Rights and Remedies. — Unsatisfactory Condition of our Law of Real Property.

<small>Lecture VIII.</small>

IN the earlier lectures of this course I considered our law in its old home, and noticed some of its distinguishing characteristics. In subsequent lectures I considered our law in its new home, — that is to say, its expansion and development in the political and judicial systems of the United States. This development we saw to be a vast extension of the area of the common law, with modifications adapting it to our special situation and circumstances, without, however, changing its generic and essential character. Generally speaking, we found the system of English and of American law to be <small>Characteristics of our law.</small> substantially the same. Having thus surveyed in its great outlines the general field of English and American law, I come in this lecture to consider more in detail its general excellences and its special defects. These defects, however, will be found to be mainly the defects of its good qualities.

No observant person can pass from State to State, from one section of our country to another, without noticing that although we are a homogeneous people, having the same traditions, language, institutions, and aspirations, yet that there are local peculiarities in almost every State or section growing out of the circumstances of its early settlement or history. The people of New England are easily distinguishable from those of New York, and these again from those of Pennsylvania. The Jerseyman has a local flavor. The Western man differs in some respects from the Eastern, and both differ in other respects from the men of the South. And there are local peculiarities among the people of the Southern States. These subordinate diversities are fortunate. They tend to prevent centralization, and to foster and sustain local pride and local government; and local self-government, it cannot be too often enforced, is the true and the only solid basis of our free institutions. A jealous State pride and watchfulness in all that justly belongs to the State, and a dominating national pride and concern in all that justly belongs to the nation, are the valid, healthful, and recognized sentiments of American citizenship and patriotism.

The American lawyer has to deal with problems which are more than ordinarily complicated by the existence of two governments exercising authority over the same territory and people, and largely, at times, over the same subject-matter. But this is unavoidable unless the frame-work of our government is to be changed, the autonomy of the States destroyed, and all power collected at the centre. Few, if any, are so rash as to advocate such changes, and we all cherish the conception of a nation founded upon the indissoluble union of indestructible States, the largest and the smallest being alike protected and secure.

A few years ago I had occasion to visit Block Island, which, although situated in the Atlantic Ocean, is part of the State of Rhode Island. I was going thither to argue by appointment a cause before one of the justices of the Supreme Court of the United States. Some of the counsel in the cause had come within the previous thirty hours on a limited train more than a thousand miles. As our vessel passed the invisible boundary-line of Connecticut into the broad Atlantic, we saw the waves of the ocean as they broke on the shores of the little State of Rhode Island. Little indeed, geographically, since it has but five counties; and it contains less than five hundred thousand people, of whom two hundred thousand live in the single county of Providence. On its north and east is the ancient and honorable Commonwealth of Massachusetts; on its west the comparatively large State of Connecticut; and on its south, almost within range of a modern cannon-shot, is Montauk Point, the eastern terminus of what is fitly called the Empire State, containing six millions of people, and whose territory in its imperial reach stretches seven hundred miles to the westward till it meets the great lakes of Ontario and Erie. There before our eyes was the little State of Rhode Island. Unlike Switzerland, no Alpine ranges of mountains stand there, faithful and indestructible, to sentinel, guard, and preserve her. The open sea washes her coasts and penetrates to her very heart. What

Providence could there be in this facile and fatal exposure to powerful neighbors? But there she was, as there she had been for more than a hundred years. What had so long preserved her existence and integrity? Armies and vessels of war she had none; and yet there she was as safe as England guarded by her royal navies and "encompassed by the inviolate sea." Fortunate nation! composed of States which stand as an impassable bulwark against dangerous centralization, and which are all and alike equally secure, because over all alike and equally is the ægis of the Constitution.

Lecture VIII.

While we all rejoice in the nation's greatness and promise for the future, we cannot overlook the fact that out of our rapidity of growth, out of our vast extent of territory, out of the universal right of suffrage, and out of our dual system of government, State and Federal, and the corresponding legislative and judicial systems, arise causes which operate to produce a complicated and in some respects an imperfect system of laws and jurisprudence; and that these originate problems of great difficulty for solution by statesmen, legislators, and lawyers.

Causes which produce intricate and difficult legal problems in the country.

We have to deal with the situation as it is. The people of forty-four States are legislating for themselves in respect of subjects over which the National Government has happily no control. With forty-four State courts of last resort and as many Federal courts sitting within these States and largely exercising a concurrent jurisdiction over the same people and the same subjects, the development of a harmonious and symmetrical system of jurisprudence is attended with unusual difficulties. Conflict of opin-

Effect of the autonomy of the States on our legal system.

ion is inevitable, and there is no common, superior tribunal, except in a limited class of cases involving Federal questions, — that is, questions arising under the Federal Constitution, treaties, and acts of Congress, which may go to the Supreme Court of the United States for authoritative settlement. It must be confessed that the legal profession in this country has done as yet but little thorough work in remedying those defects in our laws which admit of it. Mainly these must be studied, cultivated, and improved within and through the several States.[1] But State lines for commercial and social purposes have almost disappeared. Our merchants buy and sell goods, our people make contracts and engage in business of all kinds, without much, if any, reference to State boundaries and State citizenship. By means of our rivers and lakes, and especially our railways, the most distant parts of our country are nearer to Washington or New York than these cities were to each other fifty years ago.

Let us glance for a moment at the effect, actual and probable, of the rapid means of travel and communication supplied by our railway and telegraph systems upon the practice of our profession and ultimately upon the character of our laws. Lawyers have ceased to be provincial, and the freedom of intercourse between all sections of the country cannot fail to strengthen the tendency to assimilate our laws and jurisprudence and make them more uniform. Formerly causes were argued in the Supreme Court at Washington largely by members of the local bar of that city, Baltimore,

[1] See *ante* Lecture V.

and other places near at hand, and by distinguished lawyers who were members of Congress. The local counsel, except in cases of great importance, were not accustomed to follow their causes to Washington. Before the introduction of railways, the journey to the capital was difficult, wearisome, and time-consuming. Mr. Justice Story's letters show that in his time it required the greater part of two weeks to make the dreaded journey from Washington to Boston.[1] As a rule, counsel from all parts of the country now attend their cases to the Supreme Court. This is as it should be, since, everything else being equal, the counsel who have tried the cause below are better qualified to argue it above than counsel who are first engaged after the appeal. Besides, it brings the court into contact with the bar of the country at large, to the manifest advantage of both.

As illustrative of the changed condition in the practice of the law resulting from the ease and rapidity of railway travel, you may be interested in the following extract from a letter written to me by a leading lawyer of St. Louis, now the Secretary of the Interior.[2] Of three cases which he named, he says: "To get and serve an injunction in the first, "I travelled sixteen hundred miles. To argue the "second at Denver, I travelled both ways two thou-

Lecture VIII.

Effect of railways and telegraphs upon the practice of the profession.

---

[1] Mr. Justice Story writing to his wife, March 12, 1812, from Washington, says: "It will probably take me twelve days to reach home after I set out on the journey." "Life and Letters of Joseph Story, edited by his son, William W. Story," Little & Brown, Boston, 1851, vol. i., p. 219. The same journey is now made without change of cars in less than twelve hours.

[2] The Hon. John W. Noble.

"sand miles. In the Bank case I also travelled two thousand the last trip, and had previously travelled in the same case over four thousand miles. At Denver I met a judge of the Federal Court, and also lawyers, who had travelled further than I. How striking the contrast," he adds, "with the practice *in the old times*." When I was a Federal circuit judge in a circuit which embraced seven States, and which extended on the north from the international boundary-line. between the United States and the Dominion of Canada to Louisiana on the south, and from the Mississippi on the east to the Rocky Mountains on the west, I habitually travelled more than ten thousand miles every year, and my successor did the same. And within the last few years, I have, in the practice of my profession, been called upon to argue cases in Iowa, Missouri, Kansas, North Carolina, Michigan, Illinois, and other States often more than a thousand miles from my residence; and I know lawyers in New York and elsewhere who go to places equally distant whenever their professional business requires it.

You will perhaps excuse my reading the following leaf from my own experience, since it exhibits in a somewhat striking manner, as it seems to me, the conditions under which modern American lawyers practise their profession.

A few years ago a cause arose in New Mexico which involved the ownership of a line of railway from Yuma to El Paso, extending through Arizona, New Mexico, and part of Texas. On the one side lawyers from New York and elsewhere went in a special car twenty-five hundred miles to Santa Fé, the place of trial. I had arranged a telegraphic circuit, and had sent over the wire to the local counsel the text of the entire bill of complaint. On arriving there our car, which contained a parlor, dining-room, sleeping apartments, and a kitchen, was placed upon the side track of our railroad and served as a hotel; and immediately opposite to us, on another railroad, we saw a like car containing the opposing counsel who had journeyed nearly two thousand miles from the West. There, in the heart and centre of the continent, in the shadow of the Rocky Mountains, in the old historic city of Santa Fé, which was founded more than two generations before the "Mayflower" landed at Plymouth, and more than one hundred years before the first English colony sailed into the Ashley River, were these two movable habitations, one of which had come from the Atlantic and the other from the Pacific, drawn up, as it were, in battle array. In an adobe building, one story high, with walls six feet thick, which had been the governor's palace under the Mexican *régime*, and which our government had converted into a court-house, with the old Baldy Mountain, scalped and uncovered, standing in silent majesty and stately grandeur, looking down upon us, we fought for six long midsummer days our legal battle. We fought like lawyers long and well, — that is, earnestly contesting every inch of ground, but with mutual respect and courtesy, and then departed, the one party to the east and the other to the west, leaving our troubles behind us, or rather having unloaded them on the court.

Lecture VIII.

Effect of railways and telegraphs upon the practice of the law.

I have referred to this in order to observe that in no other country on the globe would a similar experience be possible, nor would it have been possible in this country prior to the building of our transcontinental railways.[1] A legislature in a State twenty-five hundred miles distant being about to adjourn, I telegraphed within a short time past the text of an act of great moment to my client, and the same was enacted within three days thereafter. Marshall's judgments and our lines of railway and telegraph have done more than any other visible agencies in making and keeping us one united nation. Let us now pass to the special subject of this lecture, — the excellences and the defects of the English and American systems of law, which I shall consider somewhat more in detail than I have heretofore done.

First, and briefly referring to the merits of these systems of law, I observe that the distinguishing excellence of the English Constitution and system of laws is that under it law is everywhere throughout English institutions and polity predominant and supreme. This, bear in mind, is not only the spirit but the very essence of the Constitution and legal institutions of England. Professor Dicey's excellent work, the "Law of the Constitution," was written mainly to bring out, illustrate, and enforce this truth.[2] Parliament is the legal sovereign, but its

---

[1] Mr. Serjeant Ballantine relates that he was applied to to defend the Gackwar of Baroda, and that he "accepted the retainer, it being the first that was ever received by a member of this bar to appear as an advocate upon any trial in India." Mr. Serjeant Ballantine's Experiences, chap. xlv., 1882.

[2] "Lectures on the Law of the Constitution," second edition, by A. V. Dicey, London, 1886.

will can only be expressed in an act of Parliament, and this at once and necessarily subjects such enactment, both as to its construction and enforcement, to the judicial courts. The crown can act only through ministers, who are *legally* responsible for the act, and thus the crown indirectly, and the minister directly, are brought under the supremacy of the law.[1] You may recall Bacon's well-known remark in his Essays, that judges though they be "lions" yet should be "lions *under* the throne, "being circumspect that they do not check or "oppose any points of sovereignty." This was a covert plea for the prerogative, which Coke fought, which Parliament resisted, and which the Revolution of 1688 finally overthrew, establishing the independence of the judges and the rule and supremacy of the law administered by the judges.[2]

The glory of the English law, establishing the rights of Englishmen, consists in the following principles: The rule of law excludes the exercise of arbitrary power; "Englishmen are ruled by the law "and by the law alone; a man may be punished "for a breach of the law, and he can be punished "for nothing else." Not only so, but equally, if not more, important is the principle that this breach of the law must be established as to all classes and all persons, official and non-official, in the ordinary courts of law. Arbitrary power and special administrative tribunals such as we find in France and other countries administering what the French call *droit administratif*, do not exist. In England the

Lecture VIII.

The essential rights of Englishmen.

[1] Dicey, p. 335.
[2] *Ib.*, pp. 206, 207, 243. See *ante* Lectures I., IV.

<small>Lecture VIII.</small> same law applies to all persons, and it is administered for and against all persons in the great law courts. "The law of England knows nothing of "exceptional offences punished by extraordinary "tribunals."[1] So also direct personal responsibility for torts — for any invasion of the legal rights of another — exists without limit or exception. No command of an official, not even of the crown, can be pleaded in bar to any wrongful act.

It is specially noteworthy in the study of our legal system that these rules of law, so all-embracing and undistinguishing in their application and so effective in their protective energy, have in the main been the work of the courts, which have defined and enforced them. They have their source in the adjudged and established rights of individuals. These rights, secured by the decisions of the courts, make the Constitution of England, and are not created by and are not the product of the Constitution.

<small>Same principles adopted in all their amplitude in this country.</small> These great and fundamental principles, these distinguishing excellences of the English law, have been adopted in all their scope and vigor in this country. We have gone further, and by constitutional limitations upon legislative power we have placed these primordial rights beyond legislative invasion, thereby giving them a theoretical if not an actual, security greater than they possess in the old country.[2] Every American lawyer knows this to be true. The judicial judgments, Federal and State, which establish it are numerous and uniform. I shall only mention a few of the leading cases on

---
[1] Dicey, p. 229.
[2] See *ante* Lectures I., VII.

the subject in the Supreme Court of the United States.[1] In these respects I insist that the law of

[1] "The government of the United States," said Chief-Justice Marshall in Marbury v. Madison, 1 Cranch, 137, "has been emphatically termed a government of laws and not of men." See *ante* Lectures IV., VII. "No man in this country," said Mr. Justice Miller, delivering the judgment of the court in U. S. *v.* Lee, 106 U. S. Rep., 196, 220, "is so high that he is above the law. No officer of the law may set that law at defiance with impunity. All the officers of the government, from the highest to the lowest, are creatures of the law, and are bound to obey it."

This great principle of personal liberty is strikingly illustrated in Kilbourn *v.* Thompson, 103 U. S. Rep., 168, which went so far as to establish that a person may recover damages for an unlawful imprisonment under an express order of the House of Representatives. Speaking of this judgment, Mr. Justice Miller, who wrote the opinion of the court, afterwards said: "This decision, which ultimately resulted in the recovery of a large judgment by Mr. Kilbourn against the serjeant-at-arms, which sum was paid by an appropriation made by the Congress of the United States out of the treasury, was everywhere received with satisfaction. It has been followed in the States of the Union where similar questions have constantly arisen, and is undoubtedly, on account of the assertion by it of the right of the citizen to be protected against the legislative body, and to be proceeded against for any offence only in the judicial branch of the government, one of the most important that has been made in recent years. It is also important as being in some sense a direct control by the Supreme Court of the United States over the decisions and acts of one of the branches of the legislative department of the government, made without authority of the law." Address, June 29, 1887, before the Law Department of the University of Michigan at Ann Arbor; Miller on the Constitution, p. 415.

"It follows, therefore," said the late Mr. Justice Matthews in his address in 1888 before the Yale Law School, "that for every trespass or wrong in person or property which the individual may suffer, the courts of justice are open to him for redress. If his adversary pleads the authority of the government, even in the form of a statute, his defence is not complete unless he further establishes that he has also the warrant of a valid law. It is not sufficient for him to assert a justification by the authority of a State, or of the United States; he is bound to prove his defence, and the Constitution must be both his witness and his judge. This doctrine is founded upon the immutable distinction between the law as it is in its essence under the Constitu-

Lecture VIII.

American liberties.

Lecture VIII.

American liberties.

England and America is superior to the Roman law, either as it anciently existed or as it exists in the States of modern Continental Europe.

tion and the acts of those who as its agents assume its administration." See *ante* Lecture VII.

"'This distinction,' said the Supreme Court in Poindexter *v.* Greenhow, 114 U. S. Rep., 270, 291, 'is essential to the idea of constitutional government. To deny it or blot it out obliterates the line of demarcation that separates constitutional government from absolutism, free self-government based on the sovereignty of the people from that despotism, whether of the one or the many, which enables the agent of the State to declare and decree that he is the State; to say, 'L.'État c'est moi.' Of what avail are written constitutions whose bills of right for the security of individual liberty have been written, too often, with the blood of martyrs shed upon the battlefield and the scaffold, if their limitations and restraints upon power may be overpassed with impunity by the very agencies created and appointed to guard, defend, and enforce them; and that too with the sacred authority of law, not only compelling obedience, but entitled to respect? And how else can these principles of individual liberty and right be maintained, if, when violated, the judicial tribunals are forbidden to visit penalties upon individual offenders who are the instruments of wrong, when they interpose the shield of the State? The doctrine is not to be tolerated. The whole frame and scheme of the political institutions of this country, State and Federal, protest against it. Their continued existence is not compatible with it. It is the doctrine of absolutism, pure, simple, and naked; and of communism which is its twin,— the double progeny of the same evil birth.' The conclusion, indeed, is inevitable that, if the powers of the general government cannot operate directly upon the State governments, considered as political bodies, they nevertheless do operate directly upon every natural and subordinate political person domiciled or being within the territorial limits of the State; and these may be held accountable for their conduct, and amenable to the judicial process of the United States in whatever character they may assume to act; they cannot divest themselves of their direct relation to the government of the nation, of which they are citizens, and of the duty of obedience which that relation necessarily implies."

On this point it was said by the Supreme Court, in delivering judgment *in re* Ayers, 123 U. S. Rep., 443, 507: " The government of the United States, in the enforcement of its laws, deals with all persons within its territorial jurisdiction as individuals owing obedience

I now proceed to present more in detail some of the leading characteristics of English and American law, and to trace the effects thereof for good and for evil on the body of that law as it exists at the present time.

Lecture VIII.

For many ages in the English law the doctrine of the authoritative force of judicial precedent has been part of it.[1] The growth of this doctrine has been briefly traced by Sir William Markby in his "Elements of Law."[2] He says: —

"The resource of the English lawyers when

Judicial precedent.

to its authority. The penalties of disobedience may be visited upon them, without regard to the character in which they assume to act, or the nature of the exemption they may plead in justification. Nothing can be interposed between the individual and the obligation he owes to the Constitution and laws of the United States, which can shield or defend him from their just authority, and the extent and limits of that authority the government of the United States, by means of its judicial power, interprets and applies for itself. If, therefore, an individual, acting under the assumed authority of a State, as one of its officers, and under color of its laws, comes into conflict with the superior authority of a valid law of the United States, he is stripped of his representative character, and subjected in his person to the consequences of his individual conduct. A State has no power to impart to him any immunity from responsibility to the supreme authority of the United States."

"By means of this judicial power," says Justice Matthews, "the supremacy of the government of the United States may be asserted and vindicated in all cases whatsoever, even to the extent of determining for itself, and against all adverse claims, the limits of its own authority. It may prescribe by its legislative power, penalties and punishments for disobedience to any of its laws, and the validity of those laws can finally be determined only in its own courts; and if, in violation of their allegiance, individual citizens organize and arm by military force to overthrow or defeat its authority, they become liable to judicial punishment as in other cases of treason against the sovereign power."

[1] See *ante* Lecture VI.   [2] §§ 90–93.

Lecture VIII.

Judicial precedent.

"called on to fill the gap which was elsewhere "supplied by the Roman law was custom. Of "this custom the judges were themselves, in the "last resort, the repository." Ages before Hale's and Blackstone's time the authoritative force of prior decisions was established.[1] "Thus it comes to pass," continues Markby, "that English case- "law does for us what the Roman law does for "the rest of Western Europe. And this difference "between our common law and the common law "of Continental Europe has produced a marked "difference between our own and foreign legal "systems. Where the principles of the Roman law

---

[1] In Horwood's Year-Book, 32 Edw. I., p. 32, A. D. 1304, Herle, J., said: "But see whether he shall be received to aver these three causes: for the judgment to be by you now given will be hereafter an authority in every *quare admissit* in England." This is cited by Professor Hammond (1 Blacks. Com., 214, notes), and he adds, "It is useless, however, to multiply quotations upon a point so thoroughly wrought into the very foundation of English law," and thereupon the learned annotator proceeds to examine the rationale of the doctrine. Freeman speaks of the "Englishman's love of precedent," ascribing to this cause not only the growth of the common law, but also the growth of the unwritten Constitution of England. "Growth of the English Constitution," chap. iii. In another place he declares that "the life and soul of English law has ever been precedent." *Ib.*, chap. ii. As to the development of the doctrine of precedent in the Court of Chancery, Spence's Equity, vol. i., pp. 410, 416, 423, 712. Lord Eldon in his judgments frequently admitted that courts of equity equally with courts of law were bound by what had been previously decided and settled. "Life of Lord Eldon," by Horace Twiss, vol. iii., pp. 440–449. See particularly what Lord Eldon says in Gee *v.* Pritchard, 2 Swanst. 414: Davis *v.* Duke of Marlborough, *Ib.*, 162, 163; Attorney-General *v.* Forster, 10 Vesey, 342; Davis *v.* Lord Strathmore, 16 Vesey, 429. But he insisted upon great carefulness in making sure that the precedents did settle the law, and also in their application, Maundrell *v.* Maundrell, 10 Vesey, 259. See further Story's Equity, vol. i., §§ 18–23, as to the general value and authority of precedents in courts of equity.

"are adopted, the advance must always be made on "certain lines. An English or American judge can "go wherever his good sense leads him. The result "has been that whilst the law of Continental Eu-"rope is formally correct, it is not always easily "adapted to the changing wants of those amongst "whom it is administered. On the other hand, the "English law, whilst it is cumbrous, ill-arranged, "and barren of principles, whilst it is obscure and "not unfrequently in conflict with itself, is yet a "system under which justice can be done. Any-"how, it stands alone in the history of the world."[1]

Lecture VIII.

The point I wish you to notice is that the authoritative force of judicial precedents is an established and up to the present time at least an essential part of the English and American systems of law. Let us trace more at large the scope and effect of this important doctrine. What is judicial precedent? Judicial precedent is not simply part of the law in a general sense, — that it is natural to yield to the influence of example and to follow what has been practised, — but it is a part of our law in a sense and with effects which are distinctively and most strikingly peculiar. The doctrine as established is shortly this: that a decision by a court of competent jurisdiction of a point of law lying so squarely in the pathway of judicial judgment that the case could not be adjudged without deciding it, is not only binding upon the parties to the cause in judgment, but the point so decided becomes, until it is reversed or overruled, evidence of what the law is in like cases, which the courts are bound to fol-

Judicial precedent an essential part of our legal system.

[1] Markby, "Elements of Law," § 92.

Lecture VIII.

low not only in cases precisely like the one which was first determined, but also in those which however different in their origin or special circumstances stand, or are considered to stand, upon the same principle. What is to be observed and remembered is that the adjudged case has an authoritative and not merely persuasive force. The doctrine is not limited in its scope and binding effect to cases which determine the true construction of a statute, but extends to the far larger class of cases which does not depend upon positive legislation, but must be determined by general reasoning. There is a difference of opinion among writers as to whether the precedent actually constitutes the law or is only authoritative evidence thereof. It is not proposed now to enter upon this discussion; it is enough to remark at this time that the precedent has in our legal system an authoritative effect. In Continental Europe a judicial decision has no authoritative force in any other case, whether in the same or any other court. But in England and in this country a point solemnly decided has the force and effect of law, binding the judges in all other cases that clearly fall within its principle, and which the judges are therefore bound to follow and apply, unless, to use Blackstone's well-known and much criticised qualification, the precedent is "flatly absurd or unjust."[1]

The scope and effect of the doctrine of judicial precedent.

[1] See 1 Blacks. Com., Introduction, § 3, pp. 69–71, and Professor Hammond's critical and learned note, 30, Hammond's Ed., pp. 213–226; also Christian's and Chitty's notes on the passage cited in the text. Hale: "The History of the Common Law," Runnington's Ed., 1779, chap. i., pp. 3, 6, 7; chap. iv., pp. 65–69. Clark: "Practical Jurisprudence," 1883, pp. 225–230, 244–246, also part ii., chap. v. Markby: "Elements of Law," § 91. Rationale, early importance

The direct and indirect consequences of the doctrine of judicial precedent in our law, for good and for evil, present a subject of such moment as to demand the most anxious consideration. It cannot, of course, be dealt with at large within the limits of a single lecture; and I shall essay to deal with it, on this occasion, only in its most general and obvious outlines.

To this doctrine we owe a weight of obligation which cannot easily be overstated. By reason of the authoritative force thus given to judicial decisions and their consequent importance, they have been reported for several hundred years, so that at this time the volumes of reports in England and this country number about eight thousand. These embody the learning, wisdom, and experience of the judges (often men of great intellectual powers) who during this long period have made the law and the practical administration of justice the subjects of profound study. Indirectly the reports embody also the results of the researches, studies, experience, and ability of the bar during the same period, since of these the judges have had the advantage in the argument of the causes so decided. Indeed, the doctrine of judicial precedent implies that the point to the decision whereof such force is attributed should have been argued by opposing counsel.[1]

Lecture VIII.

The beneficial consequences of the doctrine of judicial precedent.

---

and value of precedent in English law and politics. Pollock: "Essays in Jurisprudence and Ethics," pp. 52, 214, 216; also chap. ix. on the "Science of Case Law." *Ante* Lecture I., p. 27 *et seq.* and notes; *post* Lectures IX., X.

[1] See *ante* Lecture I. and notes.

234 LAWS AND JURISPRUDENCE.

Lecture VIII.

Value of the judicial reports.

The value of these reports to the lawyer and to the judge is, I repeat, absolutely incalculable. It is a mine of wealth possessed by none but English-speaking peoples. Here the lawyer finds his true riches. What the art collections in the Vatican, in the Tribune Room, the Pinacotheks, in the Dresden Gallery, and in the Louvre are to the artist, the judicial reports are to the English and American lawyer. I yield to no one in my estimate of the store of riches they contain. I have not yet mentioned one of the chief elements of their possible usefulness. They are capable of being made quite as valuable to the legislator as to the lawyer, since the uninterrupted light of the experience of many generations of men shines forth from them to mark out and illumine the legislator's pathway. *He need scarcely take a single step in the dark.*

The other side of the account.

Let us now glance at the other side of the account. Throughout the greater part of the long period in which this stupendous work of judicial legislation has been silently going on, whereby the law has been constantly growing and changing by what has been likened to a species of judicial alluvion, the Parliament in England and the legislative bodies in this country have not interfered (except quite recently in respect of a few subjects) for the purpose of systematizing the law or reducing distinct branches of it into written and definite form. The consequence has been that the law has necessarily had an irregular and incomplete development.

The accidental origin and the consequent irregular development of so much of the jurisprudence of England, from which ours is borrowed, are among the most singular phenomena in its history. Of this our equity system is a notable example. It is, in fact, almost accidental that unlike any other legal system we have a separate Court of Chancery, or what is equivalent to it, with all the momentous consequences which have flowed from the separation of the two jurisdictions of law and equity, and the creation of equitable rights and estates distinct from legal. The Court of Chancery came into existence by reason of the jealous spirit and narrow conservatism of the common-law judges, and could have been avoided by a timely and simple act of Parliament.

Lecture VIII.

Accidental origin and irregular development of English law; whereof the Court of Chancery is a notable example.

These two great streams have so long flowed in distinct channels that although we regret the injurious consequences of the unnecessary separation, yet with the habitual caution of our profession we hesitate to unite them because we cannot clearly foresee all the results. The tendency to their union is, however, marked and strong. The law stream is ever increasing its volume and momentum, and is, though unperceived, inexorably eating away the narrow banks which divide it from the equitable.[1] Nothing that lies in the future seems to me more certain to occur than that at no very distant period they are destined to join each other, and to form a grand and lordly stream, which after the first disturbance is over Denham's lines will fitly describe, —

"Though deep yet clear, though gentle yet not dull,
Strong without rage, without o'erflowing full."

[1] *Post* Lecture XIII.

Lecture VIII.

But whether this shall occur or not, the law and equity reports of England and America contain the recorded experience growing out of the actual transactions and affairs of men during the hundreds of years in which our jurisprudence has been making its growth and attaining the developed condition in which we find it to-day.

Judicial power can of course be exerted only as cases arise for decision. It was entirely fortuitous when, if ever, a given point would arise for judgment; and only such points as actually arose could be authoritatively dealt with by the courts. Sir Frederick Pollock, in a paper of marked excellence, has given several interesting illustrations of the wonderfully uneven and anomalous growth of case-law, as a result of its dependence upon "the casual exigen- "cies of litigation to determine what parts of it shall "be filled up and what left incomplete," observing, and truly, that "all kinds of curious little questions "receive elaborate answers, while great ones remain "in a provoking state of uncertainty."[1]

Uneven growth of case-law.

[1] Pollock, "Essays on Jurisprudence and Ethics," chap. iii., London, 1882. He refers, among others, to the very common case of a sale of goods on credit for a fixed period, the goods meantime to remain in the seller's possession, the buyer agreeing to pay for and remove them at a specified time. Suppose the time of credit expires and the buyer fails to call and pay for them according to the contract, what then are the rights of the seller? The law on such a point certainly ought to be plain, yet more than thirty years ago Lord Blackburn, in his work on Sale (the basis of Mr. Benjamin's more elaborate treatise on the same subject), said that the question was largely unsettled, and unsettled on many points it remains to this day. The courts in England have adjudged that the seller cannot *rescind* the contract and hold the goods as owner. This seems of doubtful soundness, and the law in many countries is otherwise. But as he cannot rescind, the practical question remains, May he *resell* the goods at the buyer's

He shows that until 1851 the law concerning a not uncommon commercial transaction was wholly undecided; it was then decided against the *dicta* of the Common Pleas expressed years before. When it was at length decided it was, I submit with deference, wrongly decided; and then follows the suggestion of the Judicial Committee of the Privy Council refining away a wrong decision by the usual process of exceptions, which in the course of time eats up the rule itself; but whether the suggestion of the Judicial Committee will be adopted by the House of Lords some ten or fifty years hence, and thus made law, must meanwhile remain to merchants and lawyers in doubt and uncertainty. Parliament could settle it by a single clause in a Contract Act if it would. This case is typical of scores of others in every branch of the law, to which, if time permitted, it would be easy to refer.

Lecture VIII.
——
Uneven growth of case-law: illustration.

Continuing the consideration of defects in our legal system, I have long thought that the law of Real Property, at least in this country, is in a most

risk? Fifty years ago, the Common Pleas, says Professor Pollock, was strongly inclined to the opinion (but did not adjudge the point) that the seller had this right. The question did not arise for decision until 1851, when the Queen's Bench held that he had no such right; that a resale by him would be an actionable breach of the contract, for which he would be liable to the purchaser in damages, actual or nominal, as the case might be; and if any profit was made, the seller must account therefor to the defaulting buyer. How the House of Lords may decide, if the question ever gets there, no one can foresee. And thus stands the law to-day, except that the Judicial Committee of the Privy Council, about twenty-five years ago, suggested that if the seller should give the buyer express notice of his purpose to sell, he might not be liable to an action; but we must remember that the Privy Council's opinions and judgments are not authoritative.

unsatisfactory condition. The American law is substantially borrowed from the English law. Owing to the mode of its development the English law of landed property is refined and intricate to an extent which makes an acquisition of a thorough knowledge of it the work of years, and largely confines the practice thereof to a branch of the profession known as real estate lawyers and conveyancers. If this were really necessary, it should be uncomplainingly endured.

In England and America the law of Real Property is almost wholly distinct from the law of Personal Property. Many of the distinctions do not inhere in the two classes of property. The essential qualities of all property, whether real or personal, are its duty to contribute to the rightful demands of the State in the exercise of the right of taxation and of eminent domain, its liability to creditors, and the right of the owner to enjoy it, to alien it, to have it descend to his heirs, or to dispose of it by will. The existing law in England and the United States not only makes many unnecessary distinctions between Real and Personal Property, but it has, not by design, but as the result of historical causes, divided the rights of Real Property into two great classes of legal estates and equitable interests, — the one set of rights administered by courts of law, or courts which apply legal rules, and the other by courts of chancery, or courts which apply the doctrines of equity.

The doctrines of chancery concerning equitable estates, in part self-originated and in part borrowed from the civil and in part from the feudal law, and which had their origin in the necessity of modifying the mischievous doctrine of feudal tenures so as to adapt in some measure the crude and inadequate system of the early law to the wants and necessities of advancing civilization, became refined and complicated, obscure and intricate, by the very circumstances of their anomalous and irregular development. The chancellors undertook no systematic treatment of the subject. By the very nature of their functions they could not. Guided by no fixed rules or principles, they interfered from time to time, as single cases arose, to remedy defects in the common law, or to correct certain hardships therein, which were no longer tolerable. Nor did Parliament in this period of growth and change undertake to deal with the subject at large. When some grievous abuse pressed so heavily that it could no longer be endured, the remedial interposition of the legislature was confined to redressing that. The practice and perhaps even the conception that it was the proper function of the legislature to reduce the law on a given subject to a systematic and definite form did not exist. This conception came only in more recent times.

Lord St. Leonards relates that he received at one time a letter from an American lawyer, stating that an edition of his work on Powers would probably soon be required in this country, whereupon this learned author (who might á priori have been supposed to revel in the artificial and intricate distinctions between Powers Appendant and Appurtenant, Powers Collateral and in Gross, and Powers simply Collateral), with a deep sense of their essen-

Lecture VIII.

Sources of the complexity of the law of Real Property.

tial uselessness and mischief, remarked, "I regretted "at the time that a new State should embarrass "itself with our forms of conveyancing springing "out of the doctrine of uses."

Real Property with us does not serve as the foundation for personal distinction or family grandeur, and is invested with no peculiar sanctity. Its uses are those of property simply. It is an article of commerce, and its free circulation is encouraged. Without going into further details, I insist that the law of Real Property in this country ought to be assimilated as near as possible to the law of Personal Property, and that it is practicable to emancipate it from all of the pernicious consequences of tenure, whether existing by the common law or growing out of the doctrine of uses, and to make it as simple and easily understood as the law concerning personalty. I do not deny that the English law has by means of fictions, by force of a few statutes, and by the course of decision in the courts of chancery for two hundred years, been moulded so that the combined system of legal and equitable rights and remedies meets the wants and accords with the prevailing sentiments of the English people; but it is demonstrable that even there it is unnecessarily abstruse, complex, and uncertain. But I do earnestly maintain that it is owing simply to the inertia and conservatism of our bar that it is willing to let this great department of our law remain in its present condition, — chaotic, uncertain, complex, and abounding in subtleties and refinements; and this, although it is practicable to make it as simple, clear, and certain as any other part of our laws. Let us at length have deliverance from the remaining vestiges of the bondage of the Norman conqueror, and from the heavy burdens which a long succession of English chancellors, albeit without any fault of theirs, have imposed upon us.[1]

Lecture VIII.

I shall pursue the general subject — the excellences and defects of our laws — in the next lecture.

NOTE. — Undoubtedly the American law of real property is upon a better footing than the English original. It is perhaps on a better footing than the law of real property as it contemporaneously exists in England. Some years ago a writer in the "American Jurist" thus summarized correctly the general character of the changes that had been made in the American States: —

"(1) Abolition of feudal tenure, including copyhold; (2) abolition of tithes; (3) making both the real and personal property of intestates descend to the same persons; (4) enabling parents to become heirs to their children; (5) abolition of primogeniture and preference of males in descent; (6) making all estates descend in the same course, whether acquired by purchase or by descent from paternal or maternal relations; (7) abolishing the preference of male stock in descent; (8) enabling half-blood relations to inherit; (9) making husband and wife heirs to each other in case of failure of blood relations; (10) making seisin of land pass by the mere delivery of the deed; (11) the general registration of deeds; (12) making a fee simple pass without the word 'heirs' or any equivalent, where a less estate is not expressed; (13) enabling tenants in tail to convey estates in fee simple without a fine or recovery; (14) enabling married women to convey their estates and bar their dower without a fine; (15) change of joint tenancies into tenancies in common unless otherwise expressed; (16) removing largely the disabilities of alienage with regard to real property; (17) abolition of the doctrine of tacking in mortgages; (18) placing land mortgage, as well as the debt for which it is security, at the disposal of the mortgagee's executor; (19) making all real estate liable to execution for debt; (20) rendering real estate assets for payment of all debts without any preference; (21) shortening the time of limitation."

These changes do not at all invalidate or impair the views expressed in the text as to desirableness of further amendments in the law relating to real property, of the character therein suggested.

[1] See *ante* Lecture VI.

LECTURE IX.

Our Law: Its Uncertainty and Enormous Bulk. — Suggestions as to the Scope and True Methods of Amending the Laws; and herein Codification Considered. — The True Office and Use of Adjudged Cases (Note).

<small>Lecture IX.</small>

IN my last lecture I referred to the accidental and uneven development of case-law as one of the causes which contributes to make our law defective. I am now to refer to some other causes which operate to the same end, and shall afterwards offer some suggestions as to the true scope and method of its amendment.

<small>Why case-law is necessarily incomplete.</small>

It is manifest that the judges, from the very nature and limitations of their functions, cannot develop the general principles of the law so as to take in the entire subject, or do anything except (if you will pardon the expression) automatically (that is, depending upon the accident of cases arising for judicial action) towards giving completeness to the law, or any branch of it.

Not only is case-law incomplete, but the multiplicity and conflict of decisions are among the most fruitful causes of the unnecessary uncertainty, which characterizes the jurisprudence of England and America. Thousands of decisions are reported every year. An almost unlimited number can be found upon almost any subject. This is especially true in this country where we have forty-four State courts of last resort. What any given case decides must be deduced from a careful examination of the exact facts, and of the positive legislation, if any, applicable thereto. A general principle will be found laid down by certain courts. Other courts deny or doubt the soundness of the principle. Exceptions are gradually, but certainly, introduced. Almost every subject is overrun by more than a tropical redundancy of decisions, leaving in many cases the most patient investigator entangled in doubt. In his helplessness and despair, the lawyer, wearied with the toilsomeness of an unsatisfactory and unrewarded search " through the palpable obscure," is often tempted to wish all the reports " in the deep bosom of the ocean buried."

<small>Lecture IX.

Multiplicity and conflict of decisions as causes of uncertainty in our laws.</small>

The confusion is made worse by the usual course of legislation, which is, in general, irregular and fragmentary. The Legislature, ordinarily, does not attempt a systematic enactment or complete revision of the law on a given subject. It pre-supposes that the common law is certain and known. Some change is deemed necessary. It is made by a statute, often crudely and imperfectly worded. The statute is then expounded by the courts as occasion arises. If the statute as interpreted (as is frequently the case) falls short of, or goes beyond, or fails to meet the end desired, another and often several additional enactments are passed. So the work of amendment and re-amendment and judicial interpretation " goes on, till we have a series of statutes,

<small>Fragmentary legislation as another cause.</small>

Lecture IX.

"which to an uninitiated observer might seem to deal with their whole subject, but are really mere islands scattered in an ocean of case-law."[1] And thus, of necessity, the law on any given point has to be deduced as the result of an inquiry into the common law, and a study of the legislation and of the decisions under different statutes.

Effect of uncertainty in the law on the administration of justice.

The effect of the existing uncertainty in the law upon the administration of justice was very much considered in a report to the American Bar Association at its meeting at Saratoga in August, 1885, made by a special committee appointed to consider whether the present delay and uncertainty in judicial administration could be lessened, and, if so, by what means? The report was mainly written by Mr. David Dudley Field. After considering other subjects, the report proceeds: —

"The only remaining element of certainty or uncertainty is the character of the law itself, as it is certain or uncertain. Now, the state of the law we pronounce to be one of the greatest uncertainty. Did we not see many men of fair learning and intelligence affirm the contrary, we should say that all men believed it and all men knew it. This uncertainty comes in a great degree from the nature of the sources whence the law is derived; it is made by the judiciary and not by the Legislature, made to fit particular cases and not by general rules, and made always after the fact. It will not answer the objection to say that the Legislature makes bad laws sometimes; so does

[1] Pollock, "Essays on Jurisprudence and Ethics," London, 1882, chap. iii.

"the judiciary. But the former need not make bad
"laws. If it be not able to make good ones for the
"future conduct of the citizen, leaving the judiciary
"to enforce them, still less is the judiciary able to
"make and enforce good laws for the past conduct
"of the citizen. . . .
"A single word expresses the present condition
"of the law, — chaos. Every lawsuit is an adven-
"ture, more or less, into this chaos. . . . It is idle
"to think of going on as we are going. The con-
"fusion grows worse all the time. Chaos deepens
"and thickens daily. If one would see how it
"works, he has but to look into the case of the
"Bank of the Republic against the Brooklyn City
"and Newtown Railroad Company, in the one
"hundred and second volume of the United States
"Reports,[1] where he will get a glimpse of the chaos,
"and find also an invitation to the judges of New
"York to change their law, as if they were the
"Legislature of the State."[2]

In New York, for more than fifty years, it has been held on general principles, and not by virtue of any statute, that the holder of a negotiable bill or note, who took the same merely as collateral,

Lecture IX.

Report of the American Bar Association on the subject of uncertainty in the law.

[1] Reported under name of Railroad Company v. Railroad Company, 102 United States Reports, p. 14, 1880, which re-affirmed Swift v. Tyson.

[2] The committee consisted of David Dudley Field, chairman, and Edward J. Phelps, James O. Broadhead, Richard T. Merrick, and John F. Dillon. Mr. Merrick died, and Mr. Phelps concurred in the report, "except so far as it advocated and recommended a codification of the common law." Cortlandt Parker, appointed in place of Mr. Merrick, made a separate report in 1886 declaring himself against codification. Report of Association, 1885, pp. 323-367 ; Ib., 1886, pp. 313-385.

246   LAWS AND JURISPRUDENCE.

Lecture IX.
Illustrations of conflict and uncertainty; Bay v. Coddington and Swift v. Tyson.

though without notice, is not such a holder for value as to stand free from equities between the maker and the payee. This doctrine was adopted in New York in Bay v. Coddington.[1] The general principle involved afterwards came before the Supreme Court of the United States in Swift v. Tyson,[2] in which a view different from Bay v. Coddington was taken. Chancellor Kent afterwards, in referring to the subject in his Commentaries,[3] said : " I am inclined to " concur in Swift v. Tyson as the plainer and better " doctrine." Nevertheless, the New York courts still adhere to Bay v. Coddington, but the doctrine of that case is not held to be the law in England nor in most of the States in this country.

Doctrine of Supreme Court of the United States.

The decision referred to in volume 102 of the United States Reports was made by the Supreme Court in a case which arose in New York upon a note which had been made, and was payable in that State. The Supreme Court of the United States did not under the circumstances follow the doctrine of Bay v. Coddington, but on the contrary decided that the holder of negotiable paper by way of collateral, without notice, before maturity, was a *bona fide* holder free from equities between antecedent parties. It is obvious that if the same case had been adjudged in the tribunals of the State of New York instead of the Federal Courts sitting in that State, the result to the parties would have been precisely the reverse of what it was. The case is certainly a striking illus-

---

[1] 5 Johns. Ch., 54 ; s. c., 20 Johns., 637.
[2] 16 Peters, 1.
[3] 3 Com., 81, note.

tration of the two main purposes for which it was referred to in the report; that is, to show the chaotic condition of the law, and that any certain prospect of speedy remedy must come from the Legislature and not from the courts. One of the judges of the Supreme Court, in a note addressed to a member of the committee, thought the criticism that the Supreme Court had "invited the judges of New York "to change their law, as if they were the Legisla-"ture of the State," was not sustained by anything found in the main opinion of the court, nor, as he thought, in the concurring opinion of Mr. Justice Clifford, who "meant only to express the hope that "upon a question of commercial law, not depending "upon legislative enactment, the courts of New "York would acquiesce in the rule announced by "this court, and which obtained in nearly all the "States."

Lecture IX.

Doctrine of the Supreme Court of the United States (continued).

And such, doubtless, was Mr. Justice Clifford's meaning. In my judgment, the decision of the Supreme Court was right, and I am glad that it was able to see its way clear to make it. Mr. Field, on the other hand, denies the soundness of the decision. He insists that there is no such thing as an American common law, as distinguishable from the common law of the several States. The Supreme Court seems to affirm, which he denies, that there is a general commercial law existing throughout the Union. He maintains that the case in hand having arisen on a contract made in New York, and to be performed in New York, can be judged by no other law than the law of New York, while the Supreme Court, considering the case to be one governed

Comments thereon.

by the principles of commercial law, and not depending on any statute, felt at liberty, under the circumstances, to determine for itself what the true principles of that law were, and to hold that they were not bound by what they justly regarded as the erroneous opinions of the New York courts on that subject. But whether the decision of the Supreme Court is right or wrong, the case itself is a notable proof of the existing uncertainty of the law with respect to one of the most frequent and important of commercial transactions; and for this purpose, and this only, have I referred to it at such length.

<small>Colossal bulk of our law as a source of uncertainty therein.</small> Connected with, and in fact producing much of the uncertainty in the law, is its bulk or voluminousness, caused by the large number of reported cases. The extent to which this increases the labors of the bar and bench is much greater than is apt to be supposed by those who have never reflected upon it. As matters stand, it is a work practically necessary in almost every important case, not clearly controlled by special legislation or by an established line of precedent in the particular State, to examine the English and the more important American Reports for decisions which will sustain your positions, or which oppose those of your adversary.

The report of the special committee of the American Bar Association, before referred to, contains some instructive statements on this subject, which show the loss of time and labor caused by the necessity of a resort to the reports of so many different States and countries in order to ascertain what the law is upon subjects which form the staple of current litigation.

"In proof of uncertainty," says the committee,[1] "we can easily find the number of reversals in each "State. We content ourselves with four States. "An examination of the last volume of Reports of "Decisions in the courts of last resort of New York, "Pennsylvania, Ohio, and Virginia, respectively,— "four States which may be considered representa- "tive, and which have Courts of Appeal separate "from the courts of first instance,— gives the follow- "ing results: Volume ninety-seven of the reports of "the New York Court of Appeals contains seventy- "nine decisions, of which thirty-eight were reversals. "The judges cited in their opinions four hundred "and forty-nine decisions, being three hundred and "fifty-three made in New York, fifty-six in Eng- "land, Scotland, and Ireland, eight in our Federal "Courts, seven in Massachusetts, four in Pennsyl- "vania, three in Vermont, two in Connecticut, two "in New Hampshire, two in California, two in Min- "nesota, two in Alabama, and in New Jersey, North "Carolina, Kentucky, Florida, Virginia, Indiana, "Maine, and Iowa one each. Volume one hundred "and five of the Pennsylvania Supreme Court Re- "ports contains ninety-five decisions, of which forty- "four were reversals. The citations of the judges "were four hundred and fifty-one. Volume thirty- "nine of Ohio Supreme Court Reports contains "ninety-eight decisions, of which forty-six were "reversals. The citations were many. Volume "seventy-eight of the Virginia Supreme Court Re- "ports contains eighty-one decisions, of which forty "were reversals. The citations were five hundred

Lecture IX.

Number of reversals as proof of uncertainty.

[1] Report American Bar Association, 1885, p. 329.

Lecture IX.

Loss of time and labor to the bar and bench, caused by the enormous bulk of the laws.

"and seventy-six. The sources of these citations "made by the judges of Pennsylvania, Ohio, and "Virginia, in their opinions, were as various as "those made by the judges of New York.[1]

"These were the decisions cited, examined, and "commented on by the judges in making up their "own opinion. But the decisions cited by counsel "and pressed upon the judges for their consider-"ation were, it is safe to say, ten times as many. "*In volume eighty-eight of the New York Reports,* "*the number of cases cited by counsel was five thou-*"*sand and thirty-seven.* A single case reported in "volume ninety-seven shows that counsel on the "two sides cited two hundred and eighty-five deci-"sions, of which one hundred and twenty-five had "been made in New York, sixty-one in England, "two in Ireland, four in Pennsylvania, four in "North Carolina, four in Massachusetts, two in "New Hampshire, two in New Jersey, two in Ken-"tucky, two in the Federal Reports, and from "Maine, Vermont, Iowa, and South Carolina, one "each."[2]

[1] An examination in August, 1893, of the 136th volume New York reports, 48th Ohio, 88th Virginia, 153d Pennsylvania, being the last volumes of reports in those States respectively, shows the relative number of affirmances and reversals as follows: New York, affirmed, 84, reversed, 30; Pennsylvania, affirmed, 78, reversed, 41; Ohio, affirmed, 24, reversed, 28; Virginia, affirmed, 67, reversed, 64.

[2] Not long since I received the publishers' circular announcement of the sixty-five volumes of American Decisions (a most useful and valuable series of reports), containing, says the circular, 11,119 lead-·ing cases, re-reported, and 158,563 cases cited in the discussion of questions presented. This was not much of a shower, for in the September number, 1892, of the "Green Bag Magazine" some of the merits of the "Encyclopedia of Law," now being published, are thus stated: "In the eighteen volumes already published, there are 830

Of course, many of these citations were loosely, and perhaps many of them were unnecessarily, complete legal treatises, containing 603,551 citations. Besides these treatises, there are 14,502 unusual titles and adjudged words and phrases, upon which there are given 127,302 citations." Think of it! 830 complete legal treatises, and over 600,000 cases cited! Some further details are thus stated by the publishers. "In the twenty volumes published, there are 22,238 large pages, containing 791,564 citations." And these 22,238 pages, be it remembered, are not the body of our case-law, but only a digest of a portion of it. Who shall digest the digest? As indicating what must be the bulk of the opinions digested, the publishers make the following statement of the number of cases on certain titles or subjects, which are digested in the Cyclopedia: —

Railroad law. The Cyclopedia gives 30,045 citations, against 11,461 in Redfield on Railways. *Corporation law.* 14,409 citations, against 7,740 in Morawetz on Corporations. *Real property.* 52,813 against 26,877 in Washburn on Real Property. *Judgments.* Cyclopedia in twelve volumes gives 7,970 citations, against 4,323 in Freeman on Judgments. *Livery-stable keepers.* 379 citations, against 259 in Hanover on Horses, and so on with respect to other titles. Many of these are not arranged on any system or principle, but empirically, under such "unusual titles" as appear below. I quote from the publishers' announcement.

"There are a very large number of small titles in the law which have never received treatment by text-writers, being too small for a separate book upon the subject. By treating the whole field of the law in one large work these all receive treatment. The following are a small portion of the Unusual Titles thus far treated and the number of cases cited: —

"Accidents, 214 cases; Act of God, 204; Alteration of Instruments, 1,041; Ambiguity, 636; Board of Health, 113; Bridges, 649; Civil Damage Laws, 347; Commercial Travellers, 55; Composition with Creditors, 280; Counties, 888; County Commissioners (Supervisors), 513; County Seat, 159; Coupons, 298; Crops, 809; Dams, 655; Default, 3,210; Demand, 3,851; Deputy, 364; Drains and Sewers, 454; Duress, 1,222; Equitable Conversion and Reconversion, 324; Explosion, 96; Express Companies, 1,074; Fences, 1,663; Ferries, 416; Finder of Property, 202; Fish and Fisheries, 385; Gas Companies, 366; Hawkers and Peddlers, 149; Horses, 340; Hospital, 48; Ice and Ice Companies, 160; Identity, 178; Impossible Contracts, 202; Indemnity Contracts, 748; Inns and Innkeepers, 1,225; Interstate Commerce, 350; Intoxicating Liquors, 4,739; Investment, 766; Irrigation, 208; Jeopardy, 1,287; Lakes and Ponds, 422; Literary Property, 134;

made. If we could suppose that counsel and judges all did what they ought, — that is, never cite a case, not only without a careful reading but a careful analysis and study of it and of its bearing upon the proposition it is cited to sustain or oppose, — we can readily imagine the great amount of time that has been consumed, and labor expended, in the mere examination of authorities. Much time and labor in this direction are really unavoidable; but even in the present condition of the law a great deal of such work is wasted because it is wholly unnecessary. This waste arises in part out of the very prevalent failure to appreciate the exact function and value of adjudged cases in arguments at the bar, and to limit their use accordingly. Mr. Justice Miller of the Supreme Court of the United States, having, in a conversation a few years ago, made some observations on this subject, which to me at least were instructive, I addressed him a note asking him to give me briefly his views concerning

Lecture IX.

True office of adjudged cases.

Livery-stable Keepers, 379; Lodgings and Apartments, 386; Logs and Lumber, 608; Lost Papers, 2,295; Manufacturing Corporations, 515."

Such digests are, under existing conditions, necessary or convenient tools or labor-saving instruments to the English and American lawyer, and therefore I do not make the foregoing references to the Cyclopedia by way of criticism upon the work, but as striking proof both of the enormous bulk and the unorganized condition of our case-law. This unwieldy mass of decisions is the direct, and, as I think, natural, if not inevitable result of our doctrine of judicial precedent, which stimulates the growth of case-law, whose colossal and unmanageable proportions, constantly swelling in size, constitute the most remarkable — is it too much to say appalling? — phenomenon in our jurisprudence. Is this a normal and necessary condition? Must it go on forever? Is there any expedient remedy? And if so, wherein does it consist? These are grave and vital problems, which it is the business and duty of the bar to consider and solve, and in respect whereof I have offered some thoughts and suggestions in the course of these lectures.

the true office and use of adjudged cases in our law. He obligingly complied with my request; and I am sure you will be glad to know the views of this great and experienced judge.

He admits that the use of judicial decisions by a judge in making up his judgment in cases before him is often a subject of no little anxiety. He groups the cases into classes. The first class of cases, and perhaps the largest, are cases whose decision turns upon principles that are not disputed. Here the citation or use of authorities is generally useless, since what is required is the just application of acknowledged principles to the case at hand. The second class of cases comprises those that construe constitutions and statutes; and here the decisions of the highest court of the government which adopted the constitution or statutes in question are in most cases conclusive on other courts. The third class of cases — namely, those depending upon general principles of law or equity — must, wherever the decisions are conflicting, be determined by the weight of authority; and it is, in his opinion, in this class of questions that adjudged cases, and the examination and comparison of them by counsel, are of substantial aid to the court. He also makes some useful observations concerning the discrimination that should be made in the selection of the cases to be cited.[1]

I turn now to state some practical conclusions which the brief survey in this and the preceding

[1] That it may be preserved, I print his letter as a note at the end of this lecture.

254   *LAWS AND JURISPRUDENCE.*

Lecture IX.

Suggested remedies for bulk and uncertainty.

Codification, — resolution of the American Bar Association.

lecture of the present condition of our laws leads me to suggest for your consideration.

The report of the special committee of the American Bar Association, before mentioned, stated in fourteen distinct propositions the conclusions at which the committee had arrived as to the means whereby the existing delay and uncertainty in judicial administration could be lessened. All but one of these conclusions were adopted by the Association, without any considerable dissent. The thirteenth proposition was expressed in these words :

" XIII. The law itself should be reduced so far as " possible to the form of a statute."

This proposition was the subject of an animated discussion. I am not able to say whether standing by itself, and judged by itself, the proposition would have met with any considerable dissent or opposition. But there were in the body of the report arguments which it was supposed favored codification in general, and it was thought by many members that the thirteenth proposition, above quoted, was simply the outgrowth of that argument, and that its adoption would commit, or might be construed to commit, the Association in its organized capacity to the doctrine of codification, and that this subject was one of such supreme importance as to require previous notice and separate and distinct consideration. The result was that the consideration of the thirteenth proposition was postponed until the meeting in 1886, to the end that all the members might have time for examination and reflection, and an opportunity to be present. At the meeting of the Association in 1886, the thirteenth proposition was the subject of a full and animated discussion. It was amended so as to read :

"The law itself should be reduced, so far as its substantive principles are settled, to the form of a statute."

And in this form it was adopted, but only by a small majority. And thus the matter stands to the present time, so far as it has been dealt with by the American Bar Association.[1]

The subject thus brought into view, whether in its general or partial scope, is confessedly one of great moment, — a living, vital, practical issue. It is not my purpose to enter at large into its discussion at this time. I have heretofore glanced at it,[2] and shall have occasion to refer to it in subsequent lectures.[3] I content myself with a statement

Lecture IX.

Codification, — resolution of the American Bar Association.

---

[1] The report of the committee in 1885, the debates and the action on the report in that year, will be found in the Report of the Association, 1885, pp. 42, 323 ; for 1886, in the Report for that year at pp. 5-74, 325 (majority report), 363 (minority report.) The resolution, amended as stated in the text, was adopted, ayes, 58 ; noes, 41 (*Ib.*, p. 74). In these two reports for 1885 and 1886, Mr. David Dudley Field has set forth the reasons and grounds of the proposition as proposed and adopted with his characteristic directness and ability. This vote fairly reflects the diversity of opinion on the subject which exists among the bar of the country. In the annual address before the association in 1886, Mr. Thomas J. Semmes, an eminent lawyer of Louisiana, advocated codification with great learning and force ; while in the like address in 1890 on "The Ideal and the Actual in the Law," Mr. James C. Carter, of New York, one of the acknowledged leaders of the bar of the country, presented the argument against codification with his accustomed elegance of diction and strength of reasoning. (Reports, 1890, p. 217.)

[2] See *ante* Lectures IV., V., VIII.

[3] See *post* Lectures X., XII., XIII.

for your consideration of some of the conclusions, without much elaboration, to which my own reflections have led me.

1. As I have elsewhere remarked, the word "code" is one to which such a variety of meaning is attached that it seems to me to be essential either to drop it from the discussion, or first of all to fix and define what is meant by it.[1] If it means a general abrogation of existing laws and rules and the substitution of an entirely new system, and to that end to consign the law reports to oblivion, it will have but very few advocates, and I am not among them. Such, however, is not its necessary meaning.

A code, according to my conception, differs from a mere revision, consolidation, or digest of existing statutes, since it is essential to any practicable or desirable scheme of codification, whether it is general or confined to a particular branch, that it shall derive the elements of its chief value from the existing body of case-law and statute-law, removing therefrom what is obsolete, needlessly technical, inconsistent, or superfluous, settling obscure and doubtful points, expressing well settled principles of general interest or utility, and with a cautious hand filling up the interstices which the irregular development of law as a result of the exigencies of litigation has shown to exist, and then arranging the whole in a definite and systematic form. Codification within these restricted and conservative limits, I believe to be both practicable and expedient whenever it can be well and thoroughly done, and not before. Nor would I demand quali-

[1] See *ante* Lecture VI.

fications in those charged with the work so high that they are unattainable. *"An ideal code,"* says Sir James Stephen,[1] *" ought to be drawn by a Bacon and settled by a Coke."* But we may wait forever if we wait for an ideal code, or wait to combine such qualifications in any given commission to execute the work.

Nor does it seem to me that the views of those who insist as a condition precedent to undertaking any part of the work that the whole body of the law ought thus to be subjected to the operation at one and the same time as necessary parts of a general conception and plan, are at all feasible, and therefore are not wise. The labor required is so vast, the difficulties to be overcome are so great, that unless the work is done in divisions or branches of the law, it will probably never be undertaken at all. Some modern English statutes are so comprehensive as very nearly to realize the practicable purpose of a code on the subjects that are dealt with. For example, in 1882, Parliament passed an act to " Codify the law relating to bills of exchange, checks, and promissory notes," and the gentleman charged with its execution has stated that he examined many statutes and thousands of cases in order to frame the desired enactment.[2] Why

Lecture IX.

Codification *en bloc* not feasible.

---

[1] 3 History Criminal Law, p. 300.
[2] See *ante* Lectures IV., V., VI.; *post* Lectures XII., XIII. " 'Byles on Bills' for accuracy and clearness is among the best law books in the English language. Lawyers and judges have for years turned to it for information with absolute confidence. It is not too much to say that without it the late codification of the law of bills of exchange would have been impossible." "A Generation of Judges, by their Reporter," London, 1888, article *Byles*.

258 LAWS AND JURISPRUDENCE.

<small>Lecture IX.</small>

may we not have a Contract Act, a Partnership Act, a Criminal Code, etc., without waiting for an authorized *projet* to subject to this operation the whole body of the law *en bloc ?*

<small>Codification not a panacea for defects in our laws.</small>

2. Nor must we form unreasonable expectations of the benefits to be derived from codification, no matter how well it may be performed. It is not possible, and therefore not desirable, to attempt to make any enactment so comprehensive as to embrace all cases or combinations of fact which will arise, nor is it possible to make statutes so clear and precise as to avoid the necessity of judicial interpretation and construction. Besides, the habits, modes of thought, practice, and traditions of a people, or of a great profession like that of the law, are deeply rooted and incapable of legislative extirpation if it were attempted. Within proper limits the doctrine of judicial precedent is reasonable and highly convenient, if not necessary. Its influence has probably pervaded every system of jurisprudence, even where it has been expressly attempted to exclude it. Justinian enacted that cases actually tried by the emperor should be law, not only for the case decided, but for all similar ones.[1] The French code prohibits judicial legislation, and under it judicial decisions do not constitute an authoritative rule for other judges in the sense of our doctrine of judicial precedent. And the same is true, at least, theoretically, of the contemporary Continental codes. The Prussian and Austrian codes went so far at first as to forbid a judge from referring to the opinion of a law writer or to previous judicial judgments; and

[1] Code 1, 14, 12 pr. A. D., 529.

the Prussian code expressly directed him to base his decisions upon the statutes and the general principles of the Landrecht. But this was afterwards modified in both countries, so that at this time the decisions of the Supreme Court are regularly published, and we cannot doubt that they exercise a decisive influence upon inferior judges, whether they are absolutely binding upon them as precedents or not.[1]

The sound conclusion would seem to be that "the law itself should be reduced so far as prac-"ticable to the form of a statute." Not with the expectation that the work of judicial interpretation will be no longer necessary, but with a view to reduce the necessity of interpretation and of judicial legislation to the narrowest practicable limits, and to remove as far as may be the existing uncertainty in the law.

My idea of law amendment is that of Lord Bacon. My idea of a code is that of Mr. Justice Stephen. I conclude by quoting a passage from each of these eminent men concerning these weighty subjects:

"The work, which I propound, tendeth to prun-"ing and grafting the law, and not to ploughing up "and planting it again; for such a remove I should "hold indeed for a perilous innovation. But in the "way I now propound, the entire body and sub-"stance of the law shall remain, only discharged of "idle and unprofitable or hurtful matter; and illus-

Lecture IX.

The true idea and principle of a code.

Views of Lord Bacon.

---

[1] Clark, "Practical Jurisprudence," pp. 264, 392, and addenda; Markby, "Elements of Law," §§ 26 n., 78 and note. *Ante* Lectures IV., VI., VIII.; *post* Lecture X.

260   *LAWS AND JURISPRUDENCE.*

Lecture IX.
Views of Mr. Justice Stephen.

"trated by order and other helps, towards the better
"understanding of it, and judgment thereupon."[1]

"A code ought to be based upon the principle
"that it aims at nothing more than the reduction to
"a definite and systematic shape of the results ob-
"tained and sanctioned by the experience of many
"centuries."[2]

NOTE. — In a paper prepared in June, 1893, by Mr. David Dudley Field, by request, for the Columbian Exposition in Chicago, he says that codes of civil procedure, or what are such in substance, have been adopted "in twenty-eight American States and Territories, — New York, Missouri, Wisconsin, California, Kentucky, Ohio, Iowa, Kansas, Nevada, North Dakota, South Dakota, Oregon, Idaho, Montana, Minnesota, Nebraska, Arizona, Arkansas, North Carolina, South Carolina, Wyoming, Washington, Connecticut, Indiana, Colorado, Georgia, Utah, and Maine. The example was contagious, even so far as across the sea; and in 1873 the Parliament of England took up the subject, and adopted the Judicature Act, by which the forms of action were abolished and law and equity fused together. This act extended to Ireland, and has been followed in the English colonies of Victoria, Queensland, South Australia, Western Australia, Tasmania, New Zealand, Jamaica, St. Vincent, the Leeward Islands, British Honduras, Cambia, Grenada, Nova Scotia, Newfoundland, Ontario, and British Columbia. It was not civil procedure alone that was taken up in America; criminal procedure — that is, procedure in the criminal courts — was meliorated and codified. Long before this, however, and from the very beginning of American courts, the denial of counsel to persons accused of crime had been repudiated as a gross inhumanity. . . . Besides the acts of civil procedure that I have mentioned, and which I count as codes, — though a few of them, like the practice act of Maine, are couched in not more than a dozen comprehensive and fundamental sections, to be engrafted upon the general practice of the State, — besides these acts, I repeat, there are already to be found in American jurisprudence eighteen codes of criminal procedure, five penal codes, and five general civil codes. Taken all together, here is an array of fifty-six codes which the United States are able to present to the world as the fruit of the first century of independence."

---

[1] Lord Bacon's Proposal "Touching the Compiling and Amendment of the Laws of England," vol. ii., p. 229, Montagu's Ed., American reprint.

[2] Sir James Stephen, "History Criminal Law," vol. iii., chap. xxxiv.

NOTE.

MR. JUSTICE MILLER'S VIEWS CONCERNING THE TRUE OFFICE AND USE OF ADJUDGED CASES.

NEW YORK, Nov. 13, 1885.

Note.
True office of adjudged cases in our law.

MY DEAR JUDGE, — In a casual conversation, I once heard you make some observations concerning the functions of adjudged cases, which struck me very forcibly. They probably expressed your own course or habit as a judge in considering the force and effect of "authorities." Some cases, or class of cases, you regarded as absolutely binding, without reference to the original ground of decision; others as simply persuasive, and this only, so far as they rested on sound reasons, the validity or soundness of which reasons any court asked to adopt or apply them might, and even should, look into for itself. If you have time to drop me a note giving me, ever so briefly, your views as to the true office and use of adjudged cases in our law, I shall be much obliged.

Very sincerely yours,

JOHN F. DILLON.

Mr. JUSTICE MILLER, Washington, D. C.

WASHINGTON, Nov. 16, 1885.

Hon. JOHN F. DILLON : —

MY DEAR JUDGE, — I am in receipt of yours of the 13th instant. The subject you suggest is one which necessarily demands the careful consideration of any judge of a court of last resort. The value of authorities, and especially of judicial decisions, in enabling him to make up his own judgment in cases before him is often a question of no little anxiety. The answer must have large reference to the kind of cases in which they are offered for his examination.

There is a large class of cases, perhaps the largest, which must be decided by principles that are not disputed. That is to say,

Lecture IX.

Mr. Justice Miller's views as to the true office of adjudged cases in our law.

that the propositions advanced by the counsel on opposing sides are such as will be generally conceded, and need no support from judicial decisions. In these cases, which in my experience are the most numerous, the work of the judge is to determine from the case before him, — that is, from the pleadings and the evidence, — whether it falls within the principles offered by the plaintiff or defendant for its solution, or within some modification of these principles which counsel of neither party has adopted. The decision of this question demands the highest exercise of the reasoning faculties of a mind well stored in those general rules of law which lie at its foundation as a science, and the aid given in such cases by the decisions of other courts is not much. The scientific arrangement of the facts of the case as seen in the pleadings and evidence, by a well-trained judicial mind, must in this class be always the main reliance for a sound administration of the law.

There is another class of cases, the decision of which turns upon a construction of constitutions and statutes. In these the decisions of the highest courts of the government which adopted the Constitution or enacted the statutes should be conclusive in most cases. In the construction of the Constitution of the United States, or an act of Congress, the decisions of the Supreme Court of the United States ought, until reversed by that court, to be followed almost without question. That court has given expression to the rule in regard to the construction of the State constitution and statutes by the highest courts of the States enacting them, in the adoption of the principle that even in the case of co-ordinate and concurrent jurisdiction it will follow those courts in the construction of the statutes and constitutions of their respective States.

A third class of cases are those which arising under the general rules of the common law, or in equity, and in which the abstract reasons for one rule, or for another opposed to it, are nearly balanced, where it is more important that the rule should be established and followed with uniformity, than that one or the other rule should prevail. In this class, if there are differences in the cases decided, the question should be determined by the weight of authority. It is in this class of questions that adjudged cases are most useful, and in which the examination and comparison of them by counsel are of great aid to the court, and are likely to reward the labor of those who make the examination thorough. Perhaps to this class should be added those in which the decisions of the courts have become "rules of property," governing the rights of parties to real or personal property.

As regards the relative weight to be given to the different courts whose decisions are relied on, it is more difficult to speak. I shall say nothing of the value of the decisions of the English courts in questions purely of common law or in equity. Not because I underrate them, but because every one understands their value, especially in equity and admiralty cases.

Leaving these, and the questions arising under State statutes, the value of a decision is estimated by the character of the court, or of the judge who delivered the opinion, or by both. These vary much in the courts of the United States. Without being invidious or undertaking to name other courts of high standing, there are many things in the history and character of the Supreme Judicial Court of Massachusetts which entitle its reported decisions for the last hundred years to great consideration. But a decision often has a merit apart from the standing of the court in which it is made, owing to the high character of the judges of the court, or of the judge who delivered the opinion. Opinions delivered by such judges as Marshall, Taney, Kent, and Shaw, have a value apart from the courts in which they were delivered. Even the dissenting opinions of these men and their *obiter dicta* have weight in the minds of lawyers who have a just estimate of their character, which they cannot give to many courts of last resort of acknowledged ability. After all, the convincing power of the opinion or decision in a reported case must depend very largely on the force of the reasoning by which it is supported, and of this every lawyer and every court must of necessity be his and its own judge.

Very sincerely yours,
SAMUEL F. MILLER.

Note.

Mr. Justice Miller's views as to the true office of adjudged cases in our law.

LECTURE X.

OUR LAW.—THE VAST SIZE AND RAPID ACCUMULATION OF CASE LAW CONSIDERED SPECIALLY WITH REFERENCE TO THE PRACTICABILITY OF LIMITING ITS GROWTH BY LEGISLATIVE ACTION RESTRICTING THE PUBLICATION OF THE REPORTS OF ADJUDGED CASES.—REMEDIES PROPOSED BY LORD BACON AND LORD WESTBURY FOR THE OVERGROWN BULK OF OUR STATUTE AND CASE LAW.—THE DOCTRINE OF JUDICIAL PRECEDENT AND ITS EFFECTS.—JUDGMENT OF THE AMERICAN BAR ASSOCIATION CONCERNING THE PUBLICATION OF THE LAW REPORTS.

Lecture X.

The enormous bulk of our case-law mainly the product of the rule of judicial precedent.

THE most striking phenomenon that arrests the attention of the inquirer into the condition of our laws and jurisprudence is their enormous bulk. I have already referred to this subject, but there are important aspects of it remaining to be noticed. Irregular and intermittent legislation, especially in our own time, contributes not a little to the overgrown size of our law; but its vastness is after all mainly owing to judiciary law, and the multitude of the law reports is the direct result of the authoritative force of adjudged cases. If we add to the English and American reports the statutes and the text-books of both countries, a complete working law library (and such a library is essential to thorough work) consists, probably, of not less than ten thousand volumes.[1] As case-law constitutes the chief bulk of our jurisprudence, the inquiry may well be made, Why not keep it within more restricted limits? This is the subject which I now proceed to consider.

In the annual address which in 1884 I had the honor to deliver before the American Bar Association, I made, among others, the following observations: —

"The most distinctive feature of the common law "of England and America is the rule of judicial "precedent, or the binding force of adjudged cases "as rules of decision for like causes. In no other "system of jurisprudence is such force given to "judicial judgments as in England and America. "The result is that elsewhere the judicial reports "are comparatively few, since judicial judgments "have in general no authority and theoretically no "higher rank than expositions or commentaries of "private writers. The corresponding result is, ac"cording to a recent statement, that in 1881 the "judicial reports of England numbered two thou"sand nine hundred and forty-four volumes, and in "this country about three thousand, and they are "increasing in the United States alone at the rate "of over one hundred volumes a year.[2] Where," I inquired, "is this multiplication of reports to

Lecture X.

The number of the law reports.

[1] See *ante* Lecture III., p. 94, note; Lecture IV., p. 133, and Lecture VI., pp. 172–183. The enormous bulk of case-law is further illustrated, *ante* Lecture IX. and note, p. 250.

[2] In answer to a letter which I addressed to the librarian of the New York Law Institute, inquiring as to the number of American reports in his library, I received the following: —

Lecture X.

Is the huge bulk of our case-law remediable?

"end? Is it to go on unchecked indefinitely? "Is it desirable or practicable to check it? How "far is it an evil; and if it be so, what is the "remedy? And," I added, "these, Mr. Presi- "dent, are inquiries of such serious moment that "they may well engage the attention of the "Association."[1]

In preceding lectures I have referred to the large accumulation and rapid multiplication of the law reports, and have made some observations thereon. What I have to say on this subject in the present lecture is with some revision and enlargement what I presented to the Association by request of the Committee on Judicial Administration and Remedial Procedure at its meeting in 1886, as the grounds for the conclusion which the Association reached, and which will be hereafter stated.[2] I did not in the address before the American Bar Association, above referred to, undertake to make any direct answer to these questions. The Asso-

NEW YORK, Aug. 19, 1886.

DEAR SIR, — I regret deeply my inability, at this time, to furnish you with more complete data than the following. The list below was carefully compiled by my associate, Mr. William H. Winters.

Federal Reports to December 31, 1885 409
Miscellaneous American Reports 203
American State Reports 3,186
                                                    3,798

American Law Periodicals, December, 1885 (the publication whereof had been discontinued) 575
American Law Periodicals, December, 1885 (then being published) 702

Very respectfully yours,
JOHN M. LODEWICK.

To Hon. JOHN F. DILLON.

[1] Report American Bar Association, 1884, pp. 223, 224.
[2] *Post*, p. 289.

ciation, however, adopted the following: "*Re-solved*, That so much of the annual address as refers to the evils of the system of reporting the decisions of the courts be referred to the Committee on Judicial Administration and Remedial Procedure, with a request that they report at the next annual meeting of the Association."

Whoever has attentively considered this subject, will, I think, agree that its difficulties are equalled only by its importance. He will further agree, I think, that we have reached a period in our legal history when it is at least wise to stop and take an observation, that we may know, if possible, where we are and whither we are tending.

Speaking generally, our law is composed of two main constituents: First, *statute law* (including, in this country, constitutional law); and second, *judiciary* or *case law*, — that is, the law made by the judges in the ordinary exercise of their judicial functions.

It was long a favorite fiction that the judges did not make, but only declared, the law. But it is no longer denied, nor can it be, that the judges in the process of the interpretation of statutes, especially where they extend them to cases without their letter but within their supposed reason or equity or general utility, as well in cases which, where the statutes are silent, they decide by rules deduced from previous decisions, or decide by reference to the principles of natural right or universal justice, are actually, though indirectly, engaged in legislating, since they formulate, or at least authenticate, the rules which they apply to the transactions in hand; and these rules constitute the grounds of the judgments they pronounce.[1]

Since statutes must, of necessity, be expressed in general terms, and since no human foresight is competent to anticipate, and no human wisdom able to provide for all of the cases, or even all the classes of cases, which will arise out of the endless variety and diversity of human affairs, the work of indirect judicial legislation, such as the judges have been accustomed and obliged to perform, is, as it seems to me, an essential and permanent part of any system of jurisprudence. This function of the judges may be limited, and it ought to be, by the enactment of legislative rules of conduct or decision wherever it is wise and practicable to do so. But it can never be entirely abrogated until the impossible work shall be achieved of a legislative provision in advance for all possible combination of circumstances and cases. And therefore, if we had a code as complete as human skill and care could make it, the work of judicial interpretation would still be necessary, and the duty of adjudicating cases not expressly provided for in it would still have to be performed. And thus judicial legislation would still go on. Yet it by no means follows that such a code is not highly to be desired. Indeed, according to my best judgment, — and I have given the subject, first and last, much thought, — codification, that is, a practicable and not a visionary scheme of codification, is, when reduced to its last analysis, mainly a matter of degree and form; namely, how far it is expedient and

[1] See *ante* Lecture I., p. 5.

wise to carry the process of legislation. On this subject the bar have, and no doubt will continue to have, very different views.[1]

The problem of codification will probably have to be determined bit by bit, and we must be content to take one step at a time. But whether we shall codify *en bloc*, or in compartments, or not at all, there will never come a time when all our laws will be in the form of statutes; never a time when judiciary law — that is, law which is evolved in and by the very act of administering justice — will not form a part of our legal system. It is only a question, at any given period, how far it is necessary or expedient to transmute the judiciary law into statutory form. At the bottom, this is the question that at this time the unmanageable number and constant multiplication of the reports of judicial judgments and opinions (which are the source or evidence of judiciary law) are pressing upon us for solution. There inevitably comes a stage in the legal history of every people when its laws become "so voluminous and vast" that an authoritative and systematic recompilation or restatement of them is necessary, to the end that they may be accessible and of (to use, in default of a better, Bentham's uncouth but expressive word) *cognoscible* bulk, if not to those who are governed by them, at least to those whose business it is to advise concerning them, and to those whose duty it is to administer and apply them.[2]

---

[1] See *ante* Lecture IX., p. 255, and note.
[2] See *ante* Lecture VI., p. 176. "Cognoscible" is not Austin's word. See Austin, "Jurisprudence," 5th ed., lecture xxxix., p. 660. Clark,

Lecture X.

The Roman law, by means of commentaries on the text of the Twelve Tables and on the Pretorian Edict, by imperial constitutions, decrees, edicts, and rescripts, had, before the time of Justinian, attained to such proportions that it was said to be the load of many camels. The Roman situation was tolerable compared with ours. Our judiciary law, which embraces that of England, now runs back through six centuries, without revision or authoritative restatement.[1] It is scattered through volumes so numerous that the memory is taxed to remember even their names, that only the rich can buy them, and that the practicable industry and strength of no single lawyer can examine, much less study and digest them.

Merits and advantages of our law reports; Bentham's admission.

I shall not enter upon the discussion of the characteristics and respective merits and advantages, under various conditions, of statute and case law.[2] The usefulness and value of the law reports and of the materials they contain must be admitted by all. Even Bentham, who combined the iconoclast with the reformer, and who denounced with unsparing severity judge-made law for its "confused, un-"determinate, inadequate, ill-adapted, and incon-"sistent" character, admits that if you "traverse "the whole continent of Europe, ransack all the

---

erroneously as I think, ascribes the term to Austin. "Practical Jurisprudence," p. 382. See Imperial Dictionary, — Cognoscible.

[1] See *ante* Lectures I., p. 29, VI., p. 184, note.

[2] This subject is fully presented by Austin and by his commentator Clark. Austin's "Jurisprudence," vol. ii., 5th ed., by Campbell, Lectures xxxvii.-xxxix., pp. 620-681 and notes p. 1021 *et seq.*; Clark, "Practical Jurisprudence: A Comment on Austin," part ii., chaps. iv.-vi.

"libraries belonging to the jurisprudential sys-
"tems of the several political States, add the
"contents all together, you will not be able to
"compose a collection of cases equal in variety,
"in amplitude, in clearness of statement — in a
"word, in all points taken together, in instructive-
"ness — to that which may be afforded by the col-
"lection of English 'Reports of Adjudged Cases,'
"on adding to them the 'Abridgments and Trea-
"tises,' by which a sort of order, such as it is, has
"been given to their contents." [1]

Lecture X.

Let all this be granted, yet as against the merits and worth of this colossal body of judiciary law must be set off inconveniences and defects of such a character that they have at length become positive evils, or at least serious mischiefs. I cannot stop to enumerate all of these. Those which chiefly concern the present discussion relate to the already huge bulk and to some extent the consequent uncertainty of our case-law.[2] How this state of things has been brought about is obvious enough. Thousands of useless cases — that is, cases turning on their special facts, and those of no general interest, as well as those which are mere repetitions, and which add nothing to the law — have been and are constantly being reported. Multitudes of cases have been questioned, limited, and overruled. The reports abound in cases which are conflicting. The simplest heads of the law are overlaid with a mountainous mass of decisions, which grows day by day.

Inconveniences and defects of our case-law.

---

[1] Bentham's Works, vol. iv., p. 460; 10 *Ib.*, 511. See *ante* Lecture VI.; *post* Lectures XII., XIII.

[2] See *ante* Lecture IX., p. 248 *et seq.*; *post* Lecture XII.

272   LAWS AND JURISPRUDENCE.

<small>Lecture X.</small>

To an examination, study, and comparison of this vast body of law, with such aids as digests and text-books can give, is the legal inquirer remitted and doomed in his toilsome search for the existing law in cases which are not provided for by an adequate statute.[1]

The mischiefs thus produced have long been felt, but the difficulty of remedying them has also been felt or feared to be so great that remedies, though at times suggested and urged, have never been comprehensively or systematically applied. So far as any remedy has been adopted, it has been by means of fragmentary and extemporary legislation.

<small>Lord Bacon's scheme of law amendment.</small>

Over two hundred and fifty years ago, when the evils arising from the accumulation of statutes and reports were immeasurably less than at present, the greatest intellect, as well as one of the greatest lawyers which England has produced, gave to

---

[1] Under modern conditions it has by some been doubted whether the rule of precedent, in the broad scope and imperativeness which we have given to it, is the source of more certainty than uncertainty in the law. To a considerable extent it doubtless tends to make the law certain by depriving the judges of the liberty of deciding like cases contrary to precedent unless the precedent is plainly erroneous; but what is a like case, and whether the precedent is considered erroneous, can often be known only after the judgment of the court in the very case in which the question arises. On the other hand, a most fruitful source of uncertainty, as every practising lawyer knows full well, is found in the very multiplicity of cases, sometimes conflicting and often full of the refinements and distinctions so characteristic of judicial reasoning and discussion. When the judges resort, as they frequently do, to *analogies* supposed to be furnished by previous cases for the rule of decision to apply to the case in hand, it must often be extremely uncertain in advance what the result will be, and it is frequently doubtful whether, fettered in this way, they reach as sound results as if governed by general considerations of what is right and just. See *ante* Lecture IX., pp. 248–252; *post* Lecture XII.

the subject the most thoughtful and well-advised consideration. I refer to Lord Bacon.[1] With him the amending of the laws of England was ever a favorite subject, and one to which he often turned in the intervals when he was not pursuing the baubles of official distinction, and upon the accomplishment of which, after his sad and melancholy fall, he courageously entered in his old age unaided and alone; but to use his own language, " finding it a work of assistance, and one which " he could not master by his own fancy and " pen," he reluctantly laid it aside. His plan was comprehensive. It embraced the reduction of both the statute and the common laws to a system. His method of dealing with the statute law may be outlined in his own words : " For the re- " forming and recompiling of the statute law, it " consisteth of four parts. 1. To discharge the " books of those statutes where the case, by altera- " tion of time, is vanished. . . . 2. To repeal all " statutes which are sleeping and not of use, but " yet snaring and in force. . . . 3. The grievous- " ness of the penalty in many statutes mitigated. " . . . 4. The reducing of concurrent statutes, heaped " one upon another, to one clear and uniform law."

Lecture X.

Bacon's proposed method of dealing with statute law.

What he proposed to do with judiciary or case law I shall notice more at length, because it is especially relevant to my present purpose, and shows that at that early day the subject was comprehended in all its bearings

His scheme for compiling and amending the laws of England, as proposed to King James, consisted

[1] See *ante* Lecture II., p. 46 *et seq.*; Lecture IX., p. 259.

18

Lecture X.

Bacon's plan of dealing with case-law.

of two parts, — "the digest or recompiling of the common laws, and that of the statutes."[1] By the former, he intended mainly "the reducing or perfecting of the course or corps of the common law;" by which he meant "that there is to be made a perfect course of the law," *in serie temporis*, or year-books, as we call them, "from Edward I. to this day." In compiling which there are to be observed the following points: —

1. All overruled cases are to be left out.

2. There are also to be left out "all cases, wherein "that is solemnly and long debated whereof there "is now no question at all, but the judgments only "and resolutions shall be included, without the ar-"guments, which are now become but frivolous;" that is, unnecessary. The decided cases to be accompanied, however, with a memorandum explaining why the cases are not given at length, and where they may be found.

3. All cases "merely of iteration and repetition are to be purged away;" and of "cases of identity "those which are best reported and argued to be "retained instead of the rest," with a proper reference to the omitted cases where the point is argued at large.

4. Conflicting cases to be "specially noted and "collected, that they may be put into certainty, "either by assembling all the judges in the Ex-"chequer Chamber or by Parliament."

5. "All idle queries, which are but seminaries of "doubts and uncertainties, are to be left out, and

[1] Works of Lord Bacon, Montagu's Ed., vol. ii., pp. 229, 233, American reprint.

"no queries set down but of great doubts, well "debated and left undecided for difficulty; but "no upstarting queries which were better to die "than to be put into the books."

6. Cases reported with too great prolixity to have their tautologies and impertinences cut off, and put into a more compendious report.

The course being thus compiled, for the future the cases should be reported by official reporters, " who should be grave and sound lawyers, with an honorable stipend."[1] When we consider the comparatively small number of statutes and reports which existed at that time, the scheme which he propounded was practicable, " with assistance," and if executed as proposed would have greatly reduced the bulk and improved the condition of the English law. It will be noticed that Bacon's proposal was not what would be called radical, and that it related more to the form than the substance of the law. Indeed, he was careful to say that "the " work, which I propound, tendeth to pruning and " grafting the law, and not to ploughing up and " planting again; for such a remove I should hold, " indeed, for a perilous innovation." But his scheme was not executed, and his suggestions bore no fruit.

Statutes and reports kept on accumulating for nearly two hundred years, when Bentham appeared; and for the evils arising from the inaccessibility, bulk, and uncertainty of the English law, he proposed as a remedy what he termed *codification*. Exactly what he meant by codification, and how

[1] "A Plea for Official Reporting," strongly urged by Mr. Westlake, will be found in "Juridical Society Papers" (1863), vol. ii., p. 745.

far his views are sound or practicable, are topics which I reserve for subsequent discussion. I pause only to observe that it was the character, condition, and faults of judiciary law, that mainly suggested to him the idea of a code as the proper corrective or remedy. Bentham died, but his suggestions of a code as a cure for existing evils have given rise to the still pending controversy between the advocates of statute and of judiciary law. Judgments may differ as to what a code means or implies, and how far a code is expedient, or how far it is practicable; but it is clear that resort to the legislature for comprehensive legislation on special subjects, which is in the nature of codification, if it be not codification itself, is more and more practised, and seems to be gradually leading the way to the eventual solution of the question of codification.

Action of the English Law Amendment Society. At a quite recent period the English Society for the Promotion of Law Amendment favored a method of dealing with the English reports substantially the same, it seems to me, as Lord Bacon's method above described. In March, 1863, that society adopted a resolution that "it is highly expedient that the re-"ported decisions of our superior courts of law in "England and Ireland, from the earliest to the pres-"ent time, should be forthwith expurgated and con-"solidated, and their undue accumulation for the "future be, if possible, prevented."[1]

Lord Chancellor Westbury, as late as 1865, proposed from the woolsack to the House of Lords,

---

[1] See "The History and Origin of the Law Reports," by Mr. W. T. S. Daniel, Q. C., *passim.*

among other projects of law reform, "to revise "and expurgate the unwieldy and still increas- "ing mass of the decided cases, reducing them to "such as constituted the body of existing authori- "ties, and which might, in their turn, be digested "and arranged."[1] This, it will be perceived, is substantially Lord Bacon's plan. As Lord Westbury soon afterwards closed his official career, like his great predecessor, with the loss of the public confidence, — growing out of alleged laxity of administration, and not out of anything that touched his personal honor, — the stupendous undertaking which he proposed was not enacted by Parliament. The next year (1866), however, a royal commission was appointed "to inquire into the expediency of a Di- "gest of Law, and the best means of accomplishing

Lecture X.

Lord Westbury's scheme of law amendment.

The Royal Commission of 1866 accomplished nothing.

[1] Lord Westbury's scheme was comprehensive, embracing both case-law and statute law. As to case-law, his plan was to expurgate or "eliminate every case that does not enter into or illustrate or show the application of some portion of living law." . . . "What remains after this pruning will be arranged under heads according to the most perfect analysis that can be framed; and thus will be formed a complete digest of the cases which embody or illustrate or teach the application of the existing law." "The result will be," said Lord Westbury, "a body of recorded precedents brought into a moderate compass, and occupying, we may estimate, but a tenth of the bulk of the present reports." In 1865 he proposed "a bill to complete the expurgation of the Statute-Book, by which the statutes of the realm, now extending over forty-six large quarto volumes, will be reduced to one fourth of that bulk." This to be "followed by a proposal to appoint a commission for making a complete digest of the whole body of English law," the statute and case law to be arranged as far as possible under the same heads. He explained that "the digests of the statute and case law are not regarded by me as final works; they are materials only, to serve for the formation of a code." Nash, "Life of Lord Westbury," vol. ii., pp. 61, 92, London, 1888. See, further, Mr. Hawkins's paper on Digests and Codes, "Juridical Society Papers," (1865), vol. iii., p. 110.

278   LAWS AND JURISPRUDENCE.

Lecture X.

"that object, and of otherwise exhibiting in a compendious and accessible form the law as embodied in judicial decisions." This commission was composed of some of the most eminent men of the profession. But it accomplished nothing. It neither agreed upon the plan of the work nor the manner of having it done. It was unable to settle upon any recommendation except that a Digest was expedient, and that the work, based on a comprehensive plan, and with a uniform method, should be at once undertaken.[1]

Bacon's and Westbury's scheme practicable.

Such a work as Lord Bacon and Lord Westbury proposed can be executed, but it is a work so vast and difficult that it cannot be accomplished without the authorization and aid of Parliament.[2] I venture

[1] Lord Cranworth was the chairman of the commission, and on his death Lord Westbury became the chairman. Among the commissioners were Lord Hatherley, Lord Cairns, Lord Penzance, Sir Erskine May, Sir Roundell Palmer (Lord Selborne), Mr. Justice Willes, and others. Nash, "Life of Lord Westbury," vol. ii., pp. 160, 161, 169, 170.

[2] It is not possible to doubt that the bulk of the existing law can be greatly and, if the work be properly done, advantageously reduced. This is, in fact, demonstrable both by reasoning and examples. Cases do not constitute the law, but are illustrations and practical applications of its general principles. These principles are comparatively few. Lord Mansfield went to the pith and marrow of the business when in a passage to which I have heretofore referred (ante, p. 182), he said: "The law does not consist of particular cases, but of general principles which are illustrated and explained by these cases." Rex v. Bembridge, 3 Douglas Reports, 332, 1783. It is, therefore, practicable to extract these principles and state them in authoritative form. This is, undoubtedly, as Lord Hale says, "a very choice and tender business," and must be performed deliberately and by the most competent hands. Mr. Justice Stephen's Digest of the Law of Evidence is an example, among others, of what may be done in this direction. Mr. Taylor's Treatise on Evidence contains, says Mr. Justice Stephen, 1,797 pages, refers to 9,000 judicial deci-

to add that Lord Westbury's plan — namely, first a complete digest of case-law and also a complete digest of statute law as preliminary to codification, whether gradual or *en bloc* — has always seemed to me the safe and expedient method of doing the work.

The conservatism of the English bar is shown in the comparatively small results that came from the agitation of the subject of law amendment, revived or commenced in 1863–65. The special evil which seemed to be felt, or rather perhaps the only one which the bar considered to be remediable by its action, consisted in the number of regular and irregular reports, the latter consisting of the decisions as published and duplicated in law periodicals, such as the "Law Journal," "Jurist," "Law Times," "Weekly Reporter," etc., in each of which, as well as in the regular reports, were practically given all the decisions of all the principal courts, many of which really contained nothing new or valuable. When the bar came to deal with the subject of legal reform, they shut their eyes to the past, or to any general view of the subject, and

Lecture X.

Remedy devised by the English bar for the evils in the system of law reporting.

---

sions, and cites nearly 750 Acts of Parliament. Greenleaf's work is quite as extensive. Now Mr. Justice Stephen extracts the essential principles of the law of evidence, states these with precision, illustrates them by examples, arranges them in a systematic form in 143 articles, — all of which, with annotations and references to the American cases by Professor Chase, is brought within the moderate compass of 245 pages. The codification in 1882, by authority of an Act of Parliament, of the law relating to commercial paper, is another example of the condensation to which it is practicable to subject our overgrown and expanded law. Stephen's Digest of the Criminal Law, although not enacted by Parliament, is still another striking proof of the same fact.

undertook only to deal with the minor matter of the existing methods of law reporting. What they did in this respect is, I think, well worth knowing, and I will briefly state it. It has a very direct bearing upon the special subject of this lecture, — namely, the expediency of legislation directed to the restricting of the publication of reports of adjudged cases.

In November, 1863, influential members of the English bar requested the Attorney-General to call a meeting of the bar for the purpose of ascertaining their opinion as to the existing system of law reporting, with a view to an amendment thereof. At a meeting held in December, 1863, convened by the Attorney-General, it was "*Resolved*, that, in " the opinion of this meeting, the present system of " preparing, editing, and publishing the reports of " judicial decisions in this country requires amend- " ment." A committee of twenty-two members of the bar was appointed to consider the matter, consisting of the Solicitor-General, the Queen's advocate, and eight Queen's counsel, nine members of the outer bar, and three equity draftsmen. This committee, through a sub-committee, communicated with foreign jurists to inquire into the mode of recording and reporting judicial decisions in the various European States and in the United States of America. The facts as ascertained by them are very instructive, and are stated in the margin.[1]

[1] "To begin with the system adopted in France. Every judicial decision is required to be in writing, and to be motive; that is, to disclose on the face of it the grounds and reasons on which it is

The scheme of reporting recommended was that the matter should be placed under the general confounded; and when the signature of the President of the Tribunal has been affixed to these solemn judgments, it is the business of the greffier to see them entered on the register of the courts, and only one version of them can therefore ever legally appear. The record of the tribunals thus containing an authentic version of every decision, the legal profession and the public have at all times access to the register to ascertain what has from time to time been decided, and it is competent for any one to make from the register a selection of such decisions for publication. The collections of decisions by Sirey and Dalloz and Ledru Rollin have been thus prepared. Though these works are deservedly held in great esteem, they are not official publications, any more than any series of English law reports.

Lecture X.

" In Norway and Sweden, the judgments of the ordinary tribunals are always given in writing, and every case entered on the protocols of the courts; and in the Supreme Courts of Appeal, when the votes of the judges are given separately, it is the business of the registrar of the court to enter on the records of the court, not only the final judgment or conclusion, but the grounds and reasons of the decision of each judge. Here, as in France, therefore, the records of the courts supply ample materials for the preparation of books or collections of decisions, and such publications are left wholly to free trade.

" In Denmark, though it is competent for any one to take down, print, and publish reports of cases and decisions of which he has himself taken notes, the only authentic version of judicial proceedings is the entry in the *dombistocol*, under the hand of the judge, containing not only the conclusion itself to which the court has arrived, but the facts and reasons and grounds of the decision ; and from these, selections of cases which may serve as precedents are made by the direction of the courts, though it would seem that other selections made by competent private publishers would be received with equal attention.

" In Italy, all judicial decisions, whether civil or criminal, must be read aloud in open court with the grounds in fact or law set out at length; and authentic minutes of the judicial opinions so pronounced are duly entered in the register of the court; and compilations of the principal decisions of the four Supreme Courts of Cassation at Milan, Florence, Naples, and Palermo, are published by voluntary editors, whose province it is to make a proper selection of cases for publication, to give an analysis of them in the head and marginal notes, and to explain and illustrate them in other annotations. These compilations only so far receive the protection of the State that a certain number of copies are subscribed for out of the public treasury. The

trol and management of a council composed of members appointed as follows: Two by Lincoln's Inn, two by the Middle Temple, two by the Inner Temple, one by Gray's Inn, one by Serjeant's Inn, and two by the Incorporated Law Society. The result of this movement was the establishment of the present system of law reports in England, under the direction of the Council of Law Reporting.

Let me sum up some of the conclusions to which the foregoing discussion seems to lead.

In continental Europe, the superior tribunals are, as we have seen, required not only to put their judgments, but the reasons and grounds thereof, in writing, and to enter the same of record. So in England, the superior courts either give written opinions or orally pronounce their opinions, — that is, the reasons and grounds of their judgment; and these are taken down by the reporter and revised by the judges, and when published with a statement of the case, constitute the judicial reports. In this country it is generally required by statute, or at all events it is the universal practice, for the appellate courts to give written opinions. The wisdom of this course may not only be inferred from the universality of the practice, but rests upon obvious reasons. It necessarily secures for the cases decided more thorough examination, discussion, and consid-

compilation entitled 'La Legge Romana' is a journal of judicial and legislative proceedings for the kingdom of Italy, published at short intervals (the judicial three times a week), and containing in an abridged form notes taken from the minutes in the registers of all the important cases disposed of." [a]

[a] The "Jurist" (London), New Series, vol. x., part ii., p. 249.

eration on the part of the judges. The bar are the real constituency of the bench, and the opinions of every conscientious judge are written under the eye of a scrutinizing and intelligent profession.[1]

The practice of judges of inferior courts to give, when practicable, written opinions is for like reasons to be commended rather than discouraged, since it tends to secure better results in the administration of justice. A wise rule of the Supreme Court of the United States, as well as of many of the State courts, requires any written opinion of the inferior court in the cause to be sent up as part of the record on appeal.

The next question is, How far is it desirable that judicial opinions should be reported; that is, published for the information and use of the profession?

The theoretical answer to this inquiry is in the present state of the law plain enough; namely, that only such cases ought to be reported as are useful as precedents or constitute new developments of the law, or overrule or limit former decisions, or newly construe legislative enactments, etc. But the difficulty is, who is to judge of this? It will hardly do to leave it to the reporter, and it is useless to leave it to him if he has a pecuniary interest in the multiplication of his reports. It is almost equally useless to leave it to the judges, since a judge who has laboriously examined a cause and written a careful opinion therein will very naturally conclude that it is worth reporting. As a practical result, the body of the opinions of the courts of last re-

[1] *Ante* Lecture I., p. 31, and note; Lecture VI., pp. 189-193.

Lecture X.

Whether reports of inferior courts are useful.

sort will continue to be reported, however desirable it may be that cases which wholly turn upon the facts, and cases of "mere iteration and repetition," should not be included in the official reports.

A more doubtful question, perhaps, is, Whether it is desirable that the publication of the reports of courts inferior to the courts of last resort should be discontinued. I say this is, perhaps, a more doubtful question, since many lawyers seem to be of the opinion that such reports, containing many ill-considered opinions, really embarrass (partly by reason of the doctrine of judicial precedent) rather than aid in the administration of justice. But judges will not, as a rule, write opinions if they are not to be published; and it is not, I venture to say, expedient to adopt a policy which would discourage or prevent that deliberate study of cases which written opinions tend to promote and secure. Besides, it would be impracticable to prevent their publication in some form, either officially or unofficially. Written opinions when filed belong to the public records, and it would be against first principles to prohibit their publication by statute; and without such prohibition they would find reporters and publishers, so long as there was a demand therefor which would reward the labor and expense of the publication.

Publication of dissenting opinions.

To keep the increasing bulk of case-law within smaller limits, it has been suggested that dissenting opinions should not be published. But on what ground could this be justified? Who is authorized to assume that the majority is always right? Not infrequently dissenting opinions are the sounder.

Such cases are always carefully considered, and the majority and the minority judges set forth their competing reasons and submit them to the fair judgment of the bar. If a dissenting opinion is written, it is a fact in the case, and its suppression or non-publication, simply because it is a dissenting opinion, can be defended on no ground either of principle or of public policy. Who shall establish a censorship over the publication of any class of judicial opinions? It seems to me that this cannot be done until we shall forget Milton's plea, in which he "rose to the height of the great argument," for the liberty of unlicensed printing. Even if the utility of the publication of the decisions of inferior courts or of dissenting opinions were doubtful, I know of no principle on which their publication ought to be prohibited by the legislature.

Lecture X.

To thoughtful lawyers comparative jurisprudence often suggests useful inquiries. We find in the English and American law an already unwieldy mass of reports. In twenty years they will number ten thousand volumes; in fifty years twenty thousand. The jurisprudence of the continent of Europe presents no corresponding phenomenon. What is the reason? It is owing chiefly, I think, to the doctrine of judicial precedent, which in its breadth and application is peculiar to our jurisprudence, since it gives to appellate decisions authoritative force as law, which the judges are bound to apply to all cases they find to fall within the principle of the previous decisions.[1] This doctrine makes the re-

Effect of our doctrine of judicial precedent.

---

[1] See *ante* Lectures VI., p. 173; VIII., p. 229; IX., pp. 258, 259.
" To a certain extent it is true that the courts have held themselves

ports of adjudged cases almost as much a necessity to the lawyer as the statutes.

Effect of judicial decisions in European States.

In European States, judicial decisions have generally no binding effect as precedents, and hence the judicial reports are there relatively few.[1] And it is a question which may at least excite inquiry, whether, in the present comparatively matured state of our law, the doctrine of judicial

bound by authority as firmly as the pagan deities were supposed to be bound by the decrees of fate." Sharswood, "Law Lectures," lecture ix., pp. 245, 246. "It is not to be denied that there is some difficulty in settling with accuracy the limits of the maxim *stare decisis*. But when the principle of a decision has long been acquiesced in, when it has been applied in numerous cases and become a landmark in the branch of the science to which it relates, when men have dealt and made contracts on the faith of it, — to overrule it is an act of positive injustice, and a usurpation by one branch of the government upon the powers of another." Sharswood, "Law Lectures," lecture i., p. 45. Within these limits the doctrine of *stare decisis* is of unquestionable soundness and utility. In such cases the remedy is properly with the legislature. If the courts overrule previous decisions, the new rule retroacts and is liable to work injustice. If the legislature changes the rule, the new rule acts only upon future cases.

[1] *Ante* Lecture VI., p. 173; Lecture VIII., p. 229 *et seq.*; Lecture IX., pp. 258, 259. Austin, "Jurisprudence," 5th ed., lecture xxxix., p. 668. As to the modified form of case-law on the Continent, see Pollock's "Essays in Jurisprudence and Ethics," p. 237. "The courts," he says, "not being bound by precedent as they are with us, decided cases do not make case-law as we understand it" (p. 273). But "in the present German Empire it would seem," says Professor Clark, "that the decisions of the *Supreme Gerichtshof* do practically constitute precedents." Clark, "Practical Jurisprudence," Cambridge, 1883, p. 224, note. In an addendum the same author adds: "In Austria the direct prohibition of reference to a previous judgment has been still more distinctly modified. The *Plenarentscheidungen* of the Supreme Court are binding precedents, and the *Judicatenbuch*, since 1872, is an official record of them." *Ib.*, pp. 224, 264, note; 392, 404. He adds: "In some form of more or less authority the influence of precedents has practically made its way into those very systems which profess to exclude it." *Ib.*, pp. 263, 264; *ante* Lecture IX., p. 258.

precedent, in the scope and rigor in which it exists in English and American jurisprudence, is now really a better doctrine than the modified one which prevails generally in the Continental system, which practically, although not theoretically, gives to the opinions and judgments of the highest tribunals influential, but not in the sense of our law authoritative and binding force. Judicial decisions are part of European jurisprudence; they lack simply, speaking generally, the element of *authority* which they have with us. Lecture X.
Difference between the English and Continental systems.

As case-law is a necessary and indestructible part of every jural system, and peculiarly of our system, the publication of reports of adjudged cases will probably continue in the future, as in the past, without substantial restriction. So long and so far as the bar finds the reports to be useful they will be published, and I am unable to see any material checks which we would be warranted, or which it would be practicable, to put upon such publication by legal enactment, however desirable it is to keep case-law within more circumscribed limits. Under present conditions there is no reason to doubt that the legislative function will be exercised, in the usual manner, as freely, and that the judicial reports will continue to increase as rapidly as ever, adding to the bulk, and to some extent to the uncertainty of the law, and that this will go on and on until the effect becomes at length insupportable. A remedy will then be found, for the interests of justice are primal and eternal, and are not doomed to be crushed by the very machinery which has been devised only to the end that justice may Legislative restriction on the publication of the reports not practicable.

Lecture X.

What will be the remedy.

be promoted and secured. Whether that remedy will consist in the breaking down or modification of the doctrine of judicial precedent in the extent and rigor in which it at present exists, of which even now we see many signs,[1] or in codification in some expedient and practicable shape,[2] or in both,

---

[1] "A trait distinguishing him [the late Chief Baron Kelly] from some of his younger brethren was his grasp of general principles in preference to decided cases. The modern lawyer is too apt to run to his book-shelves for a case which has some resemblance to that in hand, although the resemblance is frequently accidental. Of late years some powerful intellects on the bench have been directed to the task of breaking down this unhealthy habit; but it is still a vice of the time." "A Generation of Judges, by their Reporter," 1888, article "Kelly." The criticism does not alone apply to the modern English lawyer; it is equally applicable to his American brother.

[2] "We have given," says Professor Baldwin, "I cannot but think, an undue prominence to judicial precedents as a natural source or annunciation of the law. The multiplication of distinct sovereignties in the same land, each fully officered, and each publishing in official form the opinions of its courts of last resort, bewilders the American lawyer in his search for authority. The guiding principles of our law are few and plain. Their application to the matter we may have in hand it is the business of our profession to make, and if we spent more time in doing it ourselves, and less in endeavoring to find how other men had done it in other cases, we should, I believe, be better prepared to inform the court and serve our client. . . . The drift of American jurisprudence is towards the expression of the law in an orderly and official form; in other words, towards codification. It has approached the question from the practical side, and in a practical way. The early colonies soon put their scanty statutes into print, arranged in some convenient way for ready reference, the various heads often following each other in alphabetical order, as in our digests of reports. New York led the way towards a more systematic and comprehensive treatment of the subject, by her Revised Statutes of 1827, a revision which, though in many points revolutionary, was so well considered and well done that it has held the ground for over half a century, while in most of our States revision succeeds revision every ten or fifteen years. But there is nothing distinctively American in codification. It is simply un-English. It is the natural aim and end of every system of jurisprudence — of juris-

or in something else, we may not be able to foresee; but that some cure will be discovered or wrought is as certain as that law and justice are the permanent and paramount interests of man on earth.

Lecture X.

There are, so far as I am aware, no special evils in the mode of reporting in this country, which seem to call for correction. One fortunate circumstance in the situation is the low price at which enterprising and rival publishing houses are now furnishing the State and Federal reports. The manner in which the judges shall write their opinions cannot be prescribed to them. The profession are, however, glad to see, in more recent years, a quite general disposition in the judges to do less essay-writing, and to hand down more compact and shorter opinions, — a very desirable change, especially in cases which either turn on the facts, or contain no new principles or no novel application of old ones.

Manner of reporting.

Influenced by these and perhaps other considerations, the American Bar Association, without dissent, expressed its judgment on the subject with which this lecture mainly deals, by the adoption of the following resolution: "*Resolved*, That while this " Association records its approval of the present " tendency of the judges to write short opinions, " especially in cases turning on facts and those not " useful as precedents, and doubts the utility, in the

Resolution of the American Bar Association concerning the publication of the law reports.

prudence itself apart from any particular system of it. Jurisprudence is the science of law, and the orderly statement of its rules can be called by no better name than code." Address of Professor Baldwin, of Yale University, before the Ohio Bar Association, July, 1892.

Lecture X.

"present state of the law, of the use of decisions "of inferior or intermediate courts as precedents, it "does not deem it practicable to interfere by legis-"lation to prohibit or limit the publication of any "class of reports, and that the evils of the great vol-"ume of judiciary law must be remedied otherwise "than by legislation restricting absolute freedom in "the publication of adjudged cases."

If this is a sound conclusion, as I think lawyers of experience will agree that it is, the continued growth of our case-law, whatever its inconveniences or evils, must be remedied in some other way, if at all, than by legislation directed to restricting the publication of the reports of adjudged cases.

A systematic, critical, and thorough discussion of the English doctrine of judicial precedent, one which shall go to the root of the business, I cannot but think to be a *desideratum* in our legal literature. This would involve a consideration of the historical development of the doctrine; its rationale, policy, and purpose; its effects upon our jurisprudence as respects certainty, bulk, convenience, and utility; its true limits; its merits as compared with the Continental doctrine or practice; the wisdom, under existing conditions, of a modification of the scope and imperativeness of the rule, and the proper discrimination to be made in its application to different classes of cases.[1]

A desideratum in our legal literature.

---

[1] See *ante*, pp. 229-232 and notes, also p. 252, and Note at end of Lecture IX., pp. 261-263. For a striking illustration of the rule of judicial precedent as imperatively extending to cases which are held to fall within the *principle* of a previous decision, though the facts are different, see the important case of Lahr *v.* Metropolitan Elevated Railway Company, 104 N. Y. Rep., 268, 1887. Ruger, C. J., delivering

To prevent misapprehension it may be allowable for me to add that I do not wish it to be inferred from the observations I have made in the course of this and other lectures, that I doubt the great value of case-law or the general utility of the doctrine of *stare decisis*. A leading objection made by Austin to judiciary law is that it "compels the judge to "take the narrowest possible view of every sub- "ject," and consequently "the law he makes is "necessarily restricted to the particular case which "gives occasion for its promulgation."[1] This is true, and this in my opinion is precisely as it ought to be, since it is the surest safeguard against the two grave perils of generalization and the arbitrary and irresponsible exercise of judicial power. Judicial decisions and their proper influence and effect are of incalculable service, since counsel are thereby

Lecture X.

One of Austin's objections to case-law not well founded.

the opinion of the court, which on this point was unanimous, said: "The doctrine of the Story case (90 N. Y., 122), therefore, although pronounced by a divided court, must be considered as *stare decisis* upon all questions involved therein, and as establishing the law, as well for this court as for the people of the State, whenever similar questions may be litigated. Wherever, therefore, the principles of that case logically lead us, we feel constrained to go, and give full effect to the rule therein stated, that abutters upon public streets in cities are entitled to such damages as they may have sustained by reason of a diversion of the street from the use for which it was originally taken, and its illegal appropriation to other and inconsistent uses," although such appropriation was expressly authorized by legislative act.

In support of the view that judicial decisions are the source of the law, — that is, make it and are not merely the evidence thereof, — see Austin, "Jurisprudence," vol. i., *passim*; Digby, "History Law of Real Property," 2d ed., p. 64, note; Pomeroy's "Municipal Law," Preface, and §§ 284, 295, 298. Contrariwise, 1 Blacks. Com., Introduction, p. 69, and the critical and scholarly discussion of Professor Hammond in his edition of Blackstone, vol. i., pp. 213-226, note 30.

[1] Austin, "Jurisprudence," vol. ii., lecture xxxix., 5th ed., p. 657.

Lecture X.

Value of judicial decisions, and utility of the doctrine of stare decisis.

enabled to advise that a case clearly like those previously adjudged will be decided in the same way, and they are also enabled more certainly to predict the judicial judgment upon a new case than would otherwise be possible. My doubts relate to the pre-eminence and breadth of the doctrine of judicial precedent as it exists in our law, or more precisely to its indiscriminate application without more regard than is usually given to the character for ability and learning of the court which rendered the decision sought to be used as a precedent, and to the nature of the case which is sought to be brought within the uncontrollable authority of the previous judgment.

And now I conclude this lecture with an expression of the hope that the suggestion above made as to the desirableness of a bold, original, and searching examination of the doctrine of precedent may find lodgement in the soil of some fertile mind here present, and bring forth hereafter useful fruit. More the teacher cannot do. Paul may plant, Apollos may water, but God giveth the increase: and he giveth it in his own way, which is always the right way; and in his own time, which is always the right time, neither too early nor too late.

LECTURE XI.

OUR LAW. — BLACKSTONE AND BENTHAM AS TYPES AND EXPONENTS OF THE CONSERVATIVE AND THE RADICAL FORCES, TO WHOSE FREE PLAY IT OWES ITS PROGRESS, AS WELL AS ITS DISTINCTIVE FORM AND CHARACTER. — THE LITERARY, INSTITUTIONAL, AND HISTORICAL VALUE OF BLACKSTONE'S COMMENTARIES. — THEIR GREAT INFLUENCE IN MOULDING THE LAWS AND JURISPRUDENCE OF AMERICA.

IT is natural for some minds to revere the past, to accept the present, and consciously or unconsciously to resist agitation and change. It is equally natural for other minds to question the wisdom of the past, to refuse to accept its lessons or results as final, to be discontented with them, and to welcome novelty as the means of effecting improvement. This mental classification obtains in the profession of the law, — those who advocate change, which they call reform; and those who resist it, being content with what is, rather than to run the risks that almost inevitably accompany innovation. It has been as true in this country as it has immemorially been true in England and elsewhere, that lawyers, as the effect of their studies and position in society, have naturally been attached to what is, and averse to experiments. De Tocqueville noticed this, and

<small>Lecture XI.</small>

<small>The conservatism of the bar.</small>

Lecture XI.

The compensations of conservatism.

he declared that the profession of the law in the United States was one of the great conservative and conserving forces of the Republic. Voltaire, speaking of lawyers as a class, characterized them as "the conservators of ancient barbarous usages." Rather strongly put, doubtless; but the history of the law plainly shows that the criticism is not wholly unjust. Any legal form, doctrine, or institution sanctioned by antiquity and precedent, no matter how inadequate, archaic, or unjust it may in the course of time have become, usually finds a body of defenders in the legal profession. They are not only suspicious of changes, but contemplate them with anxiety and dread. The exceptional force of established usages and precedent with all English-speaking peoples, is intensified in the English and American lawyer, and is so inveterate that radical changes are generally unwelcome, and many necessary ameliorations in the law have been forced upon the lawyers from the outside, and have been effected only after stubborn resistance on their part. Even Bacon, who strongly felt the necessity of amending the English law,[1] declared that "new laws are like the apothe- "caries' drugs; though they remedy the disease, yet "they trouble the body."[2] This conservatism has its undoubted compensations; but its immediate effect is to obstruct and delay changes after the necessity is apparent to the general observation and judgment. The final result is, however, that every step forward is, when taken, wisely taken; and with the

---

[1] See *ante* Lecture X.
[2] Reading upon the Statute of Uses, Bacon's Works, vol. iii., p. 304, (Montagu's Ed., American reprint).

single exception of the adoption in many of the
States of the principle of an elective judiciary,[1] I do
not recall any great structural changes in the law
that have proved precipitate or unwise, or which
had to be undone. I see signs more or less ominous
of threatened changes, chief among which are those
that menace the sacredness of contracts and the full
enjoyment of private property.[2] Happy will it be
for us if in this respect we shall be as fortunate in
the future as in the past.

Because of this tendency in our profession to conservatism, it is well that there are some minds that incline in the opposite direction, and boldly call upon the Past to vindicate and support itself. The unfettered action of these contending forces and the ceaseless struggle thus engendered produce in the long run better results than the exclusive dominance and sway of either would give. Coleridge in a thoughtful passage observes: "It is the chief "of many blessings derived from the insular char- "acter and circumstances of our country, that our "social institutions have formed themselves out of "our proper needs and interests; that, long and "fierce as the birth-struggle and growing pains "have been, the antagonist powers have been of "our own system and have been allowed to work "out their final balance with less disturbance from "external forces than was possible in the continental States. . . . Now, in every country of "civilized men, or acknowledging the rights of "property, and by means of determined boun-

[1] See *ante* Lecture IV., p. 119.   [2] See *ante* Lecture VII.

"daries and common laws united into one people
"or nation, the two antagonist powers or opposite
"interests of the state, under which all other state
"interests are comprised, are those of *permanence*
"and *progression*."[1]

This lecture and the next will exemplify these truths in connection with the evolution of laws and legal institutions. The conservative would never make the needful amendments in the law. The radical would err in the opposite direction of rash or unwise action. Changes in the law of any progressive society are, from the very purposes of law and from the very nature of society, absolutely necessary. True wisdom consists in the adaptation of law to the current state and true needs of the social organism. It has been well said that " Juris-
" prudence itself has become a study of the living
" growth of human society through all its stages;
" and it is no longer possible for law to be dealt
" with as a collection of rules imposed on society,
" as it were, by accident, nor for the resemblances
" and differences of the laws of different societies
" to be regarded as casual. . . . Whatever has
" ceased to change is dead. The essence of stu-
" pidity (it was said by a great Frenchman) is the

[1] Coleridge, "Church and State," p. 19. Mr. Morley, commenting on what he calls Stuart Mill's "famous pair of essays on Bentham and Coleridge," says: " I can vividly remember how the 'Coleridge' first awoke in many of us, who were then youths at Oxford, that sense of truth having many mansions and that desire and power of sympathy with the past, with the positive bases of the social fabric and with the value of Permanence in States, which form the reputable side of all conservatisms." Critical Miscellanies by John Morley, London, 1886, paper on " The Life of George Eliot," vol. iii., p. 131.

"demand for final opinions. As Maine himself said, the principle of progress, which is the same thing as the law of healthy life, is a principle of 'destruction tending to construction.'"[1] So true is this that it may confidently be affirmed that in a living and active society all law, whatever its form, is in its very nature mutable and temporary, except those principles of justice and right that are rooted in the moral convictions of enlightened men. These and these alone endure, and it is along these lines that the development of our substantive law and jurisprudence must proceed.

The subject of this and of the following lecture is, shortly stated, "Our Law, — Blackstone and Bentham as Types or Exponents of its Conservative and Radical Forces, and the nature and influence of their respective labors."

I select Blackstone rather than Eldon as the typi-

Lecture XI.

Progress is the law of healthy life.

---

[1] Pollock, "Oxford Lectures," No. VI., on Sir Henry Maine and his Work. Sir Henry Maine has presented this subject with characteristic elegance and ability. With respect to progressive societies, he lays it down "that social necessities and social opinion are always more or less in advance of law. We may come indefinitely near closing the gap, but it has a perpetual tendency to reopen. Law is stable; the societies we are speaking of are progressive. The greater or less happiness of a people depends on the degree of promptitude with which the gulf is closed. The instrumentalities by which law is brought into harmony with society seem to me to be three in number, Legal Fictions, Equity, and Legislation." "Ancient Law," chap. ii. How rapid and great are the changes which the law undergoes in active communities like those of England and America will be seen by comparing the state of the law as it existed in Blackstone's time and its improved condition as it exists to-day in both countries. The final lecture of the course is largely devoted to setting forth and illustrating these changes. (*Post* Lecture XIII.) In short, in little more than a century a large part of Blackstone is obsolete: at all events the Commentaries have become a very incomplete mirror of existing law.

cal conservative, for the reason that the nature of Blackstone's celebrated work, the time of its publication (coincident with our separation from the mother country), and its universal use and adoption in the several colonies (afterward States of the American Union) have given him in this country an influence in moulding its laws and jurisprudence which hardly ever fell to the lot of a law-giver, and which certainly was never so extensively enjoyed by an unauthoritative law-writer. In 1769 — just six years before the commencement of the American Revolution — the first completed edition of Blackstone's Commentaries appeared[1] It was attacked and criticised on various grounds, and a disposition to undervalue it has been more or less prevalent ever since. But its institutional value, and especially its historic value as an authentic and faithful mirror of the English law as the result of legislation and adjudication, as it then existed, it is difficult to overestimate. An unedited edition — or an edited edition where the editor has kept his hands off the text, such as the recent and valuable edition of Professor Hammond, of Washington University, St. Louis, Missouri, — will show the state of the law at that time, and supply a standard that enables us readily to perceive the great changes which it has since undergone.[2]

Professor Pollock, of Oxford, a few years since made some striking and suggestive observations,

---

[1] *Post* Lecture XIII.

[2] Blackstone's Commentaries, edited for American lawyers by William G. Hammond, with copious notes (Bancroft-Whitney Company), 1890. More fully, *post* Lectures XII., XIII.

in which I fully concur: "The typical achievement of the eighteenth century," he observes, "is Blackstone's Commentaries, which reduced to a form of singular literary excellence the matter of the authorities received as classical, and for the time being accepted as sufficient. Blackstone caught and expressed the spirit of his time with consummate skill, but he caught it only just in time. Hardly was his ink dry when Bentham sounded a blast that rudely disturbed the supposed finality of the common law, and (what was even a greater matter) the Independence of the United States insured the free and ample development of English legal ideas in directions and for purposes as yet unknown. With the nineteenth century we are started in a wide and ever-expanding field of new adventures."[1]

Lecture XI.

American expansion of English law. Extract from Sir Frederick Pollock.

I select Bentham as the typical radical or progressive, because he is in an eminent sense the father of the efforts which have been made in the English law during the last one hundred years looking to its improvement or reform. He was twenty-five years younger than Blackstone; and it is a curious coincidence that Bentham attended Blackstone's lectures at Oxford, which he afterward so unsparingly attacked. To appreciate properly the respective labors of these two eminent men, it is first of all necessary to have an accurate notion of the state of the English law at that period.

As the law of a nation cannot be justly estimated

Bentham a typical radical.

[1] Law Quarterly Review, July, 1887.

Lecture XI.

State of English law and society in Blackstone's and Bentham's time.

without a study of the growth and condition of the society out of which it springs and which it in turn regulates and governs, it is obvious that the general condition of England at the period in question and the progressive improvement of the English people for the preceding seven hundred years have a direct and important bearing upon the subject of this lecture and the next. These have been so graphically set forth by Macaulay that it will be most satisfactory to you to hear his description in his own words, which, although they are those of an unrivalled rhetorician, are nevertheless words of judicial exactness. In his article on Sir James Mackintosh, written in 1835, Macaulay says:—

Macaulay's description of the progress of the English people.

"The history of England is emphatically the "history of progress. It is the history of a con-"stant movement of the public mind, of a constant "change in the institutions of a great society. We "see that society, at the beginning of the twelfth "century, in a state more miserable than the state "in which the most degraded nations of the East "now are. We see it subjected to the tyranny of "a handful of armed invaders. We see the great "body of the people in a state of personal slavery, "the multitude sunk in brutal ignorance, and the "studious few engaged in acquiring what did not "deserve the name of knowledge. In the course of "seven centuries the wretched and degraded race "became the greatest and most highly civilized peo-"ple that the world ever saw; have spread their "dominion over every quarter of the globe; have "scattered the seeds of mighty empires and republics "over vast continents, of which no dim intimation

"had ever reached Ptolemy or Strabo; have created
"a maritime power which would have annihilated in
"a quarter of an hour the navies of Tyre, Athens,
"Carthage, Venice, and Genoa together; have car-
"ried the science of healing, the means of locomo-
"tion and correspondence, every mechanical art,
"every manufacture, everything that promotes the
"convenience of life, to a perfection that our ances-
"tors would have thought magical; have produced
"a literature which may boast of works not inferior
"to the noblest which Greece has bequeathed to
"us; have discovered the laws which regulate the
"motions of the heavenly bodies; have speculated
"with exquisite subtility on the operation of the
"human mind; have been the acknowledged lead-
"ers of the human race in the career of political
"improvement. The history of England is the
"history of this great change in the moral, intel-
"lectual, and physical state of the inhabitants of
"our own island."

Nevertheless, Professor Freeman is, I think, undoubtedly right in insisting that to understand the
English Constitution and legal institutions one must
constantly keep in mind that for fourteen hundred
years, notwithstanding foreign conquests and internal revolutions, the national life has remained
unbroken. "At no moment," he says, " has the tie
"between the present and the past been wholly
"rent asunder; at no moment have Englishmen
"sat down to put together a wholly new con-
"stitution in obedience to some dazzling theory.
"The growth of the unwritten Constitution has
"much in common with the earlier growth of the

Lecture XI.

The national life of England unbroken for centuries.

Lecture XI.

Condition of the English law in Blackstone's and Bentham's time.

"common law. It is simply another application of "the Englishman's love of precedent."[1]

It more immediately concerns us, however, to inquire into the condition of the English law at the period when Blackstone wrote and Bentham's career began. Here let me avail myself of the vivid portrayal of this subject by John Stuart Mill. Although the passage is very familiar and quite lengthy, it is so pertinent to the purpose in hand and so superior to anything I could offer, I am sure you will prefer that I should give you without abridgment Mill's own language: —

"The basis of English law was, and still is, the "feudal system. That system, like all those which "existed as custom before they were established as "law, possessed a certain degree of suitableness to "the wants of the society among whom it grew up; "that is to say, of a tribe of rude soldiers, holding "a conquered people in subjection, and dividing its "spoils among themselves. Advancing civilization "had, however, converted this armed encampment "of barbarous warriors, in the midst of enemies re-"duced to slavery, into an industrious, commercial, "rich, and free people. The laws which were suit-"able to the first of these states of society could "have no manner of relation to the circumstances "of the second, which could not even have come "into existence unless something had been done to "adapt those laws to it. But the adaptation was "not the result of thought and design; it arose not "from any comprehensive consideration of the new

[1] The Growth of the English Constitution, chap. i.

"state of society and its exigencies. What was
"done, was done by a struggle of centuries between
"the old barbarism and the new civilization; be-
"tween the feudal aristocracy of conquerors holding
"fast to the rude system that they had established,
"and the conquered effecting their emancipation.
"The last was the growing power, but was never
"strong enough to break its bonds, though ever
"and anon some weak point gave way. Hence the
"law came to be like the costume of a full-grown
"man who had never put off the clothes made for
"him when he first went to school. Band after
"band had burst; and as the rent widened, then,
"without removing anything except what might
"drop off of itself, the hole was darned, or patches
"of fresh law were brought from the nearest shop,
"and stuck on. Hence all ages of English history
"have given one another rendezvous in English
"law; their several products may be seen all
"together, not interfused, but heaped one upon
"another, as many different ages of the earth
"may be read in some perpendicular section of
"its surface, the deposits of each successive period
"not substituted, but superimposed on those of the
"preceding. And in the world of law, no less than
"in the physical world, every commotion and con-
"flict of the elements has left its mark behind in
"some break or irregularity of the strata. Every
"struggle which ever rent the bosom of society is
"apparent in the disjointed condition of the part of
"the field of law which covers the spot; nay, the
"very traps and pitfalls which one contending party
"set for another are still standing, and the teeth,

Lecture XI.

John Stuart Mill's description of the state of the English law.

"not of hyenas only, but of foxes and all cunning
"animals, are imprinted on the curious remains found
"in these antediluvian caves. In the English law,
"as in the Roman before it, the adaptations of bar-
"barous laws to the growth of civilized society were
"made chiefly by stealth. They were generally
"made by the courts of justice, who could not help
"reading the new wants of mankind in the cases
"between man and man which came before them,
"but who, having no authority to make new laws
"for those new wants, were obliged to do the work
"covertly, and evade the jealousy and opposition
"of an ignorant, prejudiced, and for the most part
"brutal and tyrannical legislature." [1]

Mill's picture mainly true but over-colored.

My judgment is that this picture, although true in its great outlines, is overdrawn; the colors are too deeply laid on, and overcharged. It should, I think, also be borne in mind that for about six of those seven centuries England had a regular Parliament, which certainly for the greater part of that period cannot fairly be described by the epithets used by Mr. Mill; and yet it was a legislature so composed as to favor from the nature, if not the necessities, of its constitution the interests of particular classes whenever these came in competition with those of the general weal. This Parliament, however, legislated for the whole realm. The general statutes as well as the body of customary law compendiously called the common law were uniform in their operation, and their authority and that of the judges who administered them extended to

---

[1] "Dissertations and Discussions," by John Stuart Mill, American reprint, vol. i., p. 393, essay on Bentham.

every part of the kingdom. These were great advantages, and they were advantages which were peculiar to England.[1]

[1] The exceptional state of things from which the advantages referred to in the text as being peculiar to England arose, is set forth with clearness by Monsieur Émile Boutmy in his recent book on the "English Constitution" (chaps. i.-v.). From the date of the Norman Conquest (A. D. 1066) it is shown that the monarchy was strong in comparison with the feudal nobility; that it early had the advantage of an executive machinery throughout the entire kingdom; that the English justices in eyre held their assizes in every county; that from the twelfth century the people enjoyed the good fortune of a homogeneous existence, were free from provincialism; that a strong feeling of nationality, based on territorial unity and strengthened by the insular position of England, was early developed; that local customs gave way before the laws and justice which were administered by the King's judges, so that "after the reign of Henry II. (A. D. 1154–1189), with a few strictly local exceptions, England possessed but one single customary law, — the common law, — one and the same for the whole land." "Unity of national law was, we may consider, established in 1200, thirty years after the definite institution of an itinerant High Court." The well-known abuses by the crown of this excess of kingly power led to the confederation of the barons in the time of John (A. D. 1215).

Monsieur Boutmy's observations on the character, causes, and effects of this great transaction are extremely interesting. We have place for only a few sentences : " The surprising political intelligence of the rebels of 1215 was in no sense due to a natural gift or inborn fitness; it was the slowly ripened fruit of necessity. Consider the case of these great barons with their estates dispersed throughout the country and confronted with a tyrannical monarch. . . . Distance gave them no sense of security; a few days' march and the King's army was at their castle gates. Nothing of the kind existed in other countries. The object which the English feudatories aimed at, and the means which they employed, took their character from these exceptional circumstances. . . . If they wished to contend at an advantage with an adversary so superior in force to themselves, the barons had but one course open to them. It was necessary not merely to unite, to make common cause, and to organize their own body, but to rally to them from one end of the kingdom to the other all who were exposed to the tyranny of the crown; and no rallying cry would be listened to unless it proclaimed the grievances of all alike. The resistance had to be political if the victory, when gained, was not to prove barren; it had to be of necessity general, national, nay, even

Lecture XI.

Essential excellences of the English law.

The English law, to be sure, was idiocratic, and on many points archaic enough; though bulky, it was without scientific form or arrangement; it was often obscure and uncertain; it was needlessly refined, slow, and expensive; it was in its criminal branch mercilessly severe; and yet what with the aid of acts of Parliament, which occasionally remedied glaring evils, with the establishment of the system of equity as administered in the Court of Chancery, with the growth and recognition of the law merchant, and with the gradual breaking down of the excessive technicalities of the old law, the English law with all of its anomalies and defects, was, taken all in all, in substance, in matter, in essential excellences, — chief among which were the principles of Magna Charta, which penetrated its every part, — a better system of laws than existed in any other part of the world. Bad enough in the respects above mentioned and many others it was; but an impartial review of it will, I think, show that it as little deserved on the one hand the

democratic, if the victory was to be gained at all. . . . This is what imparts grandeur and originality to the mighty drama, of which the first act ended with the Great Charter, and which reached its climax with the constitution of Parliament about 1340. It was then that a nation came into being, or rather took visible form, a nation ranged in compact order round its natural chiefs. This new power found in Parliament at once a means of action and a permanent organ, in which the resistance of 1215 took the pacific, regular, and continuous form of political opposition and control. It is thus that we must explain the peculiar characteristics which have made it from the beginning an institution original and unique in Europe. The absence of separate provincial traditions, privileges, and interests rendered the existence of anything more than one central assembly impossible." Boutmy, "English Constitution," Eaden's translation, 1891, chap. i., pp. 27-29.

constant and unmeasured denunciations of Bentham, as on the other the unstinted and perpetual eulogies of Blackstone.¹ To borrow and adapt a thought from Mr. Mill, it is given to a progressive like Bentham to discern more particularly those truths with which existing doctrines and institutions are at variance, while to a conservative like Blackstone it is given to discern especially the truths which lay *in* them.²

Lecture XI.

To Blackstone the field of English law seemed a paradise filled with everything to delight the eye and the mind; to Bentham it was a howling wilderness, full of all sorts of unclean birds and ravening beasts. In sober fact it was neither, but a region where good land was plentiful in the midst of fen and marsh, rock and mountain, and where thought, care, and labor were required to destroy the wild beasts, to subdue nature, to extirpate weeds and brambles, and to make the soil bear blossom, fruit, and grain.

Bentham's denunciations and Blackstone's eulogies alike unmerited.

One lesson which it is a leading purpose of this lecture to inculcate is the excellence of the Commentaries of Blackstone, and their value especially to the students, the lawyers, and the jurists of this country. He did a great work; he did it well. Its merits are the best known to the careful student who appreciates the confused and dispersed condition of statutes and decisions which it reduced to order and constructed into one of the most beautiful, noble, and symmetrical outlines of a complex system ever produced by the mind of man.

Value of Blackstone's Commentaries.

¹ See *post* Lecture XIII.
² Essay on Bentham, above mentioned.

The English law, insular in its origin and spirit, growing up irregularly during many centuries, resting partly in legislation, partly in treatises (such as Britton, Littleton, Coke, and a few others, which were regarded as authoritative), but mainly in the decisions of the courts scattered through hundreds of volumes, — was remarkable for its lack of formulated rules or scientific arrangement. It had little of the method and system which characterized the civil law, and it was almost wanting in literary or artistic form and expression. Its study involved laborious researches into its sources or evidences. This want of analysis and arrangement was seriously felt by Sir Matthew Hale, who is, I think, justly to be ranked among the very greatest of English lawyers. His "Analysis of the Civil Part of the Law," wherein he attempted the "re-"duction of the several titles of the law into dis-"tributions and heads according to an analytical "method" (which in its main scope was suggested and in part borrowed from the Institutes of Justinian), is the foundation of Blackstone's arrangement. That arrangement, while by no means the best the subject admits of, does not deserve the criticism with which Austin and others have so freely assailed it.[1] It constitutes a fair working plan,

[1] Professor Hammond's learned exposition, in his introduction to Sandars's Justinian, of the classical distribution of the law and of Blackstone's classification and arrangement based thereon attracted the attention and called forth the commendation of Sir Henry Maine, who declared it to be "the best defence he had seen." "Early Law and Custom," chap. xi., p. 365 (American reprint). Hammond's Sandars's Justinian, Introduction, p. xlii, *et seq.* See also the notes of the same learned scholar to his edition of Blackstone, vol. i., p. 316, note 1; *Ib.*, p. 330, note 2. Austin has words of praise for "our admi-

as the work of the illustrious commentator based thereon has amply demonstrated. By Blackstone's time the English law was sufficiently matured (as his Commentaries show) to admit of being put into methodical form; and the need for it arising from the mass of statutes and adjudged cases, and the insufficiency of existing text-books and treatises, pressed with increasing urgency. This great work could not have fallen into the hands of any one

<small>Lecture XI.

Urgent need by Blackstone's time for an institutional work on English law.</small>

rable Hale," some of which he even bestows upon the "Analysis." But it is difficult to account for Austin's dislike of Blackstone, and his contempt of Blackstone's work. He says: "The method observed by Blackstone in his far too celebrated Commentaries is a slavish and blundering copy of the very imperfect method which Hale delineates roughly in his short and unfinished "Analysis." . . . Neither in the general conception nor in the detail of Blackstone's book is there a single particle of original and discriminating thought." And much more to the same effect, Austin's "Jurisprudence," 5th ed. (Campbell's), pp. 68, 69.

Much has been written upon legal classification by Austin, Holland, Markby, Maine, Hammond, and others. The report of the committee of the American Bar Association on the classification of the law prepared by Professor Emlin McClain, of the Iowa University, presents an instructive view of the purposes of legal classification and of the practical difficulties of the subject, and the classification proposed by the report is an interesting attempt to solve them. Reports of the American Bar Association, vol. xiv., p. 379, 1891. The bibliography of the subject is given in the appendix to the report (pp. 407, 408). I fully agree with the following views expressed in the report (pp. 380, 381): "No system of classification of any practical utility can be devised which shall be suitable to more than one legal system. Distinctions which may be important in one may be of no consequence in another. Thus, as between the civil and common law, there are some points of analogy, but at the same time the differences are so great that no common classification descending to any degree of particularity is attainable. It is true that some notions of classification developed by the Civilians have been adopted as applicable to our system, but it will be found impracticable to carry out the civil law classification to a point where it will harmonize with the divisions of the subjects recognized by writers on the common law." See on this point the preface to the present volume.

Lecture XI.

Blackstone a consummate literary artist.

better able than Blackstone to perform it. He was by no means unfamiliar with the practical work of the profession. He gave many studious years to the task of preparation. He was, moreover, a consummate literary artist. In this respect he has never been excelled, — and I must say that in my judgment he has never, among legal elementary authors, been quite equalled. Even Bentham was forced to admit that Blackstone was the "first of all institutional writers who taught "jurisprudence to speak the language of the scholar "and the gentleman." His generalizations are clear and concise; his historical researches minute and in general remarkably accurate,[1] and his book is not, like so many modern works, a mere digest and arrangement of cases, but a systematic treatise. He had, therefore, all the qualifications — learning, general and legal, professional experience, literary gifts, and an exquisite artistic sense — necessary for the work on which he entered when he took his seat in 1758 as Vinerian Professor of Law at Oxford.

---

[1] "In the reports and treatises of the last century ... there was a serious endeavor for lucidity and form as against gratuitous technicality and the literary clumsiness of the only existing legal classics. Blackstone's Commentaries were the outcome of this endeavor, and, all things considered, an admirable one. Dr. Brunner (in the introduction to Holtzendorff's 'Encyklopädie der Rechtswissenschaft') has borne splendid witness to Blackstone's merit in his account of the sources of English law." "Oxford Lectures and Other Discourses by Sir Frederick Pollock" (London, 1890), p. 29. So deep and careful a student of the English law as Mr. Digby, in his preface to the History of the Law of Real Property, says that "Blackstone still remains unrivalled as an expositor of the law of his day. . . . It will be seen," he adds, "that I throughout refer to Blackstone as the great authority on the earlier law," without going back to the original sources. This is testimony from the highest source as to Blackstone's accuracy.

In judging of his Commentaries, we must not fall into the mistake that some of Blackstone's critics make, and look at them from a wrong point of view. He was a teacher whose purpose was to set forth the English law as it then existed, and not a reformer whose purpose was to point out its defects with a view to its improvement. The two functions are, of course, not incompatible. But it is obviously not necessary in an institutional work whose design is to state the law as it is, that the author should expose and dwell upon the defects and imperfections of the system which he is expounding.

There is no faculty more rare, none which involves the exercise of higher and more admirable qualities, than the critical faculty in general. This is eminently true of the critical legal faculty, and it detracts but little from the merits of Blackstone's work, keeping in mind its purpose, that he did not possess, or at all events did not more freely exercise that faculty. While this is true, it is also true that the expounder of a system of law ought not to praise where praise is not deserved; and it must be admitted that Blackstone was strongly inclined to view the laws of England with the eye of an idolater, and like the idolater he rarely saw anything but perfection and beauty in the object of his worship. Nevertheless, let me suggest and enforce the thought that a capital need of our law to-day is for some gifted expositor who shall perform upon it the same operation performed by Blackstone more than a hundred years ago; that is, an institutional work systematically arranging and expounding its great principles as

Lecture XI.

The proper point of view from which to judge of the Commentaries.

they have been modified, expanded, and developed since Blackstone's day, so as to make it as faithful and complete a mirror of the law as it now exists as Blackstone's work was of the law as it existed when his Commentaries were produced. And such also is the weighty opinion of Sir Frederick Pollock. "A good book of Institutes "of English Law would indeed be a boon for "lawyers and students to welcome. As it is, "our young men hear systematic lectures on "jurisprudence and legal method in general, and "have meanwhile to pick up their first notions of "the law of their own country from mauled and "tinkered editions or imitations of Blackstone put "together in defiance of all rational arrangement. "Blackstone's work was an excellent one in his "time and according to his lights; we might "honour him better at this day than by a blundering lip-service, which, as a rule, effectually excludes the knowledge of what Blackstone really "wrote. The modern editions utterly spoil Blackstone as literature, without producing a good account of the modern law. One consequence of "this is that the historical value of Blackstone in "his genuine form is apt to be sadly underrated.[1]" This is sound. Hammond's Blackstone, before mentioned, is edited on the right principle. I take my leave of Blackstone and his work with the observation that if in the pressure of the cares and toils which are the common lot of the successful lawyer you will make it a point every year once

---

[1] Pollock, "Essays on Jurisprudence and Ethics," London, 1882, pp. 6, 7.

to read the "Commentaries on the Laws of England, by Sir William Blackstone, Kt., one of the "Justices of His Majesty's Court of Common "Pleas," you will thank me as often as you shall complete the reading for the advice I have thus ventured to give.[1]

Lecture XI.

I now turn your attention to Blackstone's critic and assailant, Jeremy Bentham, to the end that we may form a judgment of the value and influence of his labors. This is the more necessary because it even yet rests uncertain in some minds whether Bentham sowed the field of the law with wheat or thistles. This subject leads, as we shall see in our next lecture, to the consideration of questions of vital and practical interest to our law.

Bentham and his labors.

Bentham was the pronounced enemy of what we call case-law, — of what he styled, somewhat con-

Enemy of case-law.

---

[1] If it were not ungracious toward an author who has done so much for his profession as Blackstone, we might indeed wish that Blackstone had possessed more fully the quality that Stuart Mill ascribes to Coleridge; namely, "the spirit of philosophy within the bounds of traditional opinions. Coleridge has been, almost as truly as Bentham, 'the great questioner of things established;' for a questioner needs not necessarily be an enemy. . . . With Coleridge the very fact that any doctrine had been believed by thoughtful men and received by whole nations or generations of mankind, was part of the problem to be solved; was one of the phenomena to be accounted for. . . . It was to be expected that Bentham should continually miss the truth which is in the traditional opinions, and Coleridge that which is out of them and at variance with them." "Dissertations and Discussions by John Stuart Mill: Essay on Coleridge," vol. ii., pp. 6, 7, American reprint, Boston, 1868. The contemporary and earlier opinions of Blackstone's Commentaries, including those of Fox, Sir William Jones, Gibbon, Mansfield, Story, Mackintosh, and others, are collected in the Preface of Paterson's "Liberty of the Subject" (MacMillan & Company), 1877.

Lecture XI.

Vast size of case-law threatens revolutionary changes in English jurisprudence.

temptuously, "judge-made law." "The frightful "accumulation of case-law," says Sir Henry Maine, "conveys to English jurisprudence a menace of "revolution far more serious than any popular "murmurs, and which, if it does nothing else, is "giving to mere tenacity of memory a disgraceful "advantage over all the finer qualities of the legal "intellect." [1] Evidently the doctrine of precedent and its direct fruits — namely, the colossal and ever-growing mass of reported cases — are to-day, even more than in Bentham's time, subjects of vast and living moment, whose depths none of us has fully sounded.

The story of Bentham's life and labors shows, to use Carlyle's phrase, that "no great man lives in vain." It also lends color to Carlyle's favorite dictum, that "the history of the world is but the biography of great men." It shows, moreover, that if a man has "that last infirmity of noble mind," is willing "to scorn delights and live laborious days" that he may gain the fair guerdon of a lasting fame, he must become connected with, and his labors must become incorporate in, institutions which have the quality of living, although the individual members successively perish. "Wise or fortunate," says Gibbon in his famous chapter on Roman Jurisprudence, speaking of Justinian, "is the prince who "connects his own reputation with the honor and "interests of a perpetual body of men." Bentham did this. Although he was the inveterate assailant

---

[1] Sir Henry Maine, "Village Communities," paper on Roman Law and Legal Education (American Ed.), p. 347. See *ante* Lecture VI., p. 176 *et seq.*; Lecture VIII., p. 231; Lecture IX., *passim;* Lecture X.

and critic of the lawyers as well as of the English system of law in his day; often, indeed usually, carrying his assaults and criticisms beyond the line of fairness, — nevertheless his lifelong and disinterested labors were inspired by a desire and ambition, free of the least taint or alloy, to promote (and time has demonstrated that they did promote and are promoting) the true interests of the profession, thus connecting himself in name and memory with it, and giving him the only reward he either sought or would prize, namely, that which springs from his labors in behalf of its true and permanent welfare.

Bentham's place in our law, and the nature and influence of his labors for its improvement, will be the subject of the next lecture.

LECTURE XII.

OUR LAW: BLACKSTONE AND BENTHAM AS TYPES AND EXPONENTS OF ITS CONSERVATIVE AND RADICAL FORCES, TO WHOSE FREE PLAY IT OWES ITS PROGRESS, AS WELL AS ITS DISTINCTIVE FORM AND CHARACTER. — BENTHAM'S PLACE IN OUR LEGAL HISTORY. — CHARACTER AND INFLUENCE OF HIS WRITINGS AND LABORS UPON ENGLISH LAW AND ITS REFORMATION (CONCLUDED).

Lecture XII.

Bentham's place in our legal history.

"BENTHAM'S theories upon legal subjects have "had a degree of practical influence upon "the legislation of his own and various other coun- "tries comparable only to those of Adam Smith and "his successors upon commerce." Such is the opinion of Sir James Stephen concerning the influence and effect of Bentham's legal writings and labors.[1] As late as 1874 Sir Henry Maine went so far as to declare: "I do not know a single law reform effected "since Bentham's day which cannot be traced to "his influence; but a still more startling proof of "the clearing of the brain produced by this system "[the system of Hobbes, Bentham, and Austin], "even in an earlier stage, may be found in Hobbes. "In his 'Dialogue of the Common Laws,' he argues "for a fusion of law and equity, a registration of

[1] Sir James FitzJames Stephen, "History of Criminal Law of England," London, 1883, vol. ii., chap. xxi., p. 216.

"titles to land, and a systematic penal code,— three measures which we are on the eve of seeing carried out at this moment."[1] Opposite views are entertained by others. It is worth while, therefore, to essay to define Bentham's place in the history of our law, and to attempt an estimate of the character and influence of his writings; and such is the purpose of this hour. Bentham's fertile and active mind embraced in the scope of its operations many other subjects than those of law and legislation, such as ethics, political economy, political reform, and even practical politics. Nevertheless, his principal attention was given to the English law and to the mode by which its improvement could best be

Lecture XII.

Bentham's place in our legal history.

[1] Early History of Institutions, Lecture XIII. Others also, well qualified to judge, have assigned to Bentham a place in the foremost rank of men of extraordinary intellectual endowments. I subjoin an extract giving Macaulay's judgment. He is by no means a partial witness: he was a Whig of the Whigs; Bentham, a Radical of the Radicals. If there was anything that a Whig hated more than a Tory, it was a Radical. Macaulay had in Bentham's lifetime attacked with fierceness and rancor the Benthamic notions of politics. Yet within a few months after the death of Bentham, in reviewing (July, 1832) Dumont's "Mirabeau," Macaulay thus expresses his opinion of Bentham's character and labors: "Of Mr. Bentham," he says, "we would at all times speak with the reverence which is due to a great original thinker and to a sincere and ardent friend of the human race. In some of the highest departments in which the human intellect can exert itself he has not left his equal or his second behind him. From his contemporaries he has had, according to the usual lot, more or less than justice. He has had blind flatterers and blind detractors,— flatterers who could see nothing but perfection in his style; detractors who could see nothing but nonsense in his matter. He will now have his judges. Posterity will pronounce its calm and impartial decision; and that decision will, we firmly believe, place in the same rank with Galileo and with Locke the man who found jurisprudence a gibberish and left it a science." (A general truth, rather too strongly expressed.) See below for opinions of Brougham and others concerning Bentham's writings and labors.

effected; and this lecture will be restricted to his writings and labors concerning English law and the method of reforming or amending it.

It is essential to a correct view of the character and value of Bentham's labors to bear in mind the period of time covered thereby, and also the condition of the English law, especially as it existed when his efforts for its improvement were begun.[1] Bentham was born in London in 1748. In 1763, at the early age of sixteen, he was graduated with honors at Oxford. He was in due time called to the English bar. His first work, the Fragment on Government, being a criticism on a portion of Blackstone's Commentaries, was published (anonymously)' in 1776; his attack on Usury Laws in 1787; his Panopticon in 1791; his protest against Law Taxes in 1796; his great work (Dumont's Edition, in Paris) on Legislation, Civil and Criminal, in 1802; on Codification in 1817; on Rewards and Punishments (Dumont's Edition) in 1818; on Judicial Evidence, in Paris, in 1823, English translation thereof in 1825, and from original English manuscripts, edited by John Stuart Mill, in 1827. I omit in this enumeration, as not essential to my present purpose, some minor works concerning law or legislation, and many important writings relating to education, prison discipline, political reforms, morals, and kindred subjects.

Bentham was, broadly speaking, contemporary with what may be styled the legal reign of Eldon. The common law in its substance and procedure was by everybody in England regarded with a

[1] See *ante* Lecture XI.

veneration superstitious to the verge of idolatry. It was declared, and generally believed to be, "the perfection of reason." Lord Eldon and the Court of Chancery, with its suitorcide delays, "pressed heavily on mankind." Imprisonment for debt, and distress for rent with all its harsh and oppressive incidents, were in unabated force. The criminal law, defective and excessively technical, abounding with capricious and cruel punishments, and which denounced the penalty of death on about two hundred offences, remained in a state which no one any longer hesitates to pronounce outrageous and shocking.[1] It was on this system that Bentham, when he was under thirty years of age, solitary and alone, commenced the attack which he incessantly continued until his death in 1832, at the age of eighty-four. He was a multiform man; but it is as a law reformer that he stands the most conspicuous and pre-eminent. He had all the personal qualities of a reformer, — deep-hearted sincerity, unbounded faith in his own powers and self-sufficiency, unwearied zeal, and dauntless moral courage.[2]

One who should not bear in mind the peculiar aversion of the English people to innovation, the inveterate conservatism of the bar, and the awe and reverence with which they regarded the existing system, might suppose that the work of amendment would readily follow when the defect, were pointed out. But Bentham's voice for nearly fifty years, so far as England was concerned, was

[1] See *post* Lecture XIII.
[2] See *ante* Lecture VI., p. 180.

> Lecture XII.
>
> Bentham's devotion to his work.
>
> A legal Recluse.

like that of one crying in the wilderness. Parliament did not heed it; the bar did not heed it; nobody heeded it. For quite twenty-five years he seems to have had no following beyond Mill, senior, and a few other personal friends. Happily for him he had a competence and was able to give his days and nights to the work to which he had resolved to consecrate his life. Happily, perhaps, also, he had no domestic cares or distractions, being without wife or children. Bowring preserves an affecting letter from which it appears that at one time in his earlier life a lady had engaged his affections and rejected his proposals. In a letter written long, long years afterwards to the lady herself, the Recluse says: "I "am alive, more than two months advanced in my "eightieth year, — more lively than when you pre- "sented me in ceremony with the flower in Green "Lane. Since that day not a single one has passed "in which you have not engrossed more of my "thoughts than I could have wished." He concludes: "I have a ring with some snow-white "hair in it and my profile, which everybody "says is like; at my death you will have such "another;" and then playfully, perhaps pathetically, adds, "Should you come to want, it will be worth a good sovereign to you."

There is in this a genuine touch of nature! Alike in peasant, prince, poet, and philosopher, the human heart, once truly touched by love, becomes thence like the ocean, — restless and insurgent evermore. Amid all his engrossing pursuits, in which he wholly shut himself out from society, and indeed from every person but a few friends whom he would occasionally meet when the toil of the day was over, the vision and the memory of the giver of the flower in Green Lane, pushing aside for the while Codes, Panopticons, Chrestomathias, Pannomions, and all such, were, he confesses, present to him every day. But although " along the " plains, where Passionate Discord rears eternal " Babel, the holy stream of wedded happiness " glides on," it glided not on for him, but passed him by irreversibly. One so thoroughly absorbed in work which he regarded as so pressing and so important to the world, would have made, it is to be feared, a poor husband, just in proportion as he was a devoted philosopher. Doubtless she judged wisely. It was well for her, and perhaps well for him, that he never saluted the woman who gave him the flower in Green Lane with the tender and sacred name of wife.

In forming a judgment of Bentham's work and of the way he did it and of the efficiency of that way, it is almost as essential to see how he regarded the English law as it is to inquire precisely how far his opinions were correct. Bentham's voluminous writings leave no doubt as to his views concerning the English law. There was no health in it. Admitting, as he did, that the legislative enactments and the reports of adjudged cases contained more valuable materials for the construction of a system of laws than any other nation in the world possessed,[1] he yet maintained that the existing law, so far from being the perfection of human reason or the product

[1] See *ante* Lecture VI., p. 174; Lecture X., p. 270.

of matured experience, was (to use his own language) but "a fathomless and boundless chaos, made up of "fiction, tautology, technicality, and inconsistency, "and the administrative part of it a system of ex-"quisitively contrived chicanery, which maximizes "delay and denial of justice." Thus viewing it, he saw no remedy but its overthrow and destruction as a system, and rebuilding it anew, using old materials as far as they were useful and no farther. He regarded the whole system, as I have often thought, with much the same feeling that the French people contemporaneously looked upon the Bastille, as a monument of feudalism, oppression, and injustice, fit only to be destroyed. Blackstone, on the other hand, viewing the system with the optimistic eyes of the age in which he wrote, compared it, in his inimitable style, to "an old Gothic castle, erected "in the days of chivalry, but fitted up for a modern "inhabitant. The moated ramparts, the embattled "towers, and the trophied halls are magnificent and "venerable, but useless, and therefore neglected. "The inferior apartments, now accommodated to "daily use, are cheerful and commodious, though "their approaches may be winding and difficult." [1] What could be more charming, what more desirable! All the interest and grandeur that attach to a structure at once imposing, venerable, and historic, combined with the convenience that results from its being already fitted to the amplest modern uses, — the only defect being, if, indeed, it is such, that the approaches *may* be (he does not

[1] 3 Black. Com., 268; 2 Dillon, "Municipal Corporations" (4th ed.), § 934, *a*, and note.

feel quite sure that they are) somewhat winding and difficult.

Bentham's claims upon our regard will not be duly valued unless we keep ever in mind the difficulties which he was called upon to face. He stood alone. For more than twenty-five years he stood absolutely alone. But like Milton (whose London house it was Bentham's pride to own, although it was one of his peculiarities that he utterly disesteemed poetry), — like Milton in his blindness, through all neglect and discouragements, Bentham "bated not a jot of heart or hope, but still bore up and steered right onward."

I have not the time, if I had the power, adequately to present a picture of the obstacles Bentham met with. And yet I must not pass these entirely over, as they are the background of any portraiture of the man and his work. There was the traditional, constitutional, ingrained aversion of the English people to innovation, combined with their idolatrous regard for the existing order of things.[1] It is worth while to illustrate this. Burke was undoubtedly the most enlightened statesman of his age, — one of the profoundest political thinkers and philosophers of any age. In one of his greatest speeches[2] he thus expressed in his felicitous way the traditional and habitual regard of the English mind for the established Constitution and for ancient acts of Parliament: —

"I do not dare to rub off a particle of the venerable rust that rather adorns and preserves than

---
[1] See *ante* Lecture XI.
[2] Conciliation with America, 1775.

Lecture XII.

Illustration from Burke.

"destroys the metal. It would be a profanation
"to touch with a tool the stones. I would not vio-
"late with modern polish the ingenuous and noble
"roughness of these truly constitutional materials.
"Tampering is the odious vice of restless and un-
"stable minds. I put my foot in the tracks of
"our forefathers, where I can neither wander nor
"stumble. *What the law has said, I say.* In all
"things else I am silent. I have no organ but
"for her words. If this be not ingenious, I am
"sure it is safe."

Again, in 1791, speaking of the English Constitution, Burke says: —

"We ought to understand this admired Consti-
"tution (of England) according to our measure,
"combining admiration with knowledge if we
"can, and to venerate even where we are not
"able presently to comprehend."[1]

Than this nothing can be more opposed to Bentham's mode of thought, since he would take nothing for granted, and would not, he said, admit murder or arson or any other act to be wrong unless it could be shown by reasoning to be so. I find in Henry Crabb Robinson's Diary[2] another contemporary illustration of the difficulty of attacking *Illustration from Lord Thurlow.* things established, so pertinent that it will excuse its irreverence. He relates that in 1788 a deputation of distinguished men waited on Lord Chancellor Thurlow to secure his support in their attempt to obtain the repeal of the Corporation and Test Act.

---

[1] Appeal from the New to the Old Whigs. Burke's Works, vol. iv., p. 213 (Little, Brown, & Co.'s Ed.).

[2] Vol. i., chap. xv., American Ed., p. 243.

The Chancellor received them very civilly, and then said : " Gentlemen, I 'm against you, by G—. " I am for the Established Church, d— me! Not " that I have any more regard for the Estab- " lished Church than for any other church, but " because it *is* established. And if you can get " your d—d religion established, I 'll be for that " too ! " This national peculiarity, as well as the natural conservatism of the bar, had been greatly intensified by the French Revolution. As late as 1808 Sir Samuel Romilly, speaking of his own parliamentary labors and discouraging experience, says : " If any person be desirous of having an " adequate idea of the mischievous effects which " have been produced in this country by the French " Revolution and all its attendant horrors, he should " attempt some legislative reform on humane and " liberal principles. He will then find, not only " what a stupid dread of innovation, but what a " savage spirit it has infused into the minds of " many of his countrymen "[1]

Lecture XII.

Effect of the French Revolution on law reform in England.

Eldon was for a quarter of a century Lord Chancellor. It is certain that he never originated a reform act; and if he ever favored an act which could be fairly said to have been intended to amend the law, I do not recall it. It was difficult and almost impossible to pass any act which Eldon disapproved. He considered the existing system as perfect ; or if not, that if the least innovation were favored or allowed no one could tell where it would stop, and

Eldon's influence on law reform.

---

[1] " Life of Sir Samuel Romilly," edited by his sons, vol. i., Diary, June, 1808. See also his beautifully written Letters to C., letter iii., September, 1807, in same volume, 3d ed., London, 1842, p. 537.

Lecture XII.

Eldon's character and merits.

therefore the true course was to destroy all innovation in the egg. He was "accused by Bentham of "nipping in the bud the spread of improvement over "the habitable globe."[1] And yet I love old Eldon. He could not help his impenetrable and incorrigible conservatism. He was sincere and immovable in his sincerity. If he was true to his party and "never ratted," he was also true to his heart and conscience and sense of duty. No breath of suspicion ever rested upon him or the absolute purity of his court. What a great advance had been made from the time of Bacon to the time of Eldon. Eldon had, moreover, the qualities of a great judge. He loved right. He hated wrong He appreciated arguments of counsel and freely heard them. He was deeply learned in his profession. His judgment was sure-footed. His love of justice was so great, his sense of the fearful responsibility attaching to the exercise of judicial power so keen, that he habitually hesitated and doubted; but his doubts and hesitations all had their origin in the dread of doing injustice, and a noble anxiety to know and to do the right. If he vigorously resisted amendment or change in our law, he as vigorously

---

[1] Townsend, "Lives of Twelve Eminent Judges," vol. ii., chap. x., p. 455, London, 1846. Bowring says that Bentham hated Eldon as much as it was possible to his benevolent nature to hate, — considered him the mightiest and most mischievous of all the opponents of law reform; and he calls him, in another place, the Lord of Doubts. Defective as the laws were, they were doubtless in a vastly better condition than they would have been if Bentham could have subjected them to the full operation of his radical, and to a large extent impracticable views, which, however, were never favored in their full scope and details by such conservative reformers as Brougham, Romilly, and Bickersteth.

protected and conserved existing excellences and merits. Again I say I love old Eldon! With all his ultra-conservatism and dubitations, — his only defects, — I love his sturdy, genuine, honest nature. I have said this that you might not conceive an undue bias against Eldon from what Sydney Smith, Bentham, and other Whigs have said of him and his court.

Lecture XII.

The libel laws even were in Bentham's way. Not to mention other instances, as late as 1811 there was difficulty in obtaining a publisher for the "Introduction to the Rationale of Evidence." More than one bookseller declined, giving as a reason that the book was libellous. The "Elements of the Art of Packing," which lay six years printed but unpublished, had alarmed the " trade," and it never was fully published until after Bentham's death. But Bentham kept right on. At length he began to attract the attention of a few gifted minds. One of the earliest of these was Sir Samuel Romilly, who of all English lawyers is, as I think, the one that nearest approaches a perfect model.[1]

Libel laws in Bentham's way.

[1] Romilly was the means of rendering Bentham what turned out to be a most signal service. About 1788, when Bentham was forty years of age, Romilly sent to Genevese Dumont some of Bentham's writings. They greatly impressed this gifted man with their originality and value. Dumont gave a large portion of his life to the *redaction* and translating into French some of the most important of Bentham's works. But this required years. On April 5, 1791, Romilly writes to Dumont: "Bentham leads the same kind of life as usual at Hendon, — seeing nobody, reading nothing, and writing books which nobody reads." In 1802 Dumont's French edition of Bentham's treatise on " Legislation Civil and Criminal " appeared, and was translated into Spanish, Russian, and Italian; in 1811 " Rewards and Punishments," and in 1823 " Judicial Evidence," thus treated and translated by Dumont, were published in Paris. This gave

Lecture XII.

Bentham's friends and co-laborers.

Romilly excepted, no persons in England of distinction or official influence acknowledged adhesion to Bentham's doctrines until the early part of the Bentham a European reputation, and quickened his tardy appreciation at home. In the history of letters there is nothing more remarkable than the relation between Dumont and Bentham. Macaulay's account of the services rendered by Dumont is as interesting as it is, generally speaking, accurate. Of the character and value of Dumont's labors the great reviewer remarks:—

"They can be fully appreciated only by those who have studied Mr. Bentham's works, both in their rude and in their finished state. The difference, both for show and for use, is as great as the difference between a lump of golden ore and a rouleau of sovereigns fresh from the mint. . . . Never was there a literary partnership so fortunate as that of Mr. Bentham and M. Dumont. The raw material which Mr. Bentham furnished was most precious; but it was unmarketable. He was, assuredly, at once a great logician and a great rhetorician. But the effect of his logic was injured by a vicious arrangement, and the effect of his rhetoric by a vicious style. His mind was vigorous, comprehensive, subtle, fertile of argument, fertile of illustrations. But he spoke in an unknown tongue; and, that the congregation might be edified, it was necessary that some brother having the gift of interpretation should expound the invaluable jargon. His oracles were of high import; but they were traced on leaves and flung loose to the wind. . . . M. Dumont was admirably qualified to supply what was wanting in Mr. Bentham. In the qualities in which the French writers surpass those of all other nations — neatness, clearness, precision, condensation — he surpassed all French writers. If M. Dumont had never been born, Mr. Bentham would still have been a very great man; but he would have been great to himself alone. The fertility of his mind would have resembled the fertility of those vast American wildernesses in which blossoms and decays a rich but unprofitable vegetation, 'wherewith the reaper filleth not his hand, neither he that bindeth up the sheaves his bosom.' . . . Many persons have attempted to interpret between this powerful mind and the public. But in our opinion M. Dumont alone has succeeded. It is remarkable that in foreign countries, where Mr. Bentham's works are known solely through the medium of the French version, his merit is almost universally acknowledged. Indeed, what was said of Bacon's philosophy may be said of Bentham's. It was in little repute among us till judgments came in its favor from beyond sea, and convinced us, to our shame, that we had been abusing and laughing at one of the greatest men of the age." Essay on Mirabeau, July, 1832.

present century. Among the most eminent of these was Mill, senior, the father of the still more eminent John Stuart Mill. Mill, the father, and his family were for years members of Bentham's household; and Mill was one of the ablest exponents and advocates of Bentham's doctrines. Afterwards came Bickersteth (subsequently Lord Langdale, Master of the Rolls), who was the well-beloved disciple; for not long before the master's death he received his benediction in these words: "Of all my friends, "Bickersteth was the most cordial to law reform to "its utmost extent." Then came Brougham and Sir James Mackintosh, and at a later period others. Romilly, Langdale, Brougham, and Mackintosh each held seats in Parliament; and their efforts for the reform of the laws, civil and criminal, and the slow, tedious, and piecemeal process by which such reforms were accomplished, are known to history, and need not be related here, even if time there were. Lord Brougham thus excellently states the grounds of Bentham's title to distinction and to our regard: "The age of law reform and the age of Jeremy "Bentham are one and the same. No one before "him had ever seriously thought of exposing the "defects in our English system of jurisprudence. "He it was who first made the mighty step of try- "ing the whole provisions of our jurisprudence by "the test of expediency, fearlessly examining how "far each part was connected with the rest, and "with a yet more undaunted courage inquiring "how far even its most consistent and symmetrical "arrangements were framed according to the prin- "ciples which should pervade a code of laws, their

Lecture XII.

Lord Brougham's estimate of Bentham.

Lecture XII.

Lord Brougham's estimate of Bentham.

"adaptation to the circumstances of society, to the
"wants of men, and to the promotion of human
"happiness. Not only was he pre-eminently origi-
"nal among the lawyers and legal philosophers of
"his own country; he might be said to be the first
"legal philosopher who had appeared in the world.
"None of the great men before him had attempted
"to reduce the whole of jurisprudence under the
"dominion of fixed and general rules; none ever
"before Mr. Bentham took in the whole depart-
"ments of legislation; none before him can be said
"to have treated it as a science, and by so treating
"made it one. This is his pre-eminent distinction.
"To this praise he is justly entitled; and it is as
"proud a title to fame as any philosopher ever
"possessed."[1]

[1] Lord Brougham's Speeches, Edinburgh, 1838, vol. ii., p. 288, Black's Edition. Brougham and Bentham were well acquainted. In a sense Brougham was one of Bentham's disciples. Both aspired to be law reformers. Indeed, Brougham's most useful labors in Parliament were directed towards law reform. There were, however, radical differences of opinion between Bentham and Brougham as to the best method of effecting the desired improvement. These differences naturally arose out of the difference in the situation and surroundings of the two men. Bentham, though he was regularly bred to the law and called to the bar, never pursued the profession. Bentham thus summarized his own career as a practising lawyer: "I never pleaded in public. On my being called to the bar, I found a cause or two at nurse for me. My first thought was how to put them to death; and the endeavors were not, I believe, altogether without success. Not long after a case was brought to me for my opinion. I ransacked all the codes. My opinion was right according to the codes; but it was wrong according to a manuscript unseen by me and inaccessible to me, — a manuscript containing the report of I know not what opinion, said to have been delivered before I was born, and locked up, as usual, for the purpose of being kept back or produced according as occasion served."

Bentham's solitary habits made him unfamiliar with practical life,

Bowring once remarked to Talleyrand, "Of all modern writers, Bentham was the one from whom

Lecture XII.

and unable clearly to distinguish the attainable from the unattainable. Brougham, on the other hand, was a man of affairs, acquainted with the world of men, with the world of lawyers, with the temper of Parliament, and able to form a practical judgment concerning matters of legislation. Though a man of liberal views, and with the courage boldly to maintain them, he had in the matter of law reform not a little of the usual conservatism of the lawyer and the prudence and tact of the legislator. Bowring records that in anticipation of Brougham's great speech on Law Reform, Bentham said: "Insincere as Brougham is, it is always worth my while to bestow a day on him. I shall try to subdue him and make something of him. I shall see whether he has any curiosity to assist in tearing the established system of procedure to rags and tatters." This was Bentham's notion of the heroic, the destructive nature of the remedy required. Brougham's heralded and famous speech on the Present State of the Law, and which he entitled "Law Reform," was delivered on the seventh day of February, 1828; but the remedy proposed by him was to preserve the garment and patch it up, instead of "tearing it to rags and tatters." Two days afterward Bentham thus records his disgust and disappointment: "Mr. Brougham's mountain is delivered, and behold! a mouse. The wisdom of the reformer could not overcome the craft of the lawyer. Mr. Brougham, after all, is not the man to set up a simple, natural, and rational administration of justice against the entanglements and technicalities of our English law proceedings." I do not know that Brougham ever heard of this contemptuous opinion, although of course he knew that his proposed remedies utterly failed to meet Bentham's views of what the case demanded. In 1838 Brougham edited an edition of his own speeches (namely, the one above cited, printed by the Messrs. Black), himself preparing historical introductions to the various subjects, and among others to the speech on Law Reform. In tracing the history of this movement, he gives many pages to a consideration of Bentham's personal and intellectual qualities, and to a critical estimate of his writings upon law, jurisprudence, and legislation. Brougham excels in biographical sketches and descriptions of this kind, and this seems to me to be one of his best. It will well reward full perusal, but I have space only for the few sentences given in the text. Mr. John Stuart Mill in a note to his article on Bentham ("Dissertations and Discussions," Am. Ed., vol. i., p. 417), commends Brougham's view of Bentham, and explains and extenuates Bentham's "unreasonable attacks on individuals, and in particular on Lord Brougham on the subject of Law Reforms; they were no more

Lecture XII.

Talleyrand's observation.

"most had been stolen, and stolen without acknowledgment." "True," replied Talleyrand; "*et pillé de tout le monde, il est toujours riche,*"— "and robbed by everybody, he is always rich."

I have thus sought to give a notion of Bentham's intellectual qualities, of his times, and of the general character of his writings respecting law and legislation. This has been necessarily an outline view only. It remains to attempt, by way of summing up, a critical estimate of the value of his labors, and the nature and extent of the actual influence upon our laws and jurisprudence of his doctrines and writings.

If we are to form a sound judgment on this subject, we must not mistake the point of view from which to look at him. To be truly appreciated, Bentham must, as I have already said, be regarded primarily and essentially as a law reformer generally, and specially as a reformer of the then existing law of England. He was bold, courageous, and original. He was the first to expose its defects and to suggest the remedies required. He destroyed with his own force the professional and general superstition that the law was perfect, and

Value and influence of Bentham's labors summed up.

the effect of envy or malice, or any really unamiable quality, than the freaks of a pettish child, and are scarcely a fitter subject of censure or criticism."

The late eminent law teacher, Professor Theodore W. Dwight, wrote me, October 24, 1890, in regard to Bentham, thus: "I am astonished at his legal genius, revere him for his kindly disposition even towards brutes, am delighted with his wit and playful repartee, and enjoy his sarcasm, of which, however, he never made use except when the occasion required it."

OUR LAW: ITS PROGRESSIVE FORCES. 333

by his labors and writings he was the means of at length awakening the public mind from its stupor and inertia on this subject. His merits as a critic and censor of the law as he found it in his day and in his country, it is difficult to overvalue. Blackstone, the type of the professional mind of his age, regarded the English law as almost perfection itself; and he found his pleasurable function to be to defend, to exalt, to glorify it.[1] Bentham held precisely opposite views. To him the English law, instead of a model of excellence, was a system full of delays, frauds, snares, and uncertainties; and the lawyers were its unthinking or interested defenders. His remedy was not to stop leaks in the roof, put in new panes of glass, and otherwise repair the rotten and dilapidated structure, but to demolish it and rebuild anew. By many he was regarded for the greater part of his life as an iconoclast, and by others as a dreamer who labored under the harmless delusion that he was a benefactor of his race, while in reality he was passing his life uselessly in Utopia.[2]

Lecture XII.

Bentham's merits as a critic and censor of our law.

[1] See *ante* Lecture XI.
[2] Sir Samuel Romilly gives this interesting account of a visit which he made in 1817 to Bentham: —

"Our last visit was to my old and most valuable friend, Jeremy Bentham, at Ford Abbey. The grandeur and stateliness of the buildings form as strange a contrast to his philosophy, as the number and spaciousness of the apartments, the hall, the chapel, the corridors, and the cloisters, do to the modesty and scantiness of his domestic establishment. The society we found and left with him were Mill and his family and a Mr. Place, — the Charing Cross radical tailor. We found Bentham passing his time, as he has always been passing it since I have known him, — which is now more than thirty years, — closely applying himself six or eight hours a day in writing upon laws and legislation and in compiling his Civil and Criminal Codes, and spending the remaining hours of every day in reading, or taking exercise by way of fitting himself for his labors, or, to use his own strangely-invented

Lecture XII.

Value of Bentham's labors.

It does not essentially detract from Bentham's merits, or the regard in which posterity should hold him, that he exaggerated, as he doubtless did, the absurdities and defects of the system that he assailed, or that his invectives against lawyers, who as a body supported it and resisted all attempts to reform it, were extravagant and unjust. All this may well be pardoned to his honest convictions, to his lifelong labors and his disinterested zeal for the public good. Nor does it essentially detract from his just estimation that he is an illustration of Bacon's observation that "there is a superstition "in avoiding superstition, when men think to do "best if they go farthest from the superstition "formerly received." Nor does it materially diminish his fame that we cannot accept all of his doctrines as sound, or all of his conclusions from doctrines whose general soundness are no longer questioned.

The following, which I give in John Stuart Mill's own words, seems to me to set forth with judicial fairness Bentham's chief merits and the nature of the obligations of the world to him: —

"Bentham," he says, "is one of the great seminal "minds in England of his age." "He is the teacher "of teachers." "To him it was given to discern "more particularly those truths with which existing

phraseology, taking ante-jentacular and post-prandial walks to prepare himself for his task of codification. There is something burlesque enough in this language; but it is impossible to know Bentham, and to have witnessed his benevolence, his disinterestedness, and the zeal with which he has devoted his whole life to the service of his fellow-creatures, without admiring and revering him."

Life of Sir Samuel Romilly, edited by his sons, vol. ii., p. 473 (3d ed.), Diary, under date September, 1817.

"doctrines were at variance." "Bentham has been "in this age and country the great questioner of "things established. It is by the influence of the "modes of thought with which his writings inocu- "lated a considerable number of thinking men, that "the yoke of authority has been broken, and innu- "merable opinions, formerly received on tradition "as incontestable, are put upon their defence and "required to give an account of themselves. Who, "before Bentham, dared to speak disrespectfully, in "express terms, of the British Constitution or the "English law?... Bentham broke the spell. It "was not Bentham by his own writings; it was "Bentham through the minds and pens which those "writings fed, — through the men in more direct "contact with the world, into whom his spirit "passed. If the superstition about ancestorial wis- "dom; if the hardiest innovation is no longer "scouted *because* it is an innovation, — establish- "ments no longer considered sacred because they "are establishments, — it will be found that those "who have accustomed the public mind to these "ideas have learned them in Bentham's school, and "that the assault on ancient institutions has been, "and is, carried on for the most part with his "weapons."[1]

Lecture XII.

Mill's critical estimate of Bentham.

[1] Essay on Bentham, "Dissertations and Discussions" (Am. Ed.), vol. i., pp. 355–358. John Stuart Mill in his Autobiography says: "During the winter of 1821–22, Mr. John Austin, with whom at the time of my visit to France my father had but lately become acquainted, kindly allowed me to read Roman law with him. [John Stuart Mill was then in his seventeenth year.] My father, notwithstanding his abhorrence of the chaos of barbarism called English law, had turned his thoughts towards the bar as on the whole less ineligible for me than any other profession; and these readings with

Lecture XII.

If time permitted, it would be easy to trace Bentham's influence through other minds, and in the

Mr. Austin, who had made Bentham's best ideas his own, and added much to them from other sources and from his own mind, were not only a valuable introduction to legal studies, but an important portion of general education. With Mr. Austin I read Heineccius on the Institutes, his Roman Antiquities, and part of his exposition of the Pandects, to which was added a considerable portion of Blackstone. It was at the commencement of these studies that my father, as a needful accompaniment to them, put into my hands Bentham's principal speculations, as interpreted to the Continent, and indeed to all the world, by Dumont, in the 'Traité de Législation.' The reading of this book was an epoch in my life, one of the turning-points in my mental history" (chap. iii.).

Further legal education Stuart Mill appears not to have received. He was never called to the bar. I may here mention what, it seems to me, is a remarkable circumstance. When Bentham was seventy-seven years of age he committed to John Stuart Mill, then about nineteen years of age, who was without other legal training than that above mentioned, the work of editing and preparing for the press "The Rationale of Evidence." Speaking of this subject, Mill in his Autobiography (chap. iii.), says: "About the end of 1824, or beginning of 1825, Mr. Bentham, having lately got back his papers on Evidence from M. Dumont (whose *Traité des Preuves Judiciaires*, grounded on them, was then first completed and published), resolved to have them printed in the original, and bethought himself of me as capable of preparing them for the press. I gladly undertook this task, and it occupied nearly all my leisure for about a year, exclusive of the time afterwards spent in seeing the five large volumes through the press. Mr. Bentham had begun this treatise three times, at considerable intervals, each time in a different manner, and each time without reference to the preceding; two of the three times he had gone over nearly the whole subject. These three masses of manuscript it was my business to condense into a single treatise, adopting the one last written as the groundwork, and incorporating with it as much of the two others as it had not completely superseded. I had also to unroll such of Bentham's involved and parenthetical sentences as seemed to overpass by their complexity the measure of what readers were likely to take the pains to understand. It was further Mr. Bentham's particular desire that I should, from myself, endeavor to supply any *lacunæ* which he had left; and at his instance I read, for this purpose, the most authoritative treatises on the English Law of Evidence, and commented on a few of

way here pointed out, in England and in this country,[1] not only in modifications and changes in specific

Lecture XII.

the objectionable points of the English rules, which had escaped Bentham's notice." "My name as editor was put to the book after it was printed, at Mr. Bentham's positive desire, which I in vain attempted to persuade him to forego." "The 'Rationale of Judicial Evidence' is one of the richest in matter of all Bentham's productions. The book contains, very fully developed, a great proportion of all his best thoughts; while among more special things it comprises the most elaborate exposure of the vices and defects of English law, as it then was, which is to be found in his works, not confined to the Law of Evidence, but including, by way of illustrative episode, the entire procedure or practice of Westminster Hall."

[1] The influence of Bentham in America, not only in respect of the emendations of the Law of Evidence, but through the efforts of other men who had caught his spirit, is directly seen in the extent to which codification has been adopted. See *ante* Lecture IX., p. 260, note. The labors of the celebrated Edward Livingston afford another interesting illustration of Bentham's influence in this country. In the prime of his life misfortunes led Livingston in 1804 to quit the home of his ancestors in New York and to make a new home in New Orleans, then recently acquired by the United States. The question whether the procedure in Louisiana should be according to the common law or continue upon the basis of the civil and Spanish law having been judicially determined in favor of the latter, Livingston drew up what is in effect a Code of Procedure, which was adopted by the Legislature in 1805, consisting of twenty sections and of about twenty-five printed pages. In its essential features it anticipated the codes of nearly half a century later. Under an act of the General Assembly of Louisiana, approved February 10, 1820, which provided that a person learned in the law shall be appointed to prepare a Code of Criminal Law, Evidence, and Procedure, Livingston was on February 13, 1821, elected by the joint ballot of the Legislature to discharge this duty. He reported his plan to the next Assembly, which "earnestly solicited him to prosecute this work according to his report."

In 1829 Livingston had an interesting correspondence with Bentham, in which the former acknowledged that he received his first impulse "to the preparation of an original, comprehensive, and complete system of penal legislation from Bentham's works which had appeared in the French of Dumont in 1802." Hunt, "Life of Edward Livingston," p. 96, note. "The perusal of your works," said Livingston to Bentham, "first gave me method to my ideas, and taught me to

338   *LAWS AND JURISPRUDENCE.*

Lecture XII.

legislation and in modes of judicial procedure, but upon existing notions in respect of legal education, the necessity for and the methods of legal reform. It would be interesting, for example, to draw the parallel between Bentham and Austin, one of Ben-

consider legislation as a science governed by certain principles, applicable to all its different branches, instead of an occasional exercise of its powers, called forth only on particular occasions without relation to or connection with each other." He thus concludes: "Hereafter no one can in criminal jurisprudence propose any favorable change that you have not recommended, or make any wise improvement that your superior sagacity has not suggested." Hunt, p. 96, note; Bentham's Works (Bowring's Ed.), vol. x., p. 51. Livingston prepared a complete Code of Crimes and Punishments, of Procedure, of Evidence, and of Reform and Prison Discipline; but having been elected to Congress and practically ceasing to reside in Louisiana, his codes were never enacted into laws. Each code was accompanied with an elaborate introductory report; and these labors gave him great and deserved fame at home and abroad. Chancellor Kent declared that Livingston had "done more in giving precision, specification, accuracy, and moderation to the system of crimes and punishments than any other legislator of the age, and that his name would go down to posterity with distinguished honor." Hunt, p. 281. Bentham urged that Parliament should print the whole work for the use of the English nation. Hunt, p. 278; Bentham's Works, vol. xi., p. 37. Villemain declared it to be "a work without example from the hand of any one man." Hunt, p. 278. Sir Henry Maine pronounced Livingston to be "the first legal genius of modern times." "Village Communities," paper on "Roman Law and Legal Education," published in 1856. Although the Livingston Code was not adopted as a whole, yet Bancroft is quite justified in the observation that "it has proved an unfailing fountain of reforms suggested by its principles." Introduction to Hunt's Life of Livingston, p. xvii. The Livingston Codes and Reports were republished in full in 1873 by the National Prison Association of the United States, with an Introduction by Chief-Justice Chase, in which he expresses the satisfaction of the Association in reproducing a work marked with such "keenness of insight, clearness of statement, force of logic, beauty of diction, elevation of sentiment, and breadth of sympathy." He declared his own opinion to be that the work "will prove that if Livingston was in advance of his times, the day is at least approaching when his broad and comprehensive views will not only be appreciated but realized."

tham's most eminent disciples, and to show the partial reaction of Austin against some of Bentham's extreme views, and the extent to which the questions thus raised are profoundly agitating at this moment not only a few thinking minds but the body of the profession, — and this not only in England, but in every country which speaks the language and which has adopted the institutions of England. This would lead to a consideration of the controversies between the analytical and the historical schools of jurisprudence, which their respective advocates yet debate with much of their original warmth, tending to the result, however, that there is, after all, truth in each; that properly understood the two schools are not antagonistic but complementary; and that the true course is to combine the logical or analytical with the historical and experimental, the former mainly supplying data for scientific arrangement, the latter mainly supplying the matter for a revised, improved, and systematic jurisprudence. I must content myself with mentioning, without dwelling upon, these interesting subjects.

Lecture XII.

Bentham and Austin.

Passing from these general considerations, I proceed to notice specifically two other subjects. One is Bentham's reforms in the Law of Evidence. Here the direct fruits of Bentham's labors are plainly to be seen. In some respects his "Judicial Evidence," before mentioned, is the most important of all his censorial writings on English law. In this work he exposed the absurdity and perniciousness of many of the estab-

Bentham's direct influence on the Law of Evidence.

lished technical rules of evidence. "In certain cases," he says, "jurisprudence may be defined, "the art of being methodically ignorant of what "everybody knows." Among the rules combated were those relating to the competency of witnesses and the exclusion of evidence on various grounds, including that of pecuniary interest. He insisted that these rules frequently caused the miscarriage of justice, and that in the interest of justice they ought to be swept away. His reasoning fairly embraces the doctrine that parties ought to be allowed and even required to testify. This work appeared in Paris in 1802, and in England in 1825 and 1827; but it produced no immediate effect on the professional mind. It was generally regarded as the speculations of a visionary. As I write I have before me Starkie's Evidence, the third edition of which appeared in 1842, and the wisdom of the exclusionary rules of evidence are not so much as criticised or questioned.

But Bentham had set a few men thinking. He had scattered the seeds of truth. Though they fell on stony ground they did not all perish. But verily reform is a plant of slow growth in the sterile gardens of the practising and practical lawyer. Bentham lived till 1832, and these exclusionary rules still held sway. But in 1843, by Lord Denman's Act, interest in actions at common law ceased, as a rule, to disqualify; and in 1846 and 1851, by Lord Brougham's Acts, parties in civil actions were as a rule made competent and compellable to testify. I believe I speak the universal judgment of the profession when I say that changes more beneficial in the administration of justice have rarely taken place in our law, and that it is a matter of profound amazement, as we look back upon it, that these exclusionary rules ever had a place therein, and especially that they were able to retain it until within the last fifty years.

Lecture XII.

Let us be just. The credit of originating this great improvement is due not to Denman and Brougham, but it essentially belongs to Bentham, although he was in his grave before it was actually effected.[1] Lord Justice Stephen forcibly remarks of Bentham's assault on the system of judicial evidence that "it was like the bursting of a shell "in the powder magazine of a fortress, the frag- "ments of the shell being lost in the ruin which "it has wrought."[2] The moral is obvious. The philosophic student of our laws may often have a keener and juster insight into their vices and imperfections than the practising lawyer, whose life and studies are exclusively confined to the ascertainment and application of the law as it is, and who rarely vexes himself with the question of what it ought to be, or makes any serious effort to reform it. But let me not be misunderstood. While the philosophic student is able to point out defects in the laws, yet the history of the law shows that only practical lawyers are capable of satisfactorily executing the work of reform. Bentham's failure in *directly* realizing greater practical results grew out of his mistaken notion that the work of actual

Credit due to Bentham for improvements in the Law of Evidence.

Cause of Bentham's failure in directly realizing practical results.

---

[1] See *post* Lecture XIII.
[2] "General View of the Criminal Law of England," p. 206; also Introduction to his Digest of Evidence.

Lecture XII.

Bentham's views of codification stated.

amendment could be accomplished without experts, — that is, without the aid of the bar and without its active support.

The last matter to which I shall refer is that to which Bentham gave the name by which it is now universally known, — codification. With a view to ascertain with exactness Bentham's views, I have recently gone over anew his writings relating to this subject. Very different ideas in our day are, as I have heretofore said, attached to what is meant or implied by a code, and much of the dispute concerning codification is after all one over words, or one arising from the want of a previous definition of the subject-matter of the disputation.[1] What Bentham meant by codification, however, is plain enough. He meant that a code should embrace all general legislation, not simply as it exists, but as it ought to be amended and made to exist, — that is, all legislation except local and special statutes; that it also should embody all the principles of the common law which it were expedient to adopt, — these to be expressed in words by legislative enactment, the gaps or *lacunæ* to be filled up in like manner by the legislature; the whole to be systematically arranged, so that all possible cases would be expressly provided for by written rules; that the function of the courts to make "judge-made law," as he is fond of stigmatizing it, should cease, and that thereafter all changes or additions to this complete and authoritative body of law should be made by the law-making body, and by it alone.

[1] See *ante* Lecture VI., p. 180.

I must say that in my judgment this in its full extent is not only an impracticable scheme, but one founded in part upon wrong principles. In a refined and complex civilization no legislative foresight, no finite intelligence, can anticipate, define, catalogue, and formulate in advance rules applicable to the infinite number and the infinite variety of cases that will inevitably arise. This view of a code also exaggerates, or, to use Bentham's language, maximizes, the evils of case-law, and underrates or minimizes its advantages. It overlooks the fact that case-law is a permanent necessity. The judicial office will, at all times, under any possible code, have to deal with and determine questions and cases not possible to be provided for by any express statutory provision.[1] A well-constructed code may, and doubtless will, lessen the number of such questions and cases; but no code can do more. The rest must be left to the courts. M. Portalis, in a well-known paper relating to the French Civil Code, expresses this truth with clearness and force. "It is to jurispru-
" dence [using the term in distinction from statute
" or positive law] that the legislator must abandon
" those rare and extraordinary cases which cannot
" enter into the scheme of a rational legislation;
" the variable, unaccountable details which ought
" never to occupy the attention of the legislator,
" and all of those objects which it would be
" in vain to attempt to foresee, and dangerous
" prematurely to define."

Lecture XII.

Bentham's scheme impracticable in its full extent, and why?

[1] See *ante* Lecture X., p. 268; Dillon, Munic. Corp. (4th ed.), vol. ii., § 934, *a;* Amos, "Science of Law," chap. v.

> Lecture XII.
> Why codification necessary.

We have now, and for centuries have had, two wholly independent manufactories, so to speak, of law, — the legislature professedly making statute law, the courts silently making case-law; and this without any unity of conception, plan, or action. Statutes are piled upon statutes, and the law reports of Great Britain and America may be roundly put at eight thousand volumes, and are constantly multiplying.[1] This colossal body of case-law is wholly unorganized and even unarranged, except so far as digests and elementary treatises may be considered as an arrangement, which scientifically viewed they are not. The infinite details of this mountainous mass in its existing shape — bear me witness, ye who hear me! — no industry can master and no memory retain. The English portion of it has been aptly likened to " chaos tempered by Fisher's Digest." The American portion already exceeds in size and complexity the English portion, and as we attempt to survey it we are reminded of the dread and illimitable region described by Milton, where

> . . . " Chaos umpire sits,
> And by *decision* more embroils the fray
> By which he reigns."

I do not believe that it is practicable to codify it all in the sense that the resulting code shall supersede for all purposes the law reports; but on many subjects, and to a very large extent in respect of all, codification is practicable, and so far as it is practicable, it is, if well done, desirable. Mark the qualification, *if well done*, not otherwise.

[1] See *ante* Lectures VIII., IX., X., *passim*.

Any code that is made, whatever may be its scope, must be based upon the fundamental principle that the existing body of our law as it has been developed in the workings of our institutions and tested by our experience is in substance the law that is best fitted to our condition and wants; for all true law has its root in the life, spirit, ideas, usages, instincts, and institutions of the people. It springs from within; it is not something alien to the people, to be imposed on them from without. If a metaphor will not mislead, true law is a native, independent, natural growth, and not an exotic. Bentham did not deny this in principle, but he was too much inclined to look at laws logically rather than historically. It follows that a code must not be one imitated from or servilely fashioned after Roman or foreign models. On this subject Bentham had correct notions. His bold, original mind and his self-sufficient powers saw as little to admire in the Roman as in the English law. I repeat it as my judgment that our code must not pre-suppose that the Roman law as it anciently existed, or as it exists in the modern adaptations of it in the States of Continental Europe, is superior in matter, substance, or value, to the native, natural, indigenous product. It must assume precisely the contrary. Freeman puts a general truth epigrammatically when he says "that we, the English people, are ourselves and not somebody else. ". . . Englishmen after all are Englishmen."[1]

This is equally true of the American people. And both Englishmen and Americans want their

[1] Preface to lecture, "Chief Periods of European History."

own laws, and not those of some other people. It would be as impossible radically to change their legal systems as to change the nature of the people. The materials for such a code already exist. A period of development is at some time reached in the legal history of every people when it is necessary to restate and reconstruct their laws. It seems to me that we have reached that period. Our materials for such restatement and reconstruction, which we may, if you please, call a code, are ample. They surpass in extent, in abundance, in variety, in richness, and above all in adaptation to our wants, any supply that can come from foreign sources.[1]

What Sir Henry Maine aptly calls "tacit codification" is a process which is in constant operation, through the labors of judges and text-writers. In this work elementary writers of learning and experience take an important part. In the scattered condition of our case-law their works are indispensable. When judges and text-writers deduce from the cases a principle and formulate it, and that formula is stamped with authority, either by long usage or judicial sanction, so that the courts do not go behind it to the cases from which it was deduced, there you have to this extent codification. This "stereotyping, as it were, of certain legal rules, is," says Maine, "at this moment pro-
" ceeding with unusual rapidity, and is indeed one
" of the chief agencies which save us from being
" altogether overwhelmed by the enormous growth
" of our case-law."[2]

---

[1] See *ante* Lecture VI., p. 174; Lecture X.
[2] "Village Communities" (Am. Ed.), pp. 368, 369. The subject

What is needed is the constructive genius and practical wisdom that can take these truly rich, invaluable, native but scattered materials, — using with a wise and generous eclecticism foreign materials only when the native do not exist or the foreign are manifestly superior, — and out of all these build an edifice of law, primarily designed and adapted to daily use, which shall be at once symmetrical, harmonious, simple, and commodious. There is here room and need for all. The institutional writer, the law teacher, the philosophic student, the scientific jurist, the experienced lawyer, the learned judge, the practical legislator, has each his place. They are not repellent and antagonistic agencies, but allies and co-laborers in the noblest work that can engage the attention, and draw forth and exemplify the highest powers of the human intellect. Toward the realization of this ideal let us press on with generous ardor, guided not by the motto of Ihering, prescribed for Continental action, — "Through the Roman law, but beyond it," — but rather by this other motto : " Through our own law, and beyond it wherever it is plainly defective or incomplete."

Lecture XII.

The existing need of our law.

of text-books as one of the literary authorities of our law, their office and use, the functions of text-book writers, and the nature of textbook law, I have seen nowhere so fully or well presented as in Professor Clark's "Practical Jurisprudence," part ii., chaps. vii.-xii., inclusive.

LECTURE XIII.

Our Law: A Century's Progress and Development. — Important Contributions to our Laws made by the United States. — Specific Changes in the Laws of both Countries upon Subjects of Great and Permanent Interest. — Present Condition of our Laws and a Forecast of their Evolution.

<small>Lecture XIII.</small>
<small>The present condition of our law.</small>

HAVING in previous lectures considered our law in its old home, and its distinguishing characteristics, its extension to and development in this country, its excellences and defects, and presented some views as to the scope and methods of its reformation or amendment, I shall now ask your attention to the present condition of our law as a result of the changes which have been wrought therein since the establishment of our national independence, a little more than a century ago.

This lecture will illustrate anew how ceaseless are the movements of the social forces, and as a consequence that law inevitably undergoes constant changes, some of which are conscious and pre-determined, and others silent and irresistible but none the less actual.[1] It will also illustrate, I think, in a very striking manner the truth of Burke's philosophic statement, — and coming from him most

<small>Equity and utility the real foundations of law.</small>

---
[1] See *ante* Lecture XII.

remarkable concession, — that "in all forms of government the people is the true legislator; and whether the immediate and instrumental cause of the law be a single person or many, the remote and efficient cause is the consent of the people, either actual or implied; and such consent is absolutely essential to its validity. . . . In reality there are two, and only two, foundations of law; and they are both conditions without which nothing can give it any force : I mean equity and utility."[1]

Lecture XIII.

It will, I think, also illustrate the fact that the wisest must be content to see but a little way in advance; that neither jurist nor legislator can expect the jurisprudential millennium (if I may so phrase their ideal) to come *per saltum*, if it ever comes at all, but must be content like the good physician to aid the *vis medicatrix naturæ*, rather than rashly to resort to heroic remedies which are full more apt to hurt than to cure. It will, moreover, and chiefly, exemplify the consolatory truths that the rights of the individual man, bottomed alone on the fact that he is a man, are being more and more realized and secured; that men are becoming more humane, more benevolent and sympathetic, more regardful of the rights of others, more sensible of a common bond of humanity; and that although the paths are still toilsome, and ofttimes discouraging, the race of man is constantly reaching a higher level by rising

The development of our law on these lines justifies a cheerful forecast.

[1] Tract on the Popery Laws, vol. vi., pp. 320, 323 (Little, Brown, & Co., American Edition of Burke's Works). See *ante* Lecture VII., p. 206, as to Burke's opinion that the passions of the people ought to be restrained "by power out of themselves." But the two views are not inconsistent. Pollock, " Science of Politics," pp. 86, 87.

Lecture XIII. to higher conceptions of duty, which will in the due order and providence of God find their expression, embodiment, and glorious fruitage, in the still higher and better law of the future, — which will more and more protect the rights of the individual, from invasion both by the State and by temporary majorities of the people. It will justify, I think, the encouraging and sustaining forecast of humanity expressed with the felicitous words which your Kent Professor knows so well how to use, when in his late Bennington oration he said that "the gift of prophecy " is mercifully withheld from man, but that hope, " kindlier than prophecy, stands in the place of it, " and it beholds with the eye of faith the great prin- " ciples of civil and religious liberty working them- " selves out to their final maturity, — a prosperity " more and more widely diffused among common " men; an advancing civilization not without the " vicissitudes, the blemishes, the mistakes, the sor- " rows through which humanity's path must always " lie, but in which the gain shall surpass the loss, " and the better surmount the worse, enlightened, " from generation to generation, by an increasing " intelligence, a broader knowledge, and a higher " morality."[1]

Specific contributions to our law made by the United States. Preliminary to noticing the specific changes during the century that is past in the laws common to both countries, I will briefly refer to a few of the more important contributions which we have made to our own system of laws. We have introduced into the law of nations the important principle of

[1] Edward J. Phelps, Bennington, Vermont, Anniversary Oration, 1891.

voluntary expatriation;[1] and by the Constitution of the United States, so far as this nation is concerned, treaties are declared to be the supreme law of the land, as binding upon the courts as the Constitution or an act of Congress, and enforceable like other laws by the judicial tribunals.

We have devised and put into successful operation, as shown in a previous lecture, written constitutional limitations upon every department of the government which protect the people against the power of the State as well as against their own

---

[1] The history of this doctrine has been accurately traced by Professor Baldwin, of the Yale Law School (since raised to the Supreme Bench of the State), in his learned address on American Jurisprudence, heretofore referred to, delivered in 1892, before the Ohio State Bar Association. He says : " Into the law of nations we of America have introduced the principle of voluntary expatriation. It is, indeed, the condition of our existence. The doctrine of perpetual allegiance was undisputed in the Old World. Its application to Americans by the British Crown was one of the grievances recited in the Declaration of Independence ; but we ourselves asserted its obligation long after independence had been achieved. Jeremiah Mason once said that the development of an American jurisprudence could only be looked for from the courts of the National Government. Upon this question, however, it was a court of a State, which, following the language of her constitution, framed by Franklin, first declared expatriation an original and indefeasible right of man ; and this at a time when those of the United States adhered to the rules of the common law. See on this subject Murray *v.* McCarty, 2 Munford (Va.) Rep., 393, 1811; Williams's Case, Wharton's State Trials, 652. Thus it was left to Congress to affirm by statute the American principle, as soon as the nation felt strong enough to assert it against the world (United States Revised Statutes, § 1999; Act of July 27, 1868), and treaties which have been made, in pursuance of this declaration, have now obtained its recognition in almost every country that can call itself civilized. This new rule of American jurisprudence is the work of the bar rather than the courts. Its earliest supporters were Adams and Jefferson ; and to our attorneys-general, and the great lawyers who from time to time have had the direction of the Department of State, we owe especially its international authority."

Lecture XIII.

America's contributions.

haste and passions.[1] We have effected a complete and permanent separation of Church and State. We have established the security of titles to lands by a public registry system, which in effect compels the registration of every instrument which concerns real property. We have in every State of the Union adopted the principle of the equal inheritance of lands by all the children, male and female alike. We have made lands freely alienable and subject to the payment of debts, and in many respects ameliorated, improved, and simplified the law of real property.[2]

[1] See *ante* Lecture VII., *passim.*

[2] *Ante* Lecture VIII., p. 237 *et seq.*, and note on p. 241. Mr. David Dudley Field, in a paper entitled "American Progress in Jurisprudence," prepared by request for the World's Congress on Jurisprudence and Law Reform in connection with the Columbian Exposition in Chicago, 1893, reprinted in the American Law Review, vol. xxvii., p. 641, gives a summary account of the progress of American laws and jurisprudence. I have space for only a few extracts from this instructive paper illustrative of the text: "We began with asserting the sovereignty of the people. This was done by the Declaration of Independence in 1776. . . . In our country this supreme power is divided between the Union and the States, but so much of it as has been given to the former was given by the latter. The result is, that Congress is not sovereign, nor is the President sovereign, nor is the Judiciary sovereign; nor, indeed, are all three combined sovereign. They may exercise their part of the sovereign power, but it is only by delegation that they exercise it at all. On the other hand, the reserved powers are all with the separate States [or the people thereof], so that we have in fact a divided sovereignty, but none the less is it true, that sovereignty in this country resides with the people, partly in all the States united, and partly in the several States — '*E pluribus unum.*' (See *ante* Lectures V., VII.) . . . Following this primal and fundamental principle of sovereignty in the people, and consecrated by it, are certain rights pronounced inherent in every human being, to be lost only for crime: the right to life; the right to liberty; the right to worship God as conscience dictates; the right to choose one's home wherever he can find it; the right to speak and write freely; and the right to labor when, where, and for such reward

It is almost needless to remark that at the date of the establishment of our national existence, English

Lecture XIII.

as the laborer and his employer may agree to between themselves. Under the influence of these great principles, our political system, State and national, has been built; a fabric purely American, without precedent in the past and ready for further development in the future.... The United States have placed their constitution beyond the reach of executive or legislative power. The President may act and the Congress may act, but the judiciary may decide after all, whether the act is authorized by the constitution. Never before in any constitutional government was the organic law put under the guardianship of the judiciary. (See *ante* Lecture VII.) This is a feature purely American, and of value incalculable for the protection of individual rights.

"In the category of these individual rights I conceive that the greatest achievement ever made in the cause of human progress is the total and final separation of the State from the Church. If we had nothing else to boast of, we could claim with justice that first among the nations we of this country made it an article of organic law that the relations between man and his maker were a private concern into which other men had no right to intrude.... Besides this great act of deliverance, we have emancipated woman from the domination of her husband; we have freed the honest debtor from the possibility of passing his life in prison; we have rendered it impossible for legislation to make that act a crime which was not a crime when it was committed; we have forbidden the States to impair the obligation of a contract between man and man; we have proclaimed from sea to sea that all men are created equal in rights, and that among those rights are the rights to life, liberty, and the pursuit of happiness; we have imbedded in the fundamental law of the land as principles inviolable and eternal, that no man can be deprived of these rights without due process of law, and that all are entitled to the equal protection of the laws."

I close this note with the observation that we are thus essentially a free people. "For who," inquired the author of the famous "Farmer's Letters," A. D. 1767-68 (John Dickinson, a great and venerable name, to which history has as yet scarcely done full justice), — "*for who are a free people?*" His answer to this question has perhaps never been excelled. It was in these words: "Not those over whom government is reasonably and equitably exercised, but those who live under a government so constitutionally checked and controlled that proper provision is made against its ever being otherwise exercised." Stillé's "Life and Times of John Dickinson," p. 89.

Lecture XIII.

Substantial identity of English and American law.

law was, notwithstanding the modifications necessary to adapt it to our situation, substantially our law. The first completed edition of Blackstone was published in 1769, only six years before the American Revolution. Professor Hammond in the preface to his edition of Blackstone tells us that "there is abundant evidence of the immediate "absorption of nearly twenty-five hundred copies "of the Commentaries in the thirteen colonies "before the Declaration of Independence. The "natural result must have been that this work "became at once the standard authority upon "law in every American court."[1] We have thus, fortunately, the means of conveniently ascertaining the exact state of the English and American law at the period when our existence as a separate nation began.

Condition of the English law at the date of our Independence.

The great divisions of the English law were then definitely fixed. It consisted of the common law as modified and supplemented by acts of Parliament; of equity law, the product of the Court of Chancery; of the admiralty law, crippled indeed by the jealousy and hostility of the common lawyers and judges; and of the criminal law, resting mainly upon an enormous number of statutes, passed at different times, during several hundreds of years. If we look with an unprejudiced eye at the common law excluding equity, but including the amendments and changes which had been made therein from time to time by Parliament, our wonder is how the great Commentator, whose perpetual note is one of praise, could be so blind to its defects, both of sub-

[1] See *ante* Lecture V., p. 150, note; Lecture XI., p. 298.

stance and form. Many of its doctrines resting upon usage and custom had originated when the nation was in the twilight of its civilization, and they were not adapted to a more refined and complex state of society.[1] Conservatism patiently bore the evil and resisted change. The common-law forms of action were inelastic and inadequate, besides which the common lawyers were idolaters of the system, and regarded innovation as a species of legal sacrilege. They had, moreover, much of the fondness of the schoolmen for verbal subtilties, puerilities, and refinements, which obscured and thwarted sound reasoning, and which, being essentially sterile, could never bear any wholesome fruit.

Lecture XIII.

But, largely, the curse of the common law came from the feudal system, and from the obstinacy with which the doctrines of feudalism were adhered to, when the system, as a distinct system, had ceased to exist. The feudal doctrine of *tenure*, by which all real property was held of a superior, by which the tenancy was always to be full, by which alienation was restrained, by which land was bound up in fetters of iron and made by entail to gratify ancestral and family pride, and by legislation to escape its share of the public burdens, out of which doctrine of tenure grew uses and trusts, and equitable as distinguished from legal estates, and from thence a large portion of the extraordinary jurisdiction of the Chancellor, — the feudal doctrine of tenure pervading every part of the common law, left, in every part, its

The poisonous effects of feudalism and the doctrine of tenure.

---

[1] See *ante* Lectures XI., XII.

Lecture XIII.

baneful effects. It has always seemed to me that tenure, in its manifold ramifications and consequences, in time came to be the chief bane of the common law. Had it not been for equitable estates and rights which thus originated, it is not improbable that Chancery as a separate tribunal would long since have been rendered unnecessary, and ceased to exist by the natural enlargement of the jurisdiction and remedies of the common-law courts.[1]

Land laws of Great Britain.

The land laws of Great Britain, which to-day press with such heavy weight upon the agricultural classes, grew out of the feudal system. That system has never died at its roots in England. John Bright not many years ago declared that "ancient, "stupid, and mischievous legislation embarrassed "land in every step you take in dealing with it." In England and Wales, about five thousand persons hold nearly one half the entire acreage; in Scotland, less than one hundred persons own about one half, and less than two thousand about nine tenths of all the lands; and in Ireland, less than two thousand proprietors, many of whom are non-residents, hold two thirds of the island. As a result of primogeniture, of entailed estates and family settlements, Great Britain is to-day a land of tenants.

Our more fortunate condition.

We have not, indeed, in this country wholly escaped from the complicated system of *estates*, which characterizes the English law. We ought to be free from them. We yet shall be. Primogeniture, entails, family settlements on the English model, are here unknown; land is plenty and cheap, and the happy result is that we are a nation of proprietors

[1] See *ante* Lecture VI., pp. 169–171.

and not of tenants. Herein consists one of the chief sources of individual prosperity and national strength. In many of the countries of the Old World the landless poor are the natural enemies of the government. Here, every proprietor, however small, is the natural ally of government and of law. There may be some reason for the various forms of socialism, communism, anarchism, among the struggling and oppressed peoples of the Old World. They are the unreasoning and desperate remedies of caste, and hunger, and despair. But here, and among us, such ideas are baneful exotics, which have taken no deep root, and attract little notice except when their wild or bad adherents seek to propagate them by illegal violence or murder.

Lecture XIII.

Sydney Smith drew this graphic picture of the condition of the English laws, on the enumerated subjects, in 1802, — that is, about fifteen years after our government was established: " The Catholics " were not emancipated. The Corporation and " Test Acts were unrepealed. The game laws " were horribly oppressive. For every ten pheas- " ants which fluttered in the wood, one English " peasant was rotting in jail. Steel traps and " spring guns were set all over the country; pris- " oners tried for their lives could have no counsel. " Lord Eldon and the Court of Chancery pressed " heavily on mankind. Libel was punished by the " most cruel and vindictive imprisonments. The " laws of debt and conspiracy were little under- " stood. Not a murmur against any abuse was " permitted; to say a word against the suitorcide " delays of the Court of Chancery, or the cruel

Sydney Smith's picture of the English laws at the beginning of the century.

Lecture XIII.

"punishments of the game laws, or any abuse
"which a rich man inflicted and a poor man suf-
"fered, was treason against the *plousiocracy*, and
"was bitterly and steadily resented." Again he
said: "The abuses of the Court of Chancery have
"been the curse of England for centuries. For
"twenty-five long years did Lord Eldon sit in
"the court, surrounded by misery and sorrow,
"which he never held up a finger to alleviate.
"The widow and orphan cried to him as vainly
"as the town-crier cries when he offers a small
"reward for a full purse; the bankrupt of the
"court became the lunatic of the court; estates
"mouldered away and mansions fell down, but
"the fees came in and all was well. But in an
"instant [in 1832] the iron mace of Brougham
"shivered to atoms this house of fraud and delay."
If this picture is too highly colored, its essential
features are correct; but we are glad to know
that in all of these respects the English law has
been greatly improved, mostly within the last
sixty years.

Specific changes since wrought.

Let us now look more specifically at other
changes in the laws of England and America upon
subjects of general and permanent interest.

Imprisonment for Debt, Distress for Rent, Modern Homestead and other Exemption Laws. — One hundred years ago imprisonment for debt in Great Britain and in this country was a common remedy. I do not remember any suggestion in Blackstone that it had ever occurred to him that the law giving such a tremendous power to the creditor was unjust or impolitic. The old reasoning was this: The creditor has a legal right to his debt; if the debtor will not or does not pay, the creditor is entitled to seize and sell his property; if he has no property, the creditor is entitled to his services, and if so, then to the control and possession of his person. Cases of fraud were not distinguished from cases of misfortune. A writ of *capias ad satisfaciendum* upon which the judgment debtor was committed to prison till the debt was paid was as common a remedy one hundred years ago as an ordinary writ of execution to sell the debtor's goods. As we look back upon the absurdity, impolicy, and cruelty of imprisonment for debt, we wonder what influences had stupefied the conscience and intelligence of mankind that laws so atrocious were so long endured. About sixty-five years ago, agitation on this subject first in this country and then in England commenced, and it soon led in the various States of the Union to the total abolition of imprisonment for debt, except in cases of actual fraud and fraudulent breaches of trust. And thus was forever swept away this relic of the severity of the earlier periods of our race.[1] England followed our example. A parliamentary inquiry showed that in eighteen months after the commercial revulsion of 1825, more than one hundred thousand writs were issued, and thousands of debtors were actually confined in the English prisons. By various acts passed during the reign of the present sovereign, beginning in 1838, im-

Lecture XIII.

Abolition of imprisonment for debt.

---

[1] Kent's Com., vol. ii., p. 398, note. America, indeed, began, says Professor Baldwin, to open the prison doors of insolvent debtors at the era of the Revolution. See the Constitution of Pennsylvania of 1776, art. 1, § 28; 2 Poore's "Charters and Constitutions," p. 1546.

prisonment of honest debtors has ceased to exist. The enlarged English Act of 1869 substantially abolished imprisonment for debt. It remains only in a few cases of criminal or fraudulent character. Verily, the world does move! And happily the permanent trend and movement are ever in the direction of a higher and a more humane level.

In this connection and by reason of the striking contrast of policy which the law of our own day offers to the law of a century ago, I may refer for a moment to the existing exemption and homestead laws in this country.

When Blackstone wrote, not only did imprisonment for debt exist, but the harsh and oppressive remedy of distress for rent was in both countries in full force. Various acts of Parliament, some then comparatively recent, had given to this remedy a sharper edge than it had at common law. The landlord, without suit or adjudication, could enter the tenant's premises and seize everything, with insignificant exceptions, and hold or sell it for his rent. Our State legislatures commenced years ago to pass laws exempting from execution necessary household goods and personal apparel, the horses and implements of the farmer, the tools and instruments of the artisan, etc. Gradually the beneficent policy of such laws has been extended. In 1828, Mr. Benton warmly advocated in the Senate of the United States the policy of a national homestead law. The Republic of Texas passed the first Homestead Act, in 1836. It was the great gift of the infant Republic of Texas to the world. In 1849, Vermont followed; and this policy has since been adopted in all but eight States of the Union.[1] By these laws, a homestead (under various restrictions as to value) for the shelter and protection of the *family* is now exempt from execution or judicial sale for debt, unless both the husband and the wife shall expressly join in mortgaging it or otherwise expressly subjecting it to the claims of creditors.

Lecture XIII.

State Homestead exemption laws.

And still more recently this policy, as wise as it is humane, has been adopted by the Congress of the United States, which has provided that on the sole condition of five years' occupancy by any head of a family, of not exceeding one hundred and sixty acres of government land, the United States will, at the end of that period, convey the same in fee simple absolute, without payment therefor, to such occupant or his heirs. From 1862, when the act took effect, to June 30, 1892, 1,049,643 original entries, covering 138,195,967 acres, have been made of government lands, of which 55,420,220 acres have been patented to 423,167 heads of families or their heirs; and the remainder is being patented in due course.[2] Words are not needed to portray this beneficent result. Such legislation, while "touched with human gentleness and love," is based upon the highest wisdom. " It is twice blessed; it blesseth him that gives and him that takes." It invests the era which originated and sustains it with a halo of true glory.

National Homestead law.

The Domestic Relations. — Undeniably the most

---

[1] Treatise on the Law of Homesteads, by Hon. Seymour D. Thompson, chap. i.

[2] This statement was furnished to me by the General Land Office at Washington, and is taken from the records of the office.

Lecture XIII.

Legal relation of husband and wife at common law.

interesting and the most important relation to the persons immediately concerned, to society, and to the State, is the relation of husband and wife. Upon this relation feudalism impressed its essential character.[1] Woman could not render military service; and feudalism, as a military system, logically ignored the wife's legal rights. Hence by a fiction of the common law, the husband and wife were for most purposes a single legal person, and that person was the husband. This fiction of the wife's merger was characteristic of the common law, and the common law pressed inexorably the dogma to all of its logical consequences. Therefore, immediately upon marriage, the wife's personal property in possession became absolutely the husband's. He had the complete *jus disponendi*. It was liable for his debts. By marriage also he took a sole estate in her lands during coverture. She could not alien them; she could not dispose of them by will; she could not exercise any power over them by contract or otherwise. If the improvidence, misfortune, or dissipation of the husband compelled the wife to become the " breadwinner " of the family, her earnings belonged to him and were subject to the claims of his creditors. No matter how wealthy she was before marriage, the legal effect of that event was to impoverish her. Parliament could have changed this any day, by a single enactment, but did not. The inadequacy of the common-law rules to an advanced stage of society was daily seen, and the unjust operation of those rules was daily felt. Yet the conservatism of the profession raised no voice against them. The

[1] See *ante* Lecture VI.

anomalous manner in which the English law con- **Lecture XIII.**
cerning the rights of married women progressively
developed itself and assumed the shape in which
it existed a century ago and down even to our
own day, is a most curious, characteristic, and
suggestive history. While the common law thus
denied the separate existence of the wife, it is
certain that it did not truly reflect her domestic
situation. The English baron was an affectionate
husband and father. A song of 1596 says, " The
wife of every Englishman is counted blest."

Whatever else may be charged against feudalism, **Effect of feudalism**
it must have great credit for its appreciation of **on the**
the dignity and worth of woman, and her elevation **domestic relation.**
and companionship. Leigh Hunt happily says that
the episode of Francesca stands in the Inferno of
Dante " like a lily in the mouth of Tartarus." So
the poetic and chivalrous regard for woman and the
tender consideration of mother, wife, daughter, and
sister, is the one " bright consummate flower " which
rejoices the eye as it looks back over the feudal
desert, — a flower that still lives, and whose fragrance perennially fills home with all of its happiness and joy. We need have no fear that it will
perish because the disabilities of coverture are removed and woman is given her just legal status
and rights. The only relief which the English and **Relief**
American jurisprudence gave to the married woman **afforded by the**
against the injustice of the common-law doctrine **Court of Chancery.**
of merger was the partial relief which the Court of
Chancery afforded; namely, that under certain circumstances and to a limited extent it would recognize separate property rights in the wife, and to that

364   LAWS AND JURISPRUDENCE.

Lecture XIII.

Modern Married Women's Acts.

extent her separate existence. These opposing rules of law and equity had one hundred years ago grown up into an exceedingly complicated system, without plan, full of uncertainty, and fruitful of litigation.

About fifty years ago the legislatures in this country commenced enacting what are known as Married Women's Acts. These have been extended from time to time, and to-day throughout the entire Union it may be said, speaking generally, that married women have been secured in all their just rights of property.[1] Our example spread at length to England, and Parliament passed the Married Women's Property Acts of 1870 and 1882, based upon the principles of the American legislation. I may have dwelt upon this subject at a tedious length. I cannot, however, but regard legislation which emancipates the wife from the shackles of the common law, which enlarges her rights far beyond those which Equity recognized, and places them upon an as-

[1] A recent address to the Mississippi Bar Association by its president, Mr. R. H. Thompson, upon the changes in the organic law of that State made by the new Constitution of 1890, is printed in the American Law Review. He states that Mississippi was the first State to give married women enlarged property rights, and that the act of the Mississippi Legislature passed in 1839 has been followed by nearly every State in the Union. As Mississippi was the first to remove woman's property disabilities by statute, so that State is the first to guard her entire emancipation in this particular by constitutional provision. Section 94 of the new Constitution deprives the Legislature of all power to create by law any distinction between the rights of men and of women to acquire, own, enjoy, and dispose of all kinds of property, or their right to contract in reference to it. Mr. Thompson adds the curious statement that the sources of Mississippi's first married women's law were the tribal customs of the Chickasaw Indians then residing in the State, and that its author was a member of the Legislature who was about to marry a rich widow, and who was himself harassed by creditors.

sured statutory basis, — legislation whose considerate beneficence penetrates every household in the land, and whose blessings will be the most felt where most needed, — as meriting unqualified approval, and which the future historian of our laws will place to the lasting credit of our own era.

Criminal Law and Procedure. — If we turn to the criminal law of a century ago and compare it with the law of to-day, the exhibit of progress and improvement is yet more striking. Not to mention the doctrines of forfeiture and attainder, whose horrible injustice mainly fell upon the innocent; the cruel manner in which for many offences the death penalty was inflicted, by quartering, and disemboweling, and kindred cruelties, — the criminal law of England, even in the ameliorated state in which it existed a century ago, had two grave and fundamental faults: (1) It did not distinguish as to the heinousness of different crimes, but punished with equal severity crimes of essentially different degrees of guilt. (2) Its penalties were severe and cruel. It was a code of blood. Nothing seemed to be so cheap as human life. "Better, they said in England, kill a man than a hare."[1] That I may not be suspected of being too severe a critic of the English criminal law, I will let English pens portray it. Sir James Stephen, speaking of the older law, says: "The "common law was in all ways a most defective "system. It was incomplete. Its punishments "were capricious and cruel."[2] Sir William Black-

Lecture XIII.

Severity of the former criminal law of England.

Justice Stephen's opinion.

[1] Emerson, "English Traits."
[2] Hist. Crim. Law, vol. i., chap. vi.

stone, commenting on the severity of the English law at the time he wrote, says: "It is a melancholy "truth that among the variety of actions which men "are daily liable to commit, no less than one hun- "dred and sixty have been declared by act of Parlia- "ment to be felonies without benefit of clergy; or, "in other words, to be worthy of instant death."[1] And the Commentator so far departed from his wonted strain of eulogy as to venture to call attention to this severity, and modestly "to hint these "outrageous penalties with decency to those whose "abilities and stations enable them to apply the "remedy."[2]

Sir James Mackintosh in 1819, in moving in Parliament for a committee to inquire into the condition of the criminal law, stated that there were then "two hundred capital felonies on the statute book." Undoubtedly this apparent severity, for the reasons stated by Sir James Stephen,[3] is greater than the real severity, since many of the offences made capital were of infrequent occurrence; and juries, moreover, often refused to convict, and persons capitally convicted for offences of minor degrees of guilt were usually pardoned on condition of transportation to the American and afterwards to the Australian colonies. But this learned author admits that, "after "making all deductions on these grounds, there can "be no doubt that the legislation of the eighteenth "century in criminal matters was severe to the "highest degree, and destitute of any sort of prin- "ciple or system."

[1] 4 Blacks. Com., 18.   [2] 4 Blacks. Com., 5.
[3] Hist. Crim. Law, vol. i., chap. xiii.

The Edinburgh Review censuring, in 1826, the injustice of denying prisoners accused of felony the right to be defended by counsel, declared, "The "judges and Parliament would have gone on to this "day, hanging by wholesale for forgeries of bank "notes, if juries had not become weary of continual "butchery and resolved to acquit." And the writer added these words, — each of which legislators should " weigh like a diamond " : " The proper ex-"ecution of laws must always depend in a great "measure upon public opinion; and it is undoubt-"edly most discreditable to any man intrusted with "power, when the governed turn around upon their "governors, and say, ' Your laws are so cruel, or so "foolish, we cannot and *will not* act upon them.'"

Lecture XIII.

Defence by counsel denied.

Hallam, writing about the year 1818, says : " A "convicted criminal is at present the stricken deer "of society, whose disgrace his kindred shrink from "participating, and whose memory they strive to "forget."[1]

It is not much over fifty years since prisoners in England accused of felony have been allowed to be defended by counsel.[2] In this country this right has, in many of the States, long been secured by constitutional provision. The criminal legislation of Great Britain for the last fifty years has tended uniformly in the direction of greater mildness. It is not necessary to trace the history of the legislation from the time when Blackstone wrote to the Criminal Consolidation Acts of 1861. It suffices for present purposes to state that the only offences

Ameliorations of the criminal laws of England.

[1] Middle Ages, chap. iii., part i.
[2] 6 and 7 William IV., chap. cxiv.

Lecture XIII.

which are now capitally punished in Great Britain are treason, murder, piracy with violence, and setting fire to dockyards and arsenals.

Comparative mildness of the criminal laws in the United States.

In this country we never adopted the extreme severities of the English statutes. We were early influenced by the views of Beccaria. Instead of hanging we condemned the criminal to labor for a term of years in what we named a penitentiary. Pennsylvania led the way to this great change by a provision in her Constitution of 1776.[1] Since this we have established reformatories for young offenders. With us the list of capital offences is still smaller than in Great Britain, having long been confined to treason, and murder in the first degree; that is, to murder where the killing was intentional, deliberate, and premeditated.

The severity of the English criminal law, in addition to its injustice to the prisoner, was productive of two evil consequences of great moment, one of which operated on juries and the other on the judges.

---

[1] "Section 38. The penal laws shall be reformed by the Legislature as soon as may be, and punishments made in some cases less sanguinary, and in general more proportionate to the crimes.

"Section 39. To deter more effectually from the commission of crimes, by continued visible punishments of long duration, and to make sanguinary punishments less necessary, houses ought to be provided for punishing by hard labor those who shall be convicted of crimes not capital, wherein the criminals shall be employed for the benefit of the public and for reparation of injuries done to private persons; and all persons at proper times shall be admitted to see the prisoners at their labor." Constitution of Pennsylvania of 1776; 2 Poore's Charters and Constitutions, 1547; Professor (now Justice) Simeon E. Baldwin's Address before the Ohio State Bar Association, 1892; Beccaria's "Crimes and Punishments" was in 1766 translated into French, and in 1768 into English. A new corrected edition was reprinted in Philadelphia in 1793, with Voltaire's "Commentary," p. 230.

Where the penalties were disproportionately severe, the humanity of juries often led them, by what Blackstone calls "pious perjuries," to acquit in cases where the prisoner's guilt was clear. The same consideration operated with the judges, who mercifully allowed defendants to escape on such fine-spun technical objections to indictments, and frivolous variances, as made criminal trials seem like a game of chance or a judicial farce. " Such " scandals," says Sir James Stephen, " do not seem " to have been unpopular. Indeed, I have some " doubt whether they were not popular, as they did " mitigate, though in an irrational, capricious man-" ner, the severity of the old criminal law."[1]

Lecture XIII.

Evil effects of the undue severity of the criminal laws.

In this country the courts implicitly followed the English decisions, although the penalties here were not so severe, and acquittals upon unsubstantial technical points disfigured our administration of criminal justice until within the last forty or fifty years quite as much as they did that of England. The mischievous consequences of this course of administration were that it encouraged the commission of crime, since it was seen that punishment by no means followed upon guilt, and it also undermined the public trust in the efficiency of the laws to pro-

[1] Hist. Crim. Law, vol. i., chap. ix., p. 284. Writing in 1882, Mr. Serjeant Ballantine, certainly well qualified to speak on the subject, says: " No one can doubt that the general administration of the law has during the last half century improved in every branch, and the present generation would scarcely credit the amount of villainy, fraud, and oppression which, previous to that period, flourished under its auspices. The gaols were filled with victims, officers of the sheriff robbing both creditors and debtors. . . . Immense taxes were imposed upon legal proceedings by numerous sinecure offices paid out of suitors' pockets." " Some Experiences of a Barrister's Life," chap. l.

Lecture XIII.

tect society against evil-doers. It thus became the parent of lynch law and of vigilance committees, whereby the community, in supposed self-defence, at times irregularly and violently took the punishment of offenders into their own hands. Modern legislation has so improved the mode of criminal procedure that unsubstantial technicalities in pleadings and procedure have almost ceased, — *only a flavor of the old system remains.* A great reform this, which also redounds to the lasting credit of our own times.

Improved procedure.

Amendments in the law of Civil Procedure.

Civil Procedure. — Remedial law in civil procedure, including in the term "remedial," as here used, the pleadings, evidence, and mode of procedure in civil causes from the beginning to the end, has undergone during the period under review even more radical changes than substantive law. These changes have occurred within the last fifty and largely within the last thirty years. The practical inconvenience and the mischiefs arising from the division of rights into legal and equitable, which rights, often conflicting, had to be asserted in different suits and frequently in different tribunals, thus necessitating double litigations, with the delays and costs incident thereto, as well as the unnecessary uncertainty thus introduced into the administration of justice, had long been felt, and patiently borne. The technical forms of common-law actions, and especially the system of pleadings in such actions, abounding in arbitrary and artificial rules and subtile distinctions, whereby form was elevated over substance and the client's case oftentimes depended full more upon the skill and ingenuity of his counsel than upon its justice, produced much popular distrust of the law, and at length much professional discontent. These and other causes concurring, efforts were made in England and in this country toward a reform in the mode of pleading. In 1834 England adopted the "New Rules." These were a sort of compromise between the old notions and the new ones, and failed, as compromises usually do, to satisfy the profession or to remedy the mischief.

Lecture XIII.

The subject was earnestly taken hold of in this country; and in New York, in 1848, a Code of Civil Procedure, prepared by an able commission, was adopted. This commission was not only able, but courageous.[1] True reformers, they worked under an inspiration like that which "made the canons " of the church of Seville say, 'Let us build so that "'all men hereafter will say that we were mad- "'men.'" This commission applied a radical remedy. It abolished, without reservation, all common-law forms of action and of pleadings. It allowed all matters, legal and equitable, growing out of the same transactions, both on the part of the plaintiff and defendant, to be litigated in one and the same suit; and it was implied, if not expressed, that where the legal rule and the equitable rule conflicted, the latter should prevail.

Codes of Procedure in the United States.

The New York Code of Procedure of 1848, either in substance or principle, spread with rapidity, and has been adopted in a large majority of the States and Territories of the Union; and it is a remarkable fact that where once adopted it has never

[1] See *ante* Lecture VI., p. 183.

Lecture XIII.

English Judicature Act based on the principles of the American Codes.

been repealed, or the superseded system restored. Reforms in procedure were adopted in England in 1852; but in 1873, by the Judicature Act of that year, changes more radical and important than had before ever been made by a single enactment, were effected. That act and its amendments proceeded upon the principles of the American Codes, and they have since been followed in many of the British Colonies.[1] It was expressly provided in the Judicature Act that where the legal rule and the equitable rule were different, the latter should control. Equity had here by the express declaration of Parliament its crowning and final triumph over the common law.

Codes of Criminal Procedure.

The New York Code of Criminal Procedure, in substance or principle, has also been adopted in many of the States and Territories; and the New York Penal Code, adopted in that State in 1882, is already substantially enacted in California and Dakota. Similar legislation has been seriously proposed in England, and is there one of the leading questions which is to-day passing through the necessary stages of discussion and examination. It can have but one eventual issue. These changes in procedure were violently opposed before they were made and afterwards; but they were necessary changes, and time and experience, which are the best tests, have established their wisdom. The conclusive proof of this is the fact, above mentioned, that when *made they always come to stay.*

Codification. — One related question of great prac-

---

[1] *Ante* Lecture VI., p. 183, and note on pp. 183–186; Lecture IX., p. 260, note.

tical interest and moment still remains to a large extent undecided, and that is as to the wisdom of undertaking a *systematic restatement of the body of our statutory and case law.* This subject is actively engaging the best minds of the profession in both countries. I have in the previous lectures of this course expressed my general views upon it. In the sense that a code " aims at nothing more than " the reduction to a definite and systematic shape " of the results obtained and sanctioned by the ex- " perience of many centuries," as that experience is embodied in statutes, in the law reports, and in the writings of the sages and masters of the law, — in this practical sense, within these conservative limits, a code in England and a code in each of the United States is, I think, manifest destiny. I venture this prediction, because this is the only remedy which it is possible to suggest to make the overgrown body of our law, I will not say convenient or symmetrical, but reasonably certain, public, and accessible. Such a course has been found not simply desirable, but necessary, in the developed stage of every other jural system; and I am unable to perceive how we can permanently avoid it, whatever our timidity, and however reluctant we may be to enter upon it.

The Law of Evidence. — Many emendations in the law of evidence have been made within the last forty-five years. The principal change is that by which interest in a witness no longer disqualifies him to testify, and that far greater change, by which parties to the record are competent to testify in all civil suits, and by which also in some of the States, and

Lecture XIII.

Codification within certain limits increasingly necessary.

Reforms in the law of evidence.

Lecture XIII.

Denman's and Brougham's Acts relating to competency of witnesses and parties.

in all of the courts of the United States,[1] the defendant is competent, at his own request, to give evidence in his own behalf, in prosecutions for crimes. In this kind of legislation England led the way.[2] Bentham early in this century opened a vigorous fire upon the absurdity of the common-law rules of evidence on the competency of witnesses, which, as he maintained, were framed to exclude rather than to admit the light.[3] He was regarded as a visionary, and his criticisms were slow in ripening into practical results. But in 1843, by Lord Denman's Act,[4] interest in common-law actions, with a few exceptions, ceased to disqualify; and in 1846 and 1851,[5] by Lord Brougham's Acts, parties in civil actions, with a few enumerated exceptions, were made competent and compellable to testify. The wisdom of this legislation, especially in respect of

---

[1] Act of March 16, 1878; 20 Sts. 30.

[2] The earliest act of this kind in this country was passed by the Legislature of Connecticut in 1848. It is very broad and sweeping in its provisions. It is in these words: "No person shall be disqualified as a witness in any suit or proceeding at law, or in equity, by reason of his interest in the event of the same, as a party or otherwise, or by reason of his conviction of a crime; but such interest or conviction may be shown for the purpose of affecting his credit." (Revised Statutes of Connecticut, 1849, p. 86, § 141. In the margin of the page the time of the passage of the law is given as 1848.) This act was drafted and its enactment secured by the Hon. Charles J. McCurdy, a distinguished lawyer and the Lieutenant-Governor of that State. A member of Judge McCurdy's family, having been present at the delivery of this lecture at New Haven in 1892, called my attention to the above fact, claiming, and justly, for this act the credit of leading in this country the way to such legislation. But he was mistaken in his claim that it preceded similar legislation in England, although its provisions are an improvement on the contemporary enactments of the like kind in that country.

[3] 1 Ev. 6.   [4] 6 & 7 Vic., chap. 85.

[5] 14 & 15 Vic., chap. 99; *ante* Lecture XII.

civil suits, has been vindicated so fully by experience that I think scarcely a single objector now remains. How much these changes in procedure and evidence have simplified and improved the administration of justice is known to every lawyer. These, too, belong to the credit of our era.

Libel; Growth of Corporations and of Corporate Litigation. — It is impossible within the compass of these lectures to notice all of even the more important improvements in our law which have been made within the century. I must pass over with bare mention the Fox Libel Act of 1792 and the subsequent legislation on that subject in both countries. Truth is with us a justification, both in civil and criminal cases, if it is written with good motives and for justifiable ends, whereof the jury are the judges.[1]

Lecture XIII.

Libel laws.

---

[1] Professor, now Mr. Justice Baldwin, succinctly states the manner in which we have dealt with this important subject: "The law of libel, in any government, is one of the surest tests by which to estimate its hold upon the people. The United States was the first to renounce, for its rulers, the protection of this law. When the decemvirs were framing the Twelve Tables of Rome, few as were the subjects they thought it important to cover in their code, they were careful to make libel against the State a capital offence; for they were the State, and they were turning a republic into a despotism. When the people of England were beginning to demand a greater share in her government, it was the law of libel to which the crown resorted for its surest weapon of defence, and it was the pride of the English bar that, in criminal cases, they nullified it by the aid of the jury. With us, in the United States, the law of libel is unknown, because the Federal government has no common law, and because the only statute ever passed by Congress to replace it on this subject was swept away in the first change of administration, and, indeed, in no small part was the cause of that change of administration ; while in our State governments we have almost everywhere come to the position that, both in civil and criminal cases, truth is a justification, unless actual malice is proved." "Address before the Ohio Bar Association," 1892.

One important subject, however, I must briefly refer to. It is the growth of corporations or the use of aggregated capital by corporate associations. The results of an examination of the comparative extent of corporate and private litigation surprised me. I found that in a recent volume of the reports of the Supreme Court of the United States sixty-one cases were reported, of which twenty-eight were between natural persons on both sides; twenty-seven were cases in which private corporations and six cases in which public corporations were concerned. In May, 1879, Chief-Justice Waite wrote me that the court had at the recent term disposed of three hundred and seventy-nine causes, of which ninety-one related to the United States, one hundred and eighty-three were corporation cases, and only one hundred and five were between private individuals. To ascertain whether the amount of corporate litigation in the Supreme Court was abnormal, I personally examined three volumes of the New York Court of Appeals Reports, — that is, volumes lxxiii., lxxiv., and cv., — with the following result: civil cases reported, four hundred and twenty-four; of which two hundred and thirty-four were between private persons, and one hundred and ninety were cases in which corporations, public or private, were concerned on one side or the other. I then examined volume i., Johnson's Reports, published in 1806. I found one hundred and thirty cases reported, of which only twenty related to any sort of corporations or involved corporation law.

This change in the character of the litigation ought not perhaps to surprise us, since we know the business of banking, of manufacturing, of insurance, of railway and water transportation, of telegraphy, and of nearly every branch of industry requiring considerable capital, prefers the safe and facile form of corporate organization and ownership to the inconvenience and liabilities of the copartnership or even joint stock relation. How wisely and satisfactorily to govern our populous public and municipal corporations is yet an unsolved problem.[1] The facts here brought to view, however, present to statesmen and lawyers questions in political economy and practical legislation of exceeding interest and difficulty. They are not, I am persuaded, insoluble, but the future must considerately deal with them in the light of time and experience, which alone can supply the needed wisdom.

American Law Reports and Development of the Literature of the Law in this Country. — In the Edinburgh Review in 1820 an eminent man, in an article in which he kindly advised the Americans not to grow vain and ambitious, said: " During the " thirty or forty years of their independence, they " have done absolutely nothing for the sciences, for " the arts, for literature, for politics or political econ- " omy. . . . In the four quarters of the globe," he tauntingly inquired, " who reads an American book ? "

This was, even at that time, unjust, because untrue. Franklin had made the discovery which in its application by Morse and other American inventors has since resulted in the modern telegraph.

[1] Dillon, " Law of Municipal Corporations," chap. i.

Lecture XIII. Whitney had invented the cotton gin. Fulton had successfully introduced steam navigation. We had always supposed that the statesmen who founded our free governments and embodied their basis principles in our State and Federal Constitutions had done something worthy of respectful regard. Gladstone's well-known, though historically inexact, eulogium is that "the American Constitution "is the most wonderful work ever struck off at a "given time by the brain and purpose of man."[1]

In general literature and in the literature of the law, our development had in 1820 just fairly begun. James Russell Lowell at the Authors' Readings in New York, in a review of American literature, said that when he was a boy, sixty years ago, there were but two American writers who could have supported themselves with their pens, — Irving and Cooper. Since then our literature has had an expansion which is truly marvellous. I fancy that, in this year of grace, 1892, no one repeats the inquiry, "Who reads an American book? What "has America done for the sciences and the "arts?"

American Law and Chancery Reports. It more immediately concerns us to see what America has done for the law. At the beginning of this century, Dallas had just commenced the publication of the Reports of the Supreme Court. Reports of some of the States soon followed. Kirby's Reports and Swift's Digest were the early contributions of Connecticut. In 1817 Chancellor

---

[1] One of the principles of that Constitution, Mr. Gladstone, in February, 1893, avowed in Parliament, in introducing his so-called Home Rule measure, he had adopted in the proposed act.

De Saussure, of South Carolina, published the first volume of Equity Reports which ever appeared in this country. Kent was appointed a judge of the Supreme Court of New York in 1798, and Chancellor in 1814. He held the latter office until 1823, during which period his seven volumes of Chancery Reports were given to the world. As a judge and author, he will not suffer when compared with the greatest names which have adorned the English law. Higher praise it is not possible to give. When he had reached the constitutional limit of sixty years, at which he could no longer hold judicial office, he retired to private life and gave himself to the preparation of his Commentaries on American Law, which appeared from 1826 to 1830, and which he publicly acknowledged owed their origin to the liberality of the trustees of Columbia College. To be the Kent Professor of Law in this University is an honor, sir [addressing Mr. Phelps], which, worn by you, pales not its effectual light, even by the side of the great public honors which you have so worthily borne. The American Bar and people venerate the name and character of Chancellor Kent. Simple as a child in his tastes and habits throughout his tranquil and useful life; more than any other judge the creator of the equity system of this country; the author of Commentaries which, in accuracy and learning, in elegance, purity, and vigor of style, rival those of Sir William Blackstone, his name is admired, his writings prized, and his judgments at law and in equity respected in every quarter of the globe (and nowhere more than in England), wherever in its widening conquest the

Lecture XIII.

Chancellor Kent's labors as a judge and author.

English language, which is the language of freedom, has carried the English law.[1]

The development of our jurisprudence, National and State, progressed with astonishing rapidity. Marshall's judgments on the Federal Constitution which fixed its outlines and established its principles, and which are among the greatest and most original productions of the human reason, were pronounced between 1801 and 1835.[2] In 1832 Mr. Justice Story published his first legal work, and until his death in 1845 his pen was never idle. By reason of the greater variety of his labors he obtained, perhaps, a wider transatlantic reputation than Chancellor Kent, or any other American jurist or author. I cannot, of course, refer to our many other law writers of merit, not even to the most eminent. I endeavored not long since to ascertain the number of American elementary treatises on the law, but did not succeed. I found that down to 1881 the judicial reports in England numbered 2,944 volumes; that in this country down to December 31, 1885, the number exceeded that in England, and was as follows: Federal Reports, 409; miscellaneous reports, 203; American State Reports, 3,186, — making in all 3,798.[3] And this mostly within the last fifty years! If this multiplication continues, and no relief shall come, may

---

[1] "If," says the late Mr. Justice Stephen, "we except the Commentaries of Chancellor Kent, which were suggested by Blackstone, I should doubt whether any work intended to describe the whole of the law of any country possessed anything like the same merits" as Blackstone's work. "History of the Criminal Law of England," vol. ii., chap. xxi., p. 215.

[2] See *ante* Lecture V., p. 165. [3] See *ante* Lecture X., p. 266, note.

we not stop, and in anticipation heave a sigh of pity for the judges and lawyers of a century hence?

The first impulse of every just man is to satisfy his just obligations. So it should be with States. And it is a satisfaction to us all to know that "in the august accounting of nations" America is rapidly discharging, in law and literature, in the sciences and arts, her great indebtedness to Europe, and especially to England, and that America may not unreasonably expect a period to arrive when, in the accounting, the Old World may become the acknowledged debtor of the new.[1]

A few reflections suggested by this retrospect may have some value. The evolution of our law which has been sketched in the course of these lectures impresses me with the conviction of the general truths which underlie the leading doctrines of Savigny and the historical jurists; namely, that law is largely the outcome of all of the past conditions, circumstances, and customs of a people; that it ordinarily originates in or is introduced by custom (using this word in the broad sense of including judiciary law), and is supplemented by legislation, direct or oblique, when, and in general only when, the law is otherwise inadequate to meet difficult and complex or new situations and exigencies. This view recognizes the fact that the life of a nation or people flows ever on, though its channels may be invisible; that its workings are unseen until they show themselves in usages and acts which are its external and superficial manifestations, and

Lecture XIII.

America repaying her debt to the Old Country.

Reflections.

Truths in Savigny's conception of law.

[1] See *ante* Lecture VI., p. 186, where an extract from Webster's finished eulogy on Justice Story is given.

Lecture XIII.

Truths in Austin's conception of law.

Austin's conception defective. The highest ideal of law realized in the American Constitutions.

which we are too prone to consider as detached and unrelated: whereas, if we enlarge our view and penetrate beyond the surface to the hidden springs and causes of human action, we shall find that in a deep and real sense there is in the life of a nation no past, no present, and no future, — since the past, the present, and the future form one unbroken chain which binds the people thereof as truly to that which is to come as it does to that which is already gone.

This review, and particularly the century's retrospect we have just made, also exemplifies the truth that lies in the Austinian conception that law is the direct creation or command of the sovereign, enforced or enforceable by the State. But it also makes plain that Austin's doctrine that all law proceeds from the sovereign, and therefore is binding alone upon the subject, is defective in that it fails to realize that law has not reached its full development until it attains complete supremacy by binding alike the sovereign and the subject. This matured, and it is not extravagant to say, sublime conception — the great gift of America to the world — has only been made a reality by the American device of written constitutions, which are the supreme law of the land, since their provisions are obligatory both upon the State and upon those subjected to its rule, and equally enforceable against both, and therefore *law* in the strictest sense of the term.[1]

---

[1] See *ante* Lecture VII., p. 197; Lightwood, "Nature of Positive Law," Macmillan & Co., London, 1883, chap. xiii., where Ihering's view ("Der Zweck im Recht," pp. 324, 344, 346, 371) is clearly expounded.

This review likewise shows that under existing conditions legislation is the usual and in many cases the only effective means of making the changes and additions necessary to conform the laws to the changed sentiments and needs of people. If you will run your eyes over the great and beneficent improvements and reforms in the mode of procedure and in substantive law to which I have referred, you will see not only that they have all been wrought by legislation, but are of such a nature that they could not have been accomplished in any other way. Nor is this result peculiar to the English and American systems. Roman law and Continental law exhibit the same phenomena of the gradual evolution and amendment of the laws by the concurrent forces of jurisprudence and legislation, and of the respective spheres of each. Accordingly, Von Ihering observes that "all thorough "reforms in the mode of procedure and of positive "law may be traced back to legislation."[1]

The Century to Come. — Having looked at the century that is gone, how natural to turn our longing eyes — though dim and purblind — to the future. The folly of prophesying has passed into an adage. James Russell Lowell wisely as well as wittily says, "Don't prophesy unless you know;" but when the time of fulfilment is laid one hundred years off, one is safe at least from being overwhelmed with confusion in his own lifetime. Unadmonished and undeterred, I venture a timid forecast of some of the changes which our laws

Lecture XIII.

Increasing energy of legislative action and the reasons therefor.

Forecast of changes in our laws.

[1] Ihering, "Struggle for Law" (Lalor's translation), p. 9.

Lecture XIII.

Predicted changes in international law.

and jurisprudence will witness within the next century.

In International Law. — I predict that the rational practice of settling disputes between nations by arbitration, so successfully applied in recent years, will become general; that wars, the opprobrium of Christian civilization, if they shall not wholly cease (which is hardly to be expected), will be comparatively infrequent; and that they will no longer be regarded as making the inhabitants of each country enemies of the other, but only as a conflict between the States concerned in their organized capacity, in which private property on land and sea shall no longer be subject to capture, confiscation, or destruction, and the cruelty of what are called the laws of war will be otherwise greatly ameliorated.[1]

---

[1] As this volume is passing through the press, a cable despatch, August 15, 1893, from Paris, thus announces the arbitrators' decision in the Bering Sea Seal Controversy between Great Britain and the United States : " At eleven o'clock the arbitrators reassembled in the room in the Foreign Office in which the public sessions of the tribunal had been held. Baron de Courcel, the president of the tribunal, then delivered to the agents of the United States and Great Britain original copies of the decision signed by all the arbitrators ; and he, thereupon, addressed the arbitrators, saying that he recognized the great value of arbitration as a cause of peace between nations. He expressed the opinion that every international arbitration renders war less probable, and said he looked forward to the time in the near future when it would be the rule and not the exception to settle international differences in this way. Senator John T. Morgan, one of the American arbitrators, and Lord Hannen, one of the arbitrators appointed by Great Britain, responded to Baron de Courcel, declaring that they reciprocated the sentiments expressed by him, and recognized the hospitality extended by France to the arbitrators. The session terminated amid mutual congratulations and expressions of good feeling."

I predict that the existing apathy of the public conscience will be aroused, and that the avarice of publishers will not be able to continue the present system of literary piracy, since all civilized nations will recognize the principle that an author has by the highest of all titles — namely, that of creation — a right of property in his work, which treaties and legislation will protect on the basis of reciprocity.

I predict (in view of the universality and increasing freedom and intimacy of commercial intercourse between nations) that substantial unity in the various departments of mercantile and maritime law on the great subjects of Bills of Exchange, Marine Contracts, Marine Insurance, Marine Torts, etc., will replace the diversity and conflict which now exist.

In Municipal Law. — In municipal law I predict important changes of substance and form. Our real property law is still poisoned by the feudal taint. It is artificial, complicated, and excessively technical, — quite as much so as the almost extinct system of common-law pleadings. The remedy must be radical. In fact, the division of property into real and personal, whereby each class possesses distinct qualities and is governed by different rules as to acquisition, mode of transfer, devolution, etc., is largely, although not wholly, artificial; and so far as it is artificial, it must be abrogated, and the law of real and personal property made, as far as practicable, substantially uniform, and thereby simplified. Substantive changes only will meet the exigencies of the situation.[1]

[1] See *ante* Lecture VIII., pp. 237-241.

Lecture XIII.

Future union of legal and equitable rights and remedies.

In no other system of jurisprudence do we witness the competing and conflicting rules which mark our division of rights and remedies into legal and equitable. The separation of what we call equity from law was originally accidental,— or at any rate was unnecessary; and the development of an independent system of equitable rights and remedies is anomalous, and rests upon no principle. The continued existence of these two sets of rights and remedies is not only unnecessary, but its inevitable effect is to make confusion and conflict. The existing diversity of rights and remedies must disappear, and be replaced by a uniform system of rights as well as remedies,— what we call a legal right ceasing to exist if it is in conflict with what we now distinguish as the equitable right.[1]

Systematic restatement of our laws the work of the future.

And generally the forecast may be ventured that while the law will in its development undoubtedly keep pace with the changing wants of society, yet the work of jurists and legislators during the next century will be pre-eminently the work of systematic restatement, probably in sections, of the body of our jurisprudence. Call it a code, or what you will, this work must be done. If not done from choice, the inexorable logic of necessity will compel its performance.

It seems to me to be reasonably clear that in these and many other respects our laws and jurisprudence are likely to undergo essential changes. Scientific jurisprudence, already a necessity, will play a more important part in the future of our

[1] *Ante* Lecture VIII., pp. 234, 235.

law than it has in the past. It is a mistake to suppose that the jurist, any more than the legislator, must look only to the past. He must also study the present, and bring himself into actual contact with the existing conditions of society, its sentiments, its moral convictions, and its actual needs. And the work must be done with all the aids that the learning and experience of the past affords, and under the inspiration of a higher ideal than the existing state of our law supplies.

This work, as important, as noble, as any that can engage the attention of men, will fall to the profession to do, since it cannot be done by others. It rests therefore upon the profession as a duty. It will not be performed by men whose sun, like mine, has passed the zenith, and whose faces are already turned to follow its setting. I address young men, men who are hailing the advance of their sun up the eastern sky, and who are full of the hopes, the aspirations, the generous illusions, the sublime audacity, which give to that interesting stage of life, when animated by high resolves, a present charm and a prophetic splendor all its own. No single laborer, unassisted, can do much in a work so vast. It is, indeed, a work which must be done more or less in compartments, and it is given to every earnest and devoted lawyer to do in his day and generation his utmost part, however humble. And mayhap some young man hears me to-day, gifted beyond the common lot, with an eye couched to that wider and higher sweep of "the gladsome light" which takes in all the constructive possibilities of the rich but scattered materials of our laws, and with hand and

Lecture XIII.

Nobility and difficulties of the work of improving our laws and jurisprudence.

brain which shall tire not, day nor night, in the arduous work; — mayhap some such man will be so fortunate as to leave on the massive, the imposing, the ever-advancing but ever-uncompleted structure of our jurisprudence some visible imprint, some lasting expression, some embodied memorial of his genius and his labors. If the foregoing retrospect of a century's progress in our laws illustrates any one thing, it is that in the domain of the law, as elsewhere,

> "There are great truths that pitch their shining tents
> Outside our walls, and though but dimly seen
> In the gray dawn, they will be manifest
> When the light widens into perfect day."[1]

Conclusion. — And here the STORRS LECTURES for the current year come to an end. It has been a sincere pleasure to me to give them. I have scattered such poor seed as I had in hand, in the hope that, as sometimes happens, even a seedling may chance to spring up into something of worth. The teacher must sow in faith, and in faith the student must hear, and the lawyer must labor; but the latter will miss his highest, his noblest end and aim, if he degrades his great calling into a trade, a mere means of livelihood. Such happily are not the influences that in the past have gone forth from this famous university, which, as I speak these parting words, enjoys the rare distinction of having two of its sons worthily holding and adorning seats upon the Supreme Bench of the United

---

[1] Longfellow, "Michael Angelo."

States, honoring it and honoring their *alma mater*.[1] Young gentlemen, with tender regret, full of faith and hope, and entreating you as you shall go hence to the stern duties of your profession to wear ever "the white flower of a blameless life," I take my leave of you with the benison that of old was bestowed upon the youthful knight: BE BRAVE, LOYAL, AND SUCCESSFUL!

Lecture XIII.

[1] Justices Brewer and Brown. Since then, Mr. Justice Shiras has been added, so that Yale University has the unique and pre-eminent distinction of having three of the nine judges who now (1893) constitute the bench of the Supreme Court.

TABLE OF CASES CITED.

	PAGE
Attorney-General v. Forster (10 Vesey, 335, 342)	230
Ayers, In re (123 U. S. 443)	228
Bay v. Coddington (5 Johns. Ch. 54; 20 Johns. 637)	246
Bayard v. Singleton (1 Martin, Nor. Car. 48)	200
Booreman's Case (March Rep. 177)	90
Bowditch v. Boston (101 U. S. 16)	130
Bowman v. Middleton (1 Bay, S. C. 252)	200
Case of the Judges (4 Call, Va. 135)	200
Chicago, &c. Ry. Co. v. Minnesota (134 U. S. 418)	32
Commonwealth v. Caton (4 Call, Va. 5)	200
Davis v. Duke of Marlborough (2 Swanst. 113, 162)	230
—— v. Lord Strathmore (16 Vesey, 419, 429)	230
Gee v. Pritchard (2 Swanst. 402, 414)	230
Hallett's Estate, Re (L. R. 13 Ch. Div. 696, 710)	6
Hart's Case (Rex v. Gray's Inn, 1 Doug. 353, 354)	39, 90
Hays v. Bell (16 Mo. 496)	126
Holmes v. Walton (New Jersey)	200
Houghtaling v. Ball (19 Mo. 84)	126
Kamper v. Hawkins (1 Va. Cas. 20)	200
Kilbourn v. Thompson (103 U. S. 168)	227
Lahr v. Metropolitan El. Ry. Co. (104 N. Y. 268)	290
Legal Tender Cases (8 Wall. 603; 11 Wall. 682; 12 Wall. 457; 110 U. S. 421)	214

	PAGE
Lord Rosslyn v. Jodrell (4 Campb. 303; 1 Starkie Rep. 148)	90
Louisville & N. R. R. Co. v. Woodson (134 U. S. 614)	130
McKown v. Craig (39 Mo. 156)	126
Marbury v. Madison (1 Cranch, 137)	200, 227
Marshall v. Hubbard (117 U. S. 415)	130
Maundrell v. Maundrell (10 Vesey, 246, 259)	230
May v. Harvey (13 East, 197)	90
Munn v. Illinois (94 U. S. 113)	214
Murray v. McCarty (2 Munf. Va. 393)	351
Ogden v. Witherspoon (2 Haywood, Nor. Car. 227)	200
Pleasants v. Fant (22 Wall. 116)	130
Poindexter v. Greenhow (114 U. S. 270)	228
Railroad Co. v. National Bank (102 U. S. 14)	245
Rakestraw v. Brewer (Abridg. Cases in Equity, 162)	90
Rex v. Bembridge (3 Doug. 327, 332)	182, 278
Rex v. Gray's Inn (Hart's Case, 1 Doug. 353, 354)	39, 90
Rex v. Lincoln's Inn (Wooller's Case, 4 Barn. & Cress. 855)	90
Schofield v. Chicago, &c. R. R. Co. (114 U. S. 615)	130
Slaughter-House Cases (16 Wall. 36)	208
State v. Parkhurst (4 Halst. N. J. Law, 427, 444)	200
Story's case (90 N. Y. 122)	291
Stowel v. Lord Zouch (1 Plowd. 357)	23
Swift v. Tyson (16 Peters, 1)	246
Townshend's Case (T. Raymond, 69)	90
Trevett v. Weeden (Rhode Island)	200
United States v. Lee (106 U. S. 196)	198, 214, 227
—— v. Schurz (102 U. S. 378)	201
Williams's Case (Wharton's State Trials, 652)	351
Wooller's Case (4 Barn. & Cress. 855)	90

AUTHORS CITED.

	PAGE
A Generation of Judges, by their Reporter	92, 128, 257, 288
Alison: History of Europe	210
American Jurist	241
American Law Review	120, 352, 364
Amos: The Science of Law	7, 124, 177, 343
Arnold: History of Rhode Island	200
Austin: Jurisprudence (Campbell's)	10, 269, 270, 286, 291, 309
—— Province of Jurisprudence determined	6

Bacon: Advancement of Learning 30, 138
—— Essays 225
—— Works of (Montagu's Edition) 117, 260, 274, 294
Baldwin, Simeon E.: Address before Ohio Bar Association . . 289, 351, 368, 375
Ballantine: Some Experiences of a Barrister's Life . . 73, 224, 369
Bancroft: History of the Constitution 200
—— Introduction to Hunt's Life of Livingston 338
Beccaria: Crimes and Punishments 368
Bentham's Works 175, 271, 318, 327, 336, 338, 339, 374
Blackburn on Sale 236
Blackstone: Commentaries 10, 43, 45, 59, 63, 91, 94, 232, 291, 310, 322, 366
Boswell: Life of Dr. Johnson 41, 97
Boutmy, Émile: Studies in Constitutional Law . . . 146, 147, 211
—— The English Constitution (Eaden's Translation) 118, 164, 305, 306
Bradley, Mr. Justice: Manuscript letter 22
Brougham: Speeches (Black's Edition) 330
—— The British Constitution 31
Brown: Life of Rufus Choate 46
Bryce: American Commonwealth 200, 206, 207
Burke's Works 31, 150, 207, 208, 323, 324, 349
Byron: Childe Harold 49

	PAGE
Campbell: Lives of the Chief-Justices	111
Carson: History Supreme Court of United States	201
Carter, James C.: Address before American Bar Association	13
Chase, Chief-Justice: Introduction to the Livingston Codes and Reports	338
Chaucer: Canterbury Tales	38, 55
Choate, Rufus: Addresses and Orations	198, 200
Clark: Bibliotheca Legum	79
Clark: Practical Jurisprudence: A Comment on Austin	11, 232, 259, 270, 286, 347
Coke: Reports, Preface	37, 50, 59, 70, 74, 79, 133, 192
Coleridge, Samuel Taylor: Church and State	206
—— Translation, "The Piccolomini,"	199
Cooley: Constitutional Limitations	200
Crabb: History of English Law	74
Daniels, W. T. S.: The History and Origin of the Law Reports	276
Dicey: The Law of the Constitution	25, 117, 202, 214, 224, 225, 226
Dickens: Martin Chuzzlewit	103
Digby: History of the Law of Real Property	158, 201, 310
Dillon: Commentaries on the Law of Municipal Corporations	119, 163, 203, 322, 343, 377
Douthwaite: Article on "Gray's Inn" in Green Bag Magazine	61
—— Gray's Inn; Its History and Associations	48, 61, 78, 94
Dugdale, Sir William: Origines Juridiciales	67
Dumont: Editions of Bentham's Works	318, 327, 336
Durand and Terrel: Pref. to Prof. Lioy's "Philosophie du Droit"	84
Edinburgh Review	367, 377
Ellis: Original Letters Illustrative of English History	118
Emerson: English Traits	365
Encyclopædia Britannica	51, 53, 58, 94
Field, David Dudley: American Progress in Jurisprudence	352
Finlason: Introduction to Reeves' History of the Common Law	159
Forster: Life of Goldsmith	99
Fortescue: De Laudibus Legum Angliæ	45, 49, 50, 54, 63, 74, 117, 125, 172
—— Governance of England (Plummer's Edition)	66
Foss: Judges of England	59, 60, 61, 62, 63, 66, 67, 70, 94, 111
Freeman: Chief Periods of European History	345
—— Growth of the English Constitution	29, 157, 161, 230, 302
—— Norman Conquest	158

AUTHORS CITED.   395

	PAGE
Gardiner: History of England	80
Gibbon: Autobiography	95, 96
Glasson: Elements du Droit Français	120
Goldsmith: English Bar; or, Guide to the Inns of Court	44
Goldsmith, Oliver: Citizen of the World	100
Green Bag Magazine	61, 250
Greenleaf on Evidence	279
Guizot: History of Civilization in Europe	154, 158

Hale: Analysis of the Civil Part of the Law 308
—— History of the Common Law 20, 172, 232
Hallam: Middle Ages 121, 164, 367
Hammond: Edition of Blackstone's Commentaries   10, 24, 63, 230,
232, 291, 298, 308
—— Edition of Sandars's Justinian 308
—— On Law Schools 81
Hardcastle, Hon. Mrs.: Life of John, Lord Campbell . . . 54, 73
Hargrave's Law Tracts 173
Harrington's Oceana 197
Hawthorne: English Note-Book 109
Hearn: The Government of England 25, 30, 160
Herbert: Antiquities of the Inns of Court and Chancery, 37, 74, 93, 94
Hitchcock: Constitutional History of the United States . . . 201
Hobbes: Dialogue of the Common Laws 316
—— Leviathan 10
Holland: Elements of Jurisprudence 11, 12, 20, 27
Holtzendorff's Encyklopädie der Rechtswissenschaft 310
Horwood's Year Book (32 Edw. I., p. 32 A.D. 1304) 230
Hume: History of England 49
Hunt: Life of Edward Livingston 337, 338
Hutton: Literary Landmarks of London . 48, 76, 95, 96, 97, 98, 99, 100, 102

Ihering: Der Zweck im Recht 382
—— Struggle for Law (Lalor's Translation) 383
Imperial Dictionary 36, 270
Irving: Life of Goldsmith 98

Jesse: London 95
—— Memories of Westminster Hall 112
Johnson's Dictionary 38
Johnson: Journey to the Western Isles; Inch Kenneth . . . 41
—— Life of Milton 188
Jones, Sir William: Preface to the Speeches of Isæus 137

	PAGE
Jonson: Every Man out of his Humour	92
Juridical Society Papers, Best	121, 122
—— Hawkins: Digests and Codes	277
—— Smith: Ancient Legal Education in the Inns of Court	78
—— Stephen	122
—— Westlake: A Plea for Official Reporting	275
Jurist (London)	282
Justinian	258

Kent: Commentaries 200, 246, 359, 379
Kolb: Condition of Nations (Translated by Mrs. Brewer) . . 26

Lamb: Essay "On Some of the Old Actors" 46
—— On the "Old Benchers" 46, 101
Law Quarterly Review 209
Lee, Francis Bazley: History of the Supreme Court of New Jersey 57
Lightwood: Nature of Positive Law 382
Loftie, W. J.: The Inns of Court and Chancery. 35, 61, 75, 94, 95,
97, 98, 102, 103
Longfellow: Michael Angelo 388
Lorimer: The Institutes of Law 4

Macaulay: Article on Sir James Mackintosh 300
—— Essay on History 159
—— Essay on Warren Hastings 109
—— Review of Dumont's Mirabeau 317, 328
Maine: Ancient Law 207
—— Early History of Institutions 13, 317
—— Early Law and Custom 308
—— Essay on Popular Government 211
—— Village Communities 314, 338, 346
Mackintosh, Life of Sir James 137, 205, 212
—— History of England 35, 159
—— Speech in Defence of Jean Peltier 91
Manning: Serviens ad Legem 70
Manning's Report of the Serjeants' Case 74
Markby: Elements of Law . . 6, 11, 22, 23, 29, 229, 231, 232, 259
Martin, Benj. Ellis: Footprints of Charles Lamb . . 99, 100, 101
Merrill (in 11 Am. Law Rev. 677) 120
Mill, John Stuart: Autobiography 335, 336
—— Dissertations and Discussions 304, 307, 313, 331, 335
Miller, Justice Samuel F.: Lectures on the Constitution of the
United States 201, 209, 227
—— The System of Trial by Jury 123

	PAGE
Milton: Comus	80
Modern Reports	54
Montesquieu: Spirit of the Laws	159
Morley, John: Critical Miscellanies	296
Murphy: Essay on Johnson	97

Nash: Life of Lord Westbury 277, 278

Paston: Letters 50
Paterson: Liberty of the Subject 313
Pearce: Inns of Court 37, 51, 59, 60, 74, 78, 79, 80, 94
Pepys's Diary 47
Phelps, Edward J.: Address before American Bar Association 166
—— Bennington Anniversary Oration 350
Political Science Quarterly 197, 200
Pollock, Sir Frederick: Article in Law Quarterly Review. . 83, 299
—— Essays in Jurisprudence and Ethics, 11, 21, 233, 236, 244, 286, 312
—— History of the Science of Politics 8, 10, 349
—— Oxford Lectures and Other Discourses 21, 25, 28, 205, 297, 310
—— Oxford Studies 143
Pomeroy: Municipal Law 291
Poore's Charters and Constitutions 359, 368
Pulling: Order of the Coif, 37, 42, 43, 55, 66, 68, 70, 72, 73, 74, 94, 112

Raleigh: History of the World 50
Reeves: History of the English Law 62
—— History of the Common Law (Introduction by Finlason) . 159
Rendle, William: The Inns of Old Southwark 38
Reports of American Bar Association . 122, 245, 249, 255, 266, 309
Report of Committee of American Bar Association . . 83, 85, 309
Report of Common-Law Commissioners on subject of Serjeants'
 Inn and the Inns of Court 74
Report on Legal Education — U. S. Bureau of Education . . 18, 85
Robinson, B. Coulson: Bench and Bar . . . . 55, 56, 68 et seq.
Robinson, Henry Crabb: Diary 324
Romilly: Life of Sir Samuel 325, 334

Schiller 198
Sharswood: Law Lectures 203, 286
Skeats's Dictionary 38
Smith, Philip Anstie: History of Education for the English Bar
            39, 59, 78, 81, 94
Southey: Works of Cowper 96
Spence: Equity 19, 230

AUTHORS CITED.

	PAGE
Spenser: Prothalamion	45
Spilsbury: Lincoln's Inn	60, 93, 94
Starkie's Evidence	340
Steiger's Cyclopedia of Education	81
Stephen: Digest of the Criminal Law	279
—— Digest of the Law of Evidence	278, 341
—— General View of the Criminal Law of England	341
—— History of the Criminal Law of England,	118, 257, 260, 316, 365, 366, 369, 380
Stillé: Life and Times of John Dickinson	353
Story: Equity	230
—— Life and Letters	221
Stow: Survey of London	51
Stubbs: Constitutional History	157, 164, 212
Taylor: Evidence	278
Tennyson	178
Thackeray: Pendennis	40, 93, 96
—— English Humourists	96
Thayer: The Jury and its Development	29, 122
Thompson, R. H.: Address to Mississippi Bar Association	364
Thompson, Seymour D.: Treatise on the Law of Homesteads	361
Townsend: Lives of Twelve Eminent Judges	326
Twiss, Horace: Life of Lord Eldon	230
Tyler: Memoir of Roger Brooke Taney	167
Voltaire's Commentary on Beccaria's Work	368
Waterhouse: Edition of Fortescue's "De Laudibus"	54
Webster, Daniel: Webster's Works	26, 145, 186
Westbury, Lord: Nash's Life of	277, 278
Woolrych: Lives of Eminent Serjeants-at-Law	70, 74
Wordsworth	57, 114
Wynne, Edward: Eunomus	51, 74, 215
—— Observations touching the Antiquity and Dignity of the Degree of Serjeant-at-Law, etc.	74

INDEX.

ACTIONS,   PAGE
   reform in the law of evidence 373
   competency of witnesses 373, 374
   law of procedure (see CODIFICATION).
AMENDMENT OF LAWS (see BACON; BENTHAM; CODIFI-
   CATION; LAW; LEGISLATION),
   true motto of the legal reformer 347
AMERICA (see CONSTITUTIONS; GOVERNMENT; UNITED
   STATES).
AMERICAN BAR ASSOCIATION,
   report on legal education 83
   report on bulk and uncertainty in the law 244, 245, 248, 254, 255
   resolution as to law reporting 267
   resolution as to publication of law reports 289
   report on classification of the law . . . . 309 *note*
AMOS, PROF. SHELDON (see table, AUTHORS CITED),
   extract from, on relations between law and morality . . . 7
   classification of defects in our law 177
ANARCHISM (see SOCIALISM).
APPENZELL,
   Swiss Canton of 161
ARBITRARY POWER,
   absence of, in English and American legal polity 224
ARBITRATION,
   in international law 384
ARGUMENTS (see REPORTS),
   superior value of oral over printed 190, 191, 192
   former English practice 191
   full consultation by the judges 192
ARKANSAS,
   instructions by the judge in jury trials . . . . 127 *note*
ARTS,
   contributions of America to .   . 377

ATTORNEYS (see BARRISTERS; LAWYERS),   PAGE
  officers of the common-law courts 52
AULA REGIA . . . . 42 *note*
AUSTIN, JOHN,
  his "Province of Jurisprudence Determined," 6
  conception of law 6, 10, 382
  leading objection to case-law 291
  reaction against Bentham's extreme views 339
AUSTRIA,
  adopted the Roman law 22
  the Austrian code 258
  doctrine of judicial precedent . . . . 286 *note*

BACON, LORD,
  connection with Gray's Inn 46, 95
  disgrace and pathetic death 47, 48
  early life in Gray's Inn 48
  tarnished but enduring fame 49
  first Queen's counsel 69
  gardens of Gray's Inn laid out by . . . . 46 *note*, 48 *note*, 95
  views on law amendment 259
  scheme of law amendment 272, 278
  method of dealing with statute law 273
  with case-law 274
BALLANTINE, SERJEANT,
  on improvement in administration of law . . . . . 369 *note*
BAR (see BARRISTERS; INNS OF COURT; LAWYERS; LEGAL
  EDUCATION; SERJEANTS-AT-LAW).
BARNARD'S INN 104
BARRISTER-AT-LAW (see INNS OF COURT),
  degree in ranks of barristers 58
  exclusive power to confer degree of 91
BARRISTERS (see INNS OF COURT; LAWYERS; LEGAL EDU-
  CATION; SERJEANTS-AT-LAW).
  higher class of lawyers 52
  right to appear in superior courts 52
  rank among members of Inns of Court 53
  lowest degree in ranks of 58
  conversion into serjeant-at-law 68, 71
BEAUMONT,
  member of the Inner Temple 95
BECCARIA,
  influence of views of, on criminal law 368
BELGIUM,
  written constitution 201
BENCH (see COURTS; ENGLAND; JUDGES).

INDEX. 401

BENCHERS (see INNS OF COURT), PAGE
   governing body of Inns of Court 53
BENTHAM, JEREMY,
   as a law reformer . . . 180, 181, 299, 313, 319, 320, 330 *note*
   a typical radical 299
   a legal recluse . . . . 320, 330 *note*
   place in our legal history 316, 317
   labors of 313–315
   devotion to his work 320
   obstacles in his way 323, 327
   value and influence of his labors 332, 334
   influence in England and America . . . . . . 336, 337 *note*
      on law of evidence 339, 340, 341, 371
   his conception of a code 180, 342
   remedy for bulk and uncertainty of the law 275
   failure in directly realizing practical results 341
   his scheme impracticable in full extent 343
   enemy of case-law 313
   admission as to value of reports 174, 270
   merits as critic of our law 333
   principal works relating to law and legislation 318
   English law and society in time of 300, 302, 303, 304, 306, 318
   opinion of the English law 307, 321
      contrasted with Blackstone's 322
   friends and co-laborers 328
   Brougham's estimate of 329
   Talleyrand's observations 332
   Mill's critical estimate 335
   Sir James Stephen's opinion 316
   Austin's reaction against extreme views of 339
BERING SEA SEAL CONTROVERSY,
   value of arbitration . . . . 384 *note*
BILLS, NEGOTIABLE,
   conflict of law respecting 245, 246, 247
BILL OF RIGHTS 203
   basis of English and American liberty 35
BLACK BOOK,
   record of proceedings of Lincoln's Inn 67
BLACKSTONE,
   a consummate literary artist 310
   typical conservative 298
   state of English law and society in time of 300, 302, 303, 304, 306
   need for an institutional work 309
   value of his Commentaries . . . 150 *note*, 298, 307, 311, 354
   great influence on American law . . . . 150 *note*, 298
   eulogies of English law 307, 333, 354
   opinion of English law contrasted with Bentham's . . . 322
   opinion as to criminal law 366

26

BLACKSTONE, — *continued*. PAGE
   indebtedness to Lord Hale 308
   his definition of law 10
   need of a modern Blackstone 311, 312
BOSWELL,
   entered name at Inner Temple 97, 98
BOUTMY, ÉMILE,
   on state of England and its laws . . . . 305 *note*
   concerning Magna Charta . . . . 305 *note*
   on United States government 146, 147
BRACTON,
   as authority in our law 23
BRIEFS (see ARGUMENTS).
BRIGHT, JOHN 356
BROUGHAM, LORD,
   estimate of Bentham 329
   acts relating to evidence 340, 374
BRYCE, PROFESSOR JAMES,
   extracts from 206, 207
BULK OF OUR LAWS (see CASE-LAW; LAW).
BURKE, EDMUND,
   illustration of conservatism of English 323, 324
   remarkable concession 348
   the people the true legislator 349

CAIRNS, LORD CHANCELLOR,
   approval of codification . . . . 183 *note*
CASE-LAW (see BENTHAM; CODIFICATION; COURTS; JUDICIAL
      PRECEDENT; LAW; LEGAL EDUCATION; REPORTS),
   one of the great divisions of the law 176, 267
   permanent necessity 343
   uneven growth 236, 237, 242
   why incomplete 242
   inconveniences and defects 176, 271
   importance and value of the reports . 31 *note*, 88, 174, 234, 270
      (see REPORTS).
   bulk and uncertainty   87, 133, 174, 177, 184 *note*, 233, 242, 248,
      250 *and note*, 264, 265, 266, 278 *note*, 285, 288, 314, 344, 380
     causes of bulk and uncertainty 242, 243, 248, 264, 272 *note*, 285
     effects 244, 249, 250
     report of America Bar Association 245
     suggested remedies 254, 268, 269, 386
       Bacon's method 274
       Bentham's 275
       Lord Westbury's . . . . 277 *note*
   illustrations of conflict and uncertainty 246, 247
   objection of Austin to 291

INDEX. 403

CASES,   PAGE
  in courts of justice 31
CASE SYSTEM (see CASE-LAW; LEGAL EDUCATION),
  place in legal education 86, 88
CENTRALIZATION,
  the States an effective bulwark against 218
CHANCERY (see COURTS; EQUITY; INNS OF CHANCERY),
  court of, origin 235
CHARACTER,
  of English judges 119
CHESTER INN 62
CHICKASAW INDIANS,
  tribal customs, sources of Mississippi's married women's
  laws . . . . 364 *note*
CHOATE, RUFUS,
  eulogium on the constitution 199, 200
CHURCH AND STATE,
  complete and permanent separation in the United States 352, 353
CIVIL LAW (see PREFACE; LAW; ROMAN LAW).
CIVIL PROCEDURE (see CODIFICATION; PROCEDURE),
  amendments in law of 370
  codification of law of . . . . . . 183, 260 *note*, 371, 372, 373
CIVIL SUITS (see ACTIONS).
CIVIL WAR,
  in the United States, the fourteenth amendment result of . 211
CLEMENT'S INN 104
CLIFFORD'S INN 104
  hostel of a noble family . . . . 37 *note*
  lease of 60, 62
  antiquity . . . . 62, 67 *note*
COCKBURN, CHIEF-JUSTICE,
  charge to jury in the Tichborne case 128
  as to reform of the law . . . . 184 *note*
  progress of law in America 187
CODE (see CODIFICATION).
CODIFICATION,
  the term defined 179, 256
  why necessary 344
  systematic recompilation of our law necessary . . 269, 347, 373,
                                                                    386, 387
  as a remedy for defects in the law 179, 254
  for bulk and uncertainty 179, 254, 255, 268, 275
  objections to 182
  within what limits practicable and expedient . . 181–183, 257,
                                                                    258, 373
  reports of American Bar Association . . 244, 245, 248, 254, 255

CODIFICATION, — *continued*. PAGE
  constantly being effected 346
  tacit codification 346
  materials ample 346
  true idea and principle 259, 345
  views of Lord Bacon 259
          Justice Stephen 260
  Lord Bacon's scheme of law amendment 272, 278
  Lord Westbury's 277, 278
  Bentham's idea 180, 181, 342
  Eldon's influence 325
  aversion of English people to innovation . . . 323, 324, 325
  effect of French Revolution on law reform in England . . 325
  drift of American jurisprudence towards . . . . . 288 *note*
  Bentham and his labors 313
  action of English Law Amendment Society 276
  the Royal Commission of 1866 277
  of the law of procedure . . . 183, 260 *note*, 370, 371, 372, 373
      David Dudley Field's labors 183
      Lord Chancellor Cairns' approval . . . . . . 183 *note*
      Chief-Justice Cockburn's suggestion . . . . . . 184 *note*
      Lord Coleridge's views . . . . 185 *note*
      America led in this reform . . . . 186 *note*
  need of reform in the substantive law 184, 186
      labors of Edward Livingston . . . . 337 *note*
COIF (see SERJEANT-AT-LAW),
  order of the . . . . 68 *et seq.*
  power of conferring 71
  what it is 71
COKE, LORD,
  account of Inns of Court 50
  as to value of oral arguments 191
COLERIDGE, LORD,
  view on codification . . . . 185 *note*
COLERIDGE, SAMUEL TAYLOR,
  extract from 199
  on permanence and progression in the State 295
COLONIES,
  contest of America with England . . . . 205 *note*
"COLT,"
  in ceremony on creation of serjeant-at-law 71
COMMON LAW (see ENGLAND; LAW; ROMAN LAW; WEST-
    MINSTER HALL),
  senses in which term used 155
  localization of the courts 43
  Westminster Hall the seat of the great judicial courts . 42, 108
  in what sense "unwritten" 27

INDEX. 405

COMMON LAW, — *continued.* PAGE
expansion and influence 26, 304
compared with Civil Law 143, 169
principles of Roman Law ingrafted 171
distinct from Civil or Roman 22, 23
main artificers of 27
a distinctive system 171
general character 157, 158
pervaded by a spirit of freedom 157, 158
indigenous character 158
condition of, in 18th century 300, 302, 308, 318, 354
need of an institutional work 309
basis of American systems . 27, 115, 134, 144, 155, 156, 216, 299
to what the merits of our systems due 29
American expansion of 299
essential rights of Englishmen 225, 226
Blackstone's eulogies and Bentham's denunciations . . . 307
existing need 347
accidental origin and development 234, 235, 349
feudal system, effects 302, 355
pleading, reform in 370
COMMON PLEAS, COURT OF,
effect of clause in Magna Charta concerning 42, 43
established in Westminster Hall 42
early origin . . . . 42 *note*
COMMUNISM (see SOCIALISM).
COMPENSATION,
of judges . . . . 119, 131 *note*
CONGREVE,
had chambers in the Middle Temple 100
CONNECTICUT,
laws as to competency of witnesses . . . . 374 *note*
CONSERVATISM (see COLERIDGE, SAMUEL TAYLOR),
of the English 323, 324, 325, 326
CONSTITUTIONAL LIMITATIONS (see CONSTITUTIONS),
as affecting law 15
efficiency of, in the United States 209, 210, 213, 226, 351
CONSTITUTIONS,
constitution of England, what is 32
distinguishing excellences of 224
secured by our constitutions 33
written, our supreme law 15, 196, 197
unique feature of American legal institutions 196
rationale and purposes of written 198
devices to prevent precipitate popular action 198
successful workings of our 209, 210

CONSTITUTIONS, — *continued*.   PAGE
   efficiency of constitutional limitations . . 209, 210, 213, 226, 351
   security of personal liberty, contracts, and property   207–209, 213
      Sir Henry Maine's opinion 211
   wisdom of founders of our institutions 205
   restraints on popular power 206
   provisions of early constitutions 207
   American, praised by foreign critics 202, 378
      discriminated from European 201
   legal sanctions of 199
   power of courts respecting unconstitutional statutes . . 200 *note*
   the federal constitution 163–165, 207, 351
      the fifth amendment 208, 213
      the fourteenth 211, 212, 213
      Marshall's judgments construing 165, 380
      Choate's eulogium 199
      Gladstone's 378
      fundamental guarantees 203, 207–213
      respected and protected, exception 203
   highest ideal of law realized in America 382
   duty of bar and judiciary concerning 214
CONTINENTAL SYSTEMS OF LAW (see JUDICIAL PRECEDENT; LAW; ROMAN LAW).
CONTRACTS,
   protected by the constitutions . . . . 208, 209, 213, 353 *note*
   sacredness of, Sir Henry Maine's opinion 211
      menace to 295
CONTROVERSIES (see CASES).
COPYRIGHT,
   predicted changes in law of 385
CORPORATIONS,
   growth of, and of corporate litigation 376
   public and municipal 377
CORPUS JURIS (see ROMAN LAW).
COUNCIL,
   meeting of benchers in Lincoln's Inn so termed . . . 53 *note*
COUNCIL OF LAW REPORTING 282
COUNCIL OF LEGAL EDUCATION,
   authority and functions 82
   membership 82
COUNSEL (see BARRISTERS; LAWYERS; QUEEN'S COUNSEL).
COUNSELLOR (see BARRISTER-AT-LAW; LAWYERS; SERJEANTS-AT-LAW).
COUNTY MAGISTRACY,
   powers of 118
COURT OF CHANCERY (see CHANCERY; COURTS; EQUITY).

INDEX. 407

COURTS (see CASE-LAW; COMMON PLEAS; JUDGES; JURY; ROYAL COURTS OF JUSTICE; TRIAL BY JURY; WESTMINSTER HALL),
    merits of our legal system due to mode of evolution in . 29, 30
    essential attributes of 31
    difference between legislative tribunals and 32
    localization of the courts 43
    removal of the great courts of justice into new building . 35, 112
    the local courts in England 159
    judicial and legislative functions . . 5, 19, 152, 267, 268, 343
    for what purposes established 152
    power to declare statutes void . . . . 200 *note*
    origin of court of chancery 235

COWPER,
    residence at the Temple 96

CRIMINAL CASES (see CRIMINAL LAW),
    no substitute for jury in 124

CRIMINAL LAW AND PROCEDURE (see CODIFICATION; PROCEDURE),
    of England, severity 365, 366, 367
        grave and fundamental faults 365
        defence by counsel 367
        amelioration 367
        comparative mildness in America 368
        effects of undue severity 368, 369
        improved procedure 370
        summary procedure 117, 118, 119
        codification of 372

CROWN,
    separation of judicial from kingly office 29
    judges free from control by 29

CURIA REGIS 111, 112

CUSTOM,
    as source of the unwritten law . . . . 13 *note*, 229

DEBT,
    abolition of imprisonment for 359

DEBTOR,
    improvement in law relating to . . . . 353 *note*
    national and State homestead exemption laws 361

DECISIONS (see CASE-LAW; COURTS; JUDICIAL PRECEDENT; LAW; OPINIONS).

DECREE (see JUDGMENT).

DEFINITIONS,
    of "our law," . . . . 3 *et seq.*, 12, 21, 382
    jurisprudence 20, 21
    Inns of Court 36, 37

DEFINITIONS, — *continued*.   PAGE
   codification 179, 256
   judicial precedent 231
   of law, Hobbes's . . . . 9 *note*
      Pollock's comment . . . . 10 *note*
      Blackstone's definition 10
      Austin's 10, 382
      Holland's 11
      Markby's . . . . 11 *note*
      Savigny's conception 381
DENMAN, LORD,
   act relating to evidence 340, 374
DENMARK,
   system of law reporting . . . . 281 *note*
DE TOCQUEVILLE,
   criticism on English constitution 201
DICEY, PROF. A. V. (see table, AUTHORS CITED),
   work on the Law of the English Constitution . . 202, 214, 224
DICKINSON, JOHN,
   a free government defined 353
DISTRESS FOR RENT (see REAL PROPERTY).
DOMESTIC RELATIONS,
   legal relations of husband and wife 362, 363
   effect of feudalism 362, 363
   relief afforded by chancery 363
   modern married women's acts 364
   freedom of married women . . . . . . 353 *note*, 364 *note*
DUE PROCESS OF LAW,
   a fundamental principle . . . . 353 *note*
DWIGHT, PROF. THEODORE W.,
   his regard for Bentham . . . . 332 *note*

EDUCATION (see INNS OF COURT; LEGAL EDUCATION).
ELDON, LORD CHANCELLOR,
   influence on law reform 325
   his character and merits 326, 357, 358
EMINENT DOMAIN,
   as a means of attack on private property 204
ENGLAND (see CASE-LAW; CODIFICATION; COMMON LAW;
     COURTS; INNS OF COURT; MAGNA CHARTA; WEST-
     MINSTER HALL),
   the constitution of, what is 32
      De Tocqueville's criticism 201
   excellence of legal system 171, 306
   the Roman law excluded as a system 24, 25, 159
      fortunate results 24, 25
   common law extended to every part (see COMMON LAW) . 304
   unorganized condition of law of 308

ENGLAND, — continued. PAGE
   Bentham's opinion of law of 307, 321
   contrasted with Blackstone's 322
   state of law and society in time of Blackstone and Bentham
                                           300, 302, 303, 304, 306, 318
   Macaulay's description of progress of people of 300
   unbroken national life 301
   condition of law at the date of our Independence 354
   Sydney Smith's description 357
   identity with law of America 194, 216, 226, 354
   contest with American colonies . . . . 205 note
   essential rights of Englishmen 225
   aversion to innovation 323, 324, 325, 326
   illustrations 324, 325
   branches of the legal profession 52
   judges not a distinct branch of the profession 28
   local courts and local government 159
   Law Amendment Society 276
   system of law reporting 279, 280, 282
   land-laws of 170, 356
   number of land-owners 356
   criminal law, severity of 365, 366, 367
      two fundamental faults 365
   judicature acts . . . . 183, 184, 185, 186 note, 260 note, 372
ENGLISH LAW (see CASE-LAW; COMMON LAW; ENGLAND;
   INNS OF COURT; LAW; WESTMINSTER HALL).
ENGLISH SOCIETY FOR THE PROMOTION OF LAW
   AMENDMENT 276
ENTERTAINMENTS
   in the Inns of Court 80
EQUITY (see LAW),
   doctrines of, progressive and flexible 5
   Sir George Jessel's judgment . . . . 6 note
   origin of Court of Chancery 235
   doctrines concerning equitable estates 238
   and utility, foundations of law 348
   relief against doctrine of merger of married women . . . 363
   union of legal and equitable rights and remedies 386
ETHICS (see MORAL LAW).
EUROPE,
   basis of legal systems in 22
EVIDENCE (see WITNESSES),
   in courts of justice 31
   scintilla doctrine in jury trials 130
   Bentham's influence on law of 339, 340, 341, 374
   Denman's and Brougham's Acts relating to 340, 374
   reforms in law of . . . . 373, 374 note

INDEX.

EXEMPTION LAWS (see REAL PROPERTY).   PAGE
EXPATRIATION,
    voluntary, principle of 350
EX POST FACTO LAWS,
    rendered impossible by constitutional limitations . . 353 *note*

FEDERAL CONSTITUTION (see CONSTITUTIONS).
FEUDALISM (see FEUDAL SYSTEM).
FEUDAL SYSTEM,
    general effects of feudalism 169, 302, 355, 362
    the doctrine of tenure 169, 170, 239, 355
    basis of English law 302
    source of land-laws of Great Britain 170
    effect on domestic life and manners 170, 362
        on the domestic relation 362, 363
FIELD, DAVID DUDLEY,
    labors for legal reform 183, 244
    on codification . . . . 260 *note*
FIELDING,
    student of the Middle Temple 95
FIFTH AMENDMENT (see CONSTITUTIONS).
FLETA,
    as authority in our law 23
FORD (the dramatist),
    had chambers in the Middle Temple 100
FORECAST
    of the future development of our law 383-386
FORSTER,
    member of the Inner Temple 99
FORTESCUE, SIR JOHN,
    sketch of the Inns of Court 49, 63-65
    comments on 65, 66
    as to genuineness of his account of the Inns 66
FOSS, EDWARD,
    extracts concerning Inns of Court 59-68
FOURTEENTH AMENDMENT (see CONSTITUTIONS).
FRANCE,
    adopted the Roman law 22
    written constitution 201
    the French code 258
    system of law reporting . . . . 280 *note*
FREEMAN, EDWARD A.,
    quotation from 161, 162
FRENCH REVOLUTION,
    effect on law reform in England 325

FURNIVAL'S INN,   PAGE
    the hostel of a noble family . . . . 37 *note*
    antiquity of 62
FUTURE,
    predicted changes in our law 383–386
GERMANY,
    adopted the Roman law 22
GLANVILL,
    as authority in our law   23
GOLDSMITH, OLIVER,
    residence and life in the Inns 98–100
GOVERNMENT (see ENGLAND; FRANCE; UNITED STATES),
    science of law distinguished from 8
    popular foundation of our political systems . . . 144, 145, 146
        wisdom of the founders 205
        Lincoln's famous description 145
        Boutmy's speculations and fears 147
    success of American popular institutions 150
        force and strength thereof 150, 151, 153
        their future 148
        importance of good laws well administered . . 151, 152
        dependence upon national justice 153
    our legal system and its workings 154
    local government in England 159
        exact opposite of continental systems 160
    local government in United States 160–165, 217
    beneficial effects of local diversities 217
    complexity arising from our dual governments 217
    bulwark against centralization 218
    opposing powers of permanence and progression 295
    the Swiss Cantons of Uri and Appenzell 161
GOWER,
    member of the Middle Temple 95
GRAND JURY (see JURY; TRIAL BY JURY).
GRAY'S INN (see INNS OF COURT),
    one of the four great Inns of Court 35, 50
    the hostel of a noble family . . . . 37 *note*
    gardens of 46
        laid out by Bacon . . . . 46 *note*, 48 *note*, 95
    Lord Bacon its chiefest glory 46
    Bacon's early life in the Inn 48
    meetings of the benchers styled a " pension " . . . 53 *note*
    antiquity of 60, 62, 67
    masques performed in 61
    number of inhabited houses . . . . 75 *note*
    number of volumes in library of . . . . 94 *note*
GREAT BRITAIN (see ENGLAND).

HALE, SIR MATTHEW,   PAGE
    among the greatest of English lawyers 308
    Blackstone's indebtedness to 308
HALLAM,
    bencher of the Middle Temple 102
HAMMOND, PROF. WILLIAM G.,
    his edition of Blackstone 298
    report on legal education 83
    reference to by Sir Henry Maine 308
HAWTHORNE, NATHANIEL,
    impressions of Westminster Hall 109
HEARING (see TRIAL).
HOBBES,
    definition of law . . . . 9 *note*
HOLLAND,
    adopted the Roman law 22
HOLLAND, PROF. THOMAS ERSKINE,
    definition of law 11
HOMESTEAD LAWS (see REAL PROPERTY).
HOSTEL,
    the equivalent of inn 36
HUSBAND AND WIFE (see DOMESTIC RELATIONS).

IHERING,
    motto prescribed for Continental law amendment 347
ILLINOIS,
    instructions by the judge in jury trials . . . . . . 126 *note*
IMPRISONMENT FOR DEBT (see DEBT).
INDIA,
    dominion of English law 26
INDIVIDUAL RIGHTS (see RIGHTS).
INHERITANCE,
    of lands 352
INN,
    the equivalent of hostel 36
INNER TEMPLE (see INNS OF COURT; MIDDLE TEMPLE; TEMPLE),
    one of four great Inns of Court . . . . . 35, 50, 51 *note*, 67
    origin of 67
    location 45
    gardens of 46
    the Temple Church owned by 75
    meetings of the benchers . . . . 53 *note*
    number of inhabited houses . . . . 75 *note*
        employers . . . . 75 *note*
        volumes in library . . . . 94 *note*

INNS OF CHANCERY (see INNS OF COURT), PAGE
subordinate to the Inns of Court 35
antiquity of 62
INNS OF COURT (see GRAY'S INN; INNER TEMPLE; LEGAL
EDUCATION; LINCOLN'S INN; MIDDLE TEMPLE).
defined 36
whence the name derived 36
what the phrase signifies 37
called *hospitia* . . . . 37 *note*
origin and antiquity . . . . 39, 60, 61, 68 *note*
the sites of the inns 44, 63
why chosen 45, 63, 64
unique character 34
the four great inns 35
character of the edifices 40
buildings and halls 75
number of inhabited houses . . . . 75 *note*
provided for use of lawyers and students 42, 93
the lawyers and judges of England trained and educated there 39
their historical interest and associations 40
a legal university 50, 62
legal character 90
are voluntary societies 90
power of the Crown and courts over 90, 91
visitatorial power of the judges 90
sui generis in character 92
government of 93
modern form and mode of government 44, 66, 67
admission of students 90
exclusive power to call to the bar 91
requisites to call to the bar (see LAWYERS; SERJEANTS-AT-
LAW) 92, 106
sketch of, by Fortescue 49, 63–65
as to genuineness of Fortescue's account 65, 66
comments thereon 65, 66
Coke's account 50
effect of clause in Magna Charta concerning Court of Common Pleas 42
effect of prohibition of the law schools . . . . 51 *note*, 59
number of societies . . . . 51 *note*, 64
membership 92, 93
ranks among members 53
meetings of benchers . . . . 53 *note*
regulations concerning education (see LEGAL EDUCATION) 51 *note*
ancient legal education 78, 79
readings and mootings 78, 79, 80
defective system of legal education 81
modern system 81

INNS OF COURT, — *continued*. PAGE
   present scheme 82
   decline as seminaries of instruction 81
   the Council of Legal Education 82
   number of volumes in library . . . . 94 *note*
   number of students . . . . 51 *note*, 64
   mode of student's life and study 64, 104–107
   keeping terms 105
   tuition 106
   social life of . . . . 40 *note*, 93, 94, 105
      Thackeray's description . . . . 40 *note*
      revels, plays, and entertainments 80
      masques performed in 61, 80
   literary associations 76, 95–103
   occupied by famous poets and writers 76, 77, 95–103
INSTITUTIONS (see GOVERNMENT).
INTERNATIONAL LAW,
   voluntary expatriation 350
   value of arbitration 384
   predicted changes 384, 385
INTRODUCTION,
   course of lectures outlined 2
IOWA,
   instructions by the judge in jury trials . . . . . 127 *note*
IRELAND,
   number of land-owners 356
ITALY,
   adopted the Roman law 22
   system of law reporting . . . . 281 *note*

JESSEL, SIR GEORGE,
   judgment concerning rules of equity . . . . 6 *note*
JOHNSON, DR.,
   his passage concerning famous places 41
   residence in Inner Temple Lane 97
JUDGES (see CONSTITUTIONS; COURTS; INNS OF COURT),
   judicial and legislative functions . . 5, 19, 152, 267, 268, 343
   artificers of the English law 27, 34
   not a distinct branch of the profession 28
   free from control of Crown and Parliament 29
   selected from the bar 30
   of degree of serjeant-at-law 30, 55, 69
   character of the English judges 119
   tenure and compensation . . . . 119, 131 *note*
   a stable and independent judiciary 119
   American departure from English principle . . . 120, 294, 295
   the judiciary the organ of the law . . . . 120 *note*
      not an instrument of government or party . . 120 *note*

JUDGES, — *continued*. PAGE
  fitness to decide on questions of fact . . . . . . 123 *note*, 168
  the bar the real constituency of the bench 283
  ideal of a modern judge 188
  guardians of the constitution 202, 214
  in jury trials (see TRIAL BY JURY) 125–130, 167
JUDGMENTS,
  of court of justice 31
  source and evidence of individual rights 32
JUDICATURE ACTS OF ENGLAND,
  result of reforms originating in America 183, 186 *note*, 260 *note*, 372
  David Dudley Field's labors 183
  satisfactory working of the Acts . . . 183 *note*, 184, 185, 186
JUDICIAL COURTS (see COURTS).
JUDICIAL OPINIONS (see CASE-LAW; COURTS; OPINIONS).
JUDICIAL PRECEDENT (see CASE-LAW; REPORTS),
  the term defined 231
  doctrine of, scope and effects 132, 173, 229, 230, 231, 232, 258, 285
  beneficial consequences 233
  undue prominence to . . . . 288 *note*
  value of judicial decisions 292
  utility of doctrine of *stare decisis* 292
  its force in Continental systems 132, 286
  limits of doctrine defined . . . . 286 *note*
  striking illustration of rule of . . . . 290 *note*
  thorough discussion of doctrine, a *desideratum* 290
  judicial decisions as source of the law . . . . . 291 *note*
  multiplicity and conflict of decisions . . . 242, 243, 252 *note*
  true office of adjudged cases 252
  views of Justice Miller 252, 253, 261–263
  cause of enormous bulk of our case-law 264, 285
  effect of judicial decisions in European States 286
  source of certainty or uncertainty . . . . 272 *note*
JUDICIAL RECORDS (see RECORDS; REPORTS).
JUDICIARY (see COURTS; JUDGES).
JUDICIARY LAW (see CASE-LAW).
JURISPRUDENCE (see LAW),
  the term defined 20, 21
  distinguished from natural law . . . . 8 *note*
  synonymous with law 21
  a practical science 21, 22, 156, 296
  analytical and historical schools 339
  scientific, a necessity 386
JURY (see TRIAL BY JURY),
  historical development of . . . . 121 *note*
  part of our free institutions 123, 166, 167
  Chief Justice Taney's opinion 167

JURY, — *continued*.   PAGE
   in criminal cases 124
   character and intelligence in jurymen 125

KENT, CHANCELLOR,
   labors as a judge and author 379
KING (see CROWN).
KNIGHTS TEMPLARS,
   builders of the Temple Church 75

LAMB, CHARLES,
   life in the Temple 101, 102
LAND (see LAND-LAWS; REAL PROPERTY),
   land-laws of Great Britain 170, 356
   attacks upon property in land . . . . 210 *note*
   ownership of land in Great Britain 356
      in the United States 356, 357
LAND-LAWS (see LAND),
   of Great Britain 170, 356
LAW (see CASE-LAW; COMMON LAW; COURTS; DEFINITIONS;
   JURISPRUDENCE; LEGAL EDUCATION; LEGISLATION;
   MORAL LAW; ROMAN LAW; WESTMINSTER HALL).
   definitions . . . 3 *et seq.*, 9, *note* 10, 11 *and note*, 12, 21, 381, 382
   ethics and morality, how far excluded 3, 4, 12
   when ethical rules become legal 5
   relations between morality and 7, 18, 19
   retroaction of moral upon civil law 16, 17
   distinguished from natural law . . . . 8 *note*
      politics or government 8
   a practical science 21, 22, 156, 206
   synonymous with the *lex terræ* 8
      jurisprudence 21
   not with legislation 9, 14, 15, 16, 18
   essential quality 12
   origin, nature, and ethical foundations . . . 13, 14, 138, 348
   sources and nature 13, 14, 18, 172, 229
   chief value of our system 172
   best system of practical justice 115, 171, 306
   chief excellences of English system 115, 116
      sources 172
      rule of legal equality 116
   how administered and enforced 116
   summary procedure 117, 118, 119
   judiciary the organ of . . . . 120 *note*
   statute-law and case-law 176, 267
   defects which call for remedy . . . . . 176, 177 *note*, 271
   remedies suggested 178, 179, 254, 268, 383, 386
   importance of good laws well administered 151, 152

LAW, — *continued*. PAGE
   effective power 205
   supremacy of . . . . 224, 227 *note*, 351
   bulk and uncertainty   87, 133, 174, 177, 184 *note*, 233, 242, 248,
                           250 and *note*, 264, 265, 266, 278 *note*, 285, 314
   merits of our legal polity 224
   judicial decisions as sources . . . . 291 *note*
   Austin's objection to judiciary law 291
   need of a modern Blackstone 312, 347
   Ihering's motto 347
   union of legal and equitable rights and remedies 386
   identity of English and American . 115, 194, 216, 226, 299, 354
   American system, foundation . 27, 115, 134, 144, 155, 216, 299
      growth and excellence 134, 135, 143, 171, 306
      great expansion 136, 137
      superior to Roman and Continental 143, 227, 228
      characteristics 216
      complexity 138, 217, 219
      Blackstone's influence 298, 354
      progress 186, 187
      present and future condition 187, 348
      improvement and amendment . 135, 138, 178, 193, 383–386
         duty and difficulties 138, 195, 387
      written constitutions 15, 196, 197
      effect of autonomy of the States 219
         railways and telegraph 220–223
      threatened changes 295, 314
      changes inevitable . . . . 296, 297 *note*, 314
      specific changes 358, 384–386
         forecast 383–386
   specific contributions to, by United States 350–353
   popular foundation of our political systems 144
   Bacon's scheme of law amendment 272–274, 278
   Bentham and his labors 313–315, 334
   truths in Savigny's conception 381
      in Austin's 382
   highest ideal realized 382
LAW COURTS BUILDING (see ROYAL COURTS OF JUSTICE).
LAW REFORM (see BACON; BENTHAM; CODIFICATION; LAW).
LAW REPORTS (see JUDICIAL PRECEDENT; REPORTS).
LAW SCHOOLS (see LEGAL EDUCATION),
   abolition of, by Henry III. . . . . 51 *note*, 59
LAWYERS (see BARRISTERS; INNS OF COURT; LEGAL EDU-
   CATION; QUEEN'S COUNSEL; SERJEANTS-AT-LAW).
   artificers of the common law 27, 34
      character and form determined by 94

27

LAWYERS, — *continued.* PAGE
  concentration of, in London 43
  branches of profession in England 52
  degrees of legal precedence 53
  rank of barrister-at-law 91
  independence of 91
  requisites to call to the bar 92, 106
    mode and ceremony 103, 106
  real constituency of the bench 283
  conservatism of the bar 293, 294, 355
    De Tocqueville's and Voltaire's opinion . . . 293, 294
    compensations 294
  in the United States, duties and responsibilities 138, 149, 151,
                                                                195, 214
  effect of railways and telegraphs on practice of the pro-
    fession 221, 222, 223
LEGAL EDUCATION (see INNS OF COURT),
  theory as to sources and nature of law 18
  importance of study of principles 188
  Inns of Court, regulations . . . . 51 *note*
    defective system of education 81
    ancient system 78, 79
    modern 81
    present scheme 82
    studentship 64, 104–107
    keeping terms 105
    tuition 106
  report of American Bar Association 83
  criticism of English course 84
  practical character 81, 84, 85, 86
  reading in attorney's offices 81
  requisites to call to the bar 92, 106
  in America, unsettled and unsatisfactory 84
    scope and methods 85
    limited terms of study 85
    instruction in the Civil Law 86
    "case" and "text-book" systems 86
    difficulties in the way of teaching 86, 87
    text-books, oral instruction, cases 87, 88
    importance and value of the reports 88
    advisable mode suggested 89
    popularity of the study . . . . 150 *note*
LEGAL INSTITUTIONS (see GOVERNMENT).
LEGAL LITERATURE (see REPORTS; TEXT-BOOKS),
  enormous mass of . 14, 87, 133, 134, 174, 233, 265, 285, 344, 380
  Blackstone's Commentaries 150, 298, 307, 311, 354
  Chancellor Kent's works . . . . 379, 380 *note*
  Justice Story's works 380

INDEX. 419

LEGAL PROFESSION (see LAWYERS). PAGE
LEGISLATION (see BENTHAM; CASE-LAW; INNS OF COURT),
   a branch of ethics 19
   governed by certain principles . . . . 338 *note*
   not synonymous with law 9, 16
   differentiated from law 14, 15, 18
   improvement in our law by 178, 383
   fragmentary, cause of uncertainty in the law 243
   the people the true legislator 349
   legislative functions of judges 5, 19, 267, 268, 343
LEGISLATIVE TRIBUNALS,
   difference between judicial courts and   32
LEX TERRÆ,
   "our law" synonymous with 8
LIBEL LAWS,
   in Bentham's way 327
   improvements in 375
LIBERTY,
   provisions of constitutions securing 207
LIBRARY OF THE INNS,
   number of volumes in . . . . 94 *note*
LIFE,
   provisions of constitutions protecting 207
LINCOLN, ABRAHAM,
   famous description of our government 145
LINCOLN'S INN (see INNS OF COURT),
   one of the four great Inns of Court 35, 50
   anciently the hostel of a noble family 36
   where situated 45
   gardens of 46
   meetings of the benchers styled a "council" . . . . 53 *note*
   most ancient of the inns 60, 67
   "black book" or record of proceedings 67
   number of inhabited houses . . . . 75 *note*
   volumes in library of . . . . 94 *note*
LINCOLN'S INN FIELDS 46, 49
LITERARY ASSOCIATIONS,
   of the Inns of Court 76, 95–103
LITERATURE (see LEGAL LITERATURE),
   contributions of America to 377
LIVINGSTON, EDWARD,
   as a law reformer . . . . 337 *note*
LOCAL COURTS (see COURTS).
LOCAL GOVERNMENT (see GOVERNMENT).
LOUISIANA,
   reform of law in . . . . 337 *note*
LOWELL, JAMES RUSSELL 378, 383

LYON'S INN,   PAGE
  antiquity of 62

MACAULAY,
  occupied chambers in Gray's Inn 102
  description of Westminster Hall 109
  as to progress of the English people 300
  judgment concerning Bentham . . . . 317 *note*

MAGNA CHARTA (see COMMON LAW; GOVERNMENT; UNITED STATES),
  basis of English and American liberty . . 35, 116 *note*, 164, 212
  effect of clause concerning the Court of Common Pleas . 42, 43
  made part of our fundamental law 164, 207, 208

MAINE, SIR HENRY,
  opinion as to basis of American prosperity 211
  concerning Bentham's influence 316
  "tacit codification" 346

MARITIME LAW,
  predicted improvement 385

MARKBY, SIR WILLIAM,
  definition of law . . . . 11 *note*

MARRIED WOMEN (see DOMESTIC RELATIONS).

MARSHALL, CHIEF-JUSTICE,
  judgments construing federal constitution 165, 380
  statue to his memory 166

MASQUES,
  performed in the Inns of Court 61, 80

MEETINGS,
  of benchers, how styled . . . . 53 *note*

MERCANTILE LAW,
  predicted improvement 385

MIDDLE TEMPLE (see INNER TEMPLE; INNS OF COURT; TEMPLE),
  one of the four great Inns of Court . . . 35, 50, 51 *note*, 67
  where situated 45
  gardens of 46
  meetings of the benchers termed a "parliament" . . 53 *note*
  origin of 67
  the Temple Church used by 75
  number of employers . . . . 75 *note*
  number of volumes in library of . . . . 94 *note*

MILL, JOHN STUART,
  portrayal of condition of English law 302, 303, 304
  critical estimate of Bentham 335
  edited Bentham's Rationale of Evidence . . . . . 336 *note*

MILLER, JUSTICE SAMUEL F.,   PAGE
 views of the jury system 122
 as to true office of adjudged cases 252, 253, 261–263
MINOR OFFENCES (see PETTY OFFENCES).
MISSISSIPPI,
 instructions by the judge in jury trials . . . . 127 *note*
 legislation concerning married women . . . . . . 364 *note*
MISSOURI,
 instructions by the judge in jury trials . . . . . . 126 *note*
MONOPOLY,
 of wealth in America 148
MOORE, THOMAS,
 student in the Middle Temple 100
MOOTINGS (see READINGS AND MOOTINGS).
MORAL LAW (see LAW),
 not included in the term "our law" 3, 12, 17
 conscience a universal judge 4
 when ethical rules become legal 5
 relations between law and morality 7, 18, 19
 ethical foundation of law 13, 138
 retroaction upon civil law 16, 17
 characteristics of 17
 legislation a branch of ethics 19
MORALITY (see MORAL LAW).
MUNICIPAL CORPORATIONS (see CORPORATIONS).
MUNICIPAL LAW (see LAW).

NATIONAL JUSTICE (see GOVERNMENT).
NATIONAL LIFE (see GOVERNMENT).
NATIONAL UNITY,
 effect of railways and telegraphs upon 224
NATURAL LAW (see LAW; MORAL LAW).
NATURE OF LAW (see JURISPRUDENCE; LAW) 13
 importance of correct theory 18
NEGOTIABLE BILL (see BILLS).
NEW ENGLAND TOWN MEETINGS 162
NEW INN 104
NEW JERSEY,
 serjeants-at-law in province of 57
NEW YORK,
 code of procedure 371, 372
NORTH CAROLINA,
 instructions by the judge in jury trials . . . . . . 127 *note*
NORWAY AND SWEDEN,
 system of law reporting in . . . . 281 *note*
NOTES NEGOTIABLE (see BILLS).

422   INDEX.

OLEOMARGARINE,   PAGE
    prohibition of manufacture and sale 203
OPINIONS (see COURTS; JUDGES; REPORTS),
    importance of judicial opinions and publicity . . . 30 *and note*
    full consultation by the judges 192
    wisdom of written opinions 282
    publication of dissenting opinions 284
ORAL INSTRUCTION (see LEGAL EDUCATION).
ORDER OF THE COIF (see COIF; SERJEANT-AT-LAW).
ORIGIN OF LAW (see LAW) 13
"OUR LAW" (see LAW),
    defined . . . . 3 *et seq.*, 21, 382

PARLIAMENT,
    omnipotent power 201
    judges free from control by 29, 30
    meetings of benchers in Inner and Middle Temple . . 53 *note*
PATENT OF PRECEDENCE,
    of serjeants-at-law 53, 70
PENNSYLVANIA,
    reform in criminal law 368
PENSION,
    meetings of benchers in Gray's Inn so termed . . . . 53 *note*
PEOPLE,
    the true legislator 349
PERSONAL PROPERTY (see PRIVATE PROPERTY),
    predicted changes in law of 385
PETIT JURY (see JURY; TRIAL BY JURY).
PETITION OF RIGHTS,
    basis of English and American liberty 35
PETTY OFFENCES,
    summary procedure for 117, 118, 119
PLAYS,
    in the Inns of Court 61, 80
PLEADINGS (see PROCEDURE).
POLICE POWER,
    use of, for attack on private property 204
POLITICS (see GOVERNMENT).
POLLOCK, SIR FREDERICK,
    comment on Hobbes's definition of law . . . . . . 10 *note*
    on American expansion of English law 298, 299
    opinion concerning Blackstone's Commentaries 312
PORTALIS, M.,
    view of function of the courts 343
PRACTITIONER "BELOW THE BAR" . . . . . . 58 *note*

PRECEDENT (see JUDICIAL PRECEDENT). PAGE
PRIMOGENITURE,
    unknown in the United States 356
PRIVATE PROPERTY (see CONSTITUTIONS; REAL PROP-
ERTY),
    attacks on . . . . 204, 210 *note*, 205
    secured by the constitutions 207, 208, 209, 213
    stability of, basis of American prosperity 211
    Sir Henry Maine's opinion 211
    essential qualities of all property 238
    predicted changes in law of 385
PROCEDURE (see CIVIL PROCEDURE; CODIFICATION; CRIM-
INAL LAW AND PROCEDURE),
    pleadings in courts of justice 31
    codification of the law of . . . . 183, 260 *note*, 371, 372, 373
    (see CODIFICATION).
    David Dudley Field's labors 183
    amendments in law of 370
PROFESSION (see INNS OF COURT; LAWYERS; LEGAL
EDUCATION).
PROPERTY (see CONSTITUTIONS; EMINENT DOMAIN; PRI-
VATE PROPERTY; REAL PROPERTY; SOCIALISM).
PROUDHON,
    famous maxim concerning property 213
PRUSSIA,
    the Prussian code 258
PUBLIC CORPORATIONS (see CORPORATIONS).

QUEEN'S COUNSEL (see INNS OF COURT; LAWYERS),
    highest in rank in the profession 53
    of comparatively modern origin 69
    Lord Bacon the first 69
    difference between serjeant-at-law and 70
    position outside of the profession 70
    assumed to be in the service of the queen 70

RAILWAYS,
    effect of, upon our laws 220
    upon the practice of the law 221, 222, 223
    upon our national unity 224
READER,
    in Inns of Court 79
    how chosen 79
READINGS AND MOOTINGS,
    ancient legal education in the Inns of Court 78
    what they consisted of 79
    original object 79
    disuse 80

REAL PROPERTY (see PRIVATE PROPERTY; REGISTRY SYSTEM), PAGE
   unsatisfactory condition of law of 238
   two great classes of property 238
   doctrines of chancery 238
   sources of complexity 239
   changes and amendments . . . . 240, 241 *note*, 352, 353, 385
   uses those of property only 240
   American law as compared with English . . . . . 241 *note*
   distress for rent 358
   homestead and other exemption laws 360, 361
RECORDS (see REPORTS),
   early English judicial 28, 29
REFORM, LAW (see BACON; BENTHAM; CASE-LAW; CODIFICATION; LAW; LEGISLATION; REPORTING),
   the true motto of the legal reformer 347
REGISTRY SYSTEM,
   security of titles to lands by 352
RENT,
   distress for 358
REPORTING (see CASE LAW; REPORTS),
   evils of system of 266, 267
   resolution of American Bar Association 267
   remedy devised by English bar 279
   action of English bar concerning system of 280
   the system adopted in France . . . . 280 *note*
       in Norway and Sweden . . . . 281 *note*
       in Denmark . . . . 281 *note*
       in Italy . . . . 281 *note*
   present English system 282
   conclusions concerning 282
   wisdom of written opinions 282
   manner of 289
REPORTS (see ARGUMENTS; JUDICIAL PRECEDENT; OPINIONS; RECORDS; REPORTING),
   importance and value of . . . . . 31 *note*, 88, 174, 234, 270
   regular series from Edward II.'s reign 132
   marvellous multiplication . 87, 133, 174, 233, 265, 266, 285, 288,
                                      344, 380
       a grave problem 134
       effect of doctrine of judicial precedent 285, 286
       annual rate of increase 174
   publication a continuing necessity 175, 283, 343
   legislative restriction on publication 287
       resolution of American Bar Association 289
   issue of the existing situation 176, 288
   of inferior courts 284
   deterioration of modern reports 189

REPORTS, — continued. PAGE
  publication of dissenting opinions 284
  American law and chancery 378
REVELS,
  in the Inns of Court 61, 80
RIGHTS,
  source and evidence of individual 32
  courts established to protect and enforce 152
  equal rights guaranteed by fundamental law . . . . . 353 note
RINGS,
  given by serjeants on call to the bar . . . . . . 54 note, 71
ROMAN LAW (see COMMON LAW; LAW),
  our law distinct from 22, 23
  not inferior to 143
  at one time superior to the common law 169
  basis of systems of continental Europe and South American
    States 22
  excluded from England 24, 25, 159
  as an element of instruction 86
  doctrine of judicial precedent 132, 286
  great bulk of 270
  use of, in the work of codification 345
ROMILLY, SIR SAMUEL,
  illustration of conservatism of the English people . . . 325
  high standing as lawyer 327
  his description of a visit to Bentham . . . . 333 note
ROYAL COMMISSION OF 1866 277
ROYAL COURTS OF JUSTICE,
  removal of the great courts into new building . . 35, 112, 113
  history of the new Law Courts Building 113, 139
    inauguration ceremonies 113, 140
      the Queen's speech 140
      the Lord Chancellor's speech 140, 141
      address of the Lord Chief Justice 113, 142
RUSSELL, LORD WILLIAM,
  beheaded on Lincoln's Inn Fields 49

ST. LEONARDS, LORD 239
SALES,
  law of, uncertainty . . . . 236 note
SAVIGNY,
  conception of law 381
SCIENCES,
  contributions of America to 377
SCIENTIFIC JURISPRUDENCE (see JURISPRUDENCE;
  LAW),
  a necessity 386

SCINTILLA DOCTRINE,   PAGE
    in jury trial 130
SCOTLAND,
    number of land owners 356
SECESSION,
    in United States 148
SELBORNE, LORD,
    regard for American jurists . . . . 187 *note*
SELDEN, JOHN,
    had lodgings in the Inner Temple 95
SERJEANTS-AT-LAW (see BARRISTERS; INNS OF COURT;
       LAWYERS; QUEEN'S COUNSEL),
    rank of 53, 68, 69, 70
    ceremonies previous to creation of . . . . 72 *note*
       on creation of 71
    oath required of . . . . 70 *note*
    entrance fee 72
    retaining fees . . . . 72 *note*
    rings given by . . . . 54 *note*, 71
    judges selected from 30, 55, 69
    independent of the Sovereign 70
    distinguished from other members of the bar 69
    difference between Queen's counsel and 70
    rank independent of the profession 70
    antiquity and decay of the order 55, 69
    causes of decline 69
    approaching extinction 56
    the order in America 57
SERJEANTS' INN,
    three different clubs or societies 72
    entrance fee required 72
    sale of 73
SHADWELL,
    had chambers in the Middle Temple 100
SMITH, SYDNEY,
    picture of English laws at beginning of this century . . . 357
SHERIDAN,
    student at the Middle Temple 100
SIDNEY, PHILIP,
    member of Gray's Inn 95
SOCIALISM (see PRIVATE PROPERTY),
    relation to attacks on private property 204
    unpopular in America 357
SOLICITORS (see LAWYERS),
    officers of the court of chancery 52
SOURCE OF LAW 13, 249

SOUTH AMERICAN STATES,   PAGE
  legal systems of 22
SOUTHEY,
  was entered at Gray's Inn 100
SPAIN,
  adopted the Roman law 22
STAPLE INN, ... 62, 104
STAR CHAMBER COURT . . . . 117 *note*
STARE DECISIS (see JUDICIAL PRECEDENT).
STATE (see CHURCH AND STATE; GOVERNMENT).
STATES (see UNITED STATES).
STATUTE-LAW (see CASE-LAW; COMMON-LAW; LAW),
  one of the great divisions of the law 176, 267
  power of courts to declare statutes void . . . . . 200 *note*
  Bacon's plan of dealing with 273
  Lord Westbury's scheme . . . . 277 *note*
STATUTES (see STATUTE-LAW).
STEPHEN, SIR JAMES,
  views on codification 260
  opinion as to Bentham's influence 316
    criminal law of England 365, 366, 369
STORY, JUSTICE,
  extract from Webster's eulogy 186
  works of 380
STRAND INN (see CHESTER INN).
STUDENTS (see INNS OF COURT; LEGAL EDUCATION),
  in Inns of Court, number . . . . 51 *note*, 64
  admission 90
  rank among members of Inns of Court 53
  mode of life and study 64, 104–107
  keeping terms 105
  call to the bar 103, 106
SUITS (see ACTIONS).
SUMMARY PROCEDURE,
  for petty offences 117, 118, 119
SUPREME COURT OF THE UNITED STATES (see CONSTITUTIONS; UNITED STATES),
  practice as to oral arguments, etc. 192, 193
  Yale University well represented 388
SWEDEN (see NORWAY AND SWEDEN).
SWISS CANTONS,
  of Uri and Appenzell 161

TABARD INN . . . . 38 *note*
TALLEYRAND,
  observation concerning Bentham 332

TANEY, CHIEF-JUSTICE,   Page
    opinion of trial by jury 167
TAXATION,
    use of the power for attack on private property 204
TELEGRAPH,
    communication by, effect upon our laws 220
                effect upon the practice of the profession 221,
                                                          222, 223
                effect on our national unity 224
TEMPLE (see INNER TEMPLE; INNS OF COURT; MIDDLE
    TEMPLE),
    whence name of the society derived 39
    antiquity of 62
    Inner Temple and Middle Temple 67
TEMPLE CHURCH,
    built by the Knights Templars 75
    ownership and use 75
TENURE,
    of judges . . . . 119, 131 *note*
TENURE, DOCTRINE OF,
    result of the feudal system 169, 170, 239, 355
TEXAS, REPUBLIC OF,
    homestead act 360
TEXT-BOOKS (see LEGAL EDUCATION; LEGAL LITERATURE),
    place in legal education 86
    specially designed for teaching 87, 88
    as literary authorities of our law . . . . 347 *note*
TEXT-BOOK SYSTEM (see LEGAL EDUCATION; TEXT-
    BOOKS).
THACKERAY,
    account of social life in the Inns . . . . 40 *note*
    occupied chambers in the Temple 102
THAVIE'S INN,
    antiquity of . . . . 37 *note*, 67 *note*
THE INCORPORATED LAW SOCIETY 52
THURLOW, LORD CHANCELLOR,
    illustration of conservatism of the English people . . . 324
TOOKE, JOHN HORNE,
    was entered at the Middle Temple 100
TORTS,
    direct personal responsibility for, in our law . . 226, 227 *note*
TOWN MEETINGS,
    in New England 162
TREATIES,
    supreme law of the land 351

TRIAL (see TRIAL BY JURY). PAGE
TRIAL BY JURY (see COURTS; JURY),
 in courts of justice 31
 Justice Miller's views 122
 Chief-Justice Taney's opinion 167
 historical development . . . . 121 *note*
 essential part of our system and institutions 121, 123
 decline in popular favor 120, 121
 causes of dissatisfaction 125
 defects remediable 131
 remedies suggested 129
 in criminal cases 124
 character and intelligence in jurymen 125
 verdict by less than whole number 132
 judges, curtailment of powers . . . . 125, 126 *and note*, 167
  instructions by . . . . 126 *and note*
  right to grant new trials 125, 130
  province and duty . . . 127, 128 *and note*, 130 *and note*
  legislation implying distrust 129, 167
 scintilla of evidence doctrine 130

UNCERTAINTY IN OUR LAWS (see CASE-LAW; LAW).
UNITY (see NATIONAL UNITY).
UNITED STATES (see CONSTITUTIONS; GOVERNMENT),
 vast and varied territory 148, 149
 popular foundation of political systems 144, 145, 146
 Lincoln's famous description 145
 Boutmy's speculations and fears 146, 147
 future of institutions of 148
 success of popular institutions 150
  force and strength of 150, 151, 153
 good laws well administered, importance 151, 152
 cause of growth and prosperity 150, 211
 effect of railways and telegraphs upon national unity . . 224
 English common-law basis of legal systems of . . 27, 115, 134,
        144, 155, 156, 216, 299
  (see COMMON LAW; LAW).
 importance of this fact 155
 excellences of English law secured 32, 33
 Magna Charta part of law of 164, 207, 208
 identity of American system with English . 194, 216, 226, 354
 American expansion of English law 298, 299
 excellence of legal systems of 171
  capable of amendment 135
 general survey of legal systems of 154
 expansion of law of 136, 137
 homogeneous character of American legal systems . . . 156

UNITED STATES, — *continued*.   PAGE
   supremacy of law in . . . . 224, 227 *note*
   present and future condition 187, 348
   progress of jurisprudence . . . . 186, 187, 348 *et seq.*
   specific contributions to law by . . . . 350, 351, 352, 353 *note*
   local government in 160
      independence of federal control 163
      municipal freedom 163
   written constitutions 15, 196, 197
      praised by foreign critics 202, 211
   the federal constitution 163–165, 207
   legal education (see LEGAL EDUCATION) 84
   tenure and compensation of judges . . . . 120, 131 *note*
   stable and independent judiciary 119
   order of serjeants-at-law 57
   duties and responsibilities of legal profession 138, 149, 151, 195, 214
   reform in law of procedure (see PROCEDURE) 183
   Bentham's influence . . . . 337 *note*
   contributions to the arts, sciences, and literature 377
   law and chancery reports 378
   treaties supreme law of the land 351
   a nation of land proprietors 356
   national homestead act 361
   criminal law in 368
UNITED STATES SUPREME COURT (see SUPREME COURT OF, &c).
UNWRITTEN LAW (see CASE-LAW; COMMON LAW),
   whence derived . . . . 13 *note*, 229
   in what sense the common law " unwritten " 27
URI,
   Swiss Canton of 161
UTILITY,
   and equity, real foundations of law 348
UTTER BARRISTERS (see BARRISTERS-AT-LAW).

VERDICTS (see JURY; TRIAL BY JURY),
   by less number than the whole of the jury 132
VOLUMES,
   number of, in library of Inns of Court . . . . . . 94 *note*
VOLUNTARY EXPATRIATION (see EXPATRIATION).

WALES,
   number of land owners 356
WEALTH,
   monopoly of, in America 148
WEBSTER, DANIEL,
   extract from eulogy on Story 186

INDEX.

WESTBURY, LORD,   PAGE
   scheme of law amendment 277, 278
WESTMINSTER HALL (see COMMON LAW; COURTS; ROYAL
   COURTS OF JUSTICE),
   history and associations . . . . 108 *et seq.*, 113, 114
   earlier uses 108
   seat of great judicial courts 42, 108
   chief glory of the place 110
   wherein consists its real interest 114
   since 1399 devoted mainly to legal uses 112
   distinctive system of law administered therein . . . 110, 115
   built by William Rufus 108, 110
   rebuilt 111
   existing hall and its uses 111
   Hawthorne's impressions 109
   Macaulay's description 109
   removal of courts from 112
WILLIAM OF WYKEHAM 111
WILLIAM RUFUS,
   builder of original Westminster Hall 108, 110
WISCONSIN,
   instructions by the judge in jury trials . . . . . 126 *note*
WITNESSES (see EVIDENCE),
   laws relating to competency of 373, 374
WYCHERLEY,
   had chambers in the Middle Temple 100

YALE UNIVERSITY,
   inspiring influences 388
   well represented on Supreme Bench 388
YEAR BOOKS,
   Bracton, Fleta, and Glanvill not quoted in . . . . . 23 *note*

www.ingramcontent.com/pod-product-compliance
Lightning Source LLC
Chambersburg PA
CBHW022145300426
44115CB00006B/349